AFTERGLOW OF EMPIRE

AFTERGLOW OF EMPIRE

Egypt from the Fall of the New Kingdom
to the Saite Renaissance

Aidan Dodson

The American University in Cairo Press
Cairo New York

First published in 2012 by
The American University in Cairo Press
113 Sharia Kasr el Aini, Cairo, Egypt
420 Fifth Avenue, New York, NY 10018
www.aucpress.com

Dar el Kutub No. 11216/11
ISBN 978 977 416 531 3

Dar el Kutub Cataloging-in-Publication Data

Dodson, Aidan
          Afterglow of Empire: Egypt from the Fall of the New Kingdom to the Saite Renaissance /
     Aidan Dodson. —Cairo: The American University in Cairo Press, 2012
          p.   cm.
          ISBN 978 977 416 531 3
          1.   Egypt–Antiquities
          932

1 2 3 4 5   15 14 13 12

Designed by Adam el-Sehemy
Printed in Egypt

To Martin Davies, Esq.: President of the Egypt Society of Bristol, Vice-President of the Egypt Exploration Society—and most importantly, friend!

CONTENTS

PREFACE

This book, like my previous volumes on the ends of the Eighteenth and Nineteenth Dynasties,[1] represents a distillation of research and thinking that goes back many years. In the present case, my first real acquaintance with the intricacies of the Third Intermediate Period and its immediate precursor and successor eras was gained something over three decades ago, when as a schoolboy I first perused a copy of Kenneth Kitchen's seminal book on the topic.

The publication of the first edition of that work in 1973 (with updates in 1986 and 1996) put forward an analysis and historical reconstruction that were so impressive that for some years its conclusions became all but canonical. However, as the 1980s proceeded, scholarly studies that in many cases had originally intended to refine the Kitchen picture began to raise issues that gave rise to significant questions as to the correctness of what had now become orthodoxy.[2] These multiplied in the following years, resulting in a collapse of many significant aspects of the consensus, significant ramifications of which were explored at a conference at Leiden University in the Netherlands in October 2007.

In addition, the same period saw assaults on 'orthodox' views of the period from more radical standpoints, which questioned not only the detail, but also the whole chronological structure of ancient history prior to the seventh century BC. These new paradigms attempt to lower all dates prior to the start of the New Kingdom by a number of centuries, resulting in a very significant compression of the New Kingdom and Third Intermediate Period, requiring overlaps of reigns and dynasties far in excess of anything seriously attempted before.[3] The fact that the proponents of

ix

these views came largely from outside the established academic community prompted many 'orthodox' scholars to dismiss their proposals out of hand,[4] although others attempted to meet the challenge head-on by analyzing the evidence put forward and demonstrating its (often fatal) flaws.[5] On the other hand, the 'radicals' have not infrequently raised important issues which, if not necessarily having the implications claimed, do have an impact on the orthodox picture and can in fact be incorporated into it.[6]

A side issue is that the challenge of the radicals has driven a number of conventional scholars into the bunker, from where they attempt to defend their current orthodoxy rather more fiercely than had hitherto been the case, perhaps fearful of allowing the radicals some kind of oblique victory. As a result, attempts at challenging the chronological consensus—even in a relatively modest way—can risk being dismissed out of hand as potentially giving comfort to the radicals by showing flaws in the received wisdom, or simply as a result of having used an argument previously deployed by one of them.

For my own part, engagement with these radicals—broadly my academic contemporaries—led me to start retesting the conclusions generally reached on various aspects of the period, resulting in a series of stand-alone studies, some of which stood the test of time, some of which did not. Among the former was building on a 'radical' observation to verify the existence of a hitherto unnoticed king Shoshenq (IV);[7] among the latter an ill-fated attempt at making the reign of Pasebkhanut II entirely contemporary with that of Shoshenq I.[8] I also produced a number of more general accounts of the period[9] which, however, did not attempt to address any issues beyond those I had already dealt with separately.

However, an invitation to write entries on various individual kings for a forthcoming encyclopedia of ancient history led to my beginning to take a closer look at the *detail* of many parts of the Third Intermediate Period and the late Rameside Period. This led me away from some positions I had long accepted, and prodded me into writing the book-length treatment with which I had been toying for some years. Furthermore, my dear friend Professor Salima Ikram, who had invited the aforesaid contributions, at the same time increased pressure on me in this direction, citing the lack of an up-to-date and accessible treatment that she could set for her students.

Against this background, this book's intent is therefore to provide an 'accessible' account of the Third Intermediate Period, and the immediately preceding and succeeding decades, informed by the latest data and addressing the key issues that are presently the subject of active debate, while testing any 'received wisdom' before choosing to accept it. As always with such a work, there is an inherent tension between providing a coherent and readable narrative of events and taking into account a range of variant views that may include questioning whether some events even took place. All I can say is that I have aimed to steer a course that minimizes the number of assumptions and maximizes the reading of hard data in the most straightforward way.

Chronologically, while fully understanding and sympathizing with the issues that have given rise to ultra-radical revisionism, I find it impossible to accept the two key assumptions that make anything more than a few decades' adjustment practicable: discarding *all* conclusions predicated on the pre-Ashur-dan II (late tenth century) segment of the Assyrian King List,[10] and denying the equation between the Biblical Egyptian king 'Shishak' and Shoshenq I, founder of the Twenty-second Dynasty. On the other hand, it seems to me clear that the current strict orthodoxy concerning the absolute dating (i.e., in terms of years BC) of the New Kingdom and Third Intermediate Period is no longer viable, and that some degree of adjustment of dates—downward—is both necessary and desirable.

To do otherwise is to make the macro-level chronological tail wag the micro-level dog, a course that is particularly undesirable when this is used to damn as 'impossible' potential solutions to longstanding anomalies that are otherwise convincing and internally coherent. This becomes even more the case when it is realized that that 'tail' depends entirely on the long-held assumption that Assyrian chronology is absolutely reliable back into the fourteenth century—and thus that the earlier part of the Assyrian King List is an accurate record of pre-tenth century dynastic history.

As already noted, while I would not take the ultimately nihilistic position that this King List tradition should simply be discarded, it must certainly be tested where possible, and as a result the chronology adopted as the underlying framework of this book incorporates a modest revision of pre-tenth century dates, in particular a lowering of the long-canonical 1279 BC accession date of Rameses II to 1265. The justification will be found in Chapter 1, where I endorse a proposal that reigns in the late Twentieth Dynasty that have historically been regarded as consecutive were actually in part contemporary; and in Appendix 1, which reviews the broader chronological issues, including the Assyrian King List tradition.

As has already been indicated, my thinking on the period has been stimulated by various formal and informal discussions over the past three decades. Accordingly, I must thank in particular Peter James, Robert Morkot, and

David Rohl for their friendly provocations, and a wide range of other friends and colleagues for information and debate in both formal and informal contexts. I am also indebted to Tine Bagh and Salah El-Masekh for help in gaining access to monuments in Copenhagen and at Karnak, respectively, and to Giuseppina Lenzo, Frédéric Payraudeau, and Troy Sagrillo (as well as Peter James and Robert Morkot) for advance copies of as yet unpublished work. Reg Clarke, Martin Davies, Claire Gilmour, Salima Ikram, and my wife Dyan Hilton are also to be thanked for their scrutiny of the typescript, and Martin as usual for the free run of his photographic archive. All remaining errors and cases of fuzzy or faulty logic are of course entirely my responsibility!

ABBREVIATIONS AND CONVENTIONS

Aleppo	National Museum, Aleppo, Syria
Ashmolean	Ashmolean Museum, Oxford, U.K.
Athens	National Archaeological Museum, Athens, Greece
Berlin ÄM	Ägyptisches Museum und Papyrussamlung, Berlin, Germany
Berlin VA	Vorderasiatisches Museum, Berlin, Germany
BM	British Museum, London, U.K.
BMA	Brooklyn Museum of Art, New York, U.S.A.
Brussels	Musées Royaux d'Art et d'Histoire, Brussels, Belgium
Budapest	Szépmúvészeti Museum, Budapest, Hungary
Cairo	Egyptian Museum, Cairo, Egypt
Fitzwilliam	Fitzwilliam Museum, Cambridge, U.K.
Florence	Museo Archeologico, Florence, Italy
Geneva	Musée d'Art et d'Histoire, Geneva, Switzerland
Hamburg	Museum für Völkerkunde, Hamburg, Germany
Hamm	Gustav-Lübcke-Museum, Hamm, Germany
Harvard	Harvard University Semitic Museum, Cambridge, Massachusetts, U.S.A.
Heidelberg	Sammlung des Ägyptologischen Instituts, Universität Heidelberg, Germany
Hermitage	State Hermitage Museum, St. Petersburg, Russia
Jerusalem	Rockefeller Archæological Museum, Jerusalem
Kestner	Museum August Kestner, Hanover, Germany
Khartoum	Sudan National Museum, Khartoum, Sudan
KV	Valley of the Kings tomb number

Liverpool	National Museums Liverpool, U.K.
Louvre	Musée du Louvre, Paris, France
l.p.h.	life, prosperity, health ($\begin{smallmatrix}\end{smallmatrix}$ 𓋹𓎺𓋴, ꜥnḫ wḏꜣ snb), the wish often appended to the name of the king in inscriptions
Manchester	Manchester Museum, U.K.
Marseilles	Musée d'Archéologie mediterranéenne, Marseilles, France
MFA	Museum of Fine Arts, Boston, Mass., U.S.A.
MMA	Metropolitan Museum of Art, New York, U.S.A.
Moscow	State Pushkin Museum of Fine Arts, Moscow, Russia
Munich	Staatliches Museum Ägyptischer Kunst, Munich, Germany
Nicholson	Nicholson Museum, University of Sydney, Australia
NMS	National Museums Scotland, Edinburgh
NN	no number
NRT	Tanis royal cemetery tomb number
Nubian Mus.	Nubian Museum, Aswan, Egypt
Ny Carlsberg	Ny Carlsberg Glyptotek, Copenhagen, Denmark
o	ostracon (followed by current location/number)
p	papyrus (followed by current location/number)
Petrie	Petrie Museum, University College London, U.K.
Rio de Janeiro	Museu Nacional, Rio de Janeiro, Brazil
RMO	Rijksmuseum van Oudheden, Leiden, Netherlands
ro.	*recto*
Rochester	Rochester University Memorial Art Gallery, Rochester, New York, U.S.A.
ROM	Royal Ontario Museum, Toronto, Canada
Stockholm	Medelhavsmuseet, Stockholm, Sweden
Strasbourg	Institut d'Égyptologie, Université Marc Bloch, Strasbourg, France
TT	Theban Tomb number
Turin	Museo Egizio, Turin, Italy
UPMAA	University of Pennsylvania Museum of Archaeology and Anthropology, Philadelphia, Pa., U.S.A.
Vatican	Musei Gregoriano Egizio, Vatican City
Vienna	Kunsthistorisches Museum, Vienna, Austria
vo.	*verso*

Where titles of individuals are capitalized, they are more or less direct translations of the original Egyptian. Renderings of Egyptian names are intended as far as possible to preserve the original consonantal structure of the original written Egyptian, rather than any hypothetical ancient pronunciation. Persons of the same name are distinguished by Roman numerals (upper case for kings and certain other senior figures; lower case for others) or letters, according to a basic system that has been developing within Egyptology since the 1970s (see Dodson and Hilton 2010: 39). This is not wholly internally coherent, as it is desirable to preserve some longstanding designations for avoidance of confusion. Nevertheless, the numbering of the Shoshenq kings follows the convention agreed at the conference at Leiden University in 2007 (Broekman, Demarée, and Kaper 2008).

Dates are given in Egyptian terms, which comprise a king's regnal year together with the month and day. The Egyptian year was divided into three seasons, in succession ꜣḫt, prt, and šmw, each of which was split into thirty days; the year ended with five feast days. Thus, III prt 4 means "Third Month of prt, day 4." A correlation with years BC, based on the chronological model used in this book, is provided in Appendices 2 and 3, but it should be noted that the absolute chronology of the period prior to 690 BC remains a matter for debate (cf. Appendix 1).

Square brackets in names and translations normally enclose parts of the text that are damaged or missing in the original, and are accordingly shown as either restored (e.g., Shosh[enq]) or unrestorable (e.g., Shosh[. . .]). Uncertain readings of signs are given thus: ⌈Amen⌉hotep. Where parentheses are used within translations they contain glosses or emendations for clarity (e.g., the name of the protagonist, rather than the pronoun used in the original).

When giving bibliography for monuments and texts, references are generally restricted to Porter and Moss (various dates), Kitchen 1968–90, Jansen-Winkeln 2007–2009, and Aston 2009, which together provide all substantive references down to their dates of publication; additional references provided are generally to works published subsequently or otherwise missed from these sources. Translations and commentaries to texts compiled by Kitchen are being made available in his companion volumes, Kitchen 1993ff(a) and (b), supplemented by Peden 1994b; many of these, and those compiled by Jansen-Winkeln, are to be found in translation in Ritner 2009a and Eide et al. (eds.) 1994.

MAPS

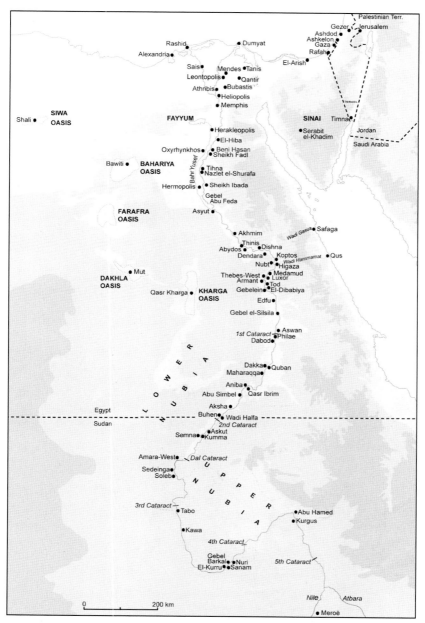

Map 1. The Nile Valley from Khartoum to the Mediterranean.

Map 2. The Near East during the earlier first millennium BC.

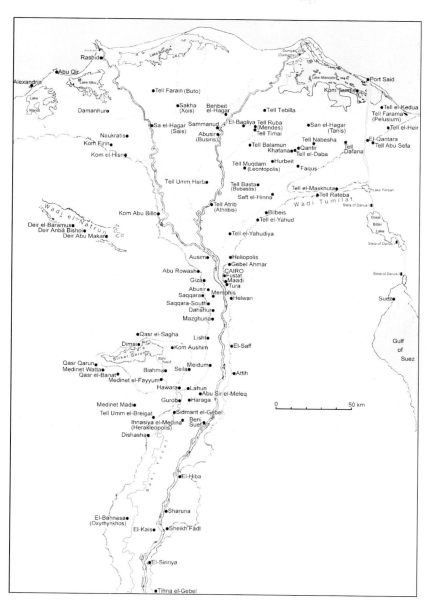

Map 3. The Nile Delta.

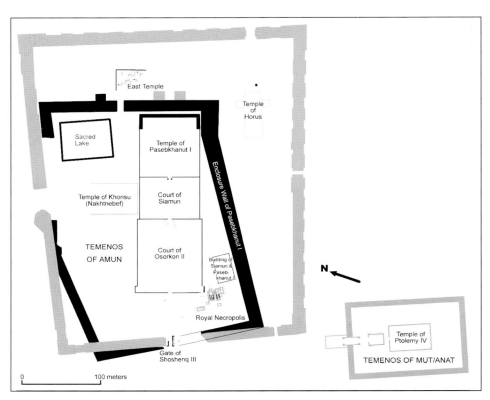

Map 4. Tanis.

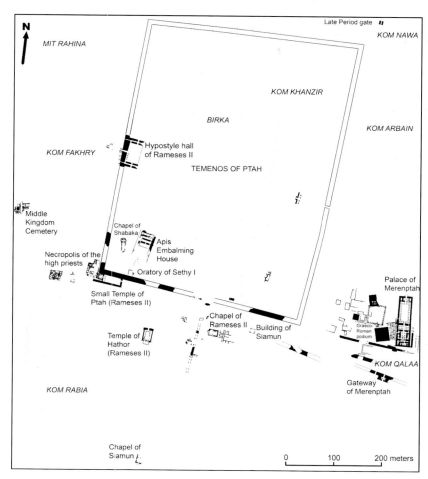

Map 5. The temple of Ptah at Memphis.

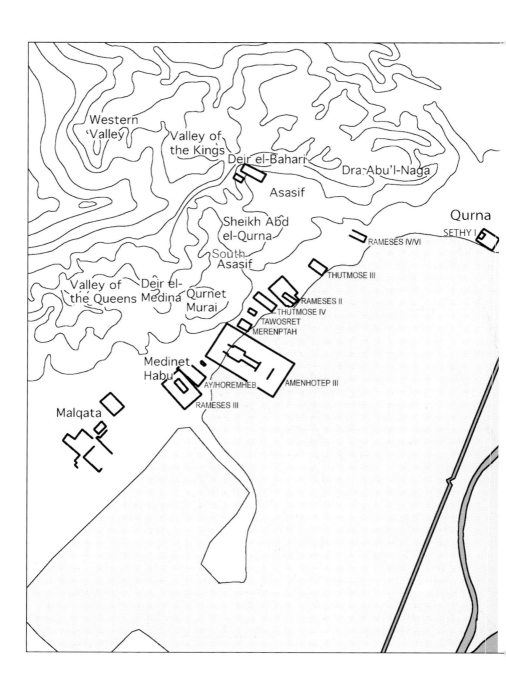

Western 'Valley

Valley of the Kings

Deir el-Bahari

Dra Abu'l-Naga

Asasif

Qurna

Sheikh Abd el-Qurna

SETHY I

RAMESES IV/VI

South Asasif

THUTMOSE III

Valley of the Queens

Deir el-Medina

Qurnet Murai

RAMESES II

THUTMOSE IV

TAWOSRET

MERENPTAH

Medinet Habu

AY/HOREMHEB

AMENHOTEP III

RAMESES III

Malqata

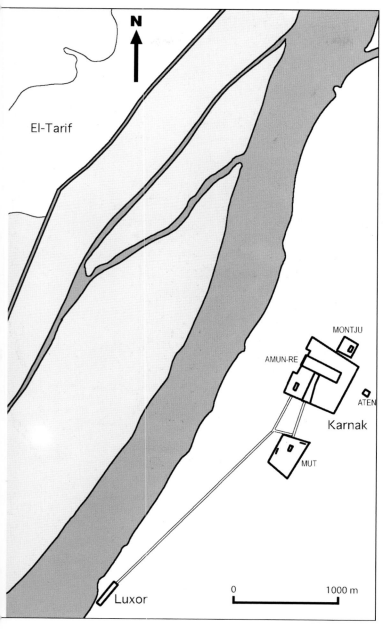

N

El-Tarif

MONTJU

AMUN-RE

ATEN

Karnak

MUT

0   1000 m

Luxor

Map 6. Thebes.

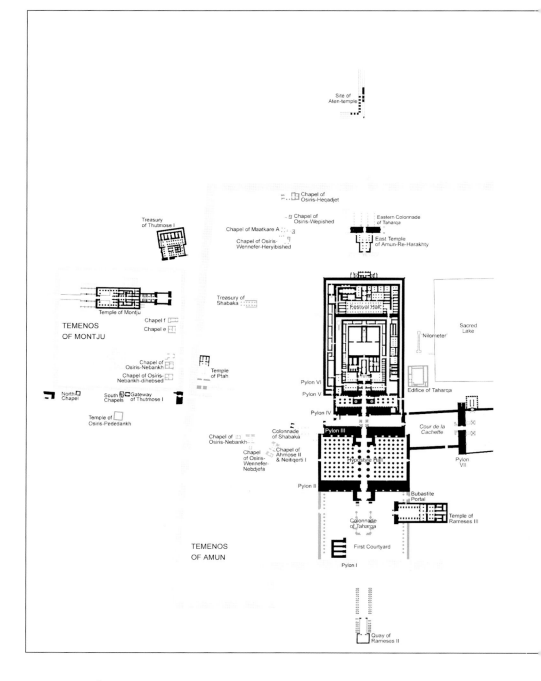

Site of
Aten-temple

Chapel of
Osiris-Heqadjet

Chapel of
Osiris-Wepished

Eastern Colonnade
of Taharqa

Chapel of Maatkare A

Treasury
of Thutmose I

Chapel of Osiris-
Wennefer-Heryibished

East Temple
of Amun-Re-Harakhty

Treasury of
Shabaka

Festival Hall

Sacred
Lake

'Nilometer'

Temple of Montju

TEMENOS
OF MONTJU

Chapel f

Chapel e

Chapel of
Osiris-Nebankh

Chapel of Osiris-
Nebankh-dihebsed

Temple
of Ptah

Edifice of Taharqa

Pylon VI

Pylon V

North
Chapel

South
Chapels

Gateway
of Thutmose I

Pylon IV

Cour de la
Cachette

Temple of
Osiris-Pededankh

Chapel of
Osiris-Nebankh

Colonnade
of Shabaka

Pylon III

Pylon
VII

Chapel of
Osiris-
Wennefer-
Nebdjefa

Chapel
of Ahmose II
& Neitiqerti I

Hypostyle Hall

Pylon II

Bubastite
Portal

Temple of
Rameses III

Colonnade
of Taharqa

TEMENOS
OF AMUN

First Courtyard

Pylon I

Quay of
Rameses II

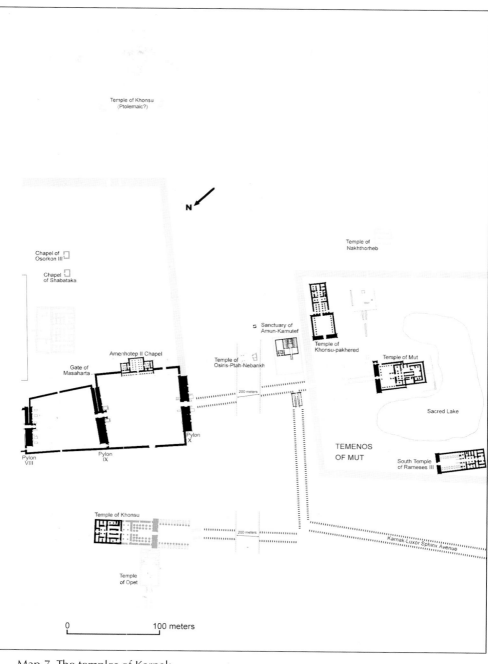

Map 7. The temples of Karnak.

Buildings in black are those extant at the end of the New Kingdom, those in dark grey are additions during the Third Intermediate Period.

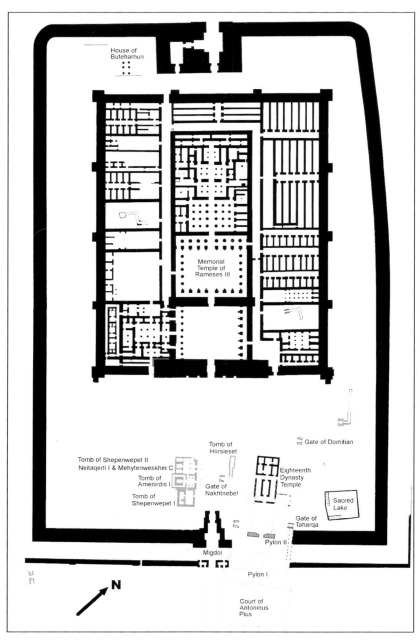

House of
Buteharnun

Memorial
Temple of
Rameses III

Tomb of
Horsieset

Tomb of Shepenwepet II
Neitaqerti I & Mehytenweskhet C

Tomb of
Amenirdis I

Tomb of
Shepenwepet I

Gate of
Nakhtnebef

Eighteenth
Dynasty
Temple

Gate of Domitian

Sacred
Lake

Gate of
Taharqa

Pylon II

Migdol

Pylon I

N

Court of
Antoninus
Pius

Map 8. The temples of Medinet Habu.

Buildings in black are those extant at the end of the New Kingdom, those in dark gray are additions during the Third Intermediate Period.

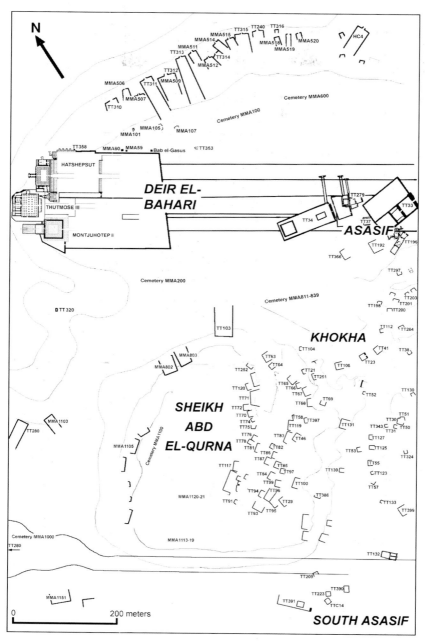

Map 9. Deir el-Bahari, Asasif, Khokha, Sheikh Abd el-Qurna, and South Asasif.

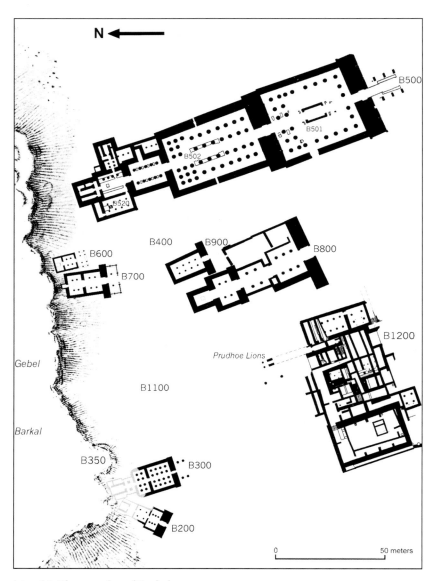

N ◄

B500
B501
B502
B520

B400 B900 B800
B600
B700

B1200

Prudhoe Lions

Gebel

B1100

Barkal

B350 B300

B200

0   50 meters

Map 10. The temples of Barkal
B200: temple of Amun-Re, built by Taharqa.
B300: rock temple of Amun, (re?)built by Taharqa.
B350: rock pinnacle in shape of uraeus.

INTRODUCTION: IMPERIAL EGYPT

During the second half of the second millennium BC, Egypt had transformed from an entity primarily focused on the Nile valley to an imperial power. At her empire's height she exercised direct or indirect control over a vast swath of territory that stretched from northern Syria into the heart of Upper Nubia. This expansion seems to have been a direct reaction to the humiliation of the Second Intermediate Period, during which much of Egypt had been under the sway of the Palestinian Hyksos rulers,[1] while Nubia, long a tributary of Egypt, had become an independent and hostile state.[2] The wars of liberation conducted by the last rulers of the Theban Seventeenth Dynasty had at length driven out the Hyksos, with the mopping-up operations of the first Eighteenth Dynasty kings transformed by Thutmose I and III into a 'forward policy' that pushed up to, and beyond, the Euphrates. An empire was thus created in Syria-Palestine that would endure, apparently with little challenge, for over a century.[3] At the same time, Nubia was once again brought under Egyptian control, with a formal viceregal regime established at least as far south as the Fifth Cataract, which replaced the looser approach that seems to have been applied during previous periods of Egyptian control in the south.[4]

However, Egypt's northern hegemony had come under pressure from the Hittites of Anatolia late in the Eighteenth Dynasty, leading to a series of campaigns into northern Syria that focused on the city of Qadesh in the Orontes valley.[5] Ultimately, an accommodation had been reached between the Egyptians and Hittites, leading to a peace treaty in Year 21 of Rameses II, and what appears to have remained a mutually supportive relationship[6] until the extinction of the Hittite empire in the first part of the twelfth

1

century. The same upheavals that had contributed to the fall of the Hittites clearly had an impact on Egypt's position in the broader Levant, culminating in Rameses III's defensive wars against the 'Sea Peoples' in his Year 8.[7]

Another invasion, this time from Libya in Year 11, saw another successful Egyptian defense, with over two thousand of the enemy being killed and their captured leaders executed. However—and very significantly for the later course of Egyptian history—the Libyan population of the western Delta continued to increase by peaceful infiltration.[8]

In parallel with these issues of foreign relations, the core of the Egyptian state had been undermined by the conflicts within the ruling elite that had arisen within a decade of the death of Rameses II, culminating with Sethnakhte's seizure of power from the female king Tawosret, and the foundation of the new Twentieth Dynasty.[9] Furthermore, by the late twenties of the reign of Rameses III, economic problems were becoming manifest, made most visible in failures to pay the Deir el-Medina workmen, which led to a sit-down strike by them in Year 29.[10] Against this background was hatched a plot against the king's life. Apparently motivated by a dispute as to which of the king's sons should be his heir, this seemingly resulted in the death of Rameses III in his thirty-second regnal year.[11]

In the wake of these unhappy events, the reigns that followed that of Rameses III saw a slow but steady national decline. On more than one occasion the conventional father-son succession of the kingship was frustrated by skulduggery, accident, or disease, leading to no fewer than three sons of Rameses III eventually occupying the throne.[12] Rameses IV[13] was succeeded by his son, Rameses V Amenhirkopeshef I, but when he died young, possibly of smallpox,[14] his own successor was his uncle, Rameses VI Amenhirkopeshef II.[15] A similar situation is seen after the death of Rameses VI, whose son, Rameses VII Itamun, was not followed on the throne by one of his own known offspring, but by another son of Rameses III, Rameses VIII Sethhirkopeshef. The regime of the eighth Rameses was short-lived, but may have ended peacefully, as none of his—admittedly scarce—memorials seem to have been mutilated. He was then followed on the throne by a ninth Rameses, whose reign was to mark a watershed in the history of Egypt.

1 THE FALL OF THE HOUSE OF RAMESES

I n contrast to Rameses III through VIII, whose mutual relationships are clear,[1] the background of Neferkare-setepenre Rameses IX Khaemwaset I is obscure. Based on the fact that Rameses IX had a son named (Rameses-)Montjuhirkopeshef (C),[2] it has been proposed that Rameses IX might have been the offspring of the son of Rameses III named Montjuhirkopeshef.[3] On the other hand the existence of a further son of Rameses IX named Nebmaatre[4] (the prenomen of Rameses VI) could also point to Rameses IX being a son of the sixth Rameses.

Montjuhirkopeshef C is known only from his tomb in the Valley of the Kings (KV19), which had originally been begun for a Prince Sethhirkopeshef, almost certainly the future Rameses VIII. Here, Montjuhirkopeshef appears with the titles of First King's Son of His Body, Eldest King's Son of his Body, First Generalissimo, and Noble at the Head of the Two Lands; the inscription of Rameses IX's name on a belt buckle guarantees his status as the original heir. Nebmaatre served as high priest at Heliopolis, named with his father on three reinscribed gateways and a column in a temple at Arab el-Hisn within the Heliopolis complex.

Of the administrators of Egypt during the reign of Rameses IX, three viziers are known: (Rameses-)Montjuerhatef, who died in Year 8,[5] a Nebmaatrenakhte who was active in Year 14,[6] and Khaemwaset (F), who was in office from at least Year 16 and survived into the reign of Rameses X (see pp. 5, 7, 10, 12). However, no other national officials are known, although a number of individuals of the viceregal administration of Nubia are attested. Two viceroys seem to have served during the reign, Wentawat and his son Ramesesnakhte (C),[7] although this is based on the internal relative chronology of the viceregal succession, rather than any explicitly dated material.[8] Among more junior office holders in Nubia, Ranefer, high priest at Quban, and Bakenwernel, Treasurer of the Lord of the Two Lands in Kush, are explicitly dated to Rameses IX's reign.[9] Indeed, a statuette of the latter came from Gebel Barkal,[10] indicating that Egyptian authority still reached into Upper Nubia.

The reign of Rameses IX saw a significant amount of work carried out at Karnak—certainly the most since the time of Rameses III (fig. 1).[11] While the Theban higher clergy of the period will be discussed below (pp. 14–16), little survives relating to their subordinates, apart from Imiseba, chief of the temple archives, attested by a text at Karnak and his impressive (albeit usurped) tomb (TT65) at Thebes-West.[12] Although high priests of the Fayyum god Sobek-shedty and of Nekhbet at el-Kab are clearly datable to the reign,[13] no information exists on the situation at Memphis, where only a handful of broadly 'late New Kingdom' high-priestly names are known.[14]

However, by far the best-known individuals of the reign are the various denizens of the Theban west bank who are mentioned in an extensive dossier of papyrus documents relating the apparent epidemic of tomb robbery that scarred the teens of Rameses IX's reign. Apart from their intrinsic interest, they also include some material that is potentially crucial to the correct reconstruction of the last years of the Twentieth Dynasty (see pp. 9ff).

Fig. 1. Relief of Rameses IX offering to the Theban triad in the *Cour de cachette* at Karnak.

Although there is one reference back to an investigation carried out by the vizier Nebmaatrenakhte in Year 14,[15] the dossier opens on III *3ht* 18 of Year 16, when a commission was sent by the vizier Khaemwaset F to inspect ancient tombs at Thebes-West. Of ten kings' tombs inspected, one (of Sobekemsaf I of the Seventeenth Dynasty at Dra Abu'l-Naga) was found to have been robbed, as had two out of four sepulchers of priestesses, while another royal pyramid had been in the process of being tunneled into. Paweraa, mayor of Thebes-West, produced a list of thieves, who were arrested and induced to confess.[16] The following day, the vizier himself led a delegation to the Valley of the Queens where all tombs were declared to be intact—even though an alleged thief taken with them had confessed[17] to having robbed the tomb of queen Iset D, wife of Rameses III (QV51).[18] In addition, following their torture and confession, those accused of robbing Sobekemsaf's tomb were taken to the site of their alleged crime and made to point out the site of their activities.[19] The confessions included the detail that the robbery had taken place some four years previously (in Year 13) and had been followed by raids on the private tombs of Tjanefer (TT158),[20] Amenkhau,[21] and others.[22] Those interrogated also included the fisherman Panakhtemopet, who had ferried the gang across to the west bank and who had also taken them to their hideout on an island in the Nile; additionally, others believed to be implicated in the crimes were also examined.[23] These results were apparently felt to be a cause for celebration by those working in the necropolis, the resulting demonstration being felt by the mayor of Thebes-East, Paser, to be aimed at him personally: he had made the allegations that had kicked off the investigation in the first place, following complaints from the two scribes of the Deir el-Medina community.[24]

On Day 21 the Great *knbt* (council) of Thebes considered Paser's charges, but heard that none of the tombs alleged by him to have been robbed had actually been plundered. Thus although *some* tombs had been robbed, the fact that they were *not* the ones on Paser's list meant that it was the mayor who was in the wrong, rather than the necropolis administrators—led by Paweraa—who had allowed *other* tombs to be robbed![25] Nevertheless, the next day saw the trial of those who had been accused of robbing Sobekemsaf's tomb. Given their previous and repeated confessions, they were found guilty and consigned to prison until the king should determine their fate.[26] That this was a grisly death—probably including impalement—is suggested by a later recollection of the (apparently horrific) fate of thieves punished during Khaemwaset F's term of office.[27]

That the aforementioned robbery of the tomb of Iset had been real, in spite of the results of the vizier's inspection, is clear from documents dating to Year 17. On I *prt* 8, eight Deir el-Medina workmen were recorded as making depositions as to who had received proceeds from the robbery,[28] while on I *prt* 13(?) they are listed as under arrest, with their loot seized.[29] On II *prt* 24 the interrogation of the accused and their wives began, which culminated in a visit on III *prt* 21 to Iset's tomb, revealing the devastation within.[30] This, however, is not the last time her tomb appears in the documentation relating to the investigation of tomb robberies (see p. 9). It was not only tombs that were receiving the attentions of Thebes's criminal elements around this time, as in the following year there was a theft of gilding from sculptures in the Ramesseum.[31]

These records of wrongdoing represent the final dated documents from the reign of the ninth Rameses, who seems to have died during I *prt* in his Year 19, to judge by the accession of Khepermaatre-setepenre Rameses X Amen-hirkopeshef III being probably datable to the period I *prt* 25–27.[32] The tomb in which Rameses IX was buried (KV6—fig. 2)[33] was not completed according to its original design, and shows signs of frequent interruptions in the continuity of work. Only the first corridor was completed in accordance with original plans, being adorned with the Litany of Re and the beginning of the Book of Caverns in fine quality relief. Beyond this point, the decorative scheme was revised, probably in conjunction with a truncation of the overall design of the tomb, a small burial chamber being constructed directly beyond the four-pillared hall, in place of the further corridors and monumental burial hall that had probably been intended. Decoration in relief only reached as far as the second corridor, after which the remainder of the tomb—apart from the pillared hall, which remained only partly cut and unadorned—was merely painted in an inferior style. It has been suggested[34] that this latter work was carried out only after the king's death, but it could also have been done following a suspension of work during his lifetime, with work then resumed at a faster tempo, perhaps owing to the king's failing health. In any case, his actual interment would prove to be the last primary burial of a king in the Valley of the Kings.

As with almost all the royal tombs there, that of Rameses IX fell victim to the inevitable robbers, and his mummy was ultimately removed to a large cache of royal bodies in the Twenty-first Dynasty tomb of the high priest Panedjem II near Deir el-Bahari (see p. 76), housed in a coffin originally made for Nesikhonsu, that high priest's wife.[35] Some items, however, remained in the tomb until the nineteenth century AD, including wooden baulks and a life-size wooden 'guardian' statue of the king (fig. 14).[36]

Material dating to the reign of Rameses X is not plentiful.[37] Apart from scarabs and other small items, his monumental attestation is limited to minor works around Pylon IV at Karnak (fig. 3),[38] an inscription on a sphinx (also at Karnak),[39] his name in the temple of Horus at Aniba,[40] and the king's unfinished tomb in the Valley of the Kings (KV18).[41] The only trace of officialdom is a graffito of Year 3 naming the vizier Khaemwaset F,[42] whom we have already met in the tomb robbery documentation of the previous reign.

On the other hand, all three[43] years of the reign are covered in documents relating to Deir el-Medina,[44] which reveal that during Year 3 only one working day in five actually saw work on the royal tomb. There are a number of cases where rations were not delivered on time and on III *prt* 6, 9, 11, 12, 18, 21, and 24 the crew were "inactive because of the foreigners," clearly an incursion of hostile individuals from the western desert, following on from previous incidents attested in Years 10, 11, 13, and 15 of Rameses IX.[45]

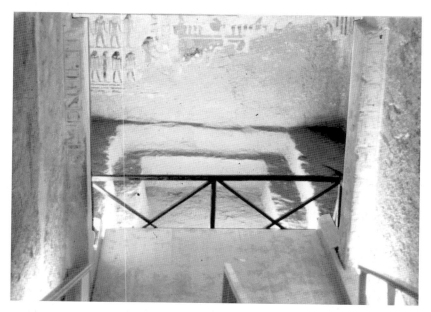

Fig. 2. Descent into the burial chamber of the tomb of Rameses IX (KV6). The cutting in the floor may have contained a wooden sarcophagus, as no trace of a stone one is known.

Fig. 3. Two-line text of Rameses X at the foot of the north tower of Pylon IV. The large cartouches below belong to Rameses IV.

Conflicts between these Libyans and the Egyptians went back many years, but had first come to a head in the middle of the Nineteenth Dynasty when, in Year 5 of Merenptah, they made an incursion into northwest Egypt in coalition with the so-called Sea Peoples from the north east Mediterranean.[46] Under Rameses III there had been further assaults, once again successfully repulsed, but from this point onward increasing numbers of Libyans infiltrated into Egypt, as peaceful settlers, but also as bandits such as those who were now disrupting work by the Theban tomb workmen.[47]

The uncertain security situation on the Theban west bank would ultimately lead to the abandonment of the Deir el-Medina village in favor of the fortified Medinet Habu temple enclosure. As well as the Libyan incursions, the fallout from the ongoing tomb robbery trials must have added to uncertainty and dislocation of normal business; in addition, it is possible that the reign of Rameses X also saw a conflict that resulted in the temporary deposition of the high priest of Amun himself (see pp. 14–16).

That circumstances were in any case not conducive to royal tomb construction is shown by the state of the sepulcher being constructed for Rameses X when work was discontinued. Only the entrance to the tomb, the first corridor, and a small fragment of the second had been cut, while decoration was limited to the entrance lintel and the initial tableaux on each wall of the first corridor. There is no indication of the tomb having been made ready for even an improvised interment,[48] and thus it is unclear where the king was buried. It has been suggested that he could have been laid to rest in the royal residence city of Per-Rameses in the northeastern Delta,[49] but it is also possible that he was interred in a modest location at Thebes. The latter may particularly have been the case given the potentially tumultuous state of the country at the end of his reign (see pp. 12–15).

The aforementioned tomb robbery documentation dated to the reign of Rameses IX is paralleled by another set of documents that covers a range of further investigations that clearly follow on from them. However, these are dated not to a king's reign but to an era known as the *wḥm-mswt*, with the literal meaning of 'repeating of births' and the implication of 'renaissance.'[50]

From Year 1 come records of more trials relating to robberies in the Valley of the Queens. These included (another?) penetration of Iset D's QV51,[51] and the robbery of both the adjacent QV52—the tomb of another of Rameses III's wives, Tyti[52]—and of the sepulcher of a "King's Wife Baketwernel of King Menmaatre," not nowadays recognized.[53] Extensive depredations of a temple, probably Karnak itself, were also catalogued in Year 1;[54] while Year 2 saw the investigation of thefts from the memorial temple of Rameses III at Medinet Habu, although the final outcome is now lost.[55] The same year also saw a trial related to the theft of a portable chest from the Ramesseum.[56]

In Year 9 came the trial of various priests accused of the wholesale theft of metals from the Ramesseum, indicating that the Year 2 trial, and that of Year 18 of Rameses IX, had not deterred the less honest members of that temple's staff.[57] Unplaced in time is a confession[58] of thieves who broke into the tomb of Rameses VI (KV9), although it may have predated Year 9 of Rameses IX, when a graffito was written on the ceiling of the tomb's burial hall.[59]

The novel era-dating used for these documents—of a kind apparently without direct parallel in ancient Egypt (but cf. pp. 40–41)—is tied into the conventional regnal scheme by a dateline "Year 1, I *ꜣḥt* 2, corresponding to Year 19."[60] That the *wḥm-mswt* was contained at least in part within the reign of King Menmaatre-setepenptah Rameses XI Khaemwaset II is indicated by the existence of an oracle text on the north wall of the Horemheb-rebuilt Amenhotep II chapel at Karnak. This is dated to "Year 7 *wḥm-mswt* III *šmw* 28 under the person of the dual king Menmaatre-setepenptah son of Re Rameses-Khaemwaset" (figs. 22–24).[61] That the Year 19 was his has been generally accepted since the late 1920s,[62] with the king's placement at the end of the sequence of Rameses kings made clear from his association with individuals who spanned the Twentieth/Twenty-first Dynasty transition.

However, if Rameses XI's Year 1 directly followed the demise of Rameses X, this would place the events related in these further tomb robbery documents more than two decades after those of Years 16 and 17 of Rameses IX. However, a number of these pieces of documentation are written on the *same* papyrus as a key text of the time of Rameses IX,[63] while they also mention individuals who featured in those previous events.[64] In particular, the fisherman Panakhtemopet, who had acted as a ferryman for thieves in Year 16 and received a share of loot in return, confesses on IV *šmw* 8 of Year 1 (unequivocally of the *wḥm-mswt*) to ferrying *the very same thieves* across the river, presumably in the recent past,[65] and is then interrogated yet again nine days later.[66] That the whole gang were all still alive, still together, and still thieving a quarter-century on from their first entanglement seems most improbable, which suggests that the two dates were actually separated by only a few years at most.

A similar conclusion springs from a number of other interrogations during the same session. First, the son of one of the tomb robbers known from the latter part of Rameses IX's reign denies his own involvement in any thefts, but is open about his father's former activities[67]—probably relevant a few years on from those events but hardly of import decades on. Second, a vivid mention of executions "during the time of the vizier Khaemwaset"[68] during another interrogation of the same series[69] would also argue against those executions having taken place decades before. Third, tomb QV51, wrecked by robbers no later than Year 17 of Rameses IX (see p. 5) was still the subject of inquiries in Year 1: it seems unlikely that these will have dragged on for some twenty-five years!

Although disturbing, the apparently secure anchoring of the *wḥm-mswt* to the end of Rameses XI's reign[70] has led to these anomalies being ignored, simply noted as puzzling, or otherwise explained away.[71] The other option, that Year 1 of Rameses XI *preceded* rather than followed the last years of Rameses IX by something approaching two decades,[72] has not generally received support, principally on the basis of the impact on the apparently settled absolute chronology of the New Kingdom as a whole. However, it can be questioned whether the current consensus on the latter is actually correct (see Appendix 1), with the result that it is indeed worth exploring the consequences of a reconfiguration of the late Twentieth Dynasty to bring the beginning of the *wḥm-mswt* rather closer to the events of the end of Rameses IX's reign.

The starting point would be to view Rameses XI as having ruled in another part of Egypt since the early years of Rameses IX, thus presaging the splits of royal authority within the country that are such a feature of the Third Intermediate Period. Perhaps significant here is that Rameses XI's prenomen was 'Menmaatre-setepenptah'—the only royal prenomen in pre-Ptolemaic history regularly to invoke Ptah, the patron god of Memphis. Since all other pre-Twenty-ninth Dynasty prenomina to do so were apparently 'specials,' for use at Memphis only, it may suggest that Rameses XI was originally a Memphite ruler.[73] In addition, it may be noted that his nomen employed the northern-referencing epithet 'netjerheqaiunu' ('divine ruler of Heliopolis'), although in this case it had previously been used by the indubitably national Rameses VI and VII, with the simple 'heqaiunu' also the universal epithet of Rameses III.[74] Nevertheless, it certainly reinforces the potential implication from his prenomen that Rameses XI might have begun his career as ruler of the north, in parallel with Rameses IX in the south. He would then have come south after the demise of both Rameses IX and X, and marked his new 'national' regime by initiating a fresh year-numbering scheme—the *wḥm-mswt*.

This model would imply that no date of Rameses XI lower than Year 19 should be present at Thebes, contrasting with the Years 1 and 18 found on a document[75] from (probably) near Herakleopolis,[76] and thus in Rameses XI's putative original territory. Unfortunately, this is not the case: on the same papyrus that contains the Deir el-Medina journal for Year 3 of Rameses X[77] we find a text that is dated to Year 1, I *ꜣḥt* 24 [. . . Men]maat[re]-setepenptah, i.e., Rameses XI. We also have other Theban documents explicitly dated to Years 8–10,[78] 12,[79] 14,[80] and 17.[81] While this might at first sight make a reconfiguration of reigns impossible, it is important to note in all these cases that these documents are administrative/private ones, rather than public monuments, and that this may influence how dates should be interpreted.

In administrative/private documents, dates tend to be reduced to the minimum required by the context—generally year/month/day; reign is only added where absolutely necessary. During the *wḥm-mswt* it appears from the only intact 'monumental' date that the full form of a dateline was "Year X *wḥm-mswt*, Y month, day Z, under the person of (Rameses XI):"[82] could this, at least on occasion, have been written with the "*wḥm-mswt*" omitted, just as other datelines indisputably omitted "under the person of . . ."?[83]

In this connection, it is worth exploring the potential purpose of the initiation of the *wḥm-mswt* in the first place. Under the conventional view of a linear succession of Rameses IX/X/XI, it is difficult to produce a clear explanation, other than to suggest that it represented a 'clean start' after a civil conflict that had seen the 'suppression' of the high priest of Amun (see pp. 14–16). But why would a new year-numbering system be instituted in such a circumstance, with all the scope for administrative confusion that would have resulted?[84] However, if Rameses XI had transitioned from being a regional king (who had fully acknowledged his counterparts, Rameses IX and X) to being a national ruler, a new year-count would have been fully appropriate. Also, from the point of view of Theban scribes, the new era would have been a new reign, making *for them* the *wḥm-mswt* and the reign of Rameses XI essentially interchangeable when it came to writing datelines.[85] Indeed, it may be significant that the *only* extant statement of correspondence between the old and new counts is of Year 1 = 19,[86] suggesting that subsequently the old count was no longer used.[87]

Using this principle to attempt to redate the above-mentioned documents that refer to the Rameses XI *wḥm-mswt* does not in most cases cause any particular problems. There are two exceptions to this. One is the Year 17 document, which was addressed to the viceroy of Kush Panehsy and sits very uncomfortably with the other documentation relating to this man and would, if belonging to the *wḥm-mswt,* would extend it well beyond its otherwise attested greatest length (cf. p. 23). Interestingly, part of the Theban necropolis journal dates to Years [17] and 18 of a reign that can only be that of Rameses XI,[88] and cannot on the basis of the personnel mentioned be placed at the end of the *wḥm-mswt*. While this could be regarded as a nail in the coffin of the potential reconfiguration, it could also indicate that there was a short hiatus between Rameses XI taking power in the south and the wholly exceptional decision to effectively restart his regnal numbering. Perhaps indicative of Year 17/18 as a period of transition is the mention in the journal of a new vizier Wennefer[89] making his first visit to Thebes, presumably as a replacement for Khaemwaset F, last seen in Rameses X's Year 3.[90] Following this, Wennefer subsequently appears with Rameses XI in the temple of Maat at Karnak.[91] Various other (Theban) documents lacking a royal name have been attributed to the earlier years of Rameses XI, but once again there are few fundamental problems with assigning them to the *wḥm-mswt;*[92] among others, they include a Year 12 list of house owners at Thebes[93] and a set of Year 14/15 agricultural accounts.[94]

In view of the foregoing, one may provisionally move forward on the basis of the hypothesis that, on the demise of Rameses X soon after I *prt* 1 in his Year 3, Rameses XI, who had been reigning in northern Egypt since the third year of Rameses IX, assumed authority over the whole of Egypt.[95] Initially continuing the regnal numbering used during the first phase of his reign, the beginning of his nineteenth personal year on III *šmw* 20 saw a

Fig. 4. 'High priest's wall' on the outside of the east wall of the southern extension of the temple of Amun-Re at Karnak. In the center are twin figures of the high priest Amenhotep G, flanked by images of Amenhotep being rewarded by Rameses IX, who is unusually shown on the same scale. The composition dates to Year 10 of the king. A similar set of scenes was carved in Dra Abu'l-Naga tomb K93.12, apparently an early Eighteenth Dynasty royal tomb-chapel, reconstructed by the God's Wife Iset E and Amenhotep late in the Twentieth Dynasty.

new era—the *wḥm-mswt*—being initiated, which was henceforth used for all dating, although not infrequently in an abbreviated form that omitted explicit mention of the era and at first sight thus attributed the years of the era to the king's personal year-count.

As to Rameses XI's origins as northern king, he would presumably have been a scion of the family of Rameses III. His personal name could point to his being a son or grandson of Khaemwaset E, son of Rameses III and *sem* priest of Ptah at Memphis,[96] a notion perhaps reinforced by Rameses XI's putative status as a northern ruler. There have been attempts to link the "King's Wife Baketwernel of King Menmaatre," the robbery of whose tomb is mentioned in Year 1 of the *wḥm-mswt* (see p. 9), with Rameses XI,[97] but this is unlikely, as the living king would be called in such a context 'his person' or 'pharaoh,' not by his prenomen. Naming the king would indicate a deceased monarch, in this case Sethy I.[98]

One result of placing the beginning of the *wḥm-mswt* within a short time of the end of Rameses X's reign is its implications for dating a well-known event. This is the 'suppression' of the high priest of Amun Amenhotep (G), which would then fall during the last year of the tenth Rameses's reign.[99] Amenhotep is well attested during the reign of Rameses IX (fig. 4), but the precise dating of his 'suppression,' alluded to in various texts of the period— including an autobiographical text of Amenhotep himself[100]—has been much debated.[101] However, it seems fairly clear that it should be placed soon before the proclamation of the *wḥm-mswt*, regardless of which reconstruction is used for the chronological relationship between Rameses IX, X, and XI.[102] Exactly what lay behind this episode, which lasted nine months,[103] is unclear, but later references to the period indicate deeply troubled times, with probable famine (the time is apparently referred to as the "year of hyenas")[104] and warfare including "when Panehsy destroyed Cynopolis."[105]

This Panehsy is universally identified as the viceroy of Kush of that name, and his role in the affair has been much debated.[106] However, a statement (made in Year 2 of the *wḥm-mswt*) that an event occurred "when

Fig. 5. Relief on pillar 7 in the temple at Buhen, showing the viceroy Sethmose adoring the cartouches of Rameses XI.

Panehsy came and suppressed my superior (i.e., the high priest), though there was no fault in him"[107] makes it fairly clear that Panehsy was indeed the opponent of the high priest.

On IV $ȝht$ 15 of Year 17 of Rameses XI (on the present reconstruction, directly after Rameses XI's assumption of national power and the last known date of Rameses X) a letter was written by the king to Panehsy, instructing him to work with a royal butler in completing a portable shrine.[108] This is very much routine business,[109] and presumably is to be dated before the outbreak of the conflict, which included the assault on Cynopolis, which lay far to the north of Thebes, near modern Beni Mazar and Sheikh Fadl[110]—well beyond the normal domain of the Nubian viceroy. This fighting is presumably the same occasion that claimed the lives of some of those accused of tomb robberies at Thebes.[111]

Fig. 6. Oracle text of Nesamun, dated to Year 7 of the whm-$mswt$ on the north wall of the chapel rebuilt by Horemheb from blocks of Amenhotep II's former portico in front of Pylon VIII on the east side of the court between Pylons IX and X at Karnak. The high priest and viceroy of Nubia, Piankh, is shown at the top.

The next we hear of Panehsy is in the aforementioned testimony of Years 1 and 2 of the *wḥm-mswt*, when his name is embellished with the 'enemy' determinative.[112] Given that Amenhotep's own account states that his 'suppression' was ended by a successful appeal to the king, it would seem that even if the action against Amenhotep had originally possessed official sanction, the high priest's appeal had then turned Panehsy into the outlaw. However, as we shall see, his career seems by no means to have been ended by this fall into disfavor (see p. 20). As for the viceroyalty itself, it seems likely that a viceroy Sethmose, known from an inscription at Buhen (fig. 5), replaced Panehsy and then governed Nubia until he was himself superseded some time before Year 7.[113]

Leaving aside the issues surrounding the 'suppression' itself, the high priesthood of Amun during the last years of the Twentieth Dynasty presents other significant difficulties. The starting point is Amenhotep, who was appointed to office no later than Year 9 of Rameses IX,[114] apparently in succession to his brother Nesamun[115] and their father Ramesesnakhte (B), the latter having served from at least the time of Rameses IV down to Year 2 of Rameses IX.[116] Following his emergence from his period of 'suppression,' it is unclear how long Amenhotep remained in office, but he had certainly gone before Year 7 of the *wḥm-mswt*, when one Piankh appears as high priest, and also viceroy of Kush, general, and army leader in an oracle text at Karnak (fig. 6).[117]

For a long time it was agreed that between the pontificates of Amenhotep and Piankh was interposed that of Herihor,[118] who combined the sacerdotal and military offices held by Piankh, but lacked—at first—the viceroyalty.[119] Primary evidence for this comes from documents naming Herihor that are dated to (undefined) Years 5 and 6—usually assumed to be years of the *wḥm-mswt*. This material comprises dockets on the coffins of Sethy I (fig. 7) and Rameses II, relating to the "repeating of their burials" on II *ꜣḥt* 7 and III *prt* 15 of that year, respectively.[120] The Year 5 document is one of the most crucial pieces of evidence surviving regarding the period.

It is ostensibly a report submitted by Wenamun, the Elder of the Portal of the Temple of Amun-Re-nesunetjeru, concerning a journey to Byblos begun at Thebes on III *šmw* 16 in that year to procure timber for the construction of a new bark of Amun.[121] The document's historical importance lies in Wenamun's 'master' being stated to be high priest Herihor, while the city of Tanis (San el-Hagar) is described as "the place where Nesibanebdjedet

Fig. 7. Docket on the restored coffin of Sethy I recording the "repeating of the burial" of the king on the orders of Herihor on II *prt* 16 of Year 6 of the *wḥm-mswt* (Cairo CG61019). Similar dockets were placed on other royal coffins and mummies.

and Tentamun are." These two then host Wenamun and send him on his way on a ship bound for the Levant; later on, it is indicated that Nesibaneb-djedet controls a significant fleet. Still later in the text, he and Tentamun are described as "the pillars whom Amun has set up for the north of his land"—and ultimately as sending goods to Byblos to pay for the wood. The document also contains a reference back to a certain Khaemwaset, emissaries from whom had died in Byblos after a seventeen-year sojourn, and who is dismissed as 'just a man.' This could be taken as referring to the vizier of that name,[122] or Rameses IX or XI, both of whom were Khaemwasets; given the dismissive context (deflating Wenamun's regard for himself and his mission), the latter seems the most likely option, timescales making Rameses IX the more probable candidate.[123]

The identity of Wenamun's Nesibanebdjedet (Greek: Smendes) with the king Hedjkheperre-setepenre Nesibanebdjedet (I)-meryamun (see pp. 39–41) is generally admitted, but his status in Year 5 is not clear. That he is not yet king is suggested by his being called by name, rather than royal title as is usual for a living king in such contexts, and the fact that he is depicted as a northern counterpoint of Herihor, who is at this point a simple high priest. Accordingly, Nesibanebdjedet is usually regarded as some kind of northern governor, under the overall authority of the pharaoh himself.

As for Tentamun, this lady is presumably Nesibanebdjedet's wife, given their close association in the Wenamun report.[124] Otherwise, we find a Tentamun as the mother of a lady Henttawy (A), who was to marry the high priest of Amun Panedjem I. However, the text in question, on Henttawy's funerary papyrus,[125] gives the latter's ancestry ambiguously as "born of the King's Wife Tentamun, begotten of the Honorable Nebseni." Does this mean that Tentamun was the daughter of Nebseni or was Nebseni another (presumably the first) husband of Tentamun? While the latter interpretation seems better grammatically,[126] the fact that Henttawy bore the title of King's Daughter would at first sight exclude the last option: on the other hand there are examples of 'King's Daughter' being applied to a granddaughter of a king.[127] A further issue here is that one of Henttawy A's sons (and a grandson) sometimes compounded their names with 'Rameses' (see pp. 39, 57, 60), implying some blood link with the Rameside royal house. Henttawy's mother Tentamun is generally seen as the link.

One option to get around the problem has been to propose two separate Tentamuns, mother and daughter.[128] Tentamun A (daughter of Nebseni) would be a wife of Rameses XI, the couple producing daughters named Henttawy (A) and Tentamun (B), who married respectively Panedjem I and Nesibanebdjedet. However, one remains uncomfortable with going against the obvious reading of Henttawy's filiation. Since it is clear that 'King's Daughter' *can* mean 'king's granddaughter,' an alternative could be to take Tentamun as a daughter of (presumably) Rameses XI, married at first to Nebseni, with whom she had Henttawy, and then as a widow espoused by Nesibanebdjedet. As both a royal granddaughter *and* a royal stepdaughter, Henttawy's title of King's Daughter would not have been inappropriate. In this connection, it may well be significant that among the titles found on Henttawy's coffin is the very unusual one of Daughter of the King's Great Wife: could this be a further clue that it was her mother who was crucial in her descent? We will return to Henttawy later.

In 1992, the conventional placement of Wenamun's adventures (and the pontificate of Herihor) in Year 5 of the *whm-mswt* was challenged by the proposition that Herihor was actually Piankh's successor.[129] This reconstruction has garnered considerable support,[130] as well as significant opposition.[131] While the proposal clearly has merits on its own terms,[132] it also creates new problems, in particular concerning the aforementioned documents naming Herihor in Years 5 and 6. If referring to the *whm-mswt*, they clearly make Herihor a predecessor, rather than successor, of Piankh. To counter this, it has been proposed that the dates were actually of Herihor himself, the high priest having arrogated the royal prerogative of a personal dating system.[133] However, the notion that a high priest might use his own 'regnal' years[134] is ultimately reliant on a single later example, which is itself problematic (see p. 65).[135] In this context it is worth noting that even such genuinely kingly figures as Hatshepsut, Neferneferuaten, and Tawosret used (or in the last case continued) the years of their associated kings, rather than superposing a sequence of their own. In this connection, it is important to emphasize that the Year 5 and 6 documents simply mention Herihor as high priest—and not as the king he later became (see pp. 22ff).

However, it is not impossible that Herihor was both predecessor *and* successor of Piankh. Piankh's period of office was dominated by a war in Nubia, which may have been split into two campaigns, one in Year 10/11 of the *wḥm-mswt*, one slightly later.[136] In prosecuting these, Piankh employed not only the titles of high priest and general, but also those of army leader and viceroy of Kush. It has generally been assumed that these operations were directed against the (ex-)viceroy Panehsy, who had become *persona non grata* after the 'War of the High Priest,' and may subsequently have maintained an irregular regime in his Nubian fastness. However, the name Panehsy is mentioned only once in the so-called Late Rameside Letters (LRL),[137] a corpus of documents written by protagonists of the Nubian war, including Piankh himself, the Chief of the Harem of Amun Herere, and the Deir el-Medina Scribes Thutmose-Tjuroy and his son Butehamun.[138] That single mention is in a letter from Thutmose to Butehamun, and simply reports Piankh's intention to "go up to meet Panehsy at the place where he is."[139] On one hand, there is no certainty that this is the same Panehsy who had been viceroy a decade earlier (it is a common name, especially in the south[140]) while on the other, there is no clear indication that the intention is to meet him in battle. Given that we know nothing of what had given rise to the southern conflict—had it really been rumbling away since the end of the War of the High Priest?—it is not impossible that a peaceful meeting was involved. Might Panehsy have been allowed to live in retirement after his disgrace, and was now being brought in to use his good offices in resolving the current problem, rather than being the rebel against whom Piankh was operating? Indeed, had his disgrace been a result of unacceptable methods, rather than actual rebellion?

While none of these propositions is susceptible to proof, neither is the general consensus that Piankh's Nubian war brought Panehsy's career to a close. Indeed, if the reconfiguration of the reigns of Rameses IX, X, and XI is accepted, we have a record of Year 12 of the *wḥm-mswt*[141] mentioning a viceroy[142] Panehsy carrying out normal functions, in conjunction with the very same Thutmose who had not long before been serving on the staff of Piankh.[143] In addition, it may be significant that the inscriptions on the doorway of Panehsy's burial chamber at Aniba (SA38) seem not to have been intentionally damaged.[144]

This mention of Panehsy falls not long after the last attestation of Piankh in (probably) Year 11,[145] and it may be that, in the light of Piankh's unexpected death and/or military defeat, circumstances conspired to bring Panehsy back into favor and office. Indeed, it is by no means clear on what basis Piankh was actually prosecuting his southern war.[146] Letters from Piankh survive that order the extrajudicial murder of two policemen,[147] and dismiss any concerns as to the king's attitude by the remarkable out-burst: "As for Pharaoh, l.p.h., how shall he reach this land? And to whom is Pharaoh, l.p.h., superior still?"[148] Against this background of skullduggery, a radical realignment of loyalties in the wake of Piankh's unexpected depar-ture from the scene would not seem particularly remarkable.[149]

Fig. 8. Stela showing the high priest Herihor (erased) and his wife Nedjmet before Osiris, Horus, Isis, and Hathor, with a hymn to Osiris below (RMO AP16).

Fig. 9. Temple of Khonsu at Karnak, with the Ptolemaic temple of Opet to the left. The Khonsu temple was begun under Rameses III, but construction and decoration continued into the early Twenty-first Dynasty.

In light of the foregoing, we need to consider a stela of Herihor (as simple high priest and general), which has his figure and name (but not those of his wife, Nedjmet) erased (fig. 8).[150] Such an erasure clearly indicates some hostility toward him personally during or following his initial high-priestly career—yet there is no sign of contemporary attacks on any of his royal monuments, or on the high-priestly ones that were produced directly before them (see just below). This could well suggest an interruption in Herihor's career, with his removal from office in favor of Piankh as a result of whatever events were to give rise to the Nubian war. Then, in the wake of Piankh's demise, he will have returned to office, along with the likewise rehabilitated Panehsy, the two of them together once again separating the viceroyalty and high priesthood that had been combined by Piankh.

On the basis of the above, one would then allocate to this putative second stage of Herihor's career the series of large-scale depictions of him as high priest in the hypostyle hall of the Khonsu temple at Karnak (fig. 9). Here, they are fully integrated into a scheme of decoration that otherwise centers on Rameses XI (fig. 10) and was explicitly executed on the king's command.[151] Although throughout he appears purely in a priestly role, these depictions break new ground for a high priest in the way that his images are juxtaposed with those of Rameses XI—he is portrayed on exactly the same scale and performing the same divine offices for the gods: no previous high priest had ever been depicted in this way.[152] In doing this he takes further the act of Amnhotep G in showing himself on the same scale as Rameses IX (fig. 5).

To the latter part of this phase of his career would belong an oracle text of Herihor as high priest in the Khonsu temple (fig. 11).[153] This seems to have predicted the future career of the high priest, but is badly broken and thus difficult to interpret. It includes the mention of one period of two decades and another of three, but exactly what these periods relate to remains obscure.[154] On the other hand, it shows that by the time the text was carved, Herihor had added the office of viceroy of Kush to his portfolio of responsibilities—on the present reconstruction in succession to the resurgent, but perhaps now defunct, Panehsy.

This exalted status for Herihor was, however, surpassed when the peristyle court of the Khonsu temple came to be decorated, where he is depicted

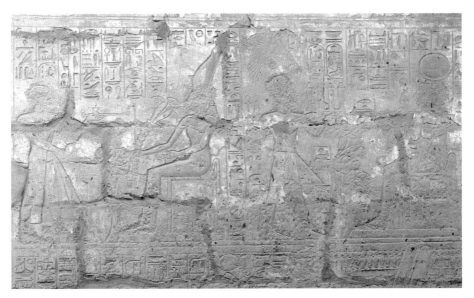

Fig. 10. Tableau in the hypostyle hall of the Khonsu temple, with Herihor as high priest on the left and Rameses XI on the right. Both men are shown on the same scale and carrying out the same kind of divine office—usually the prerogative of the king in such temple contexts.

with full royal attributes and a pharaoh's full fivefold titulary, albeit with a prenomen that is simply "First Prophet of Amun" (fig. 12).[155] While it has often been argued that this status was to a greater or lesser degree honorific,[156] it should be noted that this 'name' was used later as a prenomen of both Panedjem I (as king) and Pasebkhanut I (see pp. 50, 57). Accordingly, there seems no good reason to doubt that Herihor did indeed rule as a 'proper' pharaoh, at least in the Thebaid.

Linked in with this is the question of how long, if at all, the *wḥm-mswt* lasted beyond the Year 10 contained in the Piankh correspondence (see above). If the Rameses IX/X/XI reconfiguration is to be accepted, to this we can add Years 12 and 14 (although associated with Rameses XI's name),[157] together with a Year 15.[158] Such a period of time would nicely accommodate the joint Rameses XI/Herihor work in the hypostyle hall at the Khonsu temple and thus suggest that Herihor's kingly phase began with Rameses XI's death. Since Wenamun's report clearly shows Herihor and Nesibanebdjedet as coequal rulers of the south and north respectively, under Rameses XI, it seems not unreasonable to take the view that their respective elevations to kingship directly followed the demise of the last Rameside king, with a formal split of the country between the two new monarchs.

Like Rameses X, the last Rameside appears not to have been buried in the tomb (KV4) that he had constructed in the Valley of the Kings (fig. 13).[159] Although structurally all but complete, the decoration had hardly begun,

Fig. 11. Oracle stela of Herihor, carved to the right of the entrance to the hypostyle hall of the Khonsu temple.

and the only material relating to the king himself found in the tomb was a set of foundation deposits in the burial chamber. These were placed around the edge of the shaft that lay in the middle of the chamber, a feature that is

Fig. 12. Image of Herihor as king on a column in the peristyle court of the Khonsu temple.

unique to this tomb. Presumably he found rest in the north of Egypt, where he seems to have begun his reign, and may have perhaps already had a tomb prepared during his earliest years, perhaps in the Memphite necropolis or at Per-Rameses (Qantir).

An important issue is whether, as king, Herihor continued to act as high priest as well, or whether another individual now discharged that duty. This question brings into the equation the figure of Piankh's son, Panedjem, whose career has also been the matter of debate. He is recorded as high priest in undefined Years 1, 6, 9, 10, 11, 12, 13, and 15,[160] while a king Khakheperre Panedjem is attested in a likewise undefined Year 8, and mentioned as the father of a high priest Masaharta (A) in a Year 16. The high priest Panedjem is also depicted in the first court of the Luxor temple (figs. 22 and 27) and on the pylon of the Khonsu temple (fig. 17).[161]

Fig. 13. View down the entrance corridor of KV4, the tomb of Rameses XI. Although structurally complete, the decoration of the tomb had been hardly begun.

The general assumption has been that Panedjem served as high priest in Years 1 to 15 of one dating era, and then became king from Year 16 of that era through to at least Year 8 of a further dating era. However, it is also conceivable that the Years 8 and 16 both belong to the same dating era, which could be that of King Panedjem himself, and thus indicate a reign of 16+ years, following on from his pontificate.[162] Given that Panedjem's decoration at the Khonsu temple clearly follows on from that of Herihor (cf. pp. 28–29), it would seem most likely that the Years 1 to 15 were those of what is suggested above to be the parallel reigns of Herihor and Nesibanebdjedet. In this case, it would appear that although he retained the pontifical tag as his prenomen, on becoming king Herihor handed over the actual high priesthood to Panedjem.[163]

In view of our proposal that Piankh and Herihor had been opponents, it might seem unlikely that the former's son could have become high

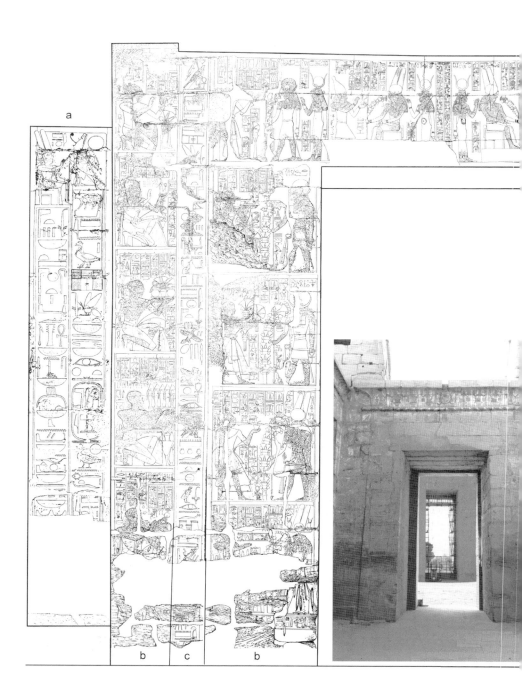

a

b   c   b

26   CHAPTER ONE

a

b   c   b

Fig. 14. Rear of the gate of the pylon of the Khonsu temple at Karnak, apparently originally laid out and partly carved under Herihor, completed by Panedjem I as high priest, and later restored by Ptolemy II. The pilaster texts (a) give the names and titles of Herihor; the scenes flanking the door (b) were initially carved with the images of a king—certainly Herihor—but were subsequently altered to show Panedjem I as high priest; the vertical texts on the door (c) refer to Panedjem as high priest, but also give him a Horus name and the title of Dual King. The lintel depicts Ptolemy II.

Fig. 15. Detail showing one of the figures of Panedjem I as high priest that had originally been carved as that of a king. To the right is the beginning of the adjacent vertical text that gives Panedjem a Horus name and the title *nsw-bity*, but no cartouches or other royal titles.

Fig. 16. Another of the figures of Panedjem I, showing the enclosure within which his name and principal titles were carved. There are some indications that this may have replaced earlier text—almost certainly the cartouches of Herihor—when the figure itself was converted from a king to a high priest.

priest under the latter. However, history is replete with erstwhile enemies reversing alliances, and it is by no means impossible that a 'deal' following Piankh's death could have provided for a division of power on Rameses XI's death that allowed Herihor to become southern king while Panedjem took his late father's pontifical and military offices.

That this putative settlement endured even after Herihor's death is suggested by the fact that in no case has any kingly image or titulary of Herihor been anciently mutilated.[164] This is in spite of Panedjem's constant emphasizing of his descent from Herihor's putative opponent, Piankh, and in spite of the fact that the numerous sons of Herihor (depicted in a procession in the Khonsu temple—see fig. 20) were bypassed for the high-priestly succession. Indeed, the only person in King Herihor's family who may have suffered after Herihor's demise was the eighteenth son in the Khonsu temple procession, where his name and titles have been replaced by those of Nespaneferhor iii, a son of Panedjem I. Thus, one must assume that the 'deal' broadly satisfied all protagonists and was essentially respected even after the passing of authority back to the line of Piankh. Indeed, the posthumous veneration of Piankh is shown by the existence of a stela from Kom el-Sultan at Abydos[165] and a relief at Luxor temple (fig. 22).

Under such a reconstruction, one might at first sight see Panedjem's transition from high priest to king as coinciding with Herihor's death—in an unknown year—and his replacement by Panedjem as southern king. However, against this are some strange occurrences on the inner part of the gateway of the pylon of the Khonsu temple. Here, figures now labeled as the simple high priest Panedjem were first carved with kingly attributes (*nemes* headdresses and a vulture hovering over their heads and certain royal titles incorporated into some texts).[166] The figures were later changed to those of a non-royal high priest, the royal attributes being plastered over (figs. 14–16).[167] In contrast, the images of Panedjem on the outer face of the pylon (e.g., fig. 17), were carved from the outset showing him as high priest.

These data have been variously interpreted, with the initially royal reliefs dismissed by some as early affectations by Panedjem that were soon reversed.[168] On the other hand, a radical interpretation has proposed that the figures were carved during a hitherto unnoticed reign between the death of Rameses XI and the accession of Herihor, identified as that of Khakheperre Panedjem—taken as a separate individual from the high priest Panedjem I.[169] However, in spite of special pleading to the contrary,[170] the location of the reliefs indicates fairly securely that they postdate Herihor's decoration of the peristyle court and, indeed, the most likely explanation is that they originally depicted King Herihor in a first phase of the decoration of the pylon, but were usurped by Panedjem I as part of his completion of the pylon's adornment after Herihor' death.[171]

An implication of this is that Panedjem I did *not* become king in Thebes directly after Herihor's death, as Panedjem's decoration of the pylon (and various other parts of the Khonsu temple) was thus necessarily carried out between Herihor's death and Panedjem's assumption of kingship. One would thus place Herihor's death early in the second decade of his joint rule with Nesibanebdjedet, leaving the latter as sole king of Egypt until Panedjem assumed the southern crown in Year 15/16—continuing the dating era initiated by Herihor and Nesibanebdjedet. The further careers of Nesibanebdjedet and Panedjem will be considered further in the next chapter, with the overall reconstruction summarized in fig. 18.

Fig. 17. Panedjem I as high priest offering to Amun, Khonsu, and Mut on the front of the pylon of the Khonsu temple.

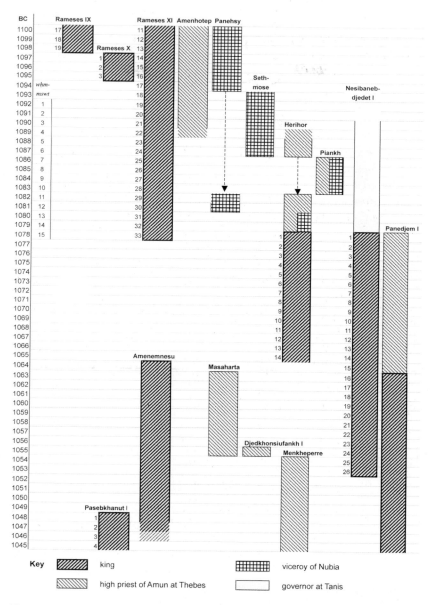

Fig. 18. Reconstruction of the careers of the principal protagonists during the period from the last years of Rameses IX to the middle of the Twenty-first Dynasty.

In the foregoing discussions we have avoided considering the family relationships of the high-priestly protagonists, as any reconstruction is heavily dependent on how one arranges the pontiffs themselves. A pivotal figure is the aforementioned Nedjmet who is attested as Herihor's wife both as high priest and as king. In the first case she bears the title of Chief of the Harem of Amun-Re-nesunetjeru, typical of the wife of a Theban high priest.

The same combination of this title with the name Nedjmet appears in a letter written by Piankh during his Nubian campaign.[172] Given the content of this letter—the murder of policemen in Thebes during the Nubian war (see p. 20),[173] and in particular its affectionate tone[174]—it seems likely that the recipient was Piankh's wife ('Nedjmet B'), rather than the aforementioned spouse of Herihor, who seems to have been one of Piankh's opponents (see p. 21). We will return to the matter of Piankh's spouse below.

In representations in the Khonsu temple dating to Herihor's kingship, *his* Nedjmet (A) is given both her original Chief of the Harem of Amun-Re-nesunetjeru title and the new royal ones of King's Great Wife and Lady of the Two Lands.[175] In her hieroglyphic Book of the Dead papyrus,[176] Nedjmet appears alongside Herihor with a cartouche and the additional title of King's Mother contained within it (fig. 19, left).

The same combination of name and title— "the King's Mother Nedjmet"—is also found in the cartouche naming the owner of a hieratic Book of the Dead/Book of Caverns papyrus.[177] This Nedjmet is stated therein to be the daughter of a King's Mother Herere (fig. 19, right). While it has been suggested that these two papyri belonged to different ladies,[178] it is important to note that the two documents are of different kinds, the second being of a particular type that appears during the earlier part of the Third Intermediate Period combining some chapters of the Book of the Dead with extracts from the Rameside "Books of the Underworld."[179] Accordingly—and further noting that there are no duplications in chapters between the two documents—this criterion cannot be used to posit two Nedjmets.[180] On the other hand, the two papyri were certainly produced by different scribes, with Nedjmet's Book of the Dead/Caverns being the earliest known example of such a compilation, most others dating to considerably later in the dynasty.[181] Its existence would suggest that this Nedjmet lived some way into the Twenty-first Dynasty.[182]

Nedjmet's mummy[183] included a bandage that bore "Year 1" in some kind of conjunction with the name of Panedjem I,[184] but is of little help in determining her date of death, as old linen could well have been used in preparing the body.[185] There is also the question, to which phase of Panedjem's career the date belonged: if it referenced him as king, this would be twenty-six years later than if it referenced him as high priest (cf. pp. 24–25).

The mummy was found in a set of coffins bearing the same cartouche and the full range of titles noted above (fig. 43),[186] accompanied by a similarly inscribed canopic chest.[187] The coffins had clearly been prepared at the same time as those of Panedjem I and Henttawy A (see p. 50), dating Nedjmet's outfit, and thus her burial, to the last decade of the reign of Nesibanebdjedet I at the earliest.[188] Nedjmet's mummy and equipment were found cached in the tomb of Panedjem II (TT320) near Deir el-Bahari along with a number of other individuals of the same period (see pp. 62–63), and it thus seems certain that the two papyri were also found here and were extracted during the years leading up to that tomb's formal archaeological 'discovery.'[189]

Fig. 19. Left: Herihor and Nedjmet A as depicted on her Book of the Dead papyrus (pBM EA10541). Right: Nedjmet A as depicted on her Book of the Dead/Book of Caverns papyrus (pBM EA10490), and naming her mother, the King's Mother Herere.

Fig. 20. Procession of the children of Herihor in the peristyle court of the Khonsu temple. From the right, the top row lists: the God's Wife and King's Great Wife Nedjmet (A); the King's Son, Steward of Amun, Prophet of Mut, Prophet of Amun, Master of Horse, Ankhef(enmut A); the King's Son, Fourth Prophet of Amun, Prophet of Onnuris, Prophet of Horus, [. . .], Preamunenamun; the King's Son, [. . .] of Amunre-nesunetjeru, Panefer[. . .]; the King's Son, Overseer of [. . .] of Amun, Amenhirwenemef B; the King's Son, Tekhui; the King's Son, Masaharta (i); the King's Son, Masaqaharta; the King's Son, Pashedkhonsu; the King's Son, [. . .] nefer; the King's Son, Amenhirkopeshef (E); the King's Son, Horkhebit; [. . .]; the King's Son, Biknetjery; the King's Son [. . .]nem; the King's Son [. . .]wasuna; the King's Son, Osorkon (i); a figure whose text was erased and relabeled for the God's Father of Amun, Nespaneferhor, son of Panedjem; Madenneb; bottom row: the Chantress of Amun, Chief of the Harem of Khonsu, Sh[. . .]e[setbaq]et; Nesyt[. . .]; [. . .]tentaneb; fifteen unlabeled women.

On the basis of this material, we learn that Nedjmet was not only the wife of Herihor, but was also both the sister of a king and also the mother of a king herself. It has sometimes been argued that the title of 'King's Mother' could also mean 'King's Mother-in-Law,' but there are no unequivocal examples of such a usage, and thus it would seem unwise to assume this except where there is no other alternative.

Looking at potential candidates for her brother, Nesibanebdjedet I seems to be the most obvious candidate, given his long-term close association with Herihor in the government of Egypt, as suggested by the scenario

depicted by Wenamun. It would seem less likely that Nesibanebdjedet could have been Nedjmet's son, and thus implicitly the son of Herihor as well[190]—the long-term coequal status of the two men might argue against their being father and son.

In this case, the only other candidate for Nedjmet's son would seem to be the obscure king Amenemnesut whose name is found just once, associated with that of the Tanite king Pasebkhanut I (Greek: Psusennês—see pp. 47–48). For the latter to be possible, Nedjmet would have to have survived until Amenemnesut's accession—which, on the basis of the aforementioned dating of certain elements of her burial assemblage (all of which include her King's Mother title), is perfectly possible.

No obvious king is, however, named in the long procession of the nineteen sons and nineteen daughters of Herihor that appears on the left-hand wall of the peristyle court of the Khonsu temple (fig. 20), headed by Nedjmet herself.[191] It is, however, conceivable that Amenemnesut is the (unnamed) infant shown carried by Nedjmet in one scene in the temple (fig. 21).[192] Whether Nedjmet was the mother of all the offspring of Herihor is, of course, a moot point, but it seems physically implausible. The procession motif is taken directly from the prototype provided by Rameses II in his various temples[193] and aped by Rameses III at Medinet Habu,[194] and was clearly adopted by Herihor to emphasize his status as a real king.

Fig. 21. Scene from left wall of the peristyle court showing Nedjmet A, nursing a baby before Mut; behind her stands the King's Daughter and Chief of the Harem of Khonsu, Shesetbaqet, who appears at the head of the row of daughters of Herihor in fig. 20. It has been suggested that the baby might be the future King Amenemnesut.

From this list, we see that the eldest son, Ankhefenmut (A), besides being a chariotry officer held the important economic post of Steward of Amun, together with posts in the priesthoods of Mut and Amun. The next son, Preamunenamun, was Fourth Prophet of Amun as well as Prophet of Onnuris and of Horus, while Panefer [. . .] and Amenhirwenemef (B) both also held priesthoods within the domain of Amun. The remaining sons are, however, not given titles, while most of the female figures are left without names or titles, raising suspicions as to whether they were intended to represent real people. The leading lady on this lower row is, however, named as the Chantress of Amun, Chief of the Harem of Khonsu, Shesetbeqet, who also appears elsewhere in the temple (fig. 21).[195]

The list is also interesting because of the names borne by some of the children. While many have purely Egyptian names, there are a number—Masaharta (i), Masaqaharta, [. . .]na, Wasuna, Osorkon (i), and Madenneb—who bear names certainly of Libyan origin; a number of these make this quite explicit by including the ⌐ ('foreign') determinative. Given that Herihor himself has a purely Egyptian name, one wonders whether the mother of these particular children was a scion of a Libyan family (cf. pp. 71–72).

If the above reconstruction is correct, we are left to explore the further affiliations of the King's Mother Herere, one of whose children became a pharaoh (Nesibanebdjedet), and another (Nedjmet A) married a man who was to become one. The identity of the father of these siblings remains uncertain; he seems unlikely to have been a king, as Herere is never called a King's Wife. A Herere bearing the title of Chief of the Harem of Amun-Re-nesunetjeru—i.e., the wife or widow of a high priest of Amun—appears in a number of letters of the time of Piankh,[196] clearly in a position of considerable authority.[197] She has been argued to be a wife of Piankh himself,[198] and thus could have later claimed the title of King's Mother via Piankh's son, Panedjem I. However, as noted above (pp. 32–36), it seems likely that Piankh's wife was a Nedjmet. While it is not impossible that Piankh could have had two contemporary wives with the 'Chief' title—Panedjem II seems to have done so (see p. 70)—his letters to Herere lack the terms of endearment found in his letter to Nedjmet and seem wholly businesslike. In addition, there is a good piece of evidence pointing to the mother of Piankh's son Panedjem I bearing the name Nedjmet.

This comes from a relief at Luxor, in which a Chief of the Harem of Amun Nedjmet is shown (alongside Amun) receiving homage from the deceased high priest Piankh and his sons: these are headed by the high priest Panedjem I (fig. 22).[199] Given that Nedjmet is here wished long life, this relief was clearly carved while she was still alive, and during Panedjem I's pontificate. She has generally been assumed to be none other than Nedjmet A, the wife of Herihor,[200] but if this were the case, why is she not called a queen, as the relief would date to either her husband's reign or a few years after his death? If sufficiently well regarded to receive the homage of Panedjem, his brothers, and their father, why is she denied the titles which Nedjmet, wife of Herihor, clearly possessed at the time and with which she would be buried some years later? Surely, it is more likely that we have here the previously posited Nedjmet B—the wife of Piankh and mother of

Fig. 22. Relief in the forecourt of the Luxor temple showing Amun and Nedjmet B being adored by the deceased Piankh (lost) and his sons, Panedjem I, Heqanefer, Heqamaat, and Ankhefenmut B.

the brothers depicted with them in the relief. Unfortunately, the one absolutely unequivocal statement of Panedjem I's maternity—in a graffito at Luxor—is damaged, so that only the first sign survives; it could equally be read as ⸢nd̲⸣ [mt] or ⸢ḥ⸣ [rr][201]—Nedjmet or Herere.[202] Nevertheless, the balance of evidence would seem to indicate that Piankh's wife and mother of his sons was Nedjmet B, although her origins and fate remain obscure.

When he became high priest, Panedjem had as his immediate deputy his brother, the Second Prophet of Amun, Heqanefer, who was presumably the direct successor of the Second Prophet Nesamun who appears with Piankh on the Year 7 oracle text. It is unclear whether this Nesamun is the same man (the son of the high priest Ramesesnakhte B) who was Second Prophet in Year 16 of Rameses IX, but given that in the Year 16 Nesamun later became briefly high priest, apparently between his father and his brother Amenhotep, this seems unlikely.[203] Panedjem's wife and children will be considered in the next chapter.

While one cannot be certain that the Chief of the Harem Herere (with whom Piankh corresponded) and the King's Mother Herere (who bore Henttawy A and, probably, Nesibanebdjedet I) were one and the same woman, it seems a reasonable assumption. As for the high priest from whom she derived the former title, the most likely candidate would seem to be the once suppressed high priest Amenhotep.[204] If this were the case, Amenhotep will in the end have been compensated posthumously for his ordeal by the fact that his children became, respectively, king of Lower Egypt and queen of Upper Egypt.

2 OF TANIS AND THEBES

Although the work attributed to the Ptolemaic historian Manetho has, since the earliest days of Egyptology, formed the basis for the dynastic structure of ancient Egyptian history, the usability of the data, and the level of reliability attributed to it by modern researchers, varies widely. For the Twentieth Dynasty, all the existing epitomes of Manetho state simply "twelve kings of Diospolis," with aggregate reigns of 135, 178, or 172 years.[1] The number of kings has usually been taken to be an error for the ten kings Sethnakhte and Rameses III through XI, but there is no reason why Herihor and Panedjem I in their kingly phases should not be included to make up the full dozen.[2]

In contrast, the Manethonic Twenty-first Dynasty enjoys considerable respect, especially as two of its members, long dismissed as phantoms, have in relatively recent times been proven to be genuine kings. All three of Manetho's excerptors give the same succession of kings "of Tanis," with only some variations around reign length:[3]

Manetho		Monuments		
Name	Reign length (years)	Prenomen	Nomen	Highest unequivocal regnal year
Smendês/ Smendis	26	Hedjkheperre-setepenre	Nesibanebdjedet-meryamun	——
Psusennês	46/41	Akheperkare-setepenamun/ Hemnetjertepyenamun	(Rameses-) Pasebkhanut-mery-amun	——
Nephercherês	4	Neferkare-heqawaset	Amenemnesut	——

Manetho		Monuments		
Name	Reign length (years)	Prenomen	Nomen	Highest unequivocal regnal year
Osochôr	6	Akheperre-setepenre	Osorkon(-mery-amun)	2[4]
Psin(n)achês	9	Netjerkheperre-mery/setepenamun	Siamun-meryamun	17[5]
Psusennês	14/35	Tyetkheperre-setepenre	(Hor-) Pasebkha-nut-meryamun	11[6]

From the above, it may be seen that while a candidate can be identified for each of Manetho's kings, reign lengths to be attributed to them are a different matter. As recorded above when discussing the career of Panedjem I, there are, however, a considerable number of year-dates that are not linked explicitly with any reign, covering not only the late Twentieth Dynasty, but the whole of the Twenty-first as well.

In many cases, this is not particularly exceptional: they include the dates of manufacture of linen bandages and personal graffiti, together with dockets placed on ancient mummies restored during this period to record the activity. As with many of the records of the Rameside Period at Deir el-Medina, which also lack explicit reign information, these were ephemeral workaday datelines, where the reign was obvious to the scribe and no useful purpose would have been served by adding the usual "under the person of King X" to the notation. However, there are other cases where one *would* normally have expected a royal name: it is not until the reign of Amenemopet that we start once again to find royal names unequivocally attached to year-dates on a regular basis.[7]

As noted above, p. 19, it has been suggested that at least some of the high priests of Amun of the Twentieth/Twenty-first Dynasty transition employed their own dating eras, and that it is because of this that kings' names are not found on dated Theban documents. However, as also noted, such a solution creates as many problems as it potentially solves, and the view that such regnal years do in fact belong to kings' reigns remains the most likely solution. One wonders whether the use of regnal years in this way could have been a hangover from the *whm-mswt*, which had created the concept of a dating era not directly coincidental with a king's reign. In addition, on the model proposed in the previous chapter, the *whm-mswt* had been followed by the parallel pharaonic regimes of Nesibanebdjedet I in the north and Herihor in the south, in effect a further 'era' without a single king. Mixed in with the accession to kingship of Panedjem I (and possibly another as well—see pp. 47–48), sheer practicality dictated keeping things as simple as possible by using one king's reign as a dating era and thus avoiding any need to be too specific in datelines. Accordingly, one would retain the long-standing overarching model that takes the years associated with Panedjem I as high priest as being those of Nesibanebdjedet I (and in our view Herihor as well), with Panedjem continuing to count by this era even after his assumption of kingship.[8] That Nesibanebdjedet I is identical with the "Smendes" of Manetho is fairly clear: the king's Egyptian name means "He of Banebdjedet"—the ram god of the city of Mendes (Tell Raba). The twenty-six years given to him by the Hellenistic historian are consistent with the succession of datelines explicitly associated with Panedjem I and his sons, running through to a Year 25, after which we find them using a new dating era—presumably that of Nesibanbdjedet's successor.[9]

Very little survives of Nesibanebdjedet I himself as king. A fragment of stela in the quarry at el-Dibabiya[10] relates that, when resident at Memphis, the king received reports of flooding in Luxor temple and ordered repairs to be made, which were then carried out. One wonders whether these were in any way linked with the reliefs of Panedjem I and his family in the

Fig. 23. Figure of Nesibanbdjedet I added to a relief of Sethy I within the gateway of Thutmose I on the western margin of the Montju precinct at Karnak.

temple (figs. 22, 27). A relief of Nesibanebdjedet himself was carved within the gateway of Thutmose I on the edge of the Montju precinct at Karnak (fig. 23),[11] but beyond this only a lapis lazuli bead preserves his royal names.[12] The king's tomb may be represented by NRT-I at Tanis (fig. 24):[13] it was ultimately reused by Osorkon II, but its location shows clearly that its construction preceded that of NRT-III, built by Pasebkhanut I, while its structure shows many signs of rebuilding (see p. 109). Of the contents of his tomb, only a pair of canopic jars survives (fig 25).[14] At Thebes, however,

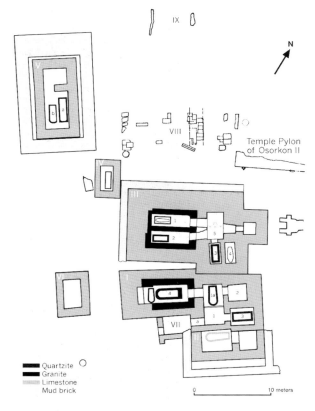

Fig. 24. Royal necropolis at Tanis:
NRT-I: Osorkon II
(ex-Nesibanebdjedet I?)
  1. Karomama B?; later
    Shoshenq V?
  3. Takelot I
  4. Osorkon II and Hornakhte
NRT-II: Pamiu
NRT-III: Pasebkhanut I
  1. Pasebkhanut I.
  2. Mutnedjmet B; later
    Amenemopet.
  3. Ankhefenmut.
  4. Wendjebaendjed.
  5. Shoshenq IIa; Siamun;
    Pasebkhanut II.
NRT-IV: Amenemopet
NRT-V: Shoshenq III
  a. Shoshenq III.
  b. Shoshenq IV.
NRT-VI: Unknown (Twenty-
first Dynasty?)
NRT-VII: Unknown (Shoshenq
V?)
NRT-VIII & IX: Unknown—
possible traces only

Temple Pylon
of Osorkon II

■ Quartzite ○
■ Granite
▒ Limestone
  Mud brick

0 _____ 10 meters

a considerable number of monuments and records can be attributed to the
Nesibanebdjedet/Herihor era. Most impressive are the reliefs in the peristyle court of the Khonsu temple depicting Herihor offering to the Theban
gods (fig. 26), including some of him presiding over the Opet festival. Most
interestingly, an Opet tableau on the west wall depicts what seems to be the
new bark of Amun constructed from the very timber whose acquisition had
so tried Wenamun a few years earlier.[15]

Dated material of the period relates largely to the restoration of royal
mummies—either the actual activity or the manufacture of linen used in
rewrapping.[16] In Year 6, Thutmose II and Amenhotep I received the attention of Panedjem I, followed in Year 12(?) by Amenhotep III, in Year 13
by Rameses III, and in Year 15 by Rameses II. The latter's mummy was on
that occasion moved to the tomb of his father, Sethy I (KV17). Rameses

III's reburial included bandages made in Years 9 and 10: linen of the latter date was also used for rewrapping Sethy I—probably at the time of his own reburial in Year 7 of Pasebkhanut I (see p. 62).

Beyond this, other datelines attributable to the first part of the Nesibanebdjedet/ Herihor era belong to the West Theban peregrinations of the Scribe of the Necropolis Butehamun, son and successor of Thutmose-Tjuroy,[17] who had acted as Piankh's aide during his Nubian campaign. Both alone and with his sons Ankhefenamun (ii) and Nebhepet he left a number of graffiti around the Theban *gebel* when going out "to see the mountains."[18]

Fig. 25. Canopic jar of Nesibanebdjedet I (Aubert Collection, Paris).

The key figure at Thebes was, however, the high priest Panedjem I. Among undated memorials of this first phase of his career are not only the various texts in the Khonsu temple at Karnak discussed in the previous chapter (see pp. 29–30), but also texts added to the bases of ram-headed sphinxes flanking the main approach from the quay into the temple of Amun-Re at Karnak.[19] A key document is the second of his reliefs in the Rameside forecourt of the Luxor temple (fig. 27—for the other relief, see pp. 36–37).[20] It is dominated by a large image of the high priest offering to Amun, with three ladies depicted behind him. The first, shown on a much smaller scale than the others, is the "King's Daughter of his body, his beloved, the God's Wife of Amun, Lady of the Two Lands, Maatkare." Her name is enclosed in a cartouche, but it seems clear that this enclosure had been added secondarily. Behind her, and now almost totally lost,[21] is the "King's Daughter of his body whom he loves, Chantress of Amun-Re-nesu-netjeru, Lord (*sic*) of the Two Lands,[22] Henttawy;" and then the remains of the "King's Daughter of his body, his beloved, [...] of Amun, Mutnedjmet."[23]

These women are usually regarded as Panedjem's daughters,[24] but it is curious that all three are called 'King's Daughter,' while Panedjem himself is here unequivocally called simply high priest, with no other title than that of Noble *(iry-pˁt)*. There seem to be two options here: one is that these filiations actually mean 'king's female descendant'; the other is that they were the actual offspring of someone other than Panedjem—with Herihor in particular springing to mind.[25]

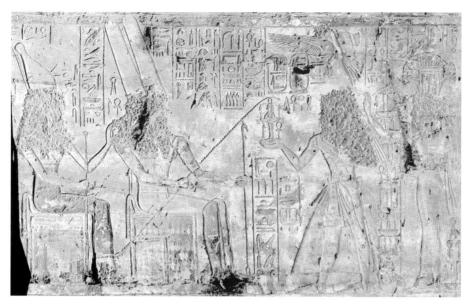

Fig. 26. Scene of Herihor, accompanied by Hathor, offering to Amun-Re and Mut on the east wall of the peristyle court.

Fig. 27. Relief in the forecourt of the Luxor temple, showing Panedjem I as high priest offering to Amun. Directly behind him is the small figure of Maatkare A. Behind her is probably a further daughter Henttawy B (although this could be a figure of Panedjem's wife, Henttawy A) and Mutnedjmet B, later to become sister-wife of Pasebkhanut I.

Against the latter solution is that neither Maatkare (A), Henttawy (B), nor Mutnedjmet (B) feature among the daughters named in Herihor's Khonsu temple procession of children. Although they could of course be among the numerous female figures left unnamed, Maatkare's status as God's Wife would seem to suggest a level of seniority that would have been recognized by her being named in the procession. Also, there is the somewhat subjective issue that Maatkare was presumably named for the prenomen of Hatshepsut, and that Panedjem I had a son named Menkheperre (B)—i.e., for Thutmose III: both names are unusual at this period and one would feel far more comfortable to see them as siblings named by the same parent with antiquarian interests. One might also cite the fact that Panedjem I himself was buried in what had once been the coffin of Thutmose I.[26] Also possibly relevant (but even more subjective!) is that the mummy of Maatkare seems to be of someone who tended toward obesity,[27] which is also true of that of Panedjem I's son Masaharta A.[28]

A further argument for making Maatkare a daughter of Panedjem is the fact that the latter's wife Henttawy A was, at the end of her life[29] (among many other things), Mother of the God's Wife of Amun. While it is possible that another God's Wife is meant, for example Henttawy D—who is, however, more usually regarded as the daughter of an Isetemkheb (see p. 70)—the most economical assumption would be that she was none other than the Maatkare with whom Henttawy is shown at Luxor. On this basis, one tends toward the view that Maatkare's title should be taken as indicating her descent from royalty via her mother, the King's (grand)Daughter Henttawy. That the latter had a royal status independent of her husband's ultimate kingship is shown by the fact that she was already using a cartouche while simply Chief of the Harem alongside Panedjem in purely high-priestly mode.[30] This cartouche contains the additional epithet of "Adoratrix of Hathor" (*dwȝt-Ḥwthr*), which henceforth was to be generally the standard form of Henttawy's name-dating era, although it is not found on her *shabti*s.

Of the other two Luxor ladies, Henttawy B's claim to being Panedjem I's daughter is supported by the fact that the latter definitely had a daughter of that name.[31] The combination of individuals at Luxor would thus suggest that both Henttawy and Mutnedjmet were also Panedjem I's daughters by Henttawy A.[32]

Key data on the ramifications of Panedjem's family are provided by the titles on the coffins of Henttawy.[33] These include, apart from the aforementioned Mother of the God's Wife: King's Daughter; Daughter of the King's Great Wife; First King's Great Wife; King's Wife; King's Mother; Mother of the King's Great Wife; First Chief of the Harem of Amun; Mother of the high priest of Amun; Mother of the generalissimo. The high-priestly link seems perfectly clear, as no fewer than three high priests are known who call themselves explicitly the "King's Son of Panedjem"—Masaharta A, Djedkhonsiufankh I, and Menkheperre A. At least one of these must have been her son, although probably not Menkheperre, as the latter's (unknown) mother appears to have been married at least once prior to espousing Panedjem.[34] As the role of generalissimo had been combined with that of high priest since the days of Piankh and Herihor (see pp. 19, 21) this aspect of her maternity seems also straightforward.

It is Henttawy's royal links that have been most debated over the years, but it is now generally agreed that Henttawy was the mother of Pasebkhanut I and his sister-wife Mutnedjmet.[35] In particular, a bracelet from Pasebkhanut I's tomb at Tanis names him alongside a King's Mother Henttawy-duathathor,[36] who from the context can hardly be anyone other than his own mother. On this basis, it seems likely that the Mutnedjmet on the Luxor relief is the same lady, who would later espouse her brother and become queen at Tanis.

A second wife of Panedjem I, Isetemkheb (A), is also known, named alongside him (as high priest) on bricks from el-Hiba (fig. 28a),[37] which

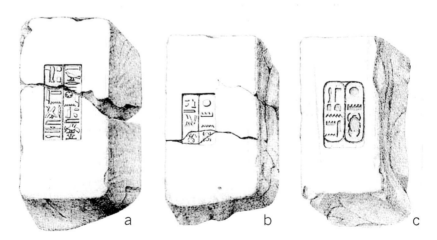

Fig. 28. Stamped bricks: a. Panedjem I and Isetemkheb A; b. Menkheperre B and Isetemkheb D. From el-Hiba (Berlin ÄM1566, 1616); c. Menkheperre A. From Luxor (Berlin ÄM1572).

seems to have been the northern outpost of the territory governed by the Thebans. Apart from the fact that she there bears the titles of Leading Lady and Chief of the [Harem], usual designations of the wife of a high priest, nothing is known of her—including whether she was Panedjem's first wife, after whose death he married Henttawy, or whether he had two contemporary spouses.[38]

Panedjem's standing probably derived from a combination of his own descent from the late Twentieth Dynasty strongman Piankh, and his wife's status both as the sister of the northern king Nesibanebdjedet and as a blood heir to the old Rameside line. Given this background, it seems strange that Panedjem's transition to the southern kingship after the demise of Herihor was seemingly delayed by at least as long as it took to decorate the pylon of the Khonsu temple, where both Panedjem and Henttawy are found in pontifical mode (figs. 17, 29)— albeit with Henttawy already a cartouche user and wearer of a queenly vulture headdress. Their daughter Maatkare is also shown in the role of God's Wife (fig. 30). Probably dating to the same period are restoration texts at Medinet Habu, which give Panedjem the titles of Overseer of the City, vizier, and generalissimo, in addition to his pontifical title.[39]

Fig. 29. Henttawy A as depicted on the pylon of the Khonsu temple at Karnak. Although still only the wife of the high priest, she has a cartouche and a queen's vulture-headdress.

One wonders whether the existence of Herihor's putative son, Amenemnesut, may have been an issue. His only contemporary memorial is a pair of bow caps with his names paired with those of Pasebkhanut I (fig. 31),[40] but he is also included in a much later genealogy of a Memphite priest (fig. 32)[41] as well as featuring in Manetho as Nephercherês. Interestingly, these latter two sources disagree over whether he should be placed before or after Pasebkhanut, with the genealogy giving Amenemnesut priority. Indeed, the direct juxtaposition of the kings' names on the bow caps might suggest that the two kings were northern and southern contemporaries, perhaps reinforced by the fact that Amenemnesut was explicitly "ruler of Thebes" in his

Fig. 30. Depiction of the God's Wife Maatkare A offering to Amun and Khonsu on the pylon of the Khonsu temple.

prenomen. It is thus possible that on Herihor's death, Amenemnesut immediately succeeded him as king in the south, but after a while was sidelined by Panedjem I when he finally achieved kingship as his co-ruler.[42] Amenemnesut will then have continued in obscurity until after the accession of Pasebkhanut I (given the manufacture of the bow caps), with his final end wholly obscure. It is possible that Amenemnesut could have at first continued the Herihor/Nesibanebdjedet year-count until Nesibanebdjedet's death, and then shared that of Pasebkhanut I, Amenemnesut's Manethonic reign length of four years reflecting his demise in their joint Year 4.

That this putative Nesibanebdjedet/Herihor/Amenemnesut dating era lasted for the full twenty-six years given to Nesibanebdjedet in Manetho seems guaranteed by datelines that seem to follow on from those discussed earlier in the chapter, and run into the 20s.[43]

Fig. 31. Pair of bow caps from NRT-III at Tanis. The one on the left bears the paired prenomina of Pasebkhanut I and Amenemnesut; the one on the right, their nomina (Cairo JE85886–7).

Fig. 32. Section of the genealogy of a Memphite priest, showing the generations under Amenemnesut (Ashakhet A, left) and Pasebkhanut I (Pipi A, <Hor>sieset J and Pipi B) (Berlin ÄM23673).

However, the Theban political scene during the last decade of the era changed dramatically in Year 15/16. On III *prt* 6 of Year 15 the restoration of the mummy of Rameses II had been ordered by the high priest Panedjem I, but on Year 16, IV *prt* 11 an order was issued by the high priest "Masaharta son of king Panedjem" to renew the burial of Amenhotep I.[44]

It has already been noted that Panedjem's wife Henttawy had begun to use royal titles and attributes while her husband was yet a simple high priest. However, between this phase and his assumption of full pharaonic style in the aforementioned Year 15/16, we find two intermediate stages. First, Panedjem affected royal dress while retaining his high-priestly titulary. This stage is evidenced only by a pair of statues, one small (fig. 33)[45] and one colossal (fig. 34):[46] it remains a matter of debate as to whether these pieces were manufactured for Panedjem or are usurpations of earlier works.[47] The second involved the use of a Horus name, and the title of Dual King, but no cartouche, as seen in the vertical columns of text either side of the inner face of the doorway of the pylon of the temple of Khonsu (figs. 14c,15).

Even when he adopted the twin cartouches of a fully fledged king, an evolution is to be seen. Initially, his prenomen was that used by Herihor, "First Prophet of Amun." This, however, is found only once, in the unused tomb of Rameses XI (KV4), where on the left-hand wall, just beyond the point where the last initial sketch for Rameses XI's decoration had been applied, was sketched a figure of Amun-Re-Horakhty, together with columns of text containing the god's speech (fig. 35).[48] This was copied from

Fig. 33. Royal statuette bearing the priestly titulary of Panedjem I. From Karnak Cachette (Cairo CG42191).

an adjacent scene left by Rameses XI's artists, with the exception that the prenomen was the aforementioned "First Prophet of Amun" and the nomen "Panedjem-true-of-voice." The implication of this initial sketch is presumably an intent to take over the tomb for burial of the newly minted king, even before he had adopted his definitive titulary. However, nothing else was done in the tomb, which was apparently later used as a workshop by those salvaging material from robbed tombs in the Valley of the Kings, before being used for a private burial during the Twenty-second Dynasty.[49] Finally, as found on the remainder of his royal monuments, Panedjem adopted a titulary that included the alternate Horus names *kꜣ-nḫt-mry-imn* and *kꜣ-nḫt ḥꜥ-m-wꜣst* and the latter Khakheperre-setepenamun (see Appendix 3), the prenomen being of Middle Kingdom vintage, having originally been used by Senwosret I.

In addition to the previously noted abortive appropriation of the tomb of Rameses XI, Panedjem's plans for ultimate burial included something else deriving from the burial arrangements of an earlier pharaoh: the outer coffin of Thutmose I, who had died over four centuries earlier (fig. 36).[50] This cedarwood case was entirely covered with a new gesso layer and decorated in accordance with the latest design, also seen on the coffins of Nedjmet A and Henttawy: indeed, they all seem to have been prepared at the same time.[51] To this was added a mummy board,[52] made during the Twenty-first Dynasty to match the Thutmose I coffin. The latter's origins were made apparent, however, when much of the new surface was roughly removed within a few decades of Panedjem's death, prior to the coffin's reburial in the TT320 cache (see pp. 62–64).

It is possible that the taking over of this coffin was opportunistic, it having been found empty during the ongoing program of salvage in the wake of tomb robberies that had generated the various rewrappings and

Fig. 34. Colossus in the First Courtyard at Karnak inscribed for Panedjem I as high priest; its manufacture has been attributed to his time (reusing an earlier block) and also to that of Rameses II (reusing a whole statue).

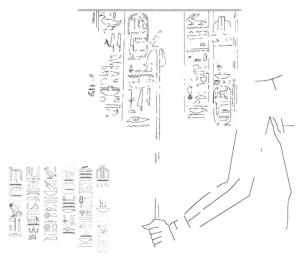

Fig. 35. Text of Panedjem I in KV4. It was first begun to the right of its ultimate location, but then started again further to the left, the 'new' first columns being destroyed. However, these can be restored through the palimpsest traces of the beginning of the first version, shown here in a lighter color. The full version of the text is provided in hieroglyphic type.

Fig. 36. Coffin lid and mummy cover (or inner coffin lid?) of Panedjem I, the first to be usurped from Thutmose I of the Eighteenth Dynasty. From TT 320 (CG61025).

reburials already noted.[53] Certainly no trace of the mummy of Thutmose I has been identified in any cache.[54] On the other hand, as noted above (p. 45), Panedjem I had offspring named Maatkare and Menkheperre, respectively the prenomina of Hatshepsut and Thutmose III, and not hitherto regularly found as children's names. Could it be that Panedjem was personally interested in the classic phase of the Eighteenth Dynasty, and thus took the opportunity of acquiring Thutmose I's vacant coffin to cement his links with that bygone era? Certainly, there is previous evidence for this kind of physical linking of a king with earlier monarchs, for example the potential implications of the reuse of Fourth Dynasty material in the pyramid of Twelfth Dynasty founder Amenemhat I at Lisht,[55] and the apparent removal of Third Dynasty sarcophagi from under the Step Pyramid to the pyramid complex of Senwosret III at Dahshur.[56]

Interestingly, alongside a son and daughter whose names evoked a wholly Egyptian past, Panedjem also had a son whose name, Masaharta (A), was wholly Libyan and had previously been found among the sons of Heri-hor. It was this man (fig. 37) who was appointed to the Theban pontificate on Panedjem's elevation to kingship, and would serve for much of the next decade.

As the new pontiff, Masaharta undertook work in the area of Pylons IX and X at Karnak (fig. 38),[57] as well as adding inscriptions to at least two pieces of ancient sculpture in the temple.[58] Otherwise he continued the work that he had begun with the restoration of Amenhotep I in Year 16, by attending to the burial of that king's wife Meryetamun B in TT358. Rewrapping of the queen's mummy was completed on III *prt* 28, bandages made under his direction in Year 18 being employed in this work.[59] As well as being named with the Scribe Ankhefenamun ii in some Theban graffiti of Year 16,[60] Masaharta is also known from a fragment of stela from Koptos (Qift).[61] It is probable that Masaharta's wife was the Chief of the Harem of Amun-Re Tayuheret, whose burial was found in TT320 and had coffins similar to those of Masaharta.[62] A daughter has been attributed to Masaharta on the basis of the juxtaposition of his name with those of king Panedjem I and an Isetemkheb, called a daughter of a high priest of Amun, on a leather 'tent' found in TT320.[63] However, the 'tent' seems to have

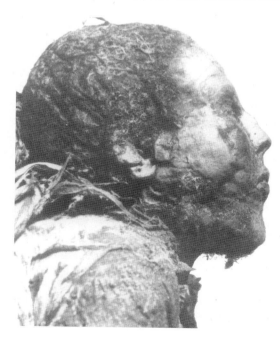

Fig. 37. Head of the mummy of Masa-harta. From TT320 (Luxor Museum of Mummification ex-Cairo CG61092).

Fig. 38. Gateway erected by Masaharta just east of Pylon IX at Karnak.

been made up from the pieces of a number of such items, and it has been suggested that the Isetemkheb in question was actually the daughter of Menkheperre—another high priest under Panedjem I—who went on to became the wife of Panedjem II (see p. 70).[64]

The coffins of Masaharta, which also ultimately found their way to the TT320 cache,[65] contained the pontiff's mummy,[66] that of a man of considerable girth, even allowing for any overpacking of the body in the elaborated form of embalming that was current at the time (fig. 38).[67] The mummy of Masaharta's sister, the God's Wife Maatkare A,[68] has a similar physique, which contributed to a major misassessment of her career. The root cause was the presence in her coffin of a small mummy alongside her own (fig. 39), which was assumed to be that of a baby. When Maatkare's own mummy was examined her "enormously enlarged" breasts were explained as being "probably" due to lactation, while the fact that the "skin of the abdomen was loose and somewhat puckered" was attributed to Maatkare having died in childbirth or soon afterward.[69]

At the time of this examination, Maatkare was assumed to have been a wife of Panedjem I.[70] However, when it became apparent that from the middle of the Twentieth Dynasty the office of God's Wife of Amun changed from a subsidiary one of a king's wife to that of a virgin princess dedicated to Amun,[71] things became more complicated. Might Maatkare have been an

Fig. 39. Inner coffin of Maatkare and the mummies found within. The gilded hands and face of the coffin lid appear to have been stolen by those carrying out the (re)burial, as the face of the outer coffin was found intact: there are a number of examples of pilfering by undertakers and burial parties during the Twenty-first Dynasty. From TT320 (Cairo CG61028, 61088–9).

exception to this new rule—or might she have had an illicit affair?[72] The situation was transformed when the 'problem child' was x-rayed and found to be that of Maatkare's pet monkey![73] However, the influence of the original interpretation of Maatkare's physique remained, and some scholars continued to follow the view that her physical characteristics were indeed the result of her having recently given birth[74]—rather than the more likely scenario that Maatkare, like her brother, simply suffered from obesity, which was maintained and perhaps overemphasized by the embalmers' packing.

As God's Wife, Maatkare's status exceeded that of the previous known incumbent, Iset E. The latter had had the titles of Noble (*irtt-pʿt*) and God's Wife of Amun, together with that of Adoratrix of the God (*dwȝt-ntr*), within her own cartouche,[75] but Maatkare's fullest style includes a cartouche-enclosed prenomen, Mutemhat, and the queenly title of Lady of the Two Lands.[76] In such things she set the pattern for most (if not all) later God's Wives and, in addition to the Khonsu temple representations already noted, included her names on a window frame from a chapel at Karnak.[77] It is unclear how long her career lasted, as the period of office of the next known God's Wife, Henttawy D, is not directly linked to any particular pontificate (see p. 70). Maatkare's body and funerary equipment[78] were found reburied in TT320, and may originally have been interred in a collective tomb alongside her father and other relations (see pp. 62–63).

The death of Masaharta has conventionally been placed in the early 20s of Nesibanebdjedet I's reign, since a Year 25 mentioned on a stela of his brother and ultimate successor, Menkheperre, has been taken to be of that era. It has also been suggested that Masaharta's departure from office followed a period of illness at the northern Theban stronghold of el-Hiba. This is derived from a document in which an unnamed brother of a certain Masaharta petitions the local god for his cure.[79] Unfortunately one cannot be certain that the high priest of that name is involved, nor of the date of the petition.[80]

The aforementioned stela, from Karnak, is generally referred to as the 'Maunier' or 'Banishment' stela, and recounts events beginning on III *šmw* 29 of a Year 25.[81] This has been attributed to the reign of Nesibanebdjedet I on the basis that a lost year-date later in the stela should be restored as a much lower number, indicating that the stela spanned two reigns, with those of Nesibanebdjedet and Pasebkhanut I (or just possibly Amenemnesut) as the only credible candidates.[82] However, it seems also possible for the figure '30' to be fitted into the space of the lost year,[83] which would shift the whole stela a quarter-century later, into the middle of what can only be the reign of Pasebkhanut I.[84]

The choice is of some significance, as the stela relates that on I *ȝḫt* 2+x of Year 25, an oracle of Amun-Re summoned Menkheperre, son of Panedjem I, to Thebes "to drive out his opponent and cause that . . . [things be] as they were in the reign of Re." The god then "established (Menkheperre) in the position of his father as First Prophet of Amun-Re-nesunetjeru and great general of Upper and Lower Egypt." It then relates that in the aforementioned later year, Menkheperre proposed to the god that a group of "quarrelsome servants"—apparently adherents of the high priest's "opponent"—who had been exiled to "the oasis where people are confined" (Kharga Oasis) should be recalled. To this the god gave his assent.

Taken at face value, the stela would indicate that some form of rebellion had occurred in Thebes, and that Menkheperre arrived, defeated what one would assume had been a usurping high priest, and then took over the Theban pontificate on the basis of his lineage. If this was indeed Menkheperre's first appointment, the Year 25 cannot be that of Pasebkhanut I, as Menkheperre is known from various dockets on mummy linen to have been in office in Years 6–8 of what must be that reign.[85]

Accordingly, the Year 25 should indeed be taken as belonging to the reign of Nesibanebdjedet, with the later year—whatever its value—referring to the time of a successor. The identity of his "opponent" is unclear, although a number of scholars have speculated that he might have been a scion of the family of Herihor,[86] but it certainly seems credible that some kind of irregularity occurred at Thebes after the death of Masaharta. A clue may lie in the existence of an ephemeral high priest Djedkhonsiufankh I, also a son of Panedjem I, known only from the now lost coffin of his son.[87] Given that Menkheperre would serve as pontiff for some five decades, Djedkhonsiufankh can only realistically be placed between his brothers Masaharta and Menkheperre.[88] It has been proposed that, having succeeded Masaharta, he was cut off prematurely during a brief pontificate by the "opponent" whom Menkheperre then had to defeat.

The king under whom the recall of exiles took place is most likely to have been Menkheperre's brother, Akheperre-setepenamun (Rameses[89]-) Pasebkhanut I, who was certainly Nesibanebdjedet I's ultimate successor. Amenemnesut could be an option if he had an independent reign at this point in time but, as discussed above, he may actually have reigned in parallel with both Nesibanebdjedet and Pasebkhanut until the latter's fourth regnal year (see fig. 18).

It is possible that these potential years of cohabitation with Amenemnesut are reflected by the fact that a number of items produced for Pasebkhanut I bear not his usual prenomen of Akheperre, but instead "First Prophet of Amun." This was not only written in a cartouche in the same way as had been affected by Herihor for his entire reign, and briefly by Panedjem I, but also as a straightforward title in front of Pasebkhanut's usual nomen cartouche.[90] In all cases, the kingly *nsw-bity* is prefixed, while the occurrence of the title on material from Pasebkhanut I's tomb, including one in the same title string as his usual prenomen and other names, makes it clear that these items refer to him, rather than to the later high priest(s) Pasebkhanut III/IV (see pp. 77–81). Unfortunately, none of these examples are datable, so it remains unclear whether there was indeed this posited development, or whether the king's use of the title might have been context-based and employed throughout his reign. In any case it can probably be assumed that the Amun cult being referred to was that at Tanis.[91] The accession of Pasebkhanut I while his father Panedjem I yet lived meant that, with the high priesthood of Amun held by Menkheperre and the office of God's Wife by Maatkare, all key posts in Thebes and Tanis were seemingly now in the hands of descendants of Piankh.

Pasebkhanut I was responsible for the construction of the first enclosure wall of the temple of Amun at Tanis, as well as the first datable parts of the temple itself.[92] Very little of this now survives, but a number of sculptures usurped by the king for installation there have been recovered.[93] Much of the temple, as built over the coming centuries, comprised reused material, in particular from the former residence city of Per-Rameses twenty kilometers to the south, which was progressively demolished as the drying up of the Pelusiac branch of the Nile delta removed its significance as a strategic and economic center (fig. 40).[94] Outside Tanis, a statue base at Tell Tennis in the far northeast Delta may reflect some activity there,[95] while a small temple was built at Giza dedicated to Isis Mistress of the Pyramids (fig. 41),[96] and a doorway with the king's name erected at Memphis.[97]

Only a few of the courtiers at Tanis are known, principally one Wendjebaendjed, who held various senior military, court, and priestly appointments, and would be buried in the king's tomb,[98] and the family of one Ankhefenamun.[99] The latter held a number of senior posts both at court and in the temples of Amun, Mut, and Khonsu which existed at Tanis, mirroring the position at Thebes.

Fig. 40. Site of the temple of Amun at Tanis. The gateway on the far left is that of Shoshenq III (cf. fig. 89), with the modern shelter for his tomb just right of center; this tomb stands at a considerably higher level than the earlier royal tombs, which lie behind. Most of the standing remains name solely Rameses II, whose city of Per-Rameses was the 'donor' for much of the stonework at Tanis, and it is thus difficult to identify what elements were actually erected by individual Third Intermediate kings.

At Memphis, three high priests of Ptah are attributed to Pasebkhanut I's reign by the later genealogy already mentioned (p. 47), including the name of Amenemnesut, under whom Ashakhet A is recorded as having served (fig. 32). The three high priests in question, Pipi A, Horsieset J, and Pi(u)p(u)i B, formed a single family line,[100] and while no contemporary material survives of the first two, Pipi B is attested as serving under Siamun (see p. 74), suggesting that he succeeded to the pontificate late in Pasebkhanut's reign.

One Memphite enigma surrounds the Apis bulls of the period. These beasts had been buried in the Serapeum at Saqqara since the time of Amenhotep III,[101] but although Apis 20.4/XVII[102] is apparently securely assigned to the reign of Rameses IX by inscribed material,[103] the next bull clearly attested by extant inscribed material is Apis 22.x+2/XXVII of Year 23 of Osorkon II. This produces a gap of some 225 years on our chronology.[104] Four bulls were allocated to the reign of Rameses XI by Auguste Mariette, the excavator of the Serapeum, and another three

Fig. 41. Temple of Isis-Mistress-of-the-Pyramids at Giza, originally the chapel of pyramid GIc, built for one of the women of the family of Khufu. However, some one and a half millennia later, under Pasebkhanut I and Amenemopet, it was enlarged as a sanctuary of Isis, with further extensions added during the Twenty-sixth Dynasty.

to the Twenty-first Dynasty, but on grounds that are impossible now to determine.[105] At 20/25 years per bull life,[106] nine or ten bulls are required to fill the gap, suggesting that three or four bull burials of this period still remain to be identified.[107]

Of the family of Pasebkhanut I, his principal wife was his sister Mutnedjmet B, whom we have already met, with other members of the family, at Luxor; her attestations as queen are limited to funerary material.[108] A further wife would seem to have been named Wiay, since Pasebkhanut I's daughter Isetemkheb (C) was almost certainly identical with the "Isetemkheb daughter of Wiay" who was the mother of the Theban high priest Panedjem II. The latter in turn called himself "King's Son of Pasebkhanut"—certainly with the meaning of (grand)son. It is generally assumed that the King's Son, etc., (Rameses-)Ankhefenmut (C), who had a burial chamber in the king's tomb (see p. 66) was a son of Pasebkhanut I,[109] although there have been attempts to equate him with one of the other apparently separate individuals of the name.[110] Whether the king's

Fig. 42. Stela showing Panedjem I and Henttawy A, as king and queen, offering to Osiris. From Koptos (Cairo JE71902).

successor on the throne, Amenemopet, was also a son is wholly unknown, but not improbable.

Following the almost simultaneous installation of Pasebkhanut and Men-kheperre in their respective offices—in which they would both remain for five decades—their father, Panedjem I, still had at least another eight years of life and kingship remaining to him. On III *prt* 29 in Year 8 (of Paseb-khanut I), Panedjem gave the order to 're-Osirify' Ahmose I and the latter's son, prince Siamun,[111] thus continuing the process of restoring royal mum-mies that had occupied Panedjem throughout his tenure as pontiff and

Fig. 43. Inner coffin lid of Nedjmet A, showing the removal of much of the gilded surface—yet leaving intact that associated with religious texts and images. From TT320 (Cairo CG61024B).

then king. The previous year, queen Ahmose-Sitkamose had also been re-Osirified,[112] while king Sethy I had been reburied in his own tomb, presumably after yet another robbery.[113]

Various items bearing Panedjem's kingly names and titles exist, but all are undated. Outside Thebes, two blocks naming him were found at Tanis,[114] with an altar deriving from Abydos[115] and a stela from Koptos that shows the king and queen Henttawy offering to Osiris (fig. 42).[116] At Karnak-North, Panedjem's names and titles were added to elements of the Treasury of Thutmose I and to a column.[117] In the main enclosure at Karnak, a reused block was found in the Chapel of Osiris-Nebankh[118] and an inscription added to the western wall of the Khonsu temple;[119] a text was also added to a figure between the paws of a ram-headed sphinx in front of the temple of Mut.[120] Queen Henttawy is also known from usurped sculpture in the Mut temple.[121]

As already noted (see pp. 45, 50), the funerary outfit of Panedjem I was built around the reworked outer coffin of Thutmose I. However, nothing is known as to where he was actually buried. On the other hand, the state of the coffin and mummy board makes it clear that—ironically, given his own involvement in the restoration of robbed royal mummies—this original burial was robbed.[122] Since collective burials seem to have been the norm at Thebes during the Twenty-first Dynasty, it would seem likely that his burial place will have been used for other members of the Theban pontifical/royal family, and this is supported by the state of many of the coffins of Panedjem's likely tombmates. The coffins of Panedjem I (fig. 36), Nedjmet A (fig. 43), Henttawy A, Maatkare A (fig. 39), Masaharta A, and Tayuheret have all had most of their gilding or gilded elements removed,[123] with the interesting aspect that divine images and religious texts were left more or less intact.[124] This suggests that while robbers caused some of the damage,

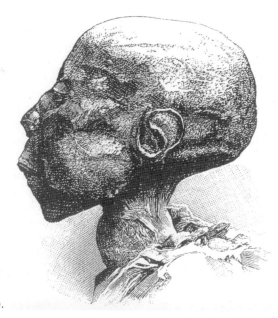

Fig. 44. Head of mummy
of Panedjem I. From
TT320 (Cairo no number).

the final state of the coffins was the result of the efforts of those charged
with reburying the mummies—officially[125] or otherwise.[126]

   The final ancient resting place of all these mummies, as well as many
earlier high-status corpses, was tomb TT320, that of the high priest Panedjem II. Some, if not all, of these secondary interments were placed in
the tomb after Year 11 of Shoshenq I, a date that appears on the wrappings
of the last certain primary interment in the tomb, Djedptahiufankh A,
probable son-in-law of Panedjem II.[127] Certainly the coffins and mummy
of Henttawy A comprised one of the very last groups to be introduced, as
they were found just inside the entrance to the tomb, with no scope for
anything else to be carried past them. It is thus likely that Panedjem and
the rest of his family group arrived at this same time, although the placement of coffins and mummies beyond the outermost few remins unclear.[128]

   In the shifting of the various mummies and coffins around the Theban
gebel, a number of bodies ended up in coffins other than their own and
Panedjem I was one of them.[129] His mummy (fig. 44)[130] was actually found
inside the Eighteenth Dynasty giant coffin of queen Ahhotep,[131] his own
coffins being occupied by an anonymous mummy of Eighteenth Dynasty
date.[132] However, a Book of the Dead papyrus[133] and two boxes of *shabti*s
(fig. 45) belonging to Panedjem were found in the tomb.[134]

Fig. 45. *Shabti* box of Panedjem I. From TT320 (Cairo JE26253A).

With the death of Panedjem I and the disappearance of Amenemnesut, Egypt had, probably for the first time in over three decades, a single king in the person of Pasebkhanut I, with his own brother Menkheperre as high priest in Thebes— and possibly their sister Maatkare A still as God's Wife. Menkheperre married his niece Isetemkheb C, suggesting that he may have been significantly younger than her father Pasebkhanut I.

Dated monuments of Menkheperre's pontificate are not plentiful. Besides his stela of Year 25 (of Nesibanebdjedet I), a mummy label bearing a Year 27 from a mass reburial of Eighteenth Dynasty royal ladies is probably attributable to the reign of Pasebkhanut I, and thus to the pontificate of Menkheperre.[135] Subsequent to this, we have the record of an inspection of Theban temples in Year 40[136] and the construction of a wall on the north boundary of the Karnak complex in Year 48.[137] Bricks deriving from such work and bearing Menkheperre's name are known not only from Karnak[138] but also Luxor (fig. 28c)[139] and sites further north. One group attests to further work on the fortifications at el-Hiba (cf. p. 65),[140] from whence apparently derive a large group of papyri dating to Menkheperre's pontificate and attesting to the city's importance.[141] Other stamped bricks suggest the addition of protective walls at Nazlet el-Shurafa in Middle Egypt, Medamud, and Gebelein.[142] A graffito including Menkheperre's name and paternity was also inscribed on the island of Biga at the First Cataract.[143]

Menkheperre's only known spouse is Isetemkheb C: with her, and possibly other unknown partners, he had at least five sons and probably at least four daughters. Two of the sons, Nesibanebdjedet II—first named on a slab from Karnak with the title of High Steward of Amun (*imy-r pr wr n imn-rꜥ*)[144] and then on a papyrus when he was titled Second Prophet of Amun[145]—and Panedjem II, would become high priests in turn, respectively espousing their sisters Henttawy C and Isetemkheb D. A third son, Pasebkhanut A, held a range of civil and military titles, and was eventually buried in a substantial brick tomb (D22) at Abydos.[146] His brother Ankhefenmut (E) was a God's Father of Amun and of Mut,[147] and was ultimately buried in the Bab el-Gasus, a collective tomb of priests and priestesses at Deir el-Bahari.[148] The mummy of the final known son, Hori C, who was a priest of Amun, Hathor, and Seth, was also found here.[149] Both of the remaining daughters[150] were also ultimately buried in the Bab el-Gasus: Meryetamun (F) had held offices in the Theban Amun, Mut, and Khonsu cults,[151] while Gautsoshen (A) had married the Third Prophet of Amun Tjanefer (A). This couple became the parents of Menkheperre C, who would succeed his father as Third Prophet, and Panedjem (A), who went on to become Fourth Prophet.[152]

At some point during his long pontificate, Menkheperre A acquired— via a mechanism that remains obscure—some royal attributes: a statuette shows him with a high-priestly skullcap, but a royal kilt and cartouche around his personal name.[153] However, while his name and high-priestly title are found enclosed in ovals on various bricks (fig. 28c),[154] with a vari- ant first oval found at el-Hiba that reads "Dual King (of) Upper Egypt & Lower Egypt,"[155] all Menkheperre's monumental attestations give him purely high-priestly titles and no cartouche—and certainly no definitive prenomen.[156] This suggests that his use of such attributes was brief, per- haps directly following his father's death: as late in his career as Year 48 (see p. 48) he was certainly a simple high priest.

That Menkheperre died not long afterward is suggested by the fact that among the items found on the mummy of Pasebkhanut I were bracelets that bore both the king's nomen and the name and titles of the high priest of Amun, Nesibanebdjedet II.[157] It would thus appear that Nesibanebdjedet succeeded his father shortly before the death of his uncle Pasebkhanut I. On the other hand, it has been suggested that Menkheperre was actually still alive at the time, with Nesibanebdjedet either serving as his deputy or having been elevated to the pontificate after Menkheperre's assumption of royal style—if one were indeed to place this at the end of his career.[158] Of course, these issues would probably be resolved by the discovery of the burial of Menkheperre, but that remains unknown—and most probably survives intact, given that nothing even potentially deriving from it or that of Isetemkheb C has ever come to light.[159]

In contrast, the intact tomb at Tanis of Menkheperre's royal brother Pasebkhanut I is well known. This sepulcher (NRT-III) was constructed directly adjacent to NRT-I—the putative tomb of Nesibanebdjedet I—and comprised a pair of granite chambers for the king and queen, with the remainder of the structure built of limestone blocks, in some cases reused

Fig. 46. Royal necropolis at Tanis, showing the originally buried substructures of the tombs. The corner of the pylon of Osorkon II is just to the left of tomb NRT-III.

(fig. 46).[160] The whole structure had originally been concealed below the courtyard in the front of the Amun temple and probably been surmounted by a now lost brick chapel.[161] The first part of the subterranean tomb to be constructed and occupied seems to have been a burial chamber for the aforementioned dignitary Wendjebaendjed, as this decorated room was not accessible from any of the other parts of the tomb and had been sealed by the addition of its roofing blocks.[162]

The remaining chambers were, however, accessible via a shaft at the eastern end (fig. 24), which presumably originally lay in a courtyard of the formerly superposed chapel. The antechamber beyond was primarily decorated with processions of genii and scenes of the king making offerings. In the south wall, a doorway led to a chamber almost completely filled with the sarcophagus intended for the king's son, Ankhefenmut C: a fall from grace on his part is suggested by the erasure of his figures, names, and titles from the walls of his chamber.

Two concealed doorways in the west wall of the antechamber, sealed with granite plugs and then covered with decorated limestone blocks, led to a pair of parallel chambers, prepared for the king and his wife, Mutnedjmet. The king's chamber was found intact, although all material not of stone or precious metal was in an advanced state of decay—including the king's mummy, resting in a silver coffin of the feathered rishi design that had been used for royal burials since the Seventeenth Dynasty, some six centuries earlier.[163] The silver coffin (fig. 47)[164] was placed inside a stone anthropoid coffin that had been usurped from an unknown late Eighteenth/early Nineteenth Dynasty nobleman,[165] which was in turn enclosed in what had originally been the innermost of the nest of three sarcophagi that had sheltered the mummy of the Nineteenth Dynasty king Merenptah.[166] This, like the coffin of Thutmose I reused by Pasebkhanut's father, had presumably been removed from the donor king's tomb, in this case KV8 in the Valley of the Kings, as part of the recycling of material from the plundered tombs after the removal of Merenptah's mummy prior to its eventual reburial, along with others, in the tomb of Amenhotep II (KV35).[167] Interestingly, while the lids of Merenptah's outer sarcophagi survived largely intact, both coffers had been demolished,[168] presumably to facilitate the extraction of the inner case for reuse, and also to allow their bottoms to be salvaged for reuse—perhaps as stelae, for which their size and thickness will have admirably suited them.

It is unclear, however, whether or for how long Mutnedjmet ever rested in her burial chamber, as the room had been usurped for the interment (or reinterment) of Pasebkhanut I's successor Amenemopet. That this was carried out soon after the latter's death is suggested by the fact that the doorway leading to the chamber from the antechamber had been filled with blocks carved with a scene of Amenemopet designed to match the adjacent decoration of Pasebkhanut: a significantly later reburial is unlikely to have taken such care. Amenemopet's name now replaced the queen's on the lid of her sarcophagus and on her chamber's wall, where it now incongruously accompanied Mutnedjmet's carved female figure. It is possible that Mutnedjmet's mummy was reburied in Amenemopet's original tomb, NRT-IV (see p. 69): remains of a coffin were found there.[169]

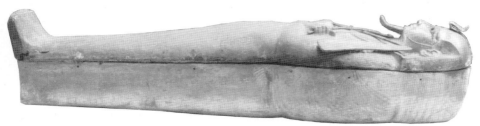

Fig. 47. Silver coffin of Pasebkhanut I. From Tanis NRT-III (Cairo JE85912).

The near simultaneous deaths of the aged Pasebkhanut I and Menkheperre A brought the new generation to office in both Tanis and Thebes. However, the tenure of the high priest Nesibanebdjedet II seems to have been brief, with only the already mentioned handful of items attributable with certainty to his lifetime.[170] His principal wife is likely to have been his sister Henttawy C, to judge by a slightly later (Years 6 and 8 of either Amenemopet or Siamun) property decree on Pylon X at Karnak,[171] which also indicates that Nesibanebdjedet II had two daughters, Isetemkheb (E) by Henttawy, and Nesikhonsu (A: see p. 70). Henttawy C was ultimately buried at Deir el-Bahari alongside her aunts Henttawy B and Djedmute-sankh A, the latter also the widow of a short-lived pontiff.[172] Nothing is known of Nesibanebdjedet's burial—perhaps in the never-found tomb of his father and mother.

Nesibanedjedet's Tanite contemporary in the new generation was king Usermaatre-setepenamun Amenemopet-meryamun, as indicated by both men being named on trappings from a mummy found in the Bab el-Gasus.[173] The background of Amenemopet, as already noted, is completely unknown, although a reasonable assumption would be that he was a son of Pasebkhanut I. It would appear that Amenemopet came to the throne prior to Pasebkhanut's death, as a fragment of bandage from the Bab el-Gasus reads "[. . .]the Dual King Amenemopet, Year 49[. . .]."[174] Year-dates never follow the name of the king, and thus the text must originally have read "[Year X under the person of] the Dual King Amenemopet, Year 49 [under the person of the Dual King Pasebkhanut]," or suchlike.[175] It would thus seem that, old and ill—he was afflicted by severe arthritis in his back and age-related problems with his right foot, not to mention a number of dental abscesses[176]—Pasebkhanut I appointed his heir as co-ruler. On the basis of the bandage fragment, Amenemopet then began his own year-count, contrasting with the situation that prevailed with the multiple parallel reigns of the earlier part of the dynasty. Perhaps this was a case of the heir simply taking over the reins of power early, rather than instituting the kind of parallel authority seen with Nesibanebdjedet I and his Theban ex-priestly contemporaries. How long this co-rule lasted is unclear, although the fact that one version of Manetho gives Pasebkhanut I a forty-six-year reign *might* suggest that the handover took place then. There are two instances where Amenemopet uses the title of high priest of Amun rather than his prenomen,[177] and it is conceivable that these date to this early phase of his reign.[178]

If the excerptors of Manetho were correct in unanimously assigning nine years of reign to Amenemopet, he may have only had a half dozen years of independent rule—or even less if Pasebkhanut lived significantly beyond his Year 49. If he was the eldest son of the long-lived Pasebkhanut I, this would not be surprising: Amenemopet's skeleton is certainly also that of an old man.[179] His own surviving monuments are scanty: at Tanis itself only his original tomb, NRT-IV, survives, containing a Middle Kingdom sarcophagus reinscribed for the king (fig. 48).[180] As already noted, Amenemopet's body and funerary equipment ended up in NRT-III. The burial was less rich than Pasebkhanut I's, the coffin being of gilded wood rather than silver,[181] with the gold mask that covered the decayed mummy's face far less massive than that of the earlier king (fig. 49).[182] Outside the sarcophagus lay the canopic jars and other vessels, along with the remains of a further gilded coffin, bearing Amenemopet's name. Perhaps too large to fit into the borrowed sarcophagus, the coffin may have been simply dumped alongside.[183] At Memphis, construction is indicated by a block with a scene of Amenemopet making an offering to Ptah,[184] while further work was carried on at the temple of Isis at Giza.[185]

Fig. 48. Middle Kingdom sarcophagus that was reinscribed for Amenemopet and installed in his original tomb (NRT-IV) at Tanis; the lid (beyond) was made from an Old Kingdom inscribed slab.

Fig. 49. Gold mummy mask of Amenemopet. From Tanis NRT-III (Cairo JE86063).

In the south, a sphinx in the avenue in front of the Mut temple at Karnak had Amenemopet's names added, but the majority of his attestations at Thebes are on bandages and trappings from mummies interred there during his reign.[186] In these contexts the king is regularly associated with the high priest of Amun, Panedjem II (fig. 50), who followed his brother Nesibanebdjedet II as pontiff and would continue in office for some two decades.

The new pontiff had two known wives, his sister Isetemkheb (D) and his niece Nesikhonsu, daughter of Nesibanbedjedet II. The relative status of these two ladies is slightly problematic, as Nesikhonsu's fairly brief tenure as Chief of the Harem of Amun (i.e., senior wife of the high priest) fell during the much longer period during which Isetemkheb held the selfsame title. Indeed, it has been suggested that Isetemkheb was for a while set aside in favor of the younger woman, and was then reconciled with her husband after Nesikhonsu's premature death, remaining a significant figure at Thebes well after Panedjem's own death.[187] Certainly Nesikhonsu's burial outfit (built around a set of coffins originally made for Isetemkheb D[188]) contained, apart from a particularly lavish provision of (more or less) usual items such as the canopic jars[189] and a papyrus, a wooden board that bore versions of a most curious oracular decree by Amun-Re. In this the god states that he will ensure that Nesikhonsu does no posthumous harm to her widower, Panedjem,[190] suggesting that something had been amiss.[191]

Whatever the nature of their mutual personal relationships, Nesikhonsu A bore Panedjem II four children,[192] while at least one son—Panedjem's heir Pasebkhanut III—and a daughter seem to have been borne by Isetemkheb D. A second daughter may well have been God's Wife of Amun Henttawy (D), known from *shabti*s,[193] if Isetemkheb D was the "Mother of the God's Wife, Isetemkheb" named on a brick from Higaza on the Qena Bend.[194] In any case, Isetemkheb D held a wide range of sacerdotal offices in the southern half of Egypt, while Nesikhonsu strikingly held the

Fig. 50. Panedjem II, as shown in his funerary papyrus. From TT320 (BM EA10793).

(masculine) title of viceroy of Nubia. No other holder of the title is known subsequent to Piankh and Herihor, and it is unclear why it (and the linked Overseer of Southern Lands) was bestowed on Nesikhonsu. By the later Twenty-first Dynasty, much of Nubia seems to have been lost to Egypt (cf. pp. 139–40), and Nesikhonsu can hardly have discharged the functions of the viceroys of old.

We have previously noted the occasional appearance of Libyan names in the royal/pontifical families of the Twenty-first Dynasty, but without an immediate genealogical explanation. Such a link is, however, available for the first Libyan-named king to appear on the Egyptian throne—Akheperre-setepenre Osorkon (the Elder),[195] who became king on Amenemopet's demise.

This link is not, however, a record carved during the Twenty-first Dynasty: rather, it is an inscription carved some two centuries later on the roof of the Khonsu temple at Karnak. This both mentions the king as the ancestor of a priest Ankhefenkhonsu who lived under Takelot III (fig. 51),[196] and names Osorkon's mother as a Mehytenweskhet (A). She is certainly to be identified with the King's Mother Mehytenweskhet who is named in another genealogy of the eighth century—the stela of Pasenhor B from the Serapeum at Saqqara (fig. 52). Here she appears as the wife of the Libyan Great Chief (of the Ma[shwesh])[197] Shoshenq (A), mother of the Great Chief Nimlot (A) and grandmother of the pharaoh Shoshenq I, founder of the Twenty-second Dynasty.[198] The Pasenhor text takes his ancestry in the male line back through four further generations of Libyan chiefs to one Buyuwawa who must have lived around the end of the New Kingdom. The Karnak text also indicates a link back to a maternal half sister[199] of the high priest Menkhperre.

It remains wholly obscure how Osorkon came to succeed Amenemopet—and by extension, how this descendant of Libyan chieftains had come to the throne. It is of course possible that he seized the throne, but there is no substantive evidence for this, while the Libyan names of Masaharta A, and the various sons of Herihor already noted, indicate a Libyan element within the ruling elite back in the last years of the Twentieth Dynasty. It therefore seems likely that intermarriages between the Chiefs of the Ma and the house of Piankh had, upon Amenemopet's death, led to Osorkon being sufficiently close to the royal line to be a credible heir if Amen-

Fig. 51. Now lost text from the roof of the Khonsu temple. It records the induction of the priest Ankhefenkhonsu in Year 7 of Takelot III, who provides an ancestry that includes Osorkon the Elder.

Fig. 52. Stela of Year 37 of Shoshenq V, dedicated by the Prophet of Neith Pasenhor at the burial of Apis bull XXXIII, and including his own genealogy back to the eleventh century. Among Pasenhor's ancestors was Osorkon II, and as a result the stela provides the ancestry of the Twenty-second Dynasty royal line (Louvre IM2846).

emopet had died without a surviving son. That Osorkon could have been a son-in-law of Amenemopet is also possible, although no direct evidence exists for such a relationship.

In any case, the accession of Osorkon the Elder seems not to have disturbed the status quo at Thebes, where Osorkon's only certain contemporary monument is an entry in the Karnak Priestly Annals[200] that commemorates the induction of the God's Father of Amun Nespaneferhor (iv) on I šmw 20 of his Year 2 (fig. 53).[201] From the time of Osorkon the Elder may also come two items that have generally been attributed to the much later, eighth-century king Osorkon IV—a block and a faience

Fig. 53. Fragments 3 and 4 of the Karnak Priestly Annals, covering appointments to the office of God's Father of Amun-Re-nesunetjeru during the reigns of Osorkon the Elder, Siamun, Pasebkhanut II, and Shoshenq I.

seal bearing the names affected by Osorkon the Elder.[202] Apart from the record of Year 2, the only evidence for the length of the reign is Manetho's figure of six years.[203]

Nothing is known of the origins or family of the next king, Netjerkheperre-setepen/meryamun Siamun-meryamun. However, it is possible that he (or Pasebkhanut II) was the father of the King's Daughter of the Lord of the Two Lands Tetsepeh B, who was wife of a high priest of Ptah at Memphis during the latter part of the Twenty-first Dynasty.[204] Building work was carried out at Memphis during Siamun's reign by the Prophet of Ptah Ankhefenmut (D). On behalf of the high priest Pipi B (who now affected the cognomen Netjerkheperre-meryptah), he erected a building some way to the south of the Ptah temple on the edge of Kom el-Rabia (fig. 54).[205] Other activity in the Memphite region is evidenced by a Year 16 stela from Fustat.[206]

At Tanis, the capital, a number of architectural fragments attest to Siamun's extension of the Amun and Mut/Anat temples there (fig. 55),[207] while a block from Khataana[208] may be a stray from Tanis or indicate other work in the eastern Delta. A little further south, Siamun's cartouches were added to the bases of the obelisks of Thutmose III at Heliopolis,[209] and a hieratic graffito of Year 17 was inscribed in the cliffs behind Abydos.[210]

Fig. 54. Detail of the lintel of a doorway from a temple erected during the reign of Siamun to the south of the main Ptah temple at Memphis, showing the king and the priest Ankhefenmut D offering to Ptah (Ny Carlsberg ÆIN 1012).

At Thebes, Panedjem II remained in office, and it may have been during the first years of Siamun (but possibly of Amenemopet or Osorkon the Elder) that an investigation was held into alleged corruption at Karnak, recorded in a text on the outside of the western wall of the southernmost court of the Amun temple at Karnak.[211] Also deriving from Karnak, and recording decrees in Years 5, 6, and 8, are the property text of Henttawy C (see p. 68) and a stela relating an oracle in favor of Osorkon's brother, Nimlot A.[212] Otherwise, the Theban memorials of Siamun's reign are entirely concerned with burial at Thebes-West.

In Year 5, Panedjem's wife Nesikhonsu A died and became apparently the first interment in a large tomb just south of Deir el-Bahari. There has been considerable debate as to whether this sepulcher, TT320 (figs. 56–57), was a new excavation of the Twenty-first Dynasty or had been enlarged out of an earlier New Kingdom tomb, but it seems most likely to have been constructed specifically by Panedjem II as his family vault.[213] A hieratic

Fig. 55. Block from a building constructed by Pasebkhanut I and Siamun just east of the royal necropolis at Tanis, showing Siamun smiting an enemy.

text on the right doorjamb at the bottom of the shaft records Nesikhonsu's burial there on IV *šmw* 21.[214] Possibly it was at this point that one of her coffins was appropriated for Rameses IX, as a text on his shroud records a "gift that . . . Nesikhonsu (A) made in Year 5."[215] It is thus possible that she was joined in the tomb by the last of the Rameside kings to be buried in the Valley of the Kings, who thus became the first king's mummy to find rest in what was later to become the great 'Royal Cache.'[216]

Panedjem II himself followed his wife to the grave five years later. The introduction of his burial outfit (figs. 50, 58)[217] into TT320 was recorded in a pair of hieratic texts opposite that of Nesikhonsu,[218] dated to Year 10, IV *prt* 20. The funeral was directed by the God's Father of Amun Djedkhonsiufankh (Q), who had also conducted the interment of Nesikhonsu.

On the same day—perhaps to take advantage of activity surrounding Panedjem's interment as a distraction—the mummies of Rameses I, Sethy I, and Rameses II were reinterred in the (as yet unlocated) tomb of the Eighteenth Dynasty queen Inhapy.[219] Here they joined the mummy of Amenhotep I, which had apparently been introduced into the

Fig. 56. The location of TT320 in the cliffs south of Deir el-Bahari.

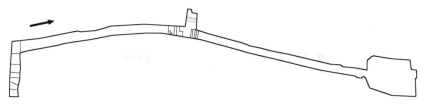

Fig. 57. Plan of TT320.

tomb earlier.[220] The two Rameses and Sethy I had been removed from the latter's KV17 three days earlier; they had rested there together since Year 15 of Nesibanebdjedet I (see p. 42).

One Bab el-Gasus burial contained linen explicitly dated to Year 8 of Siamun;[221] other burials with dated linen could refer either to his reign or to that of Pasebkhanut II (see below).

Fig. 58. Coffin lids, mummy board, and wrapped mummy of Panedjem II, the mummy equipped with the 'Osiris shroud' that is typical of the period. From TT320 (Cairo CG61029, 61094).

Panedjem II was succeeded as high priest by his son Pasebkhanut (III),[222] who seems to have served through until at least the end of the reign of Siamun. As noted above (p. 74) the king's highest known year is the Year 17 graffito, but he is generally given a nineteen-year reign on the assumption that the "Psin(n)achês" given as the successor of Osochôr (Osorkon the Elder) by Manetho is meant to be Siamun, and that the reign length given by him should be emended to read "(1)9 years." We will consider the posthumous fate of Siamun below.

That the "Psusennês" whom Manetho gives as the next king should be identified with Tyetkheperure-setepenre (Hor-)Pasebkhanut (II)-meryamun is clear. Less so is whether this king was the same person as the high priest Pasebkhanut III, or a separate homonym.[223] This question is complicated by the fact that the temple of Sethy I at Abydos contains a graffito which, although somewhat problematic, appears to show that at one point in Pasebkhanut II's reign the Theban high priest was also named Pasebkhanut (fig. 59).[224]

Fig. 59. Hieratic graffito in the southwest corner of the Ptah chapel in the temple of Sethy I at Abydos, giving the parallel names and titles of king Pasebkhanut II and a contemporary high priest of the same name.

A bandage from a mummy found in the Bab el-Gasus would at first sight be able to resolve this, as it was first reported to read "linen made by the First Prophet of Amun Pasebkhanut son of Panedjem for his lord Amun (in) Year 4."[225] Given that Pasebkhanut III became high priest only in Year 10 of Siamun, the "Year 4" bandage would have to belong to a later reign, most probably that of Pasebkhanut II—or conceivably Shoshenq I—meaning that Pasebkhanut II and III must have been separate individuals. Unfortunately, the orthography of the date as first published is strange,[226] while its second publication (by the same scholar) not only prints the date as "Year 5," but gives the date a different orthography, and adds a query to the reading.[227] The date could thus have been significantly different, and if higher than ten could refer to the reign of Siamun, leaving the question open, just as does another bandage of Pasebkhanut III, dated to a Year 12.[228] The obvious solution of rechecking the linen is not currently available, as none of the bandages from the unwrapping of the Bab el-Gasus mummies can currently be located.

Accordingly, there remain a number of potential options for reconstructing relationships and events following the death of Siamun. For clarity, one should therefore distinguish potentially three Pasebkhanuts at the end of the Twenty-first Dynasty:

Pasebkhanut II	King Tyetkheperure
Pasebkhanut III	high priest, son of Panedjem II
Pasebkhanut IV	high priest, in office under Pasebkhanut II

One could have Pasebkhanut III becoming king (Pasebkhanut II) on Siamun's death, and being succeeded as high priest by *another* Pasebkhanut (IV)—perhaps his son.[229] Another option would make Pasebkhanut II unrelated to the Panedjem family—perhaps the son of Siamun—and have Pasebkhanut III/IV as a single individual, serving as high priest under Siamun, Pasebkhanut II, and perhaps even Shoshenq I.

Leaving aside the issues surrounding the Theban high priesthood during Pasebkhanut II's reign, three entries in the Karnak Priestly Annals can be attributed to his time. One explicitly dates to his Year 11 (or possibly Year 3),[230] one to what is almost certainly his Year 13, and another to an unknown year.[231] At Abydos, a pottery ostracon naming the king was found in the shrine of Osiris in the former tomb of Djer at Umm el-Qaab.[232] It is possible that the deposition of this—and perhaps the execution of the graffito in the Sethy I temple—was linked to the erection of a stela by the Chief of the Ma Shoshenq B (later king Shoshenq I) endowing, by royal grace, a statue cult for his late father Nimlot A at Abydos.[233] Shoshenq's son, the later king Osorkon I, seems also to have been active during this period, to judge from a block from Saft el-Henna naming him as a Prophet of Sopdu, generalissimo, and Leader of the Archers of Pharaoh.[234]

The length of Pasebkhanut II's reign is unclear.[235] As noted above, the highest year-date assignable to him is Year 13, which could support the lower of the two Manethonic figures for the reign—i.e., fourteen years in all. On the other hand, a stela dating to Year 5 of the reign of Shoshenq I[236] refers back to a land register of Year 19 of "Pharaoh Pasebkhanut": it has been argued that the context implies that this must be within one generation of the date of the stela, and thus should belong to the second king of the name.[237] However, it is by no means certain that this is the necessary interpretation of the text, leaving open the possibility that the king referred to is Pasebkhanut I.[238] Overall chronological considerations (see Appendix 1) might suggest a reign of around two and a half decades.

While the ancestry of Pasebkhanut II remains problematic, at least one child is certainly known. She was Maatkare (B), who would marry the future Osorkon I and bear his eldest son, the high priest of Amun, Shoshenq Q, although seemingly she died before she could become queen (see p. 96). Like a number of other ladies of the dynasty, Maatkare B was the subject of a property decree at Karnak, in this case carved on Pylon VII at Karnak.[239] It has been suggested that Pasebkhanut II might have been the father of a king Shoshenq ("IIc"), but this king seems likely to have been the artifact of an artisan's error (see p. 259 n. 9).

While no monuments of Pasebkhanut II's reign seem to survive at Tanis or its environs,[240] a batch of crude faience *shabtis* bearing the name of a Pasebkhanut was found in the antechamber of Tanis NRT-III. These differed completely from figures definitely attributable to Pasebkhanut I, but were very similar to figures bearing the name of Siamun that were found in the same location.[241] They suggest that the last two kings of the Twenty-first Dynasty were interred in the tomb, and that their remains are to be identified with the pair of utterly decayed coffins and mummies at the north end of the antechamber. Between them was later placed the coffin of the Twenty-second Dynasty king Shoshenq IIa (fig. 79; see pp. 95–96).[242]

At least three posthumous mentions exist of Pasebkhanut II: interestingly, in all these cases the king's nomen is prefixed by "Hor-." This may be a version of the name used late in life, or coined posthumously to distinguish Pasebkhanut II from the earlier pharaoh of that name.[243] One is in a filiation of his daughter Maatkare B dating to the reign of his son-in-law Osorkon I (see p. 96). The second is on a statue of Thutmose III that was usurped to serve as a memorial to the king.[244] The final one comes from an incomplete text in Theban Tomb TTA18, which also includes another king's prenomen that should probably be read as that of Shoshenq I, and appears to form part of a biographical inscription spanning the dynastic transition.[245]

TTA18, belonging to the Chief Document/Outline Scribe of the Estate of Amun, Amenemopet,[246] is interesting in that it may be the only known (albeit now lost)[247] rock-cut tomb-chapel at Thebes to have been decorated from scratch during the pre-Twenty-fifth Dynasty phase of the Third Intermediate Period—all the others are usurpations.[248] The most extensive example of the latter is TT68, where the Head of Temple Scribes of the Estate of Amun, Nespaneferhor (i), who lived during the time of Siamun/Pasebkhanut II, substituted his name throughout the decoration that had been added to the erstwhile sepulcher of the Twentieth Dynasty priest Paenkhmun.[249] While it is possible that the basic paintings of TTA18 could have been usurped, the texts all appear to be Third Intermediate Period originals, and the same may thus also be true of the paintings themselves.[250]

Among these is a reward scene by an unnamed high priest of Amun, whose combination of sacerdotal and military titles—"high priest, generalissimo, and army leader"—indicates a date no earlier than the last years of the *wḥm-mswt* for TTA18's decoration (fig. 60). If the aforementioned Pasebkhanut II/Shoshenq I text formed part of Amenemopet's decoration, the high priest would presumably be Pasebkhanut III/IV.[251] If it were a later graffito, he could be an earlier Twenty-first Dynasty pontiff.[252]

Fig. 60. Scene from the lost tomb of Amenemopet at the south end of Dra Abu'l-Naga (TTA18), showing the tomb owner (shown twice, facing right) being rewarded by an unnamed high priest of Amun (perhaps Pasebkhanut III/IV or an immediate predecessor), depicted on the far right. The other figures are members of Amenemopet's family.

3 THE HOUSE OF SHOSHENQ

While it is clear that Shoshenq I was king after the death of Pasebkhanut II, it is possible that he obtained at least quasi-regal authority while Pasebkhanut yet lived. The significant document is the dateline in the Karnak Priestly Annals Fragment 4b (fig. 98), which cites "Year 2 . . . of the Great Chief of the Ma, Shashaq."[1] Although this has generally been dated to the first years of Shoshenq I's independent reign,[2] one remains uncomfortable with the idea that a crowned pharaoh of Egypt could be so gratuitously insulted by his being referred to, in the heart of the state temple at Karnak, by his commoner's title. The implicit view that this was because he might have been seen as an upstart foreigner seems unlikely: his uncle Osorkon the Elder had already been a pharaoh and had been referred to as such in the same set of annals.

Rather, the dateline could be attributed to a period of co-rule with Pasebkhanut II, during which Shoshenq began to count a dating era, but did not yet take pharaonic titles. Shoshenq could have been granted control of the Thebaid following the demise of the high priest Pasebkhanut III/IV, reflecting Shoshenq's status as now heir to the throne, probably by virtue of his being the nephew of Osorkon the Elder.[3] One might also suggest that it was at this point that the high priesthood itself was bestowed on Shoshenq's son, Iuput (A).[4]

The earliest dated attestation of Shoshenq I with a cartouche and his well-known prenomen of Hedjkheperre is in Year 5.[5] One wonders, however, whether he was Hedjkheperre (a name borrowed from Nesibanebdjedet I) from the outset of his formal reign. In the same general area as the aforementioned ostracon of Pasebkhanut II at Umm el-Qaab was found another, naming a Tutkheperre Shoshenq,[6] a name also found on a block at Bubastis (Tell Basta).[7] Might this and the Umm el-Qaab piece be referred to a period of full coregency between Pasebkhanut II and Shoshenq I, following on from the latter's earliest regnal years as a simple Great Chief? In that case, Shoshenq would have chosen a prenomen closely modeled on that of his senior co-ruler, changing it only later, on coming to sole power, in order to proclaim himself a new dynastic founder.[8] Shoshenq I's close links with Pasebkhanut II are in any case displayed by the statue (originally of Thutmose III) that he[9] seems to have had reinscribed in memory of his predecessor.

Two wives of Shoshenq I are definitely known, together with one representation of a spouse that has, however, lost the lady's name (fig. 61).[10] Karomama (A) is named as the mother of the future Osorkon I on a contemporary block from Saft el-Henna (see p. 80) and in the retrospective genealogy of Pasenhor B. Another son, Nimlot (B), was borne by Penreshnes, daughter of an unnamed Chieftain of the Ma.[11] The maternity of Shoshenq I's other two known children is, however, uncertain. A daughter, Tashepenbast, is named, together with her husband, the Third Prophet of Amun Djedthutiuefankh A/i, on a statue of their grandson Neseramun ii,[12]

Fig. 61. Fragment of relief showing Shoshenq I and a woman whose name has been lost—but might be queen Karomama A—making an offering. From Zagazig (NMS A.1967.67).

Fig. 62. Fragment of the granite lining of the tomb of the high priest of Amun Iuput A at Abydos, with representations from the Book of *Amduat*. White Monastery, Sohag.

while another daughter, Djedinetnebuiusankh, is named alongside her husband Djedhoriufankh on a faience seal.[13] The other known child of Shoshenq I was the aforementioned high priest of Amun, Iuput A, explicitly called Shoshenq I's son on many of his monuments. He seems ultimately to have been buried, not at Thebes as one might have expected, but in a large tomb at Abydos (fig. 62).[14]

Iuput's appointment ended the dynastic succession of Theban pontiffs that had been such a feature of the previous dynasty, although he, like them, combined his priestly title with the military ones of generalissimo and army leader. The office of Fourth Prophet was probably held by the Chief of the Mahasun, Nesy—from his title clearly also a man of Libyan extraction—and then by his son Nesankhefmaat,[15] while Djedptahiufankh A apparently combined the roles of Second and Third Prophet.[16] Perhaps a son-in-law of Panedjem II through his daughter Nesitanebetashru A, Djedptahiufankh was buried after Year 11 in Panedjem II's tomb, TT320, with his putative wife possibly following after Year 13. They were the last primary interments there before the introduction of the large cache of royal mummies for which the sepulcher is best known. While the burials of Djedptahiufankh and Nesitanebetashru provide only the earliest possible date for this last transfer, it seems likely that the later of these funerals provided the opportunity for the last great mummy transfer of the campaign that had begun back in the Twentieth Dynasty. That New Kingdom royal tombs may have been entered during Shoshenq I's reign is suggested by the fact that the king's alabaster canopic chest (fig. 63) was clearly inspired by prototypes of the mid-New Kingdom, and is without any Third Intermediate Period parallel.[17]

Wider aspects of funereal innovation are also to be seen during Shoshenq I's reign. The decoration and form of Egyptian coffins had remained conceptually rather stable since the end of the Eighteenth Dynasty, being based on polychrome adornment on a yellow ground, finished with a layer of yellowing varnish—hence the type's modern designation as the 'Yellow' coffin.[18] Thus, although coffins made early in the new dynasty differed

Fig. 63. Canopic chest of Shoshenq I, modeled on examples from the royal tombs of the mid-New Kingdom (Berlin ÄM11000).

significantly in many details from the 'ancestral' pieces of four centuries earlier,[19] they reflected the continuation of a single artistic tradition. However, while Djedptahiufankh and Nesitanebetashru were interred in this type of coffin, before the end of Shoshenq I's reign a certain Padimut had been buried in a new kind of inner container that enveloped his body in a single hard cartonnage shell, with a decoration that in both coloration and motifs owed little to the earlier tradition.[20] This new kind of mummy case—together with an associated radically simplified outer coffin—rapidly replaced the Yellow coffins[21] and became standard throughout Egypt until superseded by a new set of concepts during the eighth century.[22]

Building work carried out in the name of Shoshenq I was relatively plentiful, after the dearth seen throughout most of the preceding dynasty. Architectural fragments and usurped sculpture exist from Tanis, Bubastis, Tell el-Maskhuta, Athribis (Tell Atrib), and Heliopolis,[23] while a considerable amount of work is evidenced at Memphis. Various fragments bearing the king's name survive from the Ptah temple, where the high priest Shedsunefertum A continued the Twenty-first Dynasty pontifical line and dedicated a number of monuments, including a new embalming table for

Fig. 64. Temple at el-Hiba, built by Shoshenq I.

Fig. 65. Relief from the temple at el-Hiba (Heidelberg 562).

the sacred Apis bull.[24] Interestingly, nothing of Shoshenq I's time has been identified at the Serapeum at Saqqara, continuing the hiatus already noted during the Twenty-first Dynasty (see pp. 59–60). On the other hand, a block from a chapel of the king has been found at Saqqara, indicating some potential royal interest there.[25] Just south of the Fayyum, the King's Son and Army Leader of the Entire Army, Nimlot B, decreed an enhanced offering regime for the god Heryshef at Herakleopolis (Ihnasiya el-Medina),[26] while on the opposite side of the Nile at el-Hiba a new temple was begun in the name of the king (figs. 64–65).[27]

The majority of monumental material dating to the reign derives from Thebes. Here, Shoshenq I was responsible for laying out a new peristyle court in front of Pylon II at Karnak, which had hitherto been the principal frontage of the temple. The first phase seems to comprise the building of a monumental gateway, generally referred to as the Bubastite Portal (fig. 66), in the southeast corner between the temple of Rameses III and the south tower of Pylon II. The interior of the gateway, which was still being decorated at the king's death, contained various scenes of the king (and often the high priest Iuput) in the presence of the Theban gods (fig. 67).[28]

The southern exterior of the gate, where it overlapped Pylon II, was adorned by a large tableau of the king[29] smiting enemies before Amun (fig. 68).[30] The names of the conquered towns included in the composition make clear that the scene commemorated an extensive campaign

Fig. 66. The Bubastite Portal from the south, with the temple of Rameses III on the left, the outer wall of the Hypostyle Hall on the far right, and Pylon II behind the victory relief of Shoshenq I in the center.

into Palestine, whose exact itinerary has been much discussed.[31] In particular, the relationship between the tableau and an event recorded in the Old Testament has been a crucial issue:

> And it came to pass in the fifth year of king Rehoboam that Shishak king of Egypt came up against Jerusalem: and he took away the treasures of the house of the Lord.[32]

Since the days of the hieroglyphic pioneer Jean-François Champollion[33] it has been generally accepted that "Shishak" was simply a rendering of "Shoshe(n)q,"[34] and thus that the campaigns recorded in the Bible and

Fig. 67. Shoshenq I and
Iuput A before Amun.
Bubastite Portal, Karnak.

at Karnak were one and the same. However, Jerusalem is not actually mentioned in the Karnak texts,[35] an omission potentially explained in various
ways—at one extreme, that the name lay among those now unreadable; at
the other, that Shishak was not Shoshenq I after all.[36]

An option taking a middle path is that the omission of Jerusalem from
the Bubastite Portal tableau simply indicates that *this* particular campaign—explicitly called the king's "first [campaign of vi]ctory"—did not
include Jerusalem. There could then have been *another* campaign that *did*
include Jerusalem in its itinerary, but was not recorded in any extant Egyptian document. In favor of this is the fact that the Bubastite Portal was but
one part of Shoshenq I's much larger building progam at Karnak.[37]

In Year 21, II *šmw*, a stela at the Gebel el-Silsila quarries records a royal
decree to the Overseer of Works Horemsaf to extract stone there for the
construction at Karnak of "very great pylon towers . . . to make a festival

Fig. 68. Victory relief of Shoshenq on the Bubastite Portal. The king's figure was formerly on the right, but having been modeled in plaster it has now fallen away, leaving only the ghostly top of his white crown. On the left is Amun, below and behind whom are name rings containing the names of conquered

court . . . surround(ed) with statues and a colonnade" (fig. 69).[38] This is clearly what is now the First Court of the temple (figs. 70–71),[39] with the projected pylon occupying the site now occupied by the (probably) Thirtieth Dynasty Pylon I.[40]

The date of the stela decree presents problems as, if one follows Manetho, Year 21 was the king's last. If quarrying began only in II *šmw* of that year there would clearly have been insufficient time for stone not only to be cut, but to be shipped and erected to produce the extant structures within the remaining few months of the king's life. Two principal options exist. First, the Manethonic data could be corrupt and Shoshenq lived for several years more, perhaps surviving almost until the *sed* festival that the decree implies was the intended purpose of the court. Second, it could be that while the decree describes the ultimate outcome of the building program, it was made up of several sequential projects, beginning with the Bubastite Portal. In that case, the Year 21 work at Silsila may actually have been for the final building phase, the construction of the (almost certainly

Fig. 69. Stela 100 at Gebel el-Silsila, marking quarry work by Shoshenq I. At the top, the king and Iuput A are led into the presence of Amun, Re-Horakhty-Atum, and Khonsu by Mut.

never completed) pylon potentially requiring the opening of a new part of the quarry to provide sufficient stone. Of these, the second is perhaps the more attractive, as it explains well the differential state of the principal elements of the project and does not require what would be a significant revision of the chronology of the period.

In the context of the history of Shoshenq I's campaigning, this latter option would remove the building and exterior decoration of the Bubastite Portal from the very end of the reign, where it is usually placed,[41] taking the view that the decoration of its interior was a separate piece of work, indeed being carried out around the time of the king's death. The campaign commemorated on the portal could thus have been, at the very latest, somewhat earlier than the Year 20 usually proposed—although it is not impossible that a significant period actually elapsed between the event, and the space for its commemoration becoming available.[42] In addition, the intention will certainly have been to cover the side walls of the court with reliefs, and any further campaigns would have been prime subjects for the exterior

surfaces (not to mention the pylon). Battle scenes would have been particularly appropriate for the outside of the north wall, as here they would
have been contiguous with the battle reliefs of Sethy I on the northern
exterior surface of the Hypostyle Hall, just as the Bubastite Portal tableau
was juxtaposed with campaign reliefs of Rameses II on the south wall of the
Hypostyle Hall.[43]

On this basis, Shoshenq I's military activities probably spread over a
number of years and comprised at least two campaigns, that of the Bubastite
Portal *and* that of the Biblical 'Jerusalem' operation. It is of course quite possible that further campaigns also occurred. Perhaps the first of them was the
subject of a fragmentary stela found in the North Court just beyond Pylon
VI,[44] which relates how a border skirmish led to a campaign culminating in
a successful battle on the shore of the Bitter Lakes. Victory scenes are also
to be found at the temple at el-Hiba (fig. 72),[45] with a probable reference to
one or other of the campaigns on the mummy cartonnage of the Prophet

Fig. 70. South side of the First Court at Karnak, showing the Bubastite Portal and southern colonnaded wall erected by Shoshenq I, separated by the temple of Rameses III, and Pylon I, probably built during the Thirtieth Dynasty. Ram-headed sphinxes that had formerly marked the avenue from the quay to the Pylon II entrance to the temple have been moved to the margins of the new court. Under Taharqa a ten-columned kiosk was added in the center of the the courtyard, of which one column has now been re-erected.

of Amun-Re and Royal Scribe Hor "[who followed] the king on his journey in the lands of Retjenu (Syria–Palestine)."[46] That Shoshenq's engagement in Palestine might have comprised more than one extensive *razzia* is also suggested by a study of cultural material from the area, pointing to a prolonged and significant Egyptian involvement during early Iron IIA times.[47]

Also in Palestine itself, a fragment of a stela found at Tell el-Mutesellim (Megiddo)[48] probably serves as a confirmation that this city was indeed conquered by Shoshenq I, as stated in his Karnak relief. The stratigraphic

Fig. 71. Outside of the north wall of the Hypostyle Hall, built by Sethy I, and the First Court of Shoshenq I. Note the contrast between the extensive relief work on the former and the total lack of decoration on the later addition.

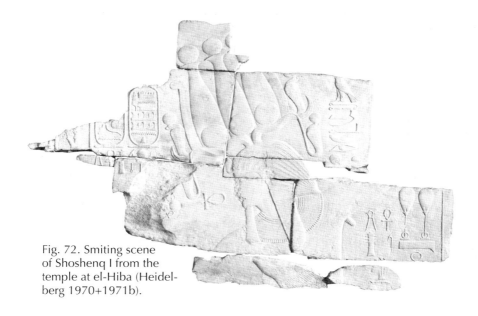

Fig. 72. Smiting scene of Shoshenq I from the temple at el-Hiba (Heidelberg 1970+1971b).

origin of this piece is somewhat problematic, and it has been suggested that it may derive from a layer conventionally dated to the ninth century,[49] suggesting secondary or even tertiary deposition.[50]

At Egypt's historic trading partner, Byblos, a seated statuette of the king was acquired by Abibaal, the local ruler, and inscribed accordingly.[51] This would probably have been sent originally as a gift for installation in the Hathor temple at Byblos, and seemingly marked the beginning of a renewed series of such donations by the kings of Egypt (cf. pp. 92, 95).

As noted above, the canopic chest of Shoshenq I has survived; unfortunately it appears to have come from the antiquities market, thus giving no indication of the place of the king's burial. Given that the kings of the Twenty-first Dynasty—and a number of rulers of the latter part of the Twenty-second Dynasty—were buried at Tanis, one might have expected the same to be true of Shoshenq I and his successor, Osorkon I. However, nothing of their burials has been identified at Tanis,[52] leaving the possibility that Shoshenq had shifted the royal necropolis elsewhere.

This is potentially supported by the fact that the two earliest kings of the Twenty-second Dynasty to be actually interred at Tanis were found buried in secondary contexts: Takelot I had been provided with a chamber in the tomb of his son, while Shoshenq IIa was found in the antechamber of Pasebkhanut I (cf. p. 101). The second case is particularly suggestive, as plant remains found on the mummy seem to have grown into the bones while the coffin lay in standing water—something that had never been present in NRT-III.[53] This might suggest that this burial had been moved to the Tanite necropolis after the evacuation of another cemetery in the wake of serious flooding—and that Takelot I's interment was a reburial undertaken at the same time, for the same reason. It is therefore possible that the lost tombs of Shoshenq I and Osorkon I were at this same location.

As to where this might have been, Manetho preserves a tradition that the dynasty was Bubastite in origin; if correct, the temple precinct at Bubastis could be a candidate for Shoshenq I's burial place.[54] On the other hand, other sites are possible, with suggestions including the area of Tanis itself,[55] Herakleopolis, and the precinct of Ptah at Memphis, the latter two of which later received high-status burials of the period (cf. pp. 104, 106), with Memphis hosting a "House of Millions of Years of Shoshenq-meryamun"—i.e., a mortuary establishment.[56]

Sekhemkheperre-setepenre Osorkon (I)-meryamun, the son and successor of Shoshenq I, had married a daughter of Pasebkhanut II, Maatkare B, a

union that may have cemented Shoshenq I's status as the heir to the last king of the Twenty-first Dynasty. However, she seems to have died before Osorkon's accession, as on the monuments of their son, Shoshenq (Q), she lacks any queenly titles, bearing only those of "King's Daughter of the Lord of the Two Lands Horpasebkhanut." Rather, the wife of Osorkon as king was Tashedkhonsu (A), mentioned in the Pasenhor genealogy, but whose only known contemporary memorial is a *shabti* found in the burial of her son, Takelot I.[57] It is likely that she was also the mother of Osorkon I's remaining known children, Iuwlot and Nesibanebdjedet (III), both of whom would ultimately become high priests of Amun at Karnak.

The first of the king's sons to become Theban pontiff was, however, Shoshenq Q,[58] who apparently succeeded his uncle Iuput A and appears in this role conducting a priestly induction in an unknown year.[59] He created or appropriated a number of sculptures at Karnak,[60] perhaps the most interesting being a quartzite figure of the personified Inundation, on which he not only names his parents and maternal grandfather, but also writes his own name in a cartouche with the epithet "-meryamun" (fig. 73).[61]

Fig. 73. Statue of the Inundation dedicated by Shoshenq Q. From Karnak (BM EA8).

Such cartouche use by someone other than a king or queen is extremely unusual at this period,[62] and clearly indicates that Shoshenq's status had risen to an exceptionally high level. As a result it has often been speculated that he might subsequently have acquired full royal titles in the person of the Heqakheperre-setepenre Shoshenq (IIa)-meryamun whose body was found secondarily buried in NRT-III at Tanis (cf. pp. 101–102).[63] However, there are a number of later items in which Shoshenq Q's descendants (see just below) remember their forebear, and in all of them he is simply a King's Son and high priest, without even a cartouche. In such circumstances it seems far more likely that Shoshenq died while still high priest than that his descendants ignored his regality.[64] As clearly the intended heir, Shoshenq must have predeceased Osorkon I, being replaced as crown prince by the future Takelot I and as high priest by Iuwlot—both his younger brothers.

From these aforementioned later pieces and his own statues, we learn that Shoshenq Q had at least three wives: Ikhya;[65] Nesi(ta)nebetashru (B), mother of Horsieset (A), Prophet of Amun;[66] and Nesitawadjetakhet, mother of another Prophet of the god, Osorkon (D)[67]—who in turn was the father of a similarly titled Iuput (B).[68] Horsieset A has in the past been regarded as a man who rose to be high priest under Osorkon II, and later became king at Thebes; however, this now seems unlikely (see p. 106).

The identity of Shoshenq Q's immediate subordinate, the Second Prophet, is unknown, although he might have been the Bakenamun who is known to have flourished under either Osorkon I or II.[69] The order of the successors of Djedptahiufankh A in the office of Third Prophet is unclear, but Shoshenq's uncle by marriage Djedthutiufankh A/i seems to have served during the latter part of Osorkon I's reign.[70] Djedthutiufankh's father Ameneminet i is posthumously given the title of Third Prophet,[71] and may have officiated in the interim, although another holder of the title, Neseramun vii, lived somewhere around the Twenty-first/Twenty-second Dynasty transition and could have been Djedptahiufankh's direct predecessor or successor.[72] Djedthutiufankh seems to have been succeeded as Third Prophet around the end of Osorkon I's reign by Djedkhonsiufankh (Q), son of Nespaneferhor (B).[73]

Fig. 74. Temple of Bastet at Tell Basta, ancient Bubastis.

Fig. 75. Relief of Osorkon I at the temple at Tell Basta.

Nesankhefmaat was succeeded as Fourth Prophet by the Great Chief of the Mehes, Pashedbast A,[74] who was probably followed directly by Djedkhonsiufankh A, a son-in-law of Iuput A.[75] A number of more junior officials are known from the Priestly Annals and inscribed pieces of sculpture.[76] Little work seems, however, to have been carried out on the fabric of the Karnak temples under the direction of these priests, as only a few reliefs were added to the Bubastite Portal to complete part of the scheme begun under Shoshenq I. An isolated block and the remains of a text in the Khonsu temple are datable to Osorkon I's reign,[77] as are (potentially) repairs to a chapel of Thoth and Amun to the south of the Sacred Lake.[78]

Further north, an inscription added to a gateway of Thutmose III at Qift may be attributed to Osorkon I,[79] while ostraka in the king's name were found at Umm el-Qaab at Abydos.[80] Decoration of the temple at el-Hiba also continued, with work being carried out as well at Atfih and Memphis.[81] At Memphis, the high priesthood was passed down in succession to Shedsunefertum A's son Shoshenq C and grandson Osorkon A, running on down to some point in the reign of Takelot I.[82]

Although no building work is attested at Heliopolis, the high priest there, Djedptahiufankh B, is known from a donation stela of Year 6.[83] The principal buildings known to have been erected under Osorkon I were, however, at Bubastis, where he made a number of additions to the Bastet temple (figs. 74–75), as well as the nearby Atum sanctuary.[84]

Abroad, a statue from Byblos (fig. 76)[85] attests to continued official links between Egypt and this important part of the Levant.

A follow-up to Osorkon's father's Palestinian exploits is suggested by an Old Testament account of a battle between king Asa of Judah and "Zerah the Kushite"—presumably a Nubian general of the Egyptian king—which resulted in the defeat of Zerah and his pursuit as far as Gerar.[86] This event has been dated to *c.* 897 BC on the basis of Biblical data,[87] which would fall in the mid-20s of Osorkon I's reign.

Fig. 76. Statue of Osorkon I from Byblos, with secondary inscription of the local king, Elibaal (Louvre AO9502).

Manetho gives fifteen years for the length of Osorkon's reign, but a Year 33 dateline on linen from a mummy whose trappings included a piece with Osorkon I's name,[88] together with the number of Third and Fourth Prophets of Amun during the period,[89] has led to the view that Manetho's figure might be an error for *35 years.[90] In any case, it would appear that on Osorkon's death he was succeeded by his son Takelot, one of the more poorly attested kings of the period.

Takelot I's position in the succession is apparently guaranteed by his position in the Pasenhor B genealogy, but for many years even his prenomen was uncertain, although it is now clear that he was Hedjkheperre-setepenamun/re Takelot (I)-meryamun,[91] the prenomen being that of Nesibanebdjet I and Shoshenq I. Nevertheless, hardly any items referable to his reign bear a royal name, including, most unusually, a series of Karnak Nile Level records (fig. 77).[92] Indeed, it has been suggested that he may have had rivals for the throne in the persons of one or more of the obscure kings Shoshenq IIa and IIb (see pp. 101, 259 n. 8, 264 n. 112).

These Nile Level records are, however, datable to this era through their citation of the successive high priests Iuwlot and Nesibanebdjedet III, both brothers of the king. Iuwlot is also known from an offering stand,[93] an ostrakon,[94] and a pair of stelae. One probably derives from Iuwlot's (unknown) tomb (fig. 78)[95] and the other recounts an oracle confirming the allocation of resources to his son Khaemwaset (Q).[96] Iuwlot's daughter, Djedisetiuesankh (i), seems to have married the Third Prophet of Amun Padimut ii-Patjenfy.[97]

Elsewhere in Egypt, a new high priest of Ptah at Memphis followed Osorkon A in office: on a block from the temple area at the Serapeum at Saqqara the new man, Merenptah (Q), is named alongside the cartouches of Takelot I.[98] It is possible that a bull was buried in the Serapeum galleries themselves in Year 14, but this remains uncertain.[99] Also found at Saqqara was a fragment of a fan bearing the king's name.[100] Other than items from his burial, three stelae, probably from Bubastis, are the only other known documents bearing Takelot I's names.[101]

The burial of Takelot I was found within the tomb (NRT-I) of his son and successor Osorkon II at Tanis (fig. 24[I/3]), and as such may have been

Fig. 77. Quay at Karnak, used from the Twenty-second Dynasty onward to record the height reached by a given year's Inundation. These provide important historical data regarding the kings and pontiffs recognized at Thebes across the second part of the Third Intermediate Period.

a reburial, moved from a perhaps flood-prone previous royal necropolis (see p. 95).[102] It is unclear whether the Middle Kingdom sarcophagus of a certain Ameny that was provided for the king's mummy[103] was part of his original tomb equipment or was provided for the reburial. On the other hand, his set of 361 *shabtis*,[104] four uninscribed canopic jars,[105] and other material[106] will certainly have derived from the initial interment.

A definite reburial at Tanis, in Pasebkhanut I's NRT-III, has already been mentioned as being that of Heqakheperre Shoshenq IIa (fig. 79). The king's bejeweled mummy[107] was enclosed in a nest of a wooden coffin, a silver coffin, a cartonnage case, and a mask with a gold face. The silver coffin and cartonnage each had the face of a raptor, the earliest example of what would be the standard approach for kingly coffins until the latter part of the Twenty-second Dynasty.[108] The body was accompanied by canopic jars and (probably) a set of uninscribed *shabtis*.[109]

The form of the king's name—with minimal epithets and using a unique prenomen—indicates that Shoshenq IIa belonged to the first part of the Twenty-second Dynasty, prior to the advent of Osorkon II, when more elaborate (but banal) forms started to be used (see pp. 130–31, 203). However, he proves difficult to place. It has been argued (see above) that the man long regarded as best candidate, Osorkon I's son Shoshenq Q, most probably died as no more than a high priest. Other suggestions that Shoshenq IIa might actually be Shoshenq I buried with a new prenomen[110] are without any parallels and unlikely, especially as Shoshenq I's canopic chest had been manufactured in the name of Hedjkheperre.[111]

Fig. 78. Stela, showing Iuwlot and his wife adoring the solar bark, and containing a solar hymn. From Thebes (BM EA1224).

One possibility is that this Shoshenq ruled briefly before or alongside Takelot I,[112] something perhaps supported by the lack of a royal name on the Nile Level inscriptions of Takelot's reign. This would, however, say nothing about Shoshenq IIa's ancestry, which must for the time being remain an open question.

Takelot I was followed on the throne by Usermaatre-setepenamun Osorkon (II)-meryamun, who not infrequently

Fig. 79. View of the antechamber of NRTIII as discovered on 17 March 1939. On the left is the raised area with the coffin of Shoshenq IIa and debris of the burials of Siamun and Pasebkhanut II. Against the far wall stand various reused canopic jars, four of which held the canopic coffinettes of Shoshenq IIa; the remainder were presumably associated with the mummies of his two Twenty-first-Dynasty companions.

added the further epithet '-sibast' to his nomen. That Osorkon II was the son of his predecessor is clear not only from the Pasenhor genealogy—which also names his mother as an otherwise unattested Kapes—but from the inscriptions in the burial chamber that Osorkon provided for Takelot I at Tanis, where the younger king is called "a son benefiting the one who sired him."[113] This chamber lay within a sepulcher whose original foundation can be dated architecturally and archaeologically before that of NRT-III, the tomb of Pasebkhanut I.[114] As already noted (p. 41), the only credible original owner for the tomb would seem to be Nesibanebdjedet I, who will either have been ejected from his tomb to make way for its new occupants, or had already suffered robbery. Either way, nothing of his funerary equipment ws left behind.

In addition to this appropriated tomb, Osorkon II undertook a significant expansion of the Amun temple at Tanis, adding a new fore-court with a pylon whose foundation deposits survived intact.[115] He also erected the East Temple, including the utilization of Old Kingdom columns that had already been reused at least once, by Rameses II.[116] Somewhere at Tanis was erected a fine stela-bearing statue of the king (fig. 80), with inscriptions apparently intended to set out the king's formal administrative program. This included the prospective assignment to his children of various key offices—including the high priesthoods of Amun and Heryshef and the Great Chiefdoms of the Ma. An interesting reference enjoins Amun to guard against any "brother being resentful of his brother"—suggesting royal concern at the inherently fissiparous nature of such a parceling out of fiefs to members of the royal lineage. There is also a reference to the royal children leading armies against the *pywd*—Libyans—presumably a troublesome tribe on Egypt's west flank.[117] The king's principal wife, Karomama (B, fig. 81), is mentioned as the mother of these children, although two other wives, Isetemkheb (G) and Djedmutesankh (iv), are known to be the mothers of two apparently younger children, respectively a daughter Tjesbastperu (A),[118] and a son Nimlot (C).[119]

Fig. 80. Statue of Osorkon II, holding a stela setting out the king's domestic program. From Tanis (UPMAA E.16199+CM CG1040).

Although the Amun high priesthoods are explicitly earmarked for Osorkon's sons, the greatest of these, at Karnak, was taken by such a son, Nimlot C, only late in the reign. During the earlier part, the office continued to be occupied by the king's brother, Nesibanebdjedet III. On the other hand, the Tanite pontificate of Amun was given to Osorkon's son Hornakhte (C) who was, however, to die young and to be buried in his father's burial chamber.[120]

The explicit mention of the high priesthood of Heryshef indicates the importance during the period of the god's city, Herakleopolis, where many local dignitaries were linked to the Twenty-second Dynasty royal family.[121] Indeed, some suggestions have made it perhaps the dynasty's city of origin.[122] Accordingly, it is no surprise to find in Osorkon II's Year 16 his son Nimlot C bearing the title of high priest of Heryshef, together with, *inter alia*, those of general and Great Chief of Per-Sekhemkheperre,[123] a military strongpoint established by Osorkon I in the vicinity of Herakleopolis. Nimlot would much later translate to Thebes to become pontiff there.

Although the pontificate of Ptah at Memphis is not mentioned as fief for a royal son, one of the offspring of Osorkon and Karomama, Shoshenq (D),[124] received this office, apparently in succession to Merenptah Q. Merenptah Q had followed the last certain member of Twenty-first Dynasty line of office holders, Osorkon A, and as such it seems that Shoshenq D's appointment was at least implicitly part of the program proclaimed on Osorkon II's Tanis statue. Shoshenq was in office by his father's Year 23, on the basis of a statue of the high priest apparently associated with the burial of an Apis bull in that year,[125] and died (or at least was buried) under Shoshenq III, given the presence of that king's name in Shoshenq D's burial (cf. further p. 115).[126] The tomb—found intact in 1942—lay just outside the southwest corner of the enclosure of the Ptah temple. It was constructed from various reused blocks (fig. 82),[127] and became the first of a series of high-priestly tombs in this location (see map 5).

No other building work at Memphis can be dated to Osorkon II's reign,[128] but further north considerable work was done at the temples at Bubastis (fig. 74), in particular a large gateway celebrating the king's *sed* festival (fig. 83).[129] Also in the Delta, a usurped statue of Senwosret III at Leontopolis (Tell Muqdam) attests to Osorkon II's work there.[130] A tomb there of a King's Wife Ka(ro)ma(ma) seems likely to have been that of queen Karomama B, although in the past she has also been regarded as being rather Karomama D, the mother of Osorkon III.[131]

Beyond Egypt's northern borders, the remains of a statue of Osorkon II are known from Byblos, the last of the series of Twenty-second Dynasty pharaohs' images to find their way to that port,[132] while from Samaria came a measuring jar bearing his names.[133] However, the remaining significant material relating to the reign comes from the south, with the remains of a stela from Elephantine[134] and a considerable number of items from Thebes.

In the main temple at Karnak, two blocks to the northeast of Pylon VI preserve the

Fig. 81. Relief of Osorkon II and Karomama B. From Bubastis (BM EA1077).

Fig. 82. Burial chamber of Shoshenq D, constructed from various reused blocks, including a lintel of Tutankhamun and a stela of Amenhotep II, used as the ceiling. From Mit Rahina-Kom el-Fakhry (Cairo JE88131).

remains of a decree of Osorkon II,[135] the king's activity also being marked by decoration in a number of the small chapels on the periphery of the Karnak complex. These included Chapel J, in the main complex, and Chapel e, on the southern enclosure wall of the Montju temple.[136] The Chapel of Osiris-Wepished at Karnak in the northeast quadrant of the Amun enclosure seems to have been built under the auspices of the Letter Writer of Pharaoh, Hor vii/viii/ix/xi, an important figure who lived on into the reign of Shoshenq VI (cf. p. 126).[137] A number of priestly inductions[138] and inundation records are dated to the reign,[139] together with a series of private statues that provide useful genealogies,[140] of a type that became increasingly common during the second half of the Third Intermediate Period.

As already noted, the earlier years of Osorkon II saw the pontificate at Karnak in the hands of his brother, Nesibanebdjedet III; however, the succession after him becomes somewhat problematic, as does the whole status of the Theban polity. In particular, a separate Theban pharaoh appears for

Fig. 83. Reconstruction of the gateway of Osorkon II's Festival Hall at Tell Basta. (Naville 1892: frontispiece.)

the first time since the Twenty-first Dynasty, in the person of Hedjkheperre-setepenamun Horsieset (I)-meryamun (fig. 84).[141] For a long time he was held to be identical with Horsieset A, son of Shoshenq Q, and to have served as high priest of Amun before becoming king. However, there is no evidence that Horsieset A had ever been a high priest,[142] while the one mention of a high priest Horsieset under Osorkon II[143] has to be placed so late in the reign that he could not have gone on to be king Horsieset. That individual was actually the high priest Horsieset B, known to have been in office under Shoshenq III and his Theban contemporaries.[144] Rather, it now seems more probable that Horsieset I was a son of the high priest Nesibanebdjedet III, to judge by the fact that the latter's wife [Isetem]kheb (S)-Ikhy bore the title of God's Mother,[145] which can be used to designate the mother of a king.[146] Horsieset's wife may have been Shebensopdet, a King's Wife who is of otherwise unknown affiliations, but was buried at Herakleopolis, whence came the evidence of the king's maternity.[147] Two daughters of Horsieset I are known: Isetweret i,[148] and [Tait]anebethen.[149]

Horsieset I had a son who was elevated to the high priesthood at Thebes, but the son's only known monument is damaged, and only two signs of the pontiff's name are partly legible, giving a reading of either [. . .]*diw*[. . .] or [. . .]ʿ*w*[. . .] (fig. 85).[150] A name of the period of the appropriate form is Padubast, and if so restored, this son of Horsieset I may be identifiable with one or other of the individuals of that name who were to play important roles in the coming decades (see pp. 121–25). Horsieset is also associated[151] with Sitamen-Mutemhat Karomama (G) meryetmut, the first God's Wife of Amun of any prominence since the time of Maatkare A.[152] Although she nowhere bears the title of King's Daughter, all other known holders of the office were royal princesses, and thus it is likely that she was indeed the offspring of a king—perhaps identical with Karomama C, shown as a daughter of Osorkon II at Bubastis.[153]

Of the lesser clergy at Karnak, the Fourth Prophet Djedkhonsiufankh A had been followed by his son Nakhtefmut A-Djedthutiufankh B, who is shown to have been a contemporary of both Osorkon II and Horsieset I by the presence of both kings' names on one of his statues, given by favor of the Theban king.[154] Horsieset I's daughter, Isetweret i, was married to Nakhtefmut's

Fig. 84. Remains of doorway with figure of Horsieset I. Karnak, Pylon IV.

son, Horsieset C, who went on to become Fourth and ultimately Second Prophet, apparently before the end of Osorkon II's reign.[155]

If Horsieset I was indeed a son of Nesibanbdjedet III, it is possible that his own kingship, and his son's pontificate, directly followed the end of Nesibanebdjedet's period of office. On the other hand, the demise of Nesibanebdjedet III could have been followed by the elevation of Nimlot C to the high priesthood in accordance with Osorkon II's intent as expressed on the Tanis statue, with the Horsieset/[Pa?]du[bast?] regime being established after Nimlot's death or other departure from office. This

Fig. 85. Fragment of granite monument showing [Pa?]du[bast?], son of Horsie-set I and high priest of Amun. From Koptos (Cairo JE37516).

may have been the first manifestation of the power struggles that would wrack the Thebaid over the next few decades, although none of the monuments of the potential protagonists seem to bear any telltale signs of intentional mutilation.[156]

This may be because Horsieset I's effective rule was brought to an end through a collapse of his health: the skull found in his tomb had "in the forehead a roughly quadrilateral hole which suggests a trepanation." The anatomist Douglas Derry commented that Horsieset "lived for a long while after the infliction, whatever its nature may have been,"[157] but it may have severely impaired his ability to function. The king's sepulcher (MH1) lay close alongside the Eighteenth Dynasty temple at Medinet Habu (fig. 117; map 8), comprising a single undecorated chamber approached by a stepped ramp, and equipped with niches for the canopic jars—now placed flanking the body, rather than at its feet as had formerly been the custom.[158] The tomb contained, apart from the remains of a skeleton, a set of canopic jars, a set of *shabti*s, and a stone anthropoid coffin, the trough usurped from Henutmire, sister-wife of Rameses II, the lid a raptor-headed Twenty-second Dynasty original (fig. 86).[159]

It may have been in the wake of Horsieset's death that his son was supplanted by Nimlot C's son, Takelot F, as high priest: the latter is mentioned in the Chapel of Osiris-Wepished at Karnak, built by Osorkon II.[160] However, before the end of the reign, yet another high priest had appeared on the stage, the aforementioned Horsieset B, who would remain on the scene—in and out of office—for some three decades. The fate of Takelot F will be discussed in the next chapter.

The length of the reign of Osorkon II is a matter of some debate. His highest certainly preserved regnal year is 23, from the stela of an Apis bull buried that year,[161] with a probable Year 29 among the Nile Level notations on the quay at Karnak.[162] On the basis of broader chronological considerations, it seems probable that he lived on into at least the mid-30s of his reign (cf. Appendix 1).

As already noted, Osorkon II had buried his father, Takelot I, in his own intended tomb at Tanis (NRT-I—figs. 24, 46), which had originally been built in the early Twenty-first Dynasty, almost certainly for Nesibanebdjedet I.[163] The full extent of Osorkon's rebuilding of this sepulcher is unclear, but certainly involved the tomb's complete decoration, and the provision of a new entrance from the west (fig. 24[I/a]), replacing the original shaft on the east (fig. 24[I/2]). The new doorway contained an unusual tableau in which the general Pashereneset son of Hori is shown mourning and reciting an elegy for the late king Osorkon (fig. 87):[164] that a king should be mourned like a mortal is a new departure. The text ends with the laconic note "Kapus made it for him." This has generally been interpreted as an indication that Osorkon II's mother Kapes (the names are slightly different, but within the potential boundaries of orthographic variation) outlived him and acted as intermediary in allowing Pashereneset to add his elegy—or even provided the king with his tomb. However, the lady in question is given no title, while Osorkon II's mother would in any case have been unlikely to be still alive at the end of her son's reign, which, as already noted, seems to have lasted some four decades. Accordingly, "Kapus" seems more likely

Fig. 86. Lid of the stone coffin of Horsieset I, with the raptor head that is typical of royal coffins of the Twenty-second Dynasty (cf. fig. 79). From Medinet Habu MH1 (Cairo JE60137).

Fig. 87. Entrance to the antechamber of the tomb of Osorkon II, showing the elegy of Pashereneset on the northern doorjamb. Tanis NRT-I.

to have been a quasi-homonym of the queen—perhaps a daughter of the king, if a member of the royal family at all.

Beyond the entrance lay what was initially a single antechamber (figs. 24[I/1, 1a], 88), decorated with extracts from various mortuary books, including the Books of the Earth, the Day, the Night, and the Dead. The last included the weighing of the heart and the Negative Confession—elements that were quite new to a kingly tomb: no longer is the king a god on earth gone to join his brothers in heaven, but one who must now submit to judgment like a mere mortal. More of the Book of the Dead adorned the adjacent square room that had probably been the Twenty-first Dynasty entrance shaft, along with elements from the Book of Amduat. The chamber used for the burial of Takelot I included material taken from the Book of the Dead, the Book of Amduat, and also the Book of the Earth (fig. 88)—all except for the tableau on the east wall, entirely in the name of Osorkon II.

The granite-lined burial chamber had minimal decoration, comprising two vignettes from the Book of the Earth. The eastern end was rebuilt to take the sarcophagus of prince Hornakhte C, while most of the remainder was occupied by a large granite sarcophagus—by its form apparently

Fig. 88. Southern part of the west wall of the burial chamber of Takelot I in the tomb of Osorkon II, bearing texts from the Book of the Earth. Tanis NRT-I.

an original Twenty-second Dynasty piece of work, rather than a usurped Middle or New Kingdom piece as had been the case in the nearby tombs of Amenemopet and Pasebkhanut I. Unfortunately, NRT-I had been robbed in antiquity, and thus only fragments of the funerary equipment of the occupants survived, although Hornakhte suffered rather less than the others.[165] Of the burial of Osorkon II himself, only the eyes from his cartonnage and the remains of a gilded coffin survived, together with canopic jars, *shabtis*, and various other debris:[166] three mummies found in the sarcophagus seem to have been those of intrusively buried children.[167]

Like Pasebkhanut I, Osorkon and his family did not retain sole occupancy of their tomb for long. A large sarcophagus was introduced into the northern half of the antechamber (fig. 24[I/1a]), and the 'new' room sealed off by a wall bearing figures of Osorkon II and Shoshenq III offering to divine figures.[168] It is unclear who was the intended occupant of the sarcophagus, as while fragments of *shabtis* of a king Shoshenq-sibast-meryamun were found,[169] Shoshenq III had his own tomb some way away (see p. 115). These might represent a later intrusive interment of Shoshenq V, replacing a member of Shoshenq III's family, perhaps after a robbery.[170]

4 DISINTEGRATIONS

The last years of the reign of Osorkon II mark a watershed in the history of the Third Intermediate Period. With it, the fissiparous tendencies that had been apparent since the last years of the New Kingdom and had been manifested in the dual kingships of the Twentieth/Twenty-first transition both recurred in the person of Horsieset I and stood on the threshold of becoming institutionalized. Indeed, Osorkon's 'manifesto' on his Tanis statue highlights the various nodes of power he wished to secure in the persons of his sons, suggesting an unease at their being held by worthies without a direct stake in the crown.

The Egypt reflected by this document now incorporated, in addition to the time-hallowed high pontificates of the principal gods, various Chiefs of the Ma(shwesh) and of Foreigners, the latter being very explicitly elements of non-Egyptian origin, and presumably including such individuals as the Chiefs of the Libu. There has been much debate over how far these foreign (Libyan) entities contributed to the breakdown of centralized authority in Egypt during the ninth and eighth centuries, and the degree to which any such contribution stemmed from the underlying nature of Libyan society, making it antithetical to the concept of a unitary monarchy.

That this Libyan admixture was indeed a key factor has been cogently argued by a number of scholars, albeit with a number of different models to underpin it.[1] Fundamentally, the issue is that the Libyan society implied by the various Rameside military entanglements to the west was one led by multiple chiefs who were linked by close family ties, rather than a single 'king.' The application of anthropological theory has provided potential insights into how such a structure could lead to a confederal approach that worked against the concept of a paramount central authority. Leading on from this, the continuing use of Libyan titles alongside Egyptian ones during the Third Intermediate Period could be seen as resulting in a Libyan tribal-based 'segmental' non-hierarchy running in parallel with, and in tension against, the historic Egyptian pharaonic hierarchy.[2] A related concern with lineage also helps explain the extensive genealogies seen on the statues dedicated at Karnak by worthies of the second half of the Third Intermediate Period. While one remains nervous at accepting this model as *the* cause of the gradual breakdown of the centralized state, which gathers pace following Osorkon II's death,[3] it certainly eases understanding of how fragmentation accelerated once the dam had been cracked.

The succession after the death of Osorkon II remains the subject of scholarly dispute. Down to this point, the succession—in the main line at least[4]—is apparently guaranteed by the genealogy of Pasenhor B (see p. 72); after this, Pasenhor's ancestry diverges from the kingly sequence and is therefore of no further help. However, the autobiographical text of the high priest Osorkon B (see pp. 118–19) states that he was a maternal great-grandson of Osorkon II, placing his own father, a king Hedjkheperre-setepenre Takelot (II)-sibast-meryamun, one generation earlier and thus a potential successor to Osorkon II.[5]

For many years it was accepted that Takelot II was indeed the direct successor of Osorkon II in the Twenty-second Dynasty line, and most material naming a Hedjkheperre Takelot was attributed to him, especially as the prenomen of Takelot I was not recognized until 1987 as *also* being Hedjkheperre-setepenre (although recognizable by his nomen lacking '-sibast').[6] This included the misattribution of the Takelotid burial in NRT-I to Takelot II, thus reinforcing the view that he was the Tanite successor of Osorkon II. However, in 1989 a reassessment of the evidence concluded that Takelot II was more likely to be a Theban king ruling in parallel with the Tanite line,[7] a reconstruction that has gained widespread acceptance[8] although doubts still remain in some quarters.[9] Among key arguments in favor of making Takelot II a southern king is that all known monuments of him and his family are in Upper Egypt. There is now no sign of him whatsoever at Tanis, despite his having had a reign of at least a quarter-century, allegedly sandwiched between those of two kings (Osorkon II and Shoshenq III—see just below) both of whom built and were buried at Tanis. Accordingly, we will proceed on the view that within a short time of Osorkon II's death—or even a little before—there was once again a separate king ruling in the south.

What then of the Tanite succession? Helpfully, Osorkon B's autobiography is dated, presumably after his father's death, by the regnal years of a king Usermaatre-setepenre/amun Shoshenq (III)-sibast-meryamun-netjerheqaiunu, which seem to have run roughly in parallel with those of Takelot II. This Shoshenq is amply attested at Tanis (see just below) and thus can be seen as the clear candidate for Osorkon II's successor there.

On the other hand, nothing is known of Shoshenq III's origins: he cannot easily have been a son of Osorkon II, as Osorkon already had a son named Shoshenq (D), who was buried in Shoshenq III's reign (see p. 104). One wonders if Shoshenq D's death occurred before his father's interment, leading to a kinsman (Shoshenq III) carrying out the burial and thus becoming the legitimate heir. It seems unlikely that this could have been a coup d'état on the part of Shoshenq III, as the family line of Shoshenq D continued to hold the key office of high priest at Memphis for at least four generations, which would seem incredible if they were in fact the rightful royal line, displaced by skullduggery following Osorkon II's death. Accordingly, Shoshenq III could actually have been a son of Shoshenq D, taking his place in the succession on his father's premature demise. The new king was in any case almost certainly a younger man, given that he was to reign for four full decades.

Of his own family, Shoshenq III's Great Wife was one Tentamenopet, with whom he had a daughter named Ankhesenshoshenq.[10] By [Ta]dibast (B), daughter of Tadibast (A), he had Bakennefi A, who seems to have been heir to the throne in Year 14.[11] A third wife was Djedbastesankh, the mother of Takelot C, a Commander of All Troops.[12] The mothers of Shoshenq III's other children are uncertain; these offspring included Pashedbast B (see p. 122); the high priest of Amun (at Tanis?), Padebehenbast, active in Year 28;[13] and probably the Great Chief of the Ma, Pamiu.[14]

At Tanis, Shoshenq III added a new monumental gateway to the brick enclosure wall of the Amun temple (figs. 40, 89),[15] as well as constructing his tomb (NRT-V—figs. 24, 94).[16] All his other known personal monuments were also built in the Delta: a chapel at Tell Umm Harb, a structure at Bendariya, a pylon at Tell Balamun, and a gateway at Kom el-Hisn.[17] We also have a number of donations of land to local cults during the reign, recorded on stelae from sites within the Delta or its margins.[18]

Other recorded activity in the north of Egypt during Shoshenq III's reign included the burial of Apis bull XXIX at Saqqara in Year 28,[19] although another bull must have been interred earlier in the reign, given that the previous known bull burial had been of Apis XXVII back in Year

Fig. 89. The collapsed remains of the gateway of Shoshenq III, as seen in 1884 (cf. fig. 40). While the portrait of the king on the nearest block is that of Shoshenq himself, others still show the names of Rameses II, from whose monuments—in particular a huge colossus—came the raw material of the gate.

23 of Osorkon II.[20] The stela that accompanied Apis XXIX to the grave reveals the Memphite hierarchy at that point in time, including their line of descent (fig. 90). The leading figure in paying homage to the deceased Apis is the Great Chief of the Ma, Padieset (A), son of a like-titled Takelot (B), who was in turn a son of the former high priest Shoshenq D. The next figure is Padieset's son, the high priest of Ptah Peftjauawybast (B), followed by another son, the *sem* priest Takelot D. What is interesting here is that on the stela of Apis XXX, buried in Year 2 of Pamiu (see p. 134), Padieset A and Takelot B are retrospectively referred to with the additional title of high priest. It would thus seem that the family of Shoshenq D continued to hold the Memphite pontificate, but that Padieset—and possibly Takelot—passed that office to a son while he yet lived, but retained the Great Chieftainship. That this dignity was regarded as senior to the pontificate—formerly second only to the king—is shown by the scale of Padieset's representation on the Apis XXIX stela, which

has been cited as an example of the way in which the tribal Libyan lineages subverted the ancient Egyptian hierarchies.[21] Padieset would ultimately be buried in a silver coffin in the necropolis of his ancestors.[22] Lastly, only a single donation stela attests to the reign of Shoshenq III at the dynastic stronghold of Herakleopolis,[23] while nothing else bearing the king's name is known between here and Thebes, to whose affairs we must now turn.

The aforementioned king Takelot II seems most likely to have been none other than the high priest Takelot F, son of the former pontiff Nimlot C and thus a grandson of Osorkon II. It is clear that he became king prior to Osorkon II's death, since his Year 24 preceded Year 22 of Shoshenq III in a chronological list of endowments by Takelot's son, Osorkon B, in the latter's 'Chronicle' text (see further p. 122).

Fig. 90. Stela from the burial of Apis XXIX, dated to Year 28 of Shoshenq III. It shows the Apis being adored by the Great Chief of the Ma Padieset A and his sons, the high priest of Ptah Peftjauawybast B and the *sem* priest of Ptah Takelot D. From Saqqara, Serapeum, Lesser Vaults (Louvre IM3749).

One would assume that Takelot F went directly from pontiff to king, but it is unclear what happened to the high priesthood at that point. The aforementioned Osorkon B held the office at various points over the following decades (see below), and a direct father-son succession is possible. However, Horsieset B was certainly high priest at some point during the short remaining period between Takelot F ceasing to be high priest and Osorkon II's death, since a statue of Horsieset was inscribed with the cartouche of the latter king.[24]

There would appear to be two basic options. First, that Takelot F was replaced as high priest by Horsieset B, and that there was a gap prior to him becoming Theban king as Takelot II, during which time Horsieset's statue was manufactured. Second, that Takelot transitioned directly from high priest to king, appointing Osorkon B as his successor, but that Horsieset immediately set up as a rival, dating his records by the Tanite king Osorkon II rather than the 'upstart' Theban. Both would reflect some

Fig. 91. Fragmentary stela dated to the reign of Takelot II. Elephantine, Khnum temple (Elephantine Museum).

degree of conflict surrounding Takelot's transition from pontiff to king, with the second in keeping with the intermittent pontificates of Osorkon B and Horsieset B over the coming decades. At present, it is not possible to choose between these two options (cf. further p. 105).

Little is known of the earlier years of the new southern regime, with the exception of a possible Karnak Nile Level text of Takelot II's Year 5.[25] Undated reliefs of Takelot and the God's Wife Karomama G in Chapel e in the Montju complex,[26] where she had previously been shown with Osorkon II (see p. 105), may date from this period. Similarly, a restoration text in the name of Takelot II in the Ptah temple at Karnak may also come from these times, as might a fragmentary stela from Elephantine, demonstrating that when this monument was erected, the king's writ embraced, or was at least acknowledged at, Aswan (fig. 91).[27]

However, it is in Year 11 that certainly dated events begin, in particular with the first episode in a long text within the Bubastite Portal at Karnak, which is a key source for the next three decades of Theban history (figs. 92–93).[28] This is the so-called Chronicle of Prince Osorkon (B), the eldest son of Takelot and his wife Karomama (D). The latter is explicitly stated in the text to be a daughter of Nimlot C, and was thus a sister of her husband.

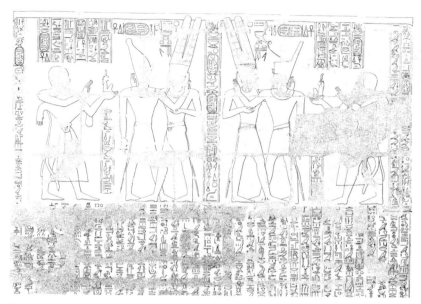

Fig. 92. Detail of the upper part of the section of the Chronicle on the north face of the eastern section of the Bubastite Portal, showing Takelot II embraced by Amun, with Osorkon B behind him.

Apart from Osorkon, who appears in the Chronicle as high priest of Amun at Thebes and generalissimo, Takelot had at least three more sons, Nimlot (F),[29] [. . .]iuankh,[30] and the general Bakenptah.[31] There were also at least three daughters: Karomama (E);[32] Isetweret (ii), who married the vizier Nakhtefmut C;[33] and Shepensopdet (v), who married the Fourth Prophet of Amun, Djedkhonsiufankh C, son of his predecessor Horsieset C, and who bore a further Fourth Prophet, Nakhtefmut B.[34]

The Chronicle is made up of two distinct sections, carved on separate occasions. The first section, dated to Year 11, is headed by a double scene of Osorkon and his father, and occupies the inside of the eastern section of the Portal (fig. 92). The second part was begun on the west wall of the porch of the Portal, with a double scene of Osorkon and Amun at the top (fig. 93), and concluded on the inside of the western section of the Portal. This covered Years 12 and 15 of Takelot II through Year 28 of Shoshenq III, with a final coda in the latter's Year 29, in which year this second section was apparently carved.

The Year 11 section is dated to I *prt* 1, and recounts Osorkon's passage southward from el-Hiba with an army, to put down a rebellion that seems

Fig. 93. Section of the Chronicle of Prince Osorkon carved on the west wall of the porch of the Bubastite Portal at Karnak.

to have caused damage to towns as far north as Hermopolis (Ashmunein). Here, the pontiff instituted repairs before the army headed on to Thebes, where captured rebels were executed and their bodies burned. This bloody episode was followed by the issuing of a series of decrees regarding the administration of the Theban temples. It was in the wake of these events that we find a priest named Hori petitioning Osorkon on I *šmw* 11 for the restoration of his hereditary rights within the Karnak temples.[35]

Concerning the question of how long before Year 11 Osorkon had been high priest, and who his opponent(s) were, one Karnak Nile Level text seems to be key. This is dated to Year 6 of Shoshenq III, and names the high priest as Horsieset (B).[36] Now, as we shall see (just below), this date seems to correspond to Takelot II's tenth regnal year, and thus reveals Osorkon's opponent as Horsieset—who was pointedly using the reign of the Tanite king as his dating era, rather than that of the Theban pharaoh. In light of our earlier discussion of Horsieset's career (see pp. 117–18), there may be two possible scenarios to explain the situation: one has Horsieset dismissed from the high priesthood some years earlier by Takelot II and replaced by Osorkon, with Horsieset making a comeback in Year 10, thus sparking the civil conflict described in the Chronicle. The other is that Horsieset remained in office during the first decade of Takelot II's reign, and rebelled on being told in or just before Year 10 to give way to Osorkon. Either way, Horsieset seemingly escaped capture and would soon reappear on the scene.

Year 12 saw Osorkon in Thebes three times, bringing with him ship-loads of offerings, his position apparently now secure. However, in Year 15 civil war broke out once again with renewed and unexpected intensity: indeed, Osorkon protests in the Chronicle that there had been no omen, such as an eclipse, which might have been expected to herald such a cataclysm.[37] This conflict was to last for some two decades.

It would appear that Horsieset had not been alone in his rebellion, as an anonymous Year 12 of another Nile Level text—which can, nevertheless, be only that of Shoshenq III—is stated to correspond to Year 5 of a king Usermaatre-setepenamun Padubast (I)-sieset-meryamun.[38] Accordingly, this Padubast must have come to power in Shoshenq III's Year 8, whose regnal years were, as noted above (p. 117), at least two years behind those of Takelot II. Padubast's advent can thus be placed in or after Takelot's Year 10, and must surely coincide with one or other of the rebellions featuring in the Chronicle. The Year 11 option seems preferable, both on broader chronological grounds and because a rebellion by Horsieset would seem more credible if backed by an alternative claimant to the Theban throne.

What then might have been the background of this further upstart king? A possibility is that he was the enigmatic son of Horsieset I, whose damaged name, we have already noted (see p. 107), could potentially be restored as [Pa]du[bast]. Certainly, as a former high priest and son of a Theban king, this individual would make a credible candidate, while Horsieset B's name could suggest that he too might have been a kinsman of Horsieset I. Certainly the two men would be closely associated over the next twenty years, with the Year 15 putsch putting them at the head of the Thebaid for the best part of a decade.

Of the new king's family, only a son, Padiamenet (iii), is known, from a record in the Karnak Priestly Annals of his induction as a God's Father in Padubast's Year 7.[39] Friendly relations between the new Theban regime and the Tanite kings suggested by Horsieset B's dating his Nile Level text by Shoshenq III back in the latter's Year 6 (see p. 120) are given more concrete form by the restoration of the doorway of Pylon X, at the southern entrance to the Karnak temple, by Pashedbast B, a son of Shoshenq III.[40]

However, while control was apparently maintained through Year 8 of Padubast I,[41] Osorkon B and Takelot II seem to have made a comeback in Takelot's Years 24 and 25: in the former year the Chronicle records donations to Amun by Osorkon, while a stela at Karnak is dated to Year 25, which is the last known for Takelot II.[42] It is possible that an oracle text potentially aimed at Horsieset B may date to this, or another, of Osorkon B's comebacks.[43] It seems likely that Takelot died shortly after the Year 25 stela was carved, as the Chronicle dates another batch of donations by Osorkon to Shoshenq III's Year 22, which would seem to correspond, at the latest, to Takelot's putative Year 26—if not Year 25 itself.

If this Takelotid revival had thus most unfortunately been followed shortly by the death of Takelot II himself, it is not surprising that shortly afterward we find Padubast I once again appearing in a Nile Level text, dated to his Year 16.[44] Most interestingly, this is stated to correspond to Year 2 of a king Iuput (I). This individual is an enigma. Although his Year 6 appears in graffiti on the roof of the Khonsu temple,[45] and a potential Year 11 in the Karnak Priestly Annals,[46] there is no unequivocal record of his prenomen, with no evidence as to his background or affiliations. A number of monuments name a king Usermaatre-setepenamun Iuput-sibast-meryamun, but seemingly he should be placed rather later in time, for while the form of his nomen fits well at this period, one representation appears stylistically to place him around a century later as Iuput II (see pp. 148–50).

The Karnak Iuput has generally been regarded as a Theban coregent of Padubast, but this by no means follows: in his Year 5 Padubast had linked his reign with that of Shoshenq III, certainly not a Theban. It has already been noted that in the brief period following Takelot II's death, Osorkon B began to date by Shoshenq III: could it be that this act implies a break in the previous link between the Padubastid regime and the one in Tanis, leading to another northern monarch (i.e., Iuput I) being henceforth recognized as the Padubastids' northern 'partner'? Given the commonality of their nomina, it is possible that both Iuputs hailed from the same city—Iuput II is known to have ruled from Leontopolis in the southeastern Delta (see p. 148).

This of course indicates that the establishment of a separate Theban kingdom had been paralleled by the setting up of another kingdom in the southeastern Delta. The potential existence of yet another fiefdom headed by somebody styling himself as a king is suggested by a series of monuments from Memphis, plus another from Bubastis, naming a king Usermaatre-setepenamun Padubast-sibast-meryamun.[47] These cartouches differ from those of Padubast I only in the epithet '-sibast' replacing '-sieset,' and some have argued that they represent the same individual, using different epithets for the north and south; others, however, have argued that they were different men, especially as the epithets were sufficient to distinguish between the cartouches of Osorkon II and III.[48]

Exactly where and when this Padubast 'II' reigned remains a problem.[49] One suggestion places him at Tanis as a successor of Osorkon IV in the eighth century (for which see pp. 150–51).[50] However, by this time royal cartouches had become radically simplified (see pp. 130–31, 203) and the compound cartouches of Padubast II sit very uncomfortably in such a late position. Rather, they would fit better if their owner were to be placed as a—probably slightly later—contemporary of Padubast I, perhaps as the successor of the putatively northern Iuput I. In any case, stelae from Memphis naming Padubast II show that he was also acknowledged at Herakleopolis,[51] suggesting a realm that stretched from the southeast Delta up to the mouth of the Fayyum.[52] The locations where Padubast II is attested include those previously containing monuments of Shoshenq III, suggesting—on our proposed timeline—that there may have been a significant realignment of allegiances in the north following the death of the third Shoshenq.[53] The potential importance of the death of Shoshenq III as a watershed in the history of the later Third Intermediate Period will be returned to later.

Considerable quantities of ink have been spilled on the matter of how this multiplicity of kings should be fitted into the Manethonic dynastic structure, with little appearance of consensus. In contrast to his apparently helpful list of Twenty-first Dynasty kings (see pp. 39–40), the Twenty-second Dynasty bequeathed by Manetho is less helpful. Two versions simply list three kings who are clearly Shoshenq I, Osorkon I, and Takelot I, with a total duration of forty-nine years.[54] The third extant redaction[55] adds three unnamed kings between Osorkon and Takelot, plus three more after the latter, boosting the dynastic length to 120 years. There then follow four kings comprising the Twenty-third Dynasty "of Tanis," headed by a Padubast and an Osorkon, who are succeeded in two versions by just a "Psammûs," who is, however, followed in the third version by a certain "Zêt."[56]

Various attempts have been made to square these successions and associated reign lengths with the evidence from the monuments.[57] However, the very range of conclusions reached by different scholars indicates the probable futility of the exercise. In particular, it is clear that the extant Manethonic model seems to be based on the underlying concept of a monolineal succession—much as was the Assyrian King List (cf. Appendix 1). This is, of course, exactly what we do *not* have during the latter part of the Third Intermediate Period, which leaves us with the resulting question of how Manetho or his original source(s) might have selected kings to comprise a probably artificial 'royal line.' Accordingly, any conclusions on royal successions or allegiances at this time based on Manetho should be regarded as unwise at best.

An illustration of this point has been the ways in which the Manethonic Twenty-third Dynasty (explicitly "from Tanis") has been variously regarded, for example, as a continuation of the Twenty-second Dynasty regime at Tanis, or a line ruling at Leontopolis, or has simply been used as a catch-all for kings of the general period other than Shoshenq III and his immediate Tanite successors. This has led to the creation of a number of wholly new 'Twenty-third Dynasties' with little or no direct link to the Manethonic scheme—in particular a 'Theban Twenty-third Dynasty' accommodating Takelot II and his lineal descendants.[58] However, such attempts tend to create more heat than light, and it is probably wiser simply to describe the locations and affiliations—where known—of a given king, rather than try to shoehorn him into an ultimately artificial numbered dynastic structure. On the other hand, one may probably retain the designation of 'Twenty-second Dynasty' as shorthand for the Tanite regime that originated with Shoshenq I and continued through Shoshenq III and beyond—although recognizing that the designation is itself strictly speaking artificial, once one gets beyond Takelot I.

Thus, by the beginning of the eighth century, one can probably detect four kingly groupings: the old Twenty-second Dynasty at Tanis, which was recognized at Memphis; a succession of kings also recognized at Memphis, but perhaps based in the southeastern Delta and recognized at Herakleopolis (Iuput I and Padubast II); the Upper Egyptian line of Takelot II, currently represented by Osorkon B, with a stronghold at el-Hiba; and their opponents, the Theban line headed by Padubast I. Further groupings would be added to these incipient 'dynasties' in the coming years. In considering this political kaleidoscope, a point to ponder is how far a given king's attestations reflect actual territorial control, or simply the personal loyalty of the individual dedicating a particular monument,[59] given the way in which the physical control of territory in the Nile valley was passing out of royal hands.

It is clear that various magnates, while not claiming kingship, were occupying fiefdoms that were increasingly independent in their day-to-day affairs, albeit dating these affairs by one or other of the lines of contemporary kings. Thus, in the western Delta we have a succession of Chiefs of the Libu, starting with Inamunnifnebu in Year 31 of Shoshenq III.[60] In the east were a series of separate Great Chiefdoms of the Ma, the best known being that at Mendes, with one Hornakhte (A) attested as Chief in Year 22 of Shoshenq III,[61] and further incumbents known down to the first part of the seventh century. Other Chiefs of the Ma included one based at Hurbeit, also first attested under Shoshenq III,[62] to whom they presumably owed some form of allegiance.

It can hardly be an accident that all these Delta fiefdoms make their first appearance in the archaeological record under Shoshenq III, suggesting that the fragmentation of the Egyptian polity gathered pace during perhaps the second decade of Shoshenq's reign. It also saw the final phase of Osorkon B's struggles against his enemies. The course of the conflict can be traced partly through the records of the years in which the Chronicle states that offerings were made by the prince-pontiff, and partly through the reigns and individuals mentioned in the period's Nile Level texts.

Thus, Osorkon seems to have been in control in Years 22, 24, 25, 28, and 29, but lost power again soon after the donations of Years 22 and 25. Thus, Years 16, 18, and 19 of Padubast I are found in the Nile level records, with Horsieset B mentioned in the latter two years.[63] Interestingly, no pontiff is given in Year 16. Following Osorkon's comeback in Years 28/9 and his triumphant inscription of the second part of his Chronicle, he was abruptly out of power again the following year—Padubast I's Year 23— when the Nile level was recorded in the names of Padubast I and a new high priest, Takelot (E).[64]

For the next decade Osorkon B was apparently excluded from Theban affairs. Nothing is known of the origins of the new pontiff Takelot E, nor the means by which he had replaced Horsieset after the latter's intermittent tenure of some three decades. Not long afterward there was a further change of personalities, when Padubast I himself disappeared and seems to have been succeeded by Usermaatre-meryamun Shoshenq (VI)-meryamun.[65] The new king is known only from the Nile Level

Fig. 94. Tomb of Shoshenq III at Tanis (NRT V); the sarcophagus was manufactured from a Thirteenth-Dynasty architrave. When found, the chamber originally contained a second sarcophagus, that of Shoshenq IV.

record of his Year 6, accompanied by Takelot E, along with graffiti on the roof of the Khonsu temple in Years 4 and 6 and an entry in the Karnak Priestly Annals which has, however, lost its date.[66] He is also named on the funerary cones of the Letter Writer of Pharaoh, Hor vii/viii/ix/xi, who had served since the days of Osorkon II and continued in office under Padubast I.[67]

It was not long after Shoshenq VI's Year 6 that we find the following entry in the Karnak Priestly Annals:[68]

> Year 39, I *šmw* 26 (of Shoshenq III): Now (Osorkon B) was in Thebes carrying out the festival of Amun in concert with his brother, the general of Herakleopolis and army leader Bakenptah, while all the gods were satisfied with them in overthrowing everyone who had fought against them.

It thus appears that, two decades after he was appointed high priest, Osorkon had finally displaced the various kings and priests with whom he had contended for control of the Thebaid. Presumably this involved the physical overthrow of Shoshenq VI and Takelot E, but nothing is known of their actual fates.

It might seem odd that, having finally disposed of those who had not only repeatedly driven him away from Thebes, but also prevented him from ascending his father Takelot II's throne, Osorkon did not immediately declare himself king in Thebes. One may note, however, that he did not do so on previous occasions when he was apparently victorious. This may simply have been a result of caution, to ensure that his position was indeed secure before taking the final step. On the other hand, from the death of Takelot II onward, Osorkon had dated his activities by the reign of Shoshenq III, who may indeed have provided him with physical support, as a result of which Osorkon may have been unwilling to declare his own kingship while the old Tanite yet lived. That this may be a plausible explanation is suggested by the fact that the year of Shoshenq III's death did actually see the appearance of a king Usermaatre-setepenamun-netjerheqawaset Osorkon (III)-sieset-meryamun. Although no source explicitly shows that he was indeed the former Osorkon B, a stela of the new king adds the title of high priest of Amun to his royal epithets, strongly suggesting that he was none other than the son of Takelot II.[69]

The placement of Shoshenq III's death around his Year 40 can be calculated by reference to the stelae marking the burial of Apis XXX in Year 2 of Pamiu.[70] This bull had been inducted in Year 28 of Shoshenq III and lived twenty-six years, showing that fourteen years separated Shoshenq III's last known regnal year (39) from Pamiu's accession. For many years it was assumed that Pamiu was Shoshenq III's direct successor, and that Shoshenq reigned for over five decades.[71] However, it has now been recognized that a king Hedjkheperre-setepenre Shoshenq (IV)-sibast-meryamun-heqaiunu reigned for at least ten years between the two.[72]

The principal evidence came from the tomb of Shoshenq III at Tanis (NRT V—figs. 24, 94), which was built to the northwest of the earlier sepulchers at a somewhat higher level (cf. fig. 40).[73] Compared with the tombs of Pasebkhanut I and Osorkon II, it is of a much simpler design, consisting of just an antechamber and a burial chamber. The entire structure is of reused blocks, its decoration comprising extracts from the various funerary books, principally the Book of the Night, supplemented by

Fig. 95. Fragment of a canopic jar of Shoshenq IV. From Tanis NRT V (present location unknown).

certain other vignettes and the judgment scene from the Book of the Dead. Shoshenq III's own granite sarcophagus had been made from a Thirteenth Dynasty lintel, and included a figure of the king himself in slightly raised relief on the lid. Alongside it was found a second, rather smaller sarcophagus, both being accompanied by the remains of funerary equipment, which included fragments of two calcite canopic jars that bore the names of Shoshenq IV (fig. 95), identifying him as the owner of the smaller sarcophagus.

Besides this, Shoshenq IV is known from a block at Tanis (on which he seems to bear the Theban epithet '-netjerheqawaset,' rather than his usual '-netjerheqaiunu'), two donation stelae, dating to his Years 4 and 10, a statuette of Isis, and some smaller pieces.[74] The Year 10 donation stela[75] was in the name of a Chief of the Libu, Niumataped (A), who is also known from a donation stela of a Year 8, normally regarded as that of Shoshenq V.[76] Taken together, the evidence supports the view that Shoshenq IV ruled between Shoshenq III and Pamiu, reigning somewhere between ten and fourteen years, depending on how long Shoshenq III lived beyond his Year 39.

As discussed above, it is likely that Shoshenq IV's accession in Tanis was paralleled by the belated taking of the Theban throne by Osorkon B (III). We have already noted (see p. 127) that in his kingly titulary Osorkon III alluded at least once to his former pontifical career; in the earliest three Nile Level texts of his reign (on which see further below) he calls himself explicitly the son of Karomama (D).[77] Of his own spouses, his Great Wife, Ka(ro)tjet(-meryetmut), is named on a stela of Year 15 at Hermopolis and in a filiation of her daughter Shepenwepet (I) in the temple of Osiris-heqadjet at Karnak;[78] another wife, Tentsai (A), is named as the mother of Osorkon III's son Takelot (G) on a block, perhaps from Herakleopolis.[79]

The other certain child was Rudamun—later to be a king—who is called Osorkon's son on a memorial of his own daughter,[80] and may appear as such on the Hermopolis stela.[81] Less definite are Djedptahiufankh (F), son of a king Osorkon and known from the late Twenty-fifth Dynasty coffin of a great-grandson;[82] Irtiubast, a King's Daughter who was married to a king Takelot and possibly sister-wife of Takelot III (formerly G);[83] and potentially the later high priest Osorkon F (see pp. 133–34).

Perhaps as a result of his previous experiences, Osorkon III ensured his control over the Amun cult at Karnak by not only appointing Takelot G as high priest (fig. 96)[84] but also making Shepenwepet I God's Wife, an office that she would hold for some six and a half decades.[85] As such she was granted the prenomen Khnemetibamun, beginning a sequence of prominent God's Wives that would continue until the end of the Twenty-sixth Dynasty (fig. 99). By their titulary and double cartouches it can be seen that they had quasi-pharaonic status, something first seen with Maatkare A at the height of her career back in the Twenty-first Dynasty.[86] Subsequently, only Karomama G is known to have been so endowed;[87] indeed, her career could have lasted down to Osorkon III's accession,[88] although one or more (potentially rival) God's Wives could have come and gone in the interim.

It was apparently early in the reign that Nebnetjeru i/iv became Third Prophet of Amun, presumably as Padimut ii's successor.[89] An entry in the Priestly Annals and a number of private statues and other memorials are dated to Osorkon III's reign,[90] including an indication that by its end the king's nephew Nakhtefmut B had succeeded Djedkhonsiufankh C as Fourth Prophet.[91] The reign saw at least two extremely high Nile inundations:

Fig. 96. Osorkon III and the high priest Takelot G (later Takelot III) preparing to release birds during a ritual before Khonsu. Reused in the Taharqa colonnade, Karnak.

Fig. 97. Detail of the quay at Karnak, showing the exceptionally high inundations of the reigns of Taharqa, Osorkon III/Takelot III, and Psamtik I.

indeed, these are the highest whose records are preserved on the quay at Karnak, with the exception of that of Year 6 of Taharqa (see fig. 97; cf. p. 162). The higher of the two, that of Year 3, is supplemented by a graffito of III *prt* 12 in the Luxor temple.[92] This records that the local citizens were "like swimmers in a wave" and the temples of Thebes "like swamps" (Luxor would have been flooded to over sixty centimeters above the level of its pavement), and it queries why Amun had sent such a disaster, given that temple ritual and offerings had been kept in order.

Another exceptionally high flood is recorded in Year 28 of Osorkon III. This record is interesting in that it notes that this corresponded to Year 5 of "his son," [Usermaatre-]setep[enamun] Takelot (III)-sieset-meryamun[93]— clearly the former high priest Takelot G. This period of co-rule saw the commencement of the construction and decoration of the chapel of Osiris-heqadjet at Karnak (fig. 98), with both kings and Shepenwepet I depicted (fig. 99).[94] An interesting feature of some of the scenes in this chapel is that both kings' prenomina are in some (but not all) cases written without the 'setepen-X' epithets that had hitherto been integral parts of these names. However, Osorkon III's nomen is always written here in full,[95] as in many cases is that of Takelot III, although in some cases the younger king's name is simply written as "Takelot."

This is a significant change from the usual pattern of royal naming thus far during the Third Intermediate Period.[96] The basic approach had hitherto followed Rameside practice, with a prenomen comprising a 'core' element (e.g., Usermaatre, Hedjkheperre) plus an epithet (setepenre/amun or

Fig. 98. The chapel of Osiris-heqadjet at Karnak, originally built by Osorkon III and Takelot III and extended during the early Twenty-fifth Dynasty.

meryamun). Initially, nomina comprised simply the king's birth name plus the epithet 'meryamun' but, as we have seen, around the reign of Osorkon II another epithet, of the form 'si-GODDESS,' started to be added, sometimes supplemented by 'netjerheqa-CITY.' The rest of the titulary followed Rameside norms, with the 'names' being effectively variable policy statements, the Horus name prefixed with "the Strong Bull" (*k3-nḫt*), as had been the case since the early Thutmoside times.[97]

However, Osorkon III, while being the Horus "Strong Bull who appears in Thebes," had very brief Nebty and Golden Falcon names (*st-ib-t3wy* and *ms-nṯrw*) that followed pre-New Kingdom patterns—the Nebty identical with the Horus name of the Fifth Dynasty king Niuserre. Takelot III went further in taking variant Horus names of ancient type as well—*w3ḏ-t3wy*, borrowed from another Fifth Dynasty king, Unas; *ʿ3-b3w*, taken from Amenemhat III of the Twelfth Dynasty; and probably also *nb-m3ʿt*, once used by Seneferu of the Fourth Dynasty.[98] This marks an important part of a move toward a more general archaism, to which we will return later.

The co-rule between Osorkon III and his son seems, from the two kings' context at Karnak, to be the only fully verifiable example of a 'true'

Fig. 99. Osorkon III and Shepenwepet I, as shown in the chapel of Osiris-heqadjet at Karnak.

coregency during this period, rather than a definite or possible instance of mutual recognition (cf. p. 122). How long it endured beyond its attested fifth year is unknown, as this is the last dated document of Osorkon III's reign. However, as this will have seen Osorkon in office as pontiff or king for six decades, it is likely that he will have died within a relatively short time of this second great flood. It may be significant that the next Inundation record is dated to Takelot III's Year 6 alone.[99] As for Osorkon's tomb, Theban documents of the Twenty-sixth and Twenty-seventh Dynasties mention a *ḥwt* (temple/tomb) of a king *wsrtn,* which seems likely to be that of Osorkon III.[100] Given that Horsieset I had his tomb at Medinet Habu (see p. 108) and that Shepenwepet I and her successors as God's Wives were also buried there (see pp. 156, 163; figs. 117, 127) along with other notables of the period, it seems likely that this lost tomb was also located there.[101]

Takelot III attained at least a thirteenth regnal year, as recorded on a stela from Amheda in the Dakhla Oasis.[102] It is possible that a Year 19 associated with the name of a God's Wife Shepenwepet in the Wadi Gasus belonged to him—although it is quite possible that was Year 19 of Taharqa in association with the other lady of the name and title, Shepenwepet II.[103] We have already noted a wife named Irtiubast, mother of a Prophet of

Amun Osorkon (see p. 129); Takelot fathered an Irbastwedjanefu (A) with the Favorite Kakat,[104] while a King's Wife Betjat may also have been married to this Takelot.[105] The mothers of Takelot III's other known children[106] (Diesetnesyt,[107] Djedptahiufankh (D) the Second Prophet of Amun,[108] Ankhkaroma,[109] Tentsai B,[110] Ihsetamun,[111] and [. . .]ankh[112]) are unknown.

Irbastwedjanefu A married the vizier Pakharu, whose father, Pamiu i, bore a portfolio of offices. These ultimately included not only that of vizier, but also that of Third Prophet of Amun and King's Son of Kush—the last one appearing for the first time since the Twenty-first Dynasty, and perhaps reflecting increasingly close links between the Theban polity and Nubia (see p. 144).[113] Ankhkaroma also married a future Third Prophet of Amun—Padiamennebnesuttawy A/B. It would appear that two other Third Prophets were interposed between him and Pamiu i: Wennefer i-Iryiy i and Amenhotep Y, known from the memorials of their descendants.[114] Takelot's Year 6 saw a significantly lower Inundation than the previous year—actually one somewhat below average—but no other records of his survive on the Karnak quay. Aside from his work in the Osiris-heqadjet chapel, which seems to have continued after the death of his father, some blocks from another Karnak chapel,[115] and the aforementioned Dakhla stela, relatively little survives bearing Takelot III's name. Two block statues from Karnak date to the reign,[116] as does the graffito from the Khonsu temple there that included the genealogy naming Osorkon the Elder (see p. 72 and fig. 51); elsewhere, a statuette and a stela are known from the North Cemetery at Abydos.[117] Three rather curious miniature canopic jars naming a king Takelot of unknown provenance may have come from Takelot III's lost tomb.[118]

Takelot will have laid down his pontificate on becoming king, but nothing from his reign indicates the name of his successor as high priest at Karnak. However, a high priest Osorkon (F) can be placed in this general period by the stylistic dating of the stela of his daughter Shepenwepet (A) to the latter part of the eighth century.[119] There has been debate over whether this Osorkon might be identical with the son of Takelot III of that name, and/or a high priest and King's Son Oso[rkon] named on a block statuette from Karnak.[120] The issue here is that the mentions of Takelot III's son—including on what seems to be his own coffin—only call him a simple Prophet of Amun, not First Prophet (high priest).[121] Unless these are all in error—which seems unlikely—the son of Takelot III must be distinguished (as Osorkon G) from the high priest Osorkon F, leaving the latter's paternity uncertain.

While it has been suggested that Osorkon F might have been a son of Takelot III's successor, Rudamun,[122] it is not impossible that he was a younger brother of Takelot III, appointed to the high priesthood by their father Osorkon III at the time Takelot III was elevated to the kingship. If he was a very much younger son, Osorkon F's period of office could have occupied a number of decades.

In the north, Usermaatre-setepenre Pamiu-sibast-meryamun (fig. 100)[123] had succeeded Shoshenq IV and occupied the Tanite throne during the middle years of the reign of his southern counterpart, Osorkon III. He was almost certainly the Pamiu who seems to have been a son of Shoshenq III (see p. 115) and

Fig. 100. Bronze statuette of Pamiu (BM EA32747).

thus probably a brother of his predecessor. That Pamiu's reign lasted at least seven years is shown by a block originally from Heliopolis,[124] while further work at Tanis is indicated by three inscribed blocks.[125] These give the king's nomen as simply "Pamiu," indicating that the archaizing simplification of royal names seen at Thebes was already to be found on occasion in the north.

A donation stela that may be assigned to the reign is known from Bubastis,[126] but the largest group of material of the reign derives from the Serapeum at Saqqara, where Apis XXX was buried on II *prt* 1 of Pamiu's Year 2. The principal stelae[127] once again show Padieset A as the leading man at Memphis, but with his son Peftjauawybast B replaced as high priest by a younger son, Horsieset H.[128] In addition, four further stelae were dedicated by other Memphite worthies,[129] while a block statue and a stela datable to this reign also probably come from this city.[130]

Pamiu's tomb seems to have been NRT-II at Tanis, to judge from a fragment of canopic jar bearing part of an Usermaatre cartouche:[131] all remaining Tanite Usermaatres of the period are otherwise accounted for.[132] The sepulcher was built up against, and shared a wall with, NRT-I (figs. 24; 101); in basic plan, the tomb is identical to Shoshenq III's, but the walls are devoid of decoration. It yielded a limestone sarcophagus, the debris of one silver and two wooden coffins, broken canopic jars, amulets, and various other fragments.[133]

Fig. 101. Tomb NRT-II at Tanis, the probable burial place of Pamiu.

Pamiu was succeeded by his son[134] Akheperre(-setepenre) Shoshenq V(-sibast-netjerheqawaset). While he employed a full set of epithets and long-form lesser names on certain monuments—in particular his 'Jubilee Chapel' at Tanis[135]—he generally followed the lead of his Theban elder contemporary Takelot III in using simple Old/Middle Kingdom-style names.[136] This nomenclaturial archaism was now combined with the appearance of an art style that also harked back to the past—in particular the early Old Kingdom—and would become the distinctive mode of the later Third Intermediate Period and the following Saite and Late Periods.[137] An example is to be seen on blocks from a structure at Memphis on which the king was shown accompanied by the high priest Takelot H (fig. 102),[138] probably the latest scion of the line of Shoshenq D and successor of Ankhefensekhmet B, the son of Horsieset H of Pamiu's reign.[139] Interestingly, Takelot combined his pontifical title with that of Great Chief [of the Ma], indicating a unique combination of spiritual and temporal Memphite authority. He was also apparently the last person to hold the Memphite high-priestly title—*wr ḥrp ḥmwt*—until the end of the Twenty-sixth Dynasty;[140] in the interim it would appear that the *sem* priest was senior officiant.[141]

A range of material derives from Shoshenq V's reign of some four decades—his Year 37 saw the burial of Apis XXXIII, from which came fifteen stelae (inc. fig. 52).[142] Earlier parts of the reign are attested by a number of dated donation stelae,[143] and by a number of stelae from the burial of Apis XXXII in Year 11.[144] Various minor items are known from Tell el-Yahudiya, Saqqara, and Bahariya Oasis, and of unknown provenance.[145] Shoshenq V's burial place is uncertain, but *shabti*s bearing the name of a Shoshenq-meryamun-sibast[. . .] found in NRT-I at Tanis[146] would suggest that he was buried or reburied there or perhaps in its annex, NRT-VII.[147]

By the time of Shoshenq V's death it is clear that the progressive subdivision of Egypt into various independent or quasi-independent entities had been continuing apace. One that was consolidating its status was that which embraced much of the western Delta, ruled by a line of Great Chiefs of the Libu who used the reigns of the Tanite kings as their dating era. Beginning with Inamunnifnebu under Shoshenq III (see p. 125), the line continued with Niumataped, who spanned the reigns of Shoshenq IV (see p. 128), Pamiu, and probably at least the first decade of the reign of Shoshenq V, followed by Titaru in Year 15,[148] Ker in Year 19,[149] Rudamun B in Year 30,[150] and Ankhhor C, who appears at Memphis at the burial of Apis XXXIII in Year 37.[151]

Also in the western Delta seem to have been a set of the Great Chiefs of the Ma, based at Sais, of whom a certain Osorkon (C) appears to have been the earliest known.[152] His probable successor was Tefnakhte, who is known from an undated statuette of Amun[153] and two of the donation stelae from the reign of Shoshenq V. One of these dates to Year 38,[154] but leaves the king's cartouches blank, although Shoshenq V is the only option, given the reign length involved: this might suggest that Tefnakhte merely used the reign as a dating era (cf. just below)—or it might simply reflect the unfinished state of the stela. A further option might be that the king died during the carving of the stela and there was some uncertainty as to the king now to be recognized (see below). This stela gives Tefnakhte the titles of *(inter alia)* Great Chief of the Whole Land, Army Leader, Great Chief of the Libu, and Ruler of the Nomes of the West. These seem to mark a progression from the titles affected by Tefnakhte two years earlier on a donation stela of Year 36—once again an anonymous year, but in this case with no space for a royal name—where he is just Great Chief of the Ma, Army Leader, and Great Chief of the Libu.[155]

It is unclear how Tefnakhte's last title related to that possessed simultaneously by Ankhhor C: did each refer to a separate branch of the Libu tribe (cf. the multiple Great Chiefs of the Ma), or were they rivals, with

Ankhhor driven out of the western Delta and in 'exile' in Memphis when he played a part in the Apis burial of Year 37?[156] In any case, it is clear that by the close of the reign of Shoshenq V, Tefnakhte was a major figure in northern Egypt, and one who would play an important role in the events of the coming years (see next chapter).

This situation in the Delta was paralleled elsewhere in Egypt, leaving a bewildering patchwork of polities between Aswan and the Mediterranean. A document from soon after Shoshenq V's death (see pp. 146–49) shows that by this time there were kings not only in Tanis and Thebes, but also in Herakleopolis, Hermopolis, and Leontopolis, plus a dozen further independent and quasi-independent Chiefs of the Ma, counts, and high priests—as well as the aforementioned Tefnakhte.

At Thebes, it seems that Takelot III was followed, not by one of his sons, but by his brother, Usermaatre-setepenamun Rudamun-meryamun. His assumed succession in Thebes is based on the presence of his painted cartouches in the chapel of Osiris-heqadjet at Karnak,[157] although he also had connections with Herakleopolis (see p. 149). No certain year-date is known,[158] but his could possibly be the Year 3 of a now anonymous Nile Level text at Karnak.[159] Given the paucity of attestations it seems likely that

Fig. 102. Relief showing Shoshenq V, followed by the high priest of Ptah, Takelot H. It displays both the 'simple' form of the king's nomen, and a style that recalls the art of the Old Kingdom. From Memphis (Cairo JE46915).

Rudamun's reign was short, although there are ample examples during the Third Intermediate Period to undermine such an assumption! A potential successor is a king Menkheperre Iny, whose Year 5 appears in a graffito on the roof of the Karnak Khonsu temple, and who is also known from a few minor items and possibly a stela.[160] However, by this time these Theban kings had ceased to be masters of their own destinies. A new overlordship had arisen from a hitherto unlooked-to location: Nubia.

5 SAVIORS FROM THE SOUTH?

Following Piankh's campaign(s) into Nubia during the *whm-mswt*, the region of Nubia had seemingly ceased to be dependent on Egypt, although the Third Prophet of Amun, Akheperre, held the title of King's Son of Kush during the pontificate of Menkheperre,[1] while Nesikhonsu A, wife of Panedjem II, bore the Nubian viceregal title as late as the reign of Siamun (cf. pp. 70–71). Evidence for the ensuing three and a half centuries is relatively scarce, with its interpretation subject to ongoing controversy.[2]

Fig. 103. Middle Kingdom fortress at Semna-West, with the Thutmosid temple in the foreground, as seen in 1962. The temple is now in the Sudan National Museum, Khartoum.

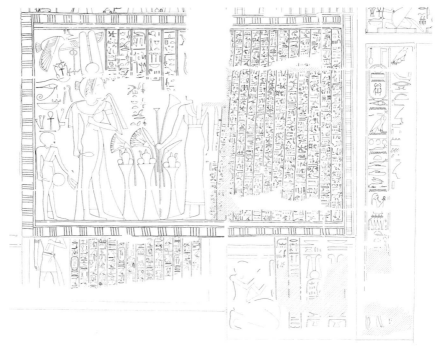

Fig. 104. Left-hand half of the façade of temple of Semna-West, on which was carved the tableau of Katimala.

In Lower Nubia, radiocarbon evidence suggests that fortification work was begun at the hilltop redoubt of Qasr Ibrim (fig. 123) some time during the tenth/ninth centuries.[3] At the Second Cataract fort at Semna-West, the façade of the temple (fig. 103) received a tableau[4] depicting a King's Great Wife Katimala,[5] with an accompanying text dated to a Year 14 and recording the events resulting from a rebellion against an unnamed king (fig. 104).[6] Its precise date remains unclear, but the style of the figures and language of the text suggest that it was carved in parallel with the Egyptian Twenty-first/early Twenty-second Dynasty.[7]

As for the identity of Katimala's spouse, two kings are known from a number of locations in Upper and Lower Nubia whose prenomina are of Rameside/earlier Third Intermediate Period pattern. One, Usermaatre-setepenre Iry-meryamun (⬭🖉🖎 🖎🖎🖎🖎), had three stelae (fig. 105) at Kawa[8] and may indeed have been the builder of the inner part of Temple B there.[9] Another, Menmaatre-setepenamun ⌐Q¬ atiaa ⌐t¬

Fig. 105. Stela of the Nubian king Iry, showing him making offerings to the Theban triad. From Kawa, temple A (Ny Carlsberg ÆIN1709).

(⟨◯══𝄐⟩ ⟨𝄐𝄐⟩),[10] is known from Gebel Barkal[11] and Nuri[12] in the heart of Upper Nubia, the core of the New Kingdom province of Kush and the core of the later independent Kushite state. These kings have conventionally been placed in the late fourth/early third century,[13] but on stylistic and archaeological grounds it is difficult to accept such a placement.[14] This reinforces the impression given by the format of the cartouches, which is very different from that current in the Late Napatan/Early Meroitic Periods.[15] Accordingly, it seems preferable to place Iry and ⌐Q⌐atiaa ⌐t⌐ during the same general period as Katimala, among the earlier local rulers in Nubia following the Egyptian withdrawal.[16] Whether these two monarchs and Katimala formed part of a single line, controlling the whole area between (at least) the Second and Fourth Cataracts, or represented separate polities, is wholly obscure.

The capital of the New Kingdom province of Kush had lain at Napata, adjacent to the holy mountain of Gebel Barkal, sacred to Amun (fig. 106).

Fig. 106. Gebal Barkal, viewed from the west, showing the peak (B350) on the south side of the mountain that seems to have been adorned to give it explicitly the form of a rearing, crowned cobra. In the foreground are pyramids Bar9–15, probably datable to the fourth and first centuries BC.

Just downstream of this is the cemetery of el-Kurru, which contains a series of tombs extending back from the mid-seventh century (fig. 107).[17] Typologically, there is a clear sequence from simple tumuli (KuTum1–6, Ku19), through mastabas (Ku9–14) to pyramids (Ku15–18, Ku51–55),[18] but far less clear is how the pre-pyramid monuments should be spread through time. For a long time the 'conventional' view assumed pairs of husband/wife tombs of a single royal line. On this basis, a simple generation count would take the sequence back to the mid-ninth century.[19] However, other views have assumed that all tombs belonged to a single line of males, thus doubling the number of generations and allowing the series to be taken back to the early eleventh century.[20] That the latter option may be the more likely is indicated by some of the material found in the tombs. This includes items of New Kingdom type, although some of them appear to be of forms that would suggest they had been manufactured and/ or imported a very considerable time before even the eleventh century.[21] A further option is that the cemetery is chronologically discontinuous, with at least some of the tumulus tombs actually contemporary with the mid-New Kingdom, thus resolving the issues around the presence of the

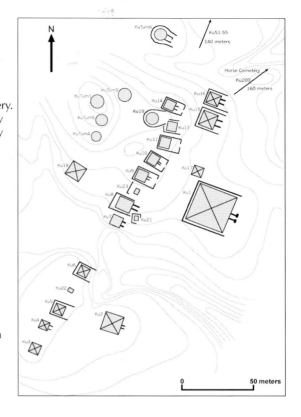

Fig. 107. Map of the el-Kurru cemetery.
Ku1. Unknown, *c.* fourth century
Ku2. Unknown, *c.* fourth century
Ku3. Ñaparaye, wife of Taharqa
Ku4. Kheñsa, daughter of Kashta
Ku5. Qalhata, wife of Shabaka
Ku6. Arty, wife of Shabataka
Ku7. Unknown
Ku8. Unknown (Kashta?)
Ku9–14. Unknown
Ku15. Shabaka
Ku16. Tanutamun
Ku17. Piye
Ku18. Shabataka
Ku19. Unknown
Ku21. Unknown
Ku23. Unknown
Ku51. Unknown, *temp.* Shabaka
Ku52. Neferukakashta
Ku53. Tabiry, wife of Piye
Ku54–55. Unknown.
KuTum1–6. Unknown

aforementioned material apparently of this date found in them.[22] The mastabas would then begin considerably later, perhaps around 900, if one were to assume about twenty-five years per generation.

That the line who occupied the last mastabas was not directly linked to their precursors is suggested by the way in which the immediate ancestor of the builders of the pyramids, Alara, is presented in later retrospectives as perhaps the originator of the family's power.[23] On the other hand, the mastaba tombs themselves seem to form a single sequence, suggesting that the polity whose rulers occupied these particular sepulchers had come into being around the time Osorkon I or Takelot I were ruling in Egypt.

No contemporary remains of Alara are known, but a daughter, Tabiry, was married to a king Piye[24]-meryamun,[25] thus placing Alara only a generation earlier than that king.[26] However, it is clear that Piye's direct predecessor was (Ni)maatre[27] Kashta. His contemporary monuments are scarce—the usual attribution of the mastaba Ku8 to him is purely an assumption based on design and location;[28] apart from an aegis and a necklace,[29] there survives just a fragment of stela dated to the reign of the king.[30] However, this stela is from Elephantine, far north of his heartland, and suggests that by Kashta's reign the Kushite kingdom had expanded to embrace the southern part of Egypt as well as Upper and Lower Nubia. Indeed, it seems possible that he obtained some form of suzerainty over the Thebaid itself, as we find his daughter Amenirdis (I—fig. 118) installed at Thebes as the adopted daughter and heir of Shepenwepet I by the last third of Piye's reign at the latest. Unfortunately, it is not certain when the installation itself took place,[31] and it is possible that it took place under Piye, rather than under Kashta: Amenirdis's first clear attestation names her alongside Nimlot D, king of Hermopolis[32] and a contemporary of Piye (see pp. 146–48). This may also have been the background to the vizier and Third Prophet of Amun Pamiu i's adoption of the ancient title of King's Son of Kush (see p. 133).

Potentially in favor of a Piye date is a group of blocks from the temple of Mut at Karnak, recording the arrival of an heir to the God's Wife of Amun (fig. 108).[33] As they now stand, incorporating texts of Sematawytefnakhte, Shipmaster of Herakleopolis, who served under Psamtik I, they seem to refer to the arrival of Neitiqerti I, in Year 9 of that king (cf. p. 170). However, it has been suggested that the Sematawytefnakhte texts are secondary and that the blocks originally referred to the installation of Amenirdis I under Piye—potentially in his Year 5.[34]

Kashta's blood relationship to Piye is unclear. Kashta married a lady named Pebatjma, with whom he had at least two daughters: the afore-mentioned Amenirdis I,[35] and Pekasater, who married Piye.[36] It has been debated[37] whether Pebatjma is identical to a King's Daughter, King's Sister, and Mother of the God's Adoratrix Paabtameri, who was the mother of a generalissimo Pegatterru-Irpaakhqenqenenef.[38] However, Pegatterru is not called a King's Son, which would be expected if he were the son of Kashta. On the other hand, he may have been the offspring of a second marriage by a widowed queen[39]—or else, as seems to have been the case at other points in the past, the title of King's Son was applicable only during the lifetime of the king in question.[40] That Paabtameri had been married to a king is suggested by the fact that she was the mother of an Adoratrix—all of whom at this period were king's daughters. She could thus have been a spouse of Piye (father of Shepenwepet II)[41] if not, after all, wife of Kashta (father of Amenirdis I).[42]

Fig. 108. Part of a scene that in its final form showed the arrival at Karnak of the flotilla carrying prospective God's Wife of Amun, Neitiqerti I, daughter of Psamtik I, conducted by the Shipmaster of Herakleopolis, Sematawytefnakhte. On the right (enlarged in drawing) is the Karnak quay (cf. fig. 77: the statue and sphinx are now missing, but the obelisk still stands), with a female figure that may be the incumbent God's Wife waiting to greet her heir. It has, however, been suggested that the texts naming Sematawytefnakhte are secondary and that the scene was originally carved to commemorate the arrival of Amenirdis I as heir to Shepenwepet, something also supported by the third ship being called "The Barge of King Piye." From temple of Mut, Karnak (Cairo JE31886).

Apart from Pekasater and Amenirdis, a certain Neferukakashta[43] may, on the basis of her name, have been another daughter of Kashta. A later king, Shabaka, is shown to have been a son of Kashta by the fact that Amenirdis I calls him her brother.[44] Whether Piye was himself a further sibling is not susceptible to proof, but if a wife of his named Kheñsa[45] is identical with a King's Wife, King's Sister, and King's Daughter Kheñsa,[46] Piye would also have been the offspring of a king—most probably Kashta, although Alara cannot be ruled out.

Given that Kashta was certainly present monumentally at Elephantine, it is likely that Piye had some kind of foothold in southern Egypt, and possibly the Thebaid, from the outset. Some military activity may be recorded early in the reign, on a stela from Gebel Barkal,[47] which presents Piye not only as a king, but also as a king- and chieftain-maker. This monument was found in the outer courtyard of the Great Temple of Amun (B500—

Map 9), a structure originally founded back in the early Nineteenth Dynasty, to which Piye added a southern annex (B520) and two successive pylons and courtyards (B501, B502), the earlier of which (B502) was ultimately transformed into a hypostyle hall. On the stela, Piye appropriates an entire titulary of Thutmose III, with the variation that the Horus name invokes Napata, rather than Thutmose's Thebes. During his reign Piye was to affect a range of titularies, apparently including three prenomina (cf. Appendix 3),[48] although he continued to prefer to use his unadorned nomen on most of his monuments.

This or a further campaign seems to be dated to Year 4 by fragments of another stela from Gebel Barkal.[49] On the basis of back calculation from fixed point synchronisms later in the Kushite royal line (see pp. 157–58), this would seem to lie close to the end of the reign of Takelot III, which may suggest that Piye's intervention was linked to troubles on his demise. In this connection, it may be significant that none of Takelot III's sons reigned, and that his brother Rudamun's claim to have actually controlled the Thebaid is equivocal (p. 137). A takeover of Thebes by Piye in Year 4 would also tie in with the aforementioned possible installation of Amenirdis I in Piye's Year 5. It may thus have been during his first half-decade on the Kushite throne that Piye also became overlord of the south of Egypt and imposed his probable sister Amenirdis on the college of Amun at Karnak. On the other hand, for the time being at least, some native kings—Rudamun and Iny—were apparently able to play some role at Thebes, although by the beginning of Piye's third decade as king there seems to be no longer any sign of anyone else recognized as a pharaoh south of Middle Egypt.

At that point in time, Egypt was convulsed by a series of events related in a further Gebel Barkal stela, dated to Year 21 of Piye and presumably relating events of the immediately preceding year or two.[50] It begins with Piye receiving a report that the Chief of the West Tefnakhte had taken control of much of northern Egypt and was now besieging Herakleopolis. This is itself interesting in indicating that Piye's existing area of authority had extended well beyond the Thebaid as far north as Herakleopolis—implicitly his vassal on account of its resistance to Tefnakhte's conquest. The stela also relates that the remaining loyalists in the north reported that Nimlot (D), the ruler of Hermopolis, had thrown off an allegiance to Piye and gone over to Tefnakhte.

Piye then ordered his Egypt-based subordinates to advance against Tefnakhte while concurrently sending a fresh army from Nubia. This force made offerings to Amun at Karnak on arrival in Thebes before heading northward by boat. They were met by Tefnakhte's own riverine forces somewhere south of Hermopolis, but in the ensuing battle it was the Kushites who were triumphant, their captives being sent back upriver to Piye at Napata.

The Kushite armies then advanced on Hermopolis, whence Nimlot returned from the siege of Herakleopolis to direct its defense. Soon after he had arrived, the army of Piye reached the area of Hermopolis and sealed it off, while sending reports back to the king in Nubia. Displeased that complete victory had not yet been achieved, Piye resolved to proceed down to Egypt himself. There he participated in the Opet festival at Thebes and then personally directed the conclusion of the campaign. His desire to participate in the festival illustrates Piye's piety toward Amun, the god not only of Thebes but also of his home city of Napata. While the king made his way northward, his armies in Egypt continued operations against Tefnakhte's coalition, with Oxyrhynkhos (Bahnasa), *t3-thn wr-nḥtw*, and *ḥwt-bnw* (precise locations uncertain, but nearby) falling next, and one of Tefnakhte's sons being killed at the second of these cities.

Having paid his respects to Amun at Thebes, Piye joined the forces investing Hermopolis. There, its inhabitants suffered not only from Kushite arrows and stones projected from slingshots, but also from hunger, until at length the city surrendered. Rich gifts were sent out to Piye, followed by Nimlot's own wife, Nesitentmehu, tasked by her husband to intercede with the Kushite king's womenfolk, and finally by Nimlot himself. Piye then entered Hermopolis, making sacrifices at the temple of Thoth, before proceeding to Nimlot's palace, where his wives and daughters were presented to Piye. In the palace stables, Piye recounts discovering starving horses, whose parlous condition was denounced as the worst of Nimlot's crimes—

Fig. 109. Detail of the lunette of Piye's Victory Stela, showing the four kings of Egypt paying homage to him (erased). Top: Nimlot D, leading a horse; Bottom, left to right: Osorkon IV; Iuput II; Peftjauawybast. From Gebel Barkal B501 (Cairo JE48862).

conveniently ignoring the fact that their lack of food had been caused by the Nubian's own siege tactics! A particular Nubian regard for horses is displayed by a horse cemetery attached to the Kushite royal necropolis at el-Kurru[51] and much later by the fourth-to-seventh century AD X-Group horse burials at Ballana and Qustul.[52]

The fall of Hermopolis and the continuing success of Piye's northern army seems to have lifted the siege of Herakleopolis, as its ruler, Neferkare Peftjauawybast (A), then arrived to thank Piye for having delivered him from "darkness" and swearing his devotion. From Hermopolis, Piye and his army sailed northward—presumably along the Bahr Yusuf—to the fortress of Per-Sekhemkheperre, which guarded the entrance to the Fayyum canal near Lahun. The stronghold, under command of a son of Tefnakhte, surrendered without a fight, as did Meidum and Lisht, but Memphis was directed to hold out by Tefnakhte, who then returned to Sais for reinforcements.

However—apparently using ships and boats as a means of scaling the ramparts of the city—Memphis was entered by Piye's forces and surrendered after two days' fighting. In the wake of this victory, a king Iuput (II) of Leontopolis, together with a range of other northern Egyptian rulers, came to pay homage to Piye. The following morning Piye crossed to the east bank, proceeding via what is now Fustat to Heliopolis, where he was met by a king Osorkon (IV), ruler of Bubastis and a hinterland that probably included Tanis (see pp. 150–51). The next day Piye pushed on to Athribis where he received a delegation of sixteen Delta rulers, headed by Padieset G of Athribis itself, and the two kings Iuput II and Osorkon IV. Between them they represented all the various polities of the region—except for the West, the domain of Tefnakhte, the chief whose expansionism had been the immediate cause of the whole conflict. Although he sent a groveling letter of submission to Piye, Tefnakhte remained in his stronghold of Sais, where he later received ambassadors from the Kushite king, sending them away with rich gifts and an assurance that he would henceforth be Piye's loyal liege. Piye, for his part, accepted his assurances and left him in control of his domains.

In the meantime, the Kushite army had finished mopping up the remaining cities in the Nile valley that had continued to hold out, including Atfih and Medinet el-Fayyum, while Piye prepared to return to Nubia. First, however, there was a final act of submission to the conqueror, when all five of the Egyptian rulers who held the title of king came to prostrate themselves before the palace (fig. 109). Only Nimlot, however, was allowed to enter: the others had rendered themselves ritually unclean by having eaten fish—another manifestation of Piye's pious nature.[53] The Kushite then sailed south, his ships laden with booty, acknowledged overlord of the whole Nile valley from the Fifth Cataract to the Mediterranean, the first ruler to be so since the Twentieth Dynasty.

Of the kings who had prostrated themselves before Piye, Neferkare Peftjauawybast of Herakleopolis is one of the better known. Two metal statuettes of his time survive, one of the ram god Heryshef, and one of the king himself (fig. 110),[54] while two Herakleopolitan donation stelae are dated to Year 10 of his reign.[55] They both seem to name one Irutj,[56] the daughter of the King's Wife and King's Daughter Tashereniset. A second wife of the king was Irbastwedjanefu (B), a daughter of Rudamun, and thus a clear link between Peftjauawybast and the Theban line of kings. By her he had another daughter, Sopdet(em)haa(wt),[57] but there is no sign of any son and successor. That he continued to rule for a while after Piye's conquest is suggested by the fact that his statuette wears the cap crown that became distinctive of the Kushite kings. It has been suggested that Peftjauawybast was not only the son-in-law of Rudamun but also a successor, as part of the same 'Herakleopolitan/ Theban Twenty-third Dynasty.'[58] However, as noted above (pp. 123–25), such classifications are problematic, and it is perhaps better to regard Peftjauawybast as occupying part of the former Theban kingdom after the advent of Piye, rather than as the 'legitimate' successor of Osorkon III and his heirs—although it is certainly not impossible that he was regarded as such by his contemporaries.

The other Upper Egyptian king, Nimlot, is far more poorly attested outside Piye's account— no prenomen is known, and only two small items naming him have been identified.[59] On the basis of his name, Nimlot is likely to have been a scion of the Twenty-second Dynasty royal line, and was followed[60] by a further Hermopolite king, Neferkheperre-khakha(u) Thutemhat,[61] at a date that cannot be determined.

Usermaatre(-setepenre/amun) Iuput II(-sibast-meryamun) of Leontopolis rivals Peftjauawybast in numbers of attestations outside Piye's narrative. Most impressive of these is a granite statue base from Tell el-Yahudiya (fig. 111), together with a

Fig. 110. Bronze statuette of Peftjauawybast (MFA 1977.16).

bronze door-socket, perhaps from Leontopolis itself, and a faience plaque bearing the king's image.[62] Like the statuette of Peftjauawybast, this shows him with a Nubian cap crown, suggesting that it dates to a period after Piye's invasion. Also from Iuput's reign is a Mendesian donation stela dating to his own Year 21,[63] but exactly when his reign began and ended is wholly obscure, likewise whether he had any predecessor or successor on the Leontopolite throne.[64]

The remaining king, Osorkon IV, is in some ways the most elusive of the four, although a representation of him, together with his cartouche names, may have come to light in 2011, with the discovery of blocks naming Usermaatre Osorkonu at Tanis. Their style is very much in the archaizing style of the time, while the writing of the nomen without epithets and with a final 'nw' separates this Osorkon from all others known[65] (cf. p. 212). On the other hand, it seems clear that Osorkon IV's mother was named Tadibast (iii), distinguishing him from the previous royal possessors of the name.[66] Piye places Osorkon in Bubastis and the district of r^c-nfr, the latter centered on what is now Tell Tebilla some fifty kilometers to the north and generally regarded as embracing the area to the east, including Tanis.[67] As such, Osorkon IV has been regarded as a scion of the main Twenty-second Dynasty line, either as direct successor of Shoshenq V or after an intervening reign of Padubast III.[68] On the chronology adopted here, with the invasion of Piye following directly on from the death of Shoshenq V, a

Fig. 111. Statue base of Iuput II from Tell el-Yahudiya (Cairo, number not known).

direct succession by Osorkon IV seems the only possibility, with Padubast to be placed as probably the last of the line in the mid-seventh century (see just below).

Nevertheless, it seems likely that the wraith-like Osorkon IV played a role in the history of Palestine over the next two decades. He is most likely to have been the "So, king of Egypt" to whom the Israelite king Hoshea sent (unsuccessfully) for aid against Shalmaneser V of Assyria in 726/5.[69] This works chronologically and geographically: Osorkon IV's realm was the easternmost of the era and thus best placed to intervene in the Levant, while "So" is a credible abbreviation of (O)so(rkon).[70] Osorkon was probably also the ruler who sent his army commander "Re'u" to aid a Palestinian rebellion against the new Assyrian king, Sargon II, in 720—only to be defeated in battle at

Fig. 112. Statue of Padubast III from Memphis–Kom el-Fakhry.

Rafah.[71] On the other hand, the Assyrian depiction of the battle[72] seems to show a Nubian,[73] which may suggest that the force commanded by "Re'u" was a joint Egyptian–Kushite one, reflecting the fact that Osorkon IV's realm was now a dependency of Nubia.

A few years later, in 716, Osorkon IV was probably the "Shilkanni, king of Egypt" who sent a gift of horses to Sargon II of Assyria, whose forces had at that time penetrated as far as el-Arish in the northeastern Sinai.[74] It is unknown when Osorkon's reign terminated, but he would appear to have been followed in his local kingship by a series of monarchs, including Shepseskare-irenre Gemenefkhonsubak and Sehetepib(en)re Padubast (III), both known from items at Tanis.[75] The latter king is also known from a statue at Memphis (fig. 112)[76] and would appear to be the individual of that name cited by the Assyrians as ruling Tanis during 671–667/6 (see p. 166).

After his triumph, Piye seems to have adopted the prenomen Seneferre, superseding the previous Usermaatre[77] and (probably) Menkheperre (see p. 146), to judge from a votive piece of linen dated to Year 20 or later.[78] This piece is the key document for determining the minimum length of Piye's reign, with the most likely reading of its date apparently "Year 30,"

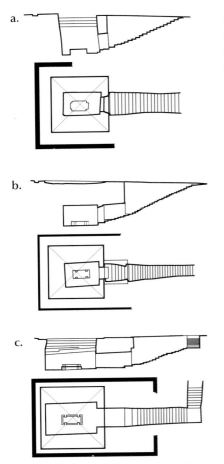

Fig. 113. Sections and plans of the el-Kurru tombs of:
a. Piye (Ku17)
b. Shabaka (Ku15)
c. Shabataka (Ku18)

rather than the "Year 40" that has also been suggested.[79] Piye would thus seem to have survived his great expedition by at least a decade. From Year 23 comes a stela from Dakhla,[80] which has a protagonist, the Chief of the Shamin, Nesthuty, who had previously been attested in office back in Year 13 of Takelot III (see pp. 132, 269 n. 102).

In addition to Tabiry, Kheñsa, and Pekasater, discussed above (p. 144), Piye had another wife, Abar, with whom he sired the later king Taharqa close to the end of his life (see p. 158). It is unknown, however, which wives bore Piye's remaining known children: two sons, Khaliut[81] and Har,[82] together with at least six daughters. The latter were headed by the future God's Wife, Shepenwepet II, identified as Piye's daughter on various of her monuments (e.g., fig. 128);[83] along with Qalhata, a wife of Shabaka (see p. 155); Arty, a spouse of Shabataka (see p. 158); and Ñaparaye and Takahatamun, sister-wives of Taharqa (see p. 162). Tabakenamun, who was a King's Daughter, Wife, and Sister, may have been Piye's daughter, but this is unclear since the identity of her husband is not certain—perhaps Shabaka or Taharqa.[84]

Piye was buried at el-Kurru below a monument (Ku17) that, while wholly vanished, seems likely to have been the first in a long series of pyramids of steep elevation to be built for kings of Kush (fig. 113a).[85] The burial chamber itself was equipped with a bench for the body in place of a sarcophagus—a typical feature of Nubian burials since at least Kerma times—and had a corbelled roof. Of the funerary equipment, only the (dummy) canopic jars,[86] *shabti* figures, and a few other fragments survived.[87] A number of Piye's wives were also certainly buried in a series of tombs at el-Kurru: Kheñsa in Ku4 by Taharqa, Tabiry in Ku53, and possibly an unnamed lady in Ku51 by Shabaka.[88]

Fig. 114. Donation Stela dated to Year 8 of Tefnakhte (Archaeological Museum, Athens).

It appears that once Piye had returned south, the various Egyptian dynasts were left in charge of their dominions—presumably bound to the Kushite by oaths of loyalty, although this is not stated in Piye's stela. These included Tefnakhte of Sais, and it has generally been assumed that he was the man of that name who shortly afterward assumed royal titles under the prenomen Shepsesre and reigned for at least eight years (fig. 114).[89] On the other hand, it has also been suggested that this Tefnakhte is not Piye's erstwhile opponent, but a putative later "Tefnakhte II," to be equated with the "Stephinatês" listed by Manetho as one of the later Saite local kings whom he classified as the first rulers of the Twenty-sixth Dynasty—a grouping that would ultimately rule the whole country in the person of Psamtik I.[90] Nevertheless, the older view seems on balance to be the better one—that as soon as Piye was safely back in Nubia, Tefnakhte resumed his expansionist career, albeit now with full royal titles.[91]

That Tefnakhte's area of control included Memphis is suggested by the fact that his successor, Wahkare Bakenrenef, was responsible for the burial there of Apis XXXIV=XXXV/24.1 in his Year 6. It is generally assumed that Bakenrenef was a son of Tefnakhte, supported by a later tradition that made him the offspring of "Tnephtichthus" and also praised him for his wisdom and as a lawgiver.[92] It is by no means clear

Fig. 115. Relief of Shabaka, reused near the Sacred Lake at Karnak. The double uraeus affected by the king symbolized the dual kingdom of the Kushite kings.

how he attained this posthumous fame,[93] nor what lay behind a further late tradition that during his reign a lamb spoke, prophesying the future.[94] Apart from various items related to the Apis burial,[95] a donation stela, perhaps from the eastern Delta,[96] and a fragment from Tanis[97] are also known. Among smaller pieces are two faience vases and a scarab that were found in tombs in Italy, which may link in with the king's aforementioned Classical reputation.[98]

A further 'fact' provided by a later source (Manetho, who makes him the sole king of his Twenty-fourth Dynasty) is that Bakenrenef was captured and burned alive by the Twenty-fifth Dynasty "Ethiopian" king "Sabacôn"—i.e., Neferkare[99] Shabaka, Piye's brother and successor. The coincidence of Shabaka's second year and Bakenrenef's sixth is strongly indicated by the presence in the Serapeum of an inscription of Shabaka's Year 2,[100] suggesting that the transition of power between Bakenrenef and Shabaka in Memphis occurred while the bull of Bakenrenef's Year 6 was still in burial.[101] Whether or not Bakenrenef indeed suffered a fiery death, it does seem that, soon after his succession, Shabaka took the decision to directly rule in Egypt, rather than simply act as remote overlord of the northern potentates and absentee monarch of southern Egypt. While some local kings—in particular Osorkon IV and his successors in the northeast—continued to exist, monuments of Shabaka exist from Memphis southward, implying that quasi-pharaohs were no longer tolerated in the Nile valley proper. Shabaka's status as king of both his dominions was indicated by his adoption of twin uraei (fig. 115)—something that would be continued by the later rulers of the dynasty.

As already noted (see p. 145), Shabaka was a son of Kashta and thus a brother of his predecessor. As Piye left a number of sons, one of whom would eventually become king, there has been considerable discussion as to the succession mechanism employed in Nubia. On the basis of such sibling successions, simple primogeniture seems not to have been employed, with what has become the broad scholarly consensus positing a system whereby the throne passed between brothers before reverting to the son of the eldest brother.[102] However, the actual evidence does not precisely match such a model, leaving a significant question mark over the fundamental dynamics of the Kushite royal succession.[103]

Shabaka's family relationships have largely had to be reconstructed from indirect data. One woman, Isetemkheb H, is explicitly called his daughter, and since she also bore the title of King's Sister (as well as King's Great Wife)[104], one of Shabaka's sons must have ruled. This corroborates statements in Assyrian records that the later king Tanutamun was an offspring of Shabaka[105] and a sister of Taharqa.[106] Tanutamun's own monuments name his mother as Qalhata,[107] who thus becomes one wife of Shabaka. On the other hand, a further son, Horemakhet, offspring of the King's Wife Masabat, who was to become high priest of Amun, has his parents explicitly named on monuments.[108]

The aforementioned Year 2 of Shabaka is also found at Karnak in a Nile Level record[109] and on a donation stela from the Delta (possibly Hurbeit), dedicated by the Great Chief of the Ma, Patjenfy, one of the local rulers who had submitted to Piye a decade earlier.[110] Further donation stelae from the north of Egypt are dated to Years 3,[111] 4,[112] and 6.[113] Various structural elements from Memphis (map 5) attest to Shabaka's building work there, including a chapel in the southwest of the temenos of Ptah,[114] as do statuary[115] and the remains of a slab bearing an important theological text, the so-called 'Shabaka Stone' or 'Memphite Theology.'[116] This is either a genuine copy of an ancient text or a pastiche imitating Old Kingdom concepts: whichever is correct, it highlights the antiquarian aspects of Twenty-fifth Dynasty thought, also seen in the continuation of the archaizing art styles already present under the later Libyan pharaohs.[117] However, it is at Thebes that the largest assemblage of Shabaka's monuments is to be found. At Karnak, various pieces of building work were carried out, including a colonnade north of the Hypostyle Hall (fig. 116);[118] while work was also undertaken at Luxor,[119] and a pylon (now Pylon II) was begun in front of the small temple at Medinet Habu (fig. 117).[120] There are also traces of activity out at Bahariya Oasis;[121] while back in Nubia, work was carried out in Temple B at Kawa.[122]

Sacerdotally, Shabaka's reign probably saw the death of Shepenwepet I and her replacement before Year 12[123] by the king's sister Amenirdis I (but see also p. 159). Shepenwepet was probably buried close to Horsieset I at Medinet Habu, in a tomb (MH17) with superposed chapel, the first of a row of such structures that would form the necropolis for all later God's Wives (map 7; figs. 117, 127).[124] In addition, it was probably Shabaka who installed his son Horemakhet as high priest at Karnak,[125] either as successor of Osorkon F or following a putative successor of Osorkon.[126]

We have already noted that the year 716 had seen the approach of the Assyrian king Sargon II to the border of Egypt and his apparent buying off by Osorkon IV. The latter (or perhaps his successor(?) Gemenefkhonsubak—he is simply called "Pharaoh" in the relevant documents) was yet further embroiled in Levantine politics a few year later. In 712 the ruler of Ashdod, Iamani, attempted to put together an anti-Assyrian coalition and made overtures to "Pharaoh" to gain his support.[127] Since the Assyrians never seem to have used this title for Kushite rulers—preferring "Ruler of Kush and Egypt" or "Ruler of Kush"—this must refer to an Egyptian dynast, and thus once again one of the later representatives of the old line of Shoshenq I seems most likely.[128]

The insurrection failed and Iamani fled through Egypt to Kushite territory.[129] There he remained until "Shapataku, ruler of the land of Meluhha (Nubia),[130] heard of the mig[ht] of the gods Ashur, Nabû, (and) Marduk

Fig. 116. Colonnade of Shabaka north of the Hypostyle Hall at Karnak.

which [Sargon II] had [demonstrated] over all lands" and sent Iamani in chains to the Assyrian king.[131] The text describing this dates to 706, and while it has been suggested that this is simply the date of carving, not of the events described,[132] it seems unlikely that any gap will have been more than a short one.[133]

Such doubts have arisen because "Shapataku" must be a transcription of "Shabataka." Prior to the republication of the aforementioned text in 1999, it was generally assumed that the extradition of Iamani had occurred under Shabaka, with Shabataka not coming to the throne until *c.* 702. Attempts have been made to 'save' this lower date by assuming that in 706 Shabataka was acting as either coregent or viceroy in Nubia, while Shabaka was resident and ruling in Egypt proper,[134] but the straightforward reading of the data seems clearly to point to Shabaka being dead by April 706.[135] That a new king, Shabataka, might have been keen to mark a fresh start with Assyria by ridding himself of an embarrassing guest also seems a credible scenario.[136]

As to the actual date of Shabaka's death, his highest surviving date is Year 15.[137] Accordingly, a reign of sixteen years would seem reasonable,[138]

Fig. 117. Eastern part of the Medinet Habu complex. The Eighteenth-Dynasty temple on the left, with its later extensions including Pylon II, was begun by Shabaka and finished by Taharqa. The Migdol gate of Rameses III is in the middle, and the funerary chapels of the God's Wives of Amun on the right. The tomb of Horsieset I is located just behind the gateway (of Nakhtnebef) in the middle ground.

with a death in 707 implying Shabaka's accession in 722/1 and forming a basis for back calculation of absolute dates for Piye and earlier kings.

Shabaka's tomb at el-Kurru (Ku15) displays rather better workmanship than Piye's, in both its architecture (figs. 107, 113b) and contents. The former included a fully tunneled burial chamber that preserved a few traces of paintings, the nature of which, however, could not be determined.[139] Many fragments of funerary equipment were recovered, including some fine-quality canopic jar lids.[140] One of Shabaka's wives was buried in Ku62,[141] while also associated with Shabaka at el-Kurru were the burials of two of his horses (Ku201, Ku203).[142]

Djedkaure Shabataka's reign appears to have lasted around eighteen years, based on the externally fixed dates of the accession of his successor in 690 and his own accession no later than 706, as discussed just above. However, only Year 3 is recorded by a contemporary source, a Nile Level text at Karnak,[143] which has led to suggestions of a fairly short reign.[144] Only one wife is known for certain: Arty, mentioned on the base of a statue of the high priest Horemakhet[145] and buried in Ku6 at el-Kurru.[146] No children seem to be attested.

As already noted, early in his reign the new king extradited to Assyria the fugitive king of Ashdod who had been living in the Nile valley for some six years. However, soon after this Sargon II had died in battle in northern Iraq, and was succeeded by his son Sennacherib, which may have led to a reassessment of Egyptian foreign policy.

At some point during the first five years of his reign, Shabataka summoned north a group of young men among whom was his kinsman, and ultimate successor, Taharqa, then aged twenty.[147] Taharqa's age at the time of his journey north indicates that this cannot have occurred later than 702, given the latest possible death date for his father Piye. In 701, Sennacherib launched a campaign into Palestine, where he was confronted by a force that included Egyptians[148] and Nubians, as well as elements from Ekron, together with Hezekiah of Judah, who then suffered defeat at the battle of Eltekeh (*Al-ta-qu-ú* = Tell el-Shalaf?).[149] It has generally been assumed that this campaign was the same as one against Hezekiah by Sennacherib referred to in the Old Testament.[150] However, the Biblical accounts include a detail that "Tirhakah king of Kush" was involved on the Judean side during this campaign[151]—and Taharqa was not king until 690, a decade after Sennacherib's 701 campaign.

Two basic options have been proposed: one, that there were two campaigns, one in 701, and one between Taharqa's accession in 690 and

Hezekiah's death in 687/6; the second, that the gloss "king of Kush" was a later addition, Taharqa having been involved only as a general in a single war of 701.[152] Certainly in favor of the latter view is the lack of any clear Assyrian data concerning a second campaign. However, the vagaries of preservation make it impossible as things stand to definitively rule out the first option.

At home, Shabataka's reign is commemorated principally by material from the Memphite and Theban areas, although a donation stela exists that probably came from the Delta.[153] A fragmentary granite seated figure of the king and a block bearing his name were found near the southern gate of the temple of Ptah at Memphis,[154] suggesting work on that part of the complex. At Saqqara, the presence of the remains of Shabataka's prenomen in the room of the Serapeum that seems to have housed the Apis burial of Year 2 of Shabaka[155] suggests that an Apis burial in an anonymous Year 4[156] should be attributed to Shabataka.

The aforementioned Year 3 Nile Level text of Shabataka at Karnak is interesting in that it is rather more extensive than most such examples, and includes the statement that the king had "appeared in the temple as king-in-the-temple, who has given to him his appearance in the Two Lands like Horus on the throne of Re." This clearly indicates a formal visit of the king to Karnak coinciding with the Inundation, but some have attempted to read into it the king's actual coronation, or even transition from a putative coregency wth Shabaka[157]—neither of which is supported by any direct evidence.[158]

Shabataka undertook work in two chapels at Karnak. First, an outer court was added to the chapel of Osiris-heqadjet, originally built under Osorkon III and Takelot III (fig. 98). The new section included images of the king and the God's Wives Amenirdis I and Shepenwepet I (fig. 118).[159] The presence of the latter—apparently alive[160]—is surprising, as a text of Year 12 of Shabaka seems at first sight to show Amenirdis in office by then (see p. 155). On the other hand, the Year 12 record, a graffito in the Wadi Hammamat, gives only the title of "God's Adoratrix," which also applied to heirs of the office. Accordingly, it may be that the aged Shepenwepet—by now in her late 90s—survived into the early years of Shabataka, although with Amenirdis long having taken over day-to-day cultic activities.

Second, another small chapel was erected just south of the southeast corner of the Sacred Lake at Karnak with scenes of the king offering to the gods (fig. 119).[161] Similar scenes were also carved on the exterior of the

Fig. 118. Amenirdis I receiving 'life' from Amun and Mut in the forehall of the chapel of Osiris-heqadjet at Karnak.

rear wall of the temple of Luxor.[162] Over the river at Thebes-West, while no royal monuments have thus far been identified, on the South Asasif were being erected what appear to have been the first two monumental tombs built at Thebes since the end of the New Kingdom. Probably begun under Shabaka, the earlier seems to have been that of the Fourth Prophet of Amun and Mayor of Thebes Karabasken (TT391),[163] by his name clearly a Nubian, who had replaced the long-established dynasty of Fourth Prophets that stretched back to Djedkhonsiufankh A in the early ninth century.[164]

Slightly later seems to be the tomb of the First ꜥq-Priest Karakhamun (TT223),[165] some of the decoration of which can be dated on stylistic grounds to Shabataka's reign. Together, these two tombs set the pattern for the sepulchers of nobles of the highest status into the Twenty-sixth Dynasty (cf. pp. 163–64). On the other hand, modest burial places still remained the norm, as had been the case throughout the Third Intermediate Period.[166] Reuse of earlier tombs and temples also continued: the Fourth Prophet of Amun Wedjahor and his family found rest in the Eighteenth Dynasty tomb TT99,[167] while the temple of Hatshepsut at Deir el-Bahari hosted a series of vaults for priests of Montju.[168]

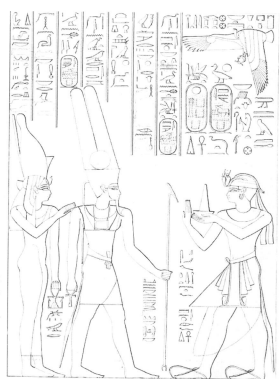

Fig. 119. West wall of the single room of the chapel erected by Shabataka near the southeast corner of the Sacred Lake at Karnak. The king's names were erased under Psamtik II, but the name of Amun (in the epithet '-meryamun') was left intact (Berlin ÄM1480).

Apart from a few small items,[169] the only Kushite monument of Shabataka is his tomb at el-Kurru (Ku18—fig. 113c).[170] The tomb represented something of a regression from that of Shabaka, the tunneled substructure of Ku15 being replaced by an open-cut structure with a corbeled roof, as had been the case in the tomb of Piye. A considerable quantity of fragments of the funerary equipment survived, including *shabtis* and three (dummy) canopic jars,[171] plus some bones, apparently of the king himself. The fragmentary skull had a number of unusual features, being "small and not prominently marked for muscular attachments [so that] its sex would have been considered doubtful if the personal identification were not known . . . ."[172]

The ancestry of the next king, Khunefertumre Taharqa (fig. 120),[173] is for once completely clear—although the mechanism by which he followed Shabataka is less so.[174] His mother is explicitly given as Abar,[175] while

Fig. 120. Head of Taharqa. From Thebes (Nubian Museum ex-CG560).

Taharqa is described as the brother of Shepen-wepet II.[176] As the latter was undoubtedly the daughter of Piye, Taharqa must thus also have been his offspring. Abar was the daughter of the sister of Alara,[177] a line of descent that seems to have been important to Taharqa.[178]

The king himself may have had four wives (fig. 121): Takahatamun is shown with Taharqa in temple B300 at Gebel Barkal,[179] where she is called his sister and First King's Great Wife; she was probably the mother of the Second Prophet of Amun Nesishutefnut.[180] Atakhe-basken, of unknown antecedents but bearing the title of King's Great Wife, was buried next to Taharqa and was thus probably his wife.[181] Also likely to have been a spouse of the king was the King's Sister and King's Wife Ñapa-raye,[182] as may have been the king's sister, Tabakenamun (see p. 152). While various individuals have been suggested as being offspring of Taharqa, only the aforementioned Nesishutefnut, and Amenirdis II, who became heir to the God's Wife of Amun (see pp. 170–71), were unequivocally his, together with "Ushanukhuru," the eldest son, who was later to be captured by the Assyrians (p. 166).[183]

Administratively, local chiefs continued to rule various northern poli-ties (those at Sais and Tanis holding kingly dignity), while at Thebes the cult of Amun remained under the direction of Horemakhet and Amenir-dis I, with the latter succeeded during Taharqa's reign by the king's sister, Shepenwepet II (fig. 128). The royal family's control over the cult was to be further consolidated by prince Nesishutefnut's appointment as Second Prophet, and the marriage of a new Fourth Prophet Montjuemhat[184] to Wadjrenes, a daughter of Taharqa's brother Har.[185] Montjuemhat was also Mayor of Thebes, succeeding his cousin Reemmakheru and father Nes-ptah.[186] The southern vizierate was held successively by Nespaqashuty C[187] and Nespamedu.[188]

In Year 6 of Taharqa a particularly high inundation was recorded, with fur-ther high floods occurring in the next three years as well (fig. 97).[189] The importance of this phenomenon is indicated by its being recorded on stelae at Tanis, Matana, Koptos, and Kawa.[190] Another interesting stela records a race run by the king's troops on a desert road some five kilometers west of Dahshur, overseen by Taharqa himself.[191] The prosperity of the Kushite king's territories is indicated by the extensive building work carried out. In Egypt proper, the temple at Athribis was rebuilt[192] and some work undertaken at Tanis,[193] Memphis,[194] Hermopolis,[195] and Akhmim.[196] At Memphis, Year 14 saw the burial of an Apis bull, the successor to that apparently interred in Year 4 of Shabataka.[197] However, the largest number of known constructions come from Thebes.

Fig. 121. Head of a fragmentary statue of a female member of the royal family during the reign of Taharqa; her name and principal titles are missing and the face has been extensively restored (Nicholson R41).

In the first court of the Amun temple at Karnak, Taharqa erected a huge kiosk of ten columns (fig. 70);[198] it is possible that Pylon I was also begun under Taharqa.[199] Adjacent to the Sacred Lake was erected the so-called Edifice of Taharqa,[200] while on the far extremity of the complex a colonnaded porch was added to the East Temple of Amun-Re-Harakhty.[201] Nearby, the chapel of Osiris-Wennefer-Heryibished was erected in the names of Amenirdis I and Shepenwepet II,[202] while the latter was responsible for a chapel of Osiris-Nebankh to the north of Pylon III.[203] Still further north, additions were made within the complex of Montju.[204] At the opposite extremity of the Karnak cluster various additions were made to the temple of Mut,[205] and also to the Luxor temple.[206]

Across the river in Thebes-West, the new pylon at the small temple at Medinet Habu was completed[207] and the God's Wife Amenirdis I buried a few meters away, adjacent to the tomb of her predecessor Shepenwepet I. Amenirdis's brick chapel was soon replaced by one of stone (fig. 128).[208]

Also at Thebes-West, the Fourth Prophet and Mayor Montjuemhat founded a massive sepulcher in the main Asasif cemetery, in front of the temples at Deir el-Bahari (TT34).[209] This would now be the principal necropolis of senior Theban officialdom into the Twenty-sixth Dynasty (fig. 122); also buried here were the stewards of the God's Wives, of whom Akhamenrau (TT404) officiated during Taharqa's reign.[210]

On the border of the Twenty-fifth Dynasty homeland of Nubia, Taharqa may have been the first king to build on the sacred island of Isis at Philae, to judge from a few fragments extant there.[211] Deeper into Lower Nubia, the clifftop fortress at Qasr Ibrim (fig. 123) was renewed and a temple erected there,[212] while at the Middle Kingdom Second Cataract fortress at Semna a new temple was built.[213] Some kind of construction also seems to have been undertaken at or near Sedeinga.[214]

The main Nubian concentrations of Taharqa's monuments were, however, between the Third and Fourth Cataracts. At Taba, on Argo Island, a large temple was built,[215] while further south, at Kawa, Taharqa extended Tutankhamun's Temple A and built Temple T,[216] the first court of the latter being the location for a series of important stelae.[217] Opposite the ancestral cemetery of el-Kurru, at the site of Sanam, a temple was built,[218] with work also being carried out at the capital, Gebel Barkal. The latter included the construction of a rock-cut temple of Mut (B300),[219] the addition of a bark stand to the Amun temple (B500),[220] together with work in temple B200,[221]

Fig. 122. The Asasif, principal cemetery of the senior officials of Twenty-fifth/sixth-Dynasty Thebes.

Fig. 123. Clifftop fortress at Qasr Ibrim, as seen in 1962.

and the addition of an inscription on one of the uraeus-form peaks at the front of the Gebel itself (cf. fig. 106).[222]

Taharqa also founded a new royal cemetery at Nuri, a few kilometers upstream of el-Kurru and on the opposite bank of the river. The pyramid he built there (Nu1—fig. 124)[223] was not only the largest of all Kushite pyramids (52 meters square, as against only 7.6 meters for the monument of Piye) but also had the most elaborate substructure of any Kushite royal tomb (fig. 125).[224] A conventional stairway below the site of the mortuary chapel led into a small antechamber, which in turn gave access to a six-pillared burial chamber, the aisles of which were vaulted. A curious corridor completely surrounded the subterranean rooms, at a slightly higher level. The usual coffin bench lay in the center of the burial chamber, while the funerary equipment included over a thousand *shabtis*, the largest assemblage ever found in any tomb.

The first decade and a half of the reign seems not to have seen any renewal of the conflict with Assyria, which had been distracted by events closer to home, culminating in the murder of Sennacherib in 681 and Esarhaddon's victory in the ensuing civil war.[225] However, by the mid-670s Assyrian suzerainty over much of Syria–Palestine had been restored, and early in 674 "the army of Assyria was defeated in a bloody battle in Egypt,"[226] clearly a fresh attempt to bring the Nile valley under control. Three years later, however, the Assyrian king returned, and in a series of battles forced a wounded Taharqa—allegedly hit with arrows five times— back to Memphis.[227] However, the ancient capital was soon itself taken, Taharqa himself retreating southward but leaving many of the royal family

Fig. 124. The pyramid of Taharqa at Nuri (Nu1). In the background are the later pyramids of, from the left, Ameninatakilebte (Nu10), Amtalqa (Nu9), Aseplta (Nu8), Siaspiqa (Nu4), and Amaniastabarqa (Nu2).

to be taken and conveyed as captives to Assyria. These included the queen and the crown prince, whom the Assyrians name as "Ushanukhuru"—the Egyptian form is unknown; he may be the royal Kushite shown kneeling before Esarhaddon on the series of stelae he erected to commemorate his victories (fig. 126).[228]

The Assyrians converted a large proportion of the country into a network of polities directly vassal to Assyria.[229] At least some of the governors of these city-states were scions of the old Libyan–Egyptian provincial chiefs, royalty, and nobility,[230] including Nekau (I) of Sais,[231] Padubast III[232] at Tanis, Shoshenq (F) of Busiris, Nimlot E at Hermopolis, Nespamedu A at Thinis, and Montjuemhat at Thebes. This Assyrian hegemony was, nevertheless, short-lived, as by 669 Taharqa had returned to Memphis, prompting Esarhaddon to once more march west, only to fall ill and die that November, while still in Palestine.[233]

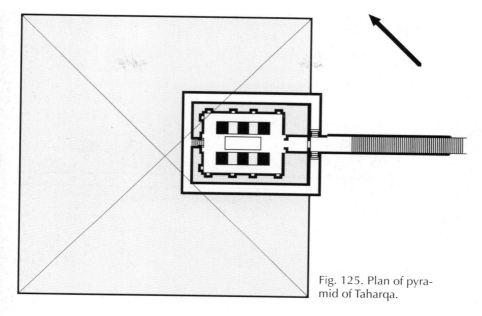

Fig. 125. Plan of pyramid of Taharqa.

Although this provided Taharqa with a brief respite, the new Assyrian king, Ashur-banipal, initiated a fresh invasion in 667/666.[234] Penetration to Memphis presumably only followed the burial of Apis bull 25.3/XXXVI, which was explicitly dated to IV *prt* 23 of Taharqa's Year 24[235] (September 667[236]): given the Assyrians' antipathy toward Taharqa it seems highly unlikely that any event would have been dated to his reign if Ashur-banipal had by then seized the city.

Nevertheless, Taharqa must have fled soon afterward, with the Assyrian troops occupying the city and Ashur-banipal returning home with booty and prisoners as soon as he had reinstalled his Delta vassals in their cities, at least some of whom had fled from the resurgent Taharqa. However, once the Assyrian king had left for home, a number of the Delta princes began to plot with Taharqa, only to be discovered, arrested and executed, along with many of the citizens of Sais, Tanis, and "Pindid." The victims were flayed and their skins nailed to the city walls as a terrible warning against further resistance. Nekau I of Sais was the only ruler spared, perhaps owing to his previous record of opposition to the Kushites. Bound by a more terrible oath, he retained the rule of Sais,[237] while his son Psamtik, invested with the new Assyrian name Nabushazzibanni, was made ruler of Athribis in place of the previous (probably executed) prince, Bakennefi C.

Fig. 126. Stela of Esarhad-
don, probably showing the
captured Kushite prince
Ushanukhuru. From Til
Barsip (Aleppo Museum
M7502).

Some degree of tranquility may have been
achieved by 664 (Taharqa's Year 26), when a
replacement for the Apis who had died in Year 24
was installed. However, that circumstances were
not 'normal' is indicated by two pieces of data. First,
the gap between the death of Apis 25.3/XXXVI and
the installation of a new bull was much longer than
would normally be expected. Second, the eventual
epitaph of this Apis (26.1/XXXVII)[238] suggests that
the birth date of the bull was not available when it
was composed in Year 20 of Psamtik I.[239] Soon afterward, Taharqa died somewhere in the south and was
interred in his Nuri pyramid, the Kushite throne
passing[240] to his nephew Tanutamun.[241]

6 FROM HUMILIATION TO RENAISSANCE

As recorded in his so-called Dream Stela, found at Gebel Barkal,[1] Bakare Tanutamun's first action after visiting Napata to ensure the acceptance of his assumption of the throne was to return northward and re-establish Kushite power successively in Thebes, Memphis, and Heliopolis. At Memphis he crushed the pro-Assyrian elements there:[2] it was probably at this time that Nekau I of Sais lost his life, his son Psamtik-Nabushazzibanni escaping to Syria.[3] The king then confronted the Delta princes, who at length came to Memphis and submitted to him.

Tanutamun's reassertion of Kushite dominion was to be short-lived, as the Assyrian armies returned, drove out the king, and pursued him to Thebes. The city was then sacked and despoiled of much of its treasure: "with full hands" Ashur-banipal returned home to Nineveh.[4] Nevertheless, once the Assyrians had retired northward, the hierarchy remained largely unchanged, with the Kushite high priest and God's Wife remaining in post. The principal exception was that the office of Second Prophet, hitherto held by prince Nesishutefnut, was added to the portfolio of the Mayor and Fourth Prophet Montjuemhat. Thebes would remain loyal to Tanutamun for nearly a decade, during which time a number of monuments were decorated in his name, including the temple of Osiris-Ptah-Nebankh, begun by Taharqa to the east of the avenue between the Amun and Mut temenoi.[5]

In the north, the enduring jigsaw of polities continued to provide the basis of government under the reimposed Assyrian dominion (cf. p. 167). Some affected royal style, including Nekau I's son at Sais, who had now become Wahibre Psamtik (I), and probably the latest of the rulers at Tanis, perhaps Neferkare P[. . .].[6] However, over the next few years Psamtik began the process of recreating a unitary Egyptian state and shaking off the bonds of Assyrian overlordship. The way in which this was initiated and progressed is not altogether clear, but the process presumably benefited from Assyrian distractions elsewhere. Herodotus attributes Psamtik's victory over eleven peers to the aid of Carian Greek mercenaries;[7] the same may also have helped the king to beat off yet another attempt by Tanutamun to regain his Egyptian throne.[8] There would subsequently be significant settlement by Carians in Egypt, with mercenaries from the Aegean forming a significant part of the Egyptian army throughout the Twenty-sixth Dynasty (cf. below).

As the end of the first decade of Psamtik's reign approached, it seems that the whole of Egypt north of the Thebaid was under the control of the Saite kings's regime. The final reunification seems to have been achieved in Year 9, when Psamtik's daughter, Neitiqerti (Greek: Nitokris), arrived in Thebes and was adopted by Amenirdis II, daughter of Taharqa and the adopted heir of the aged, but still reigning, God's Wife Shepenwepet II. In the stela that records the event,[9] Psamtik states:

> I have given to him (Amun) my daughter to be God's Wife .... Now, I have heard that a king's daughter is there (of) the Horus Qakhau, the good god, [Taharqa], true of voice, whom he gave to his sister (Shepenwepet II) to be her eldest daughter and is there as God's Adoratrix. I will not do what in fact should not be done and expel an heir from his seat .... I will give her (my daughter) to her (Taharqa's daughter) to be her eldest daughter just as she (Taharqa's daughter) was made over to the sister of her father.

Neitiqerti (I) was thus to serve only after the deaths of both Shepenwepet II and Amenirdis II—i.e., many years into the future. This was doubtless the result of negotiations that had led Tanutamun finally to give up his residual Egyptian claims. Similarly, Horkhebit, the son and successor of the Kushite high priest Horemakhet, apparently remained undisturbed.

The Kushite God's Wife Shepenwepet II and her Saite "granddaughter" Neitiqerti are seen together with Psamtik I in a rock inscription in the Wadi Gasus in the Eastern Desert (fig. 127).[10] Here, however, Neitiqerti is shown in the more prominent position, directly behind her father the king, with Shepenwepet following her and in the apparently subordinate role of "her mother"—albeit still retaining the title of God's Wife and filiation from Piye. Amenirdis II is nowhere to be seen here, and it is

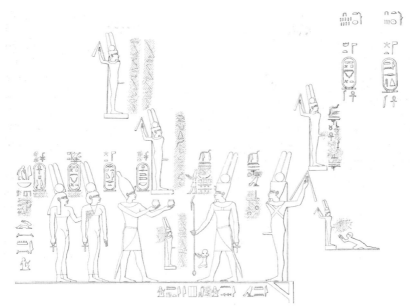

Fig. 127. Set of rock inscriptions in the Wadi Gasus, including a tableau of Psamtik I, Shepenwepet II, and Neitiqerti I offering to Amun and Min. Along with a number of individual scenes of offerings to Min, at the top right are the cartouches of a Shepenwepet, associated with a Year 19, and of an Amenirdis, associated with a Year 12.

unclear whether she ever became God's Wife, either through premature demise or through Psamtik reneging on the 'deal' once any chance of substantive Kushite reaction had faded into the past. Much depends on the date at which Neitiqerti actually became God's Wife: if it was as late as Year 26 of Psamtik I—on the basis of a reference within the autobiography of her Steward Ibi—she could not have directly followed Shepenwepet II unless the latter lived to be over one hundred, given that Shepenwepet's first appearance in the record dates to *c.* 730.[11] Amenirdis II would then thus almost certainly have officiated between Shepenwepet and Neitiqerti. However, the evidence for the Year 26 accession date is equivocal, and her succession could otherwise have been anywhere between Year 9 and Year 26. A year-date in the early teens would allow Shepenwepet II to die at an advanced, yet still credible, age, and be directly followed by Neitiqerti. In favor of this may be the fact that there is no sign of any burial place for Amenirdis II at Medinet Habu, where the tomb built directly west of that

Fig. 128. Tomb-chapels of the God's Wives of Amun at Medinet Habu. The two standing structures are respectively the sepulcher of Amenirdis I and the triple tomb of Shepenwepet II, Neitiqerti, and Neitiqerti's mother Mehytenweskhet C. These buildings were flanked on the left by the brick probable tomb of Shepenwepet I, and on the right by what may have been the site of the chapel of Neitiqerti's successor, Ankhnesneferibre.

of Amenirdis I housed only the burials of Shepenwepet II, Neitiqerti, and the latter's mother, Mehytenweskhet C (fig. 128).[12]

If Amenirdis II did not become God's Wife—and did not die prematurely—her fate is uncertain. It has been suggested variously that she might have married into the Theban nobility[13] or returned to Kush—in the latter case either to be God's Wife at Napata[14] or to marry the king and became the mother of Ñsalsa, mother of Aspelta.[15] It is also possible, however, that although passed over for the office of God's Wife she remained in Egypt as an honored member of the college perhaps into the reign of Nekau II, the last representative of the vanished world of the Nubian pharaohs.[16]

It is unknown how long Tanutamun ruled after his final loss of Egyptian dominion. His sister-wife Piankharty is depicted on her husband's Dream Stela, but no children are definitely known, and Tanutamun's successor, Atlanersa, appears to have been a son of Taharqa.[17] Tanutamun himself was ultimately buried at el-Kurru—interestingly *not* at Nuri, where Taharqa had initiated a new royal necropolis—in tomb Ku16, which was to be almost the last royal tomb to be erected there.[18] Like Shabaka's sepulcher, it had a burial chamber adorned with paintings, in this case, however, sufficiently well preserved to identify the topics covered (fig. 129).[19] The vignettes and texts essentially follow the age-old association of royal

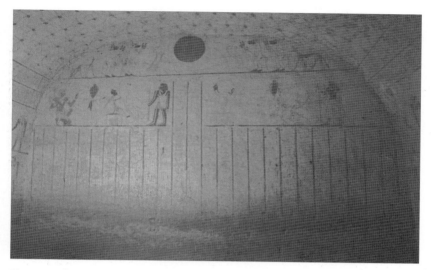

Fig. 129. The end wall of the burial chamber of Tanutamun at el-Kurru.

burials with solar matters, the entrance doorway being surmounted by painted apes adoring the sun god in his bark, a similar motif also appearing on the rear wall.

The line of the Twenty-fifth Dynasty and its successors endured in their rule in Upper Nubia until the fourth century AD.[20] They continued to contend with Egypt and her rulers, including having to resist an attack by Psamtik I's grandson (see p. 177), Lower Nubia being at least intermittently in Egyptian hands through the seventh and sixth centuries.[21] That area was, however, certainly in Nubian hands under Horsiyotef early in the fourth century, when he fought against "rebels" there,[22] although king Nastaseñ records having to repulse a riverborne attack from the north later that century.[23] Under the Ptolemies, at least northern Lower Nubia was Egyptian,[24] but the shifting allegiances of the area—and in particular of the priesthood at Philae—is evidenced by the work of the Kushite king Arqamani (Ergamenes II) at the temples at Dakka and Philae,[25] together with his successor Adkheramani's stela at the latter site, as well as his construction of the chapel that formed the core of the later temple at Dabod.[26] The Upper Egyptian revolt of Year 16 of Ptolemy IV through Year 19 of Ptolemy V may have provided a basis for a Meroitic reoccupation of Lower Nubia, and even provided military support for the rebel Egyptian king Ankhwennefer.[27] On the other hand, Arqamani's texts at Philae were later mutilated by Ptolemy V,

Fig. 130. The Northern cemetery at Meroë-Begrawiya, viewed from the south.

and Egyptian occupation extended further southward under Ptolemy VI.[28] The center of gravity of the Kushite state itself seems to have moved southward from Gebel Barkal to Meroë around the end of the fourth century, when the series of pyramids at Nuri comes to an end.[29] On the other hand, the old center remained important; pyramids were built at Gebel Barkal itself into the beginning of the first century AD (fig. 106), and there was ongoing activity at the temples. However, it is at Meroë that the major pyramid fields are to be found for the remainder of Kushite history (fig. 130).[30]

Under Roman rule, the Kushite monarchy was regarded as a client kingdom, although the Kushites were able to sack Aswan in 24 BC, provoking a Roman campaign that allegedly reached Gebel Barkal and led to a permanent border being re-established at Maharraqa.[31] Various Roman penetrations further south are recorded, but Kush remained independent and regained some control over Lower Nubia during the late third/fourth centuries AD, before being displaced by local tribes. In its Upper Nubian heartland, the Kushite kingdom remains visible into the first half of the fourth century, when the last pyramids were built in the cemeteries of Meroë, after which the state appears to have finally fragmented, leading to a range of successor states throughout Nubia, which ran on into medieval times.[32]

Now ruler of the whole of Egypt, Psamtik I secured his northeastern frontier through the construction or restoration of fortresses[33] at Tell el-Qedua,[34] Tell Dafana,[35] and Tell el-Balamun—where the temple was also extended[36]—in the east, and also at "Marua" in the west.[37] The last stronghold may link with a Libyan campaign carried out by the king in Year 11,[38] and also with the particular prominence of the Twenty-sixth Dynasty in the Western Desert oases. In the Levant, Herodotus records a siege (allegedly lasting twenty-nine years) carried out by Psamtik I against Ashdod on the Palestinian coast,[39] as well as an attempted invasion of Egypt by the Scythians (originating from the northern shores of the Black Sea) who were, however, bought off by Psamtik while still in Palestine.[40] The latter event would appear to have taken place between c. 637 and 625.[41] Greeks seem to have remained an important part of Psamtik's armies throughout his reign, the Aegean connection also being apparently furthered by the settlement of Greek traders in northern Egypt.[42]

Building projects were also a result of the renewed prosperity of the reunited state, but only fragments of constructions at the dynastic seat of Sais now survive.[43] Likewise little of Psamtik's work at Heliopolis[44] and Tanis[45] remains extant. At Karnak, various structures were erected in the name of his daughter Neitiqerti I on the southern margin of the Montju enclosure.[46]

Key to the re-establishment of the unitary state was the removal of one of the main drivers of the fissiparous tendencies of the Third Intermediate Period: the parallel authority of the Libyan tribal system (see pp. 113–14). That Psamtik I was successful in doing so is to be seen by the way in which the once mighty Chiefs of the Ma disappear from the political landscape: the last one is spotted in Year 31 as a police official at the old Libyan stronghold of Herakleopolis.[47]

Although nothing of Psamtik I's burial survives, apart from a few *shabtis*, his tomb presumably formed part of the necropolis described by Herodotus, who records that Wahibre, fourth king of this dynasty, was

> buried in the family tomb in the temple of Athena [Neith], nearest to the shrine, on the left hand as one goes in. The people of Sais buried all the kings who came from the province inside this area. The tomb of Amasis (Ahmose II) is also in the temple court, although further from the shrine than that of Apries (Wahibre) and his ancestors. It is a great cloistered building of stone, decorated with pillars carved in the imitation of palm trees, and other costly adornments.

Within the cloister is a chamber with double doors, and behind the doors stands the sepulcher.

This implies that the earliest Saite kings—including the dynastic founder—were buried in a single tomb, or perhaps that each had a separate tomb below a single superstructure. Unfortunately the whole area has been destroyed in modern times and nothing can be verified on the ground.[48]

The son and successor of Psamtik I, Wehemibre Nekau (II—fig. 131) expended considerable effort in support of his dynasty's former patron Assyria against the rising power of Babylon. Initially successful, he was able to occupy much of Syria–Palestine (including Qadesh) during his 609 campaign, killing the Judean king Josiah in battle at Megiddo.[49] However, Nekau's forces were ultimately driven back by the Babylonians to the borders of Egypt following a disastrous defeat at Carchemish in northern Syria in 605.[50]

Nekau also pursued an active maritime policy, attempting to dig a canal between the Nile and the Red Sea, and is said to have had Phoenician ships undertake a circumnavigation of Africa.[51] Of his surviving monuments, a

Fig. 131. Detail of relief of Nekau II (Ny Carlsberg ÆIN 46).

number had the king's names erased after his death in 594, but it is unclear as to why this occurred.

The six-year reign of the son of Nekau II, Neferibre Psamtik (II), likewise included an active foreign policy, in particular a thrust into Nubia that reached at least the Third Cataract.[52] Memorials to this included a large number of graffiti left by Greek mercenaries at Abu Simbel, which include the detail that the Egyptian troops on the campaign were led by General Ahmose and the foreigners by General Pediamensematawi (Potasimto).[53] This was followed by an expedition into Palestine, which included the killing of the Judean king Josiah at Megiddo in 609.[54] Psamtik II had at least two children: his son and successor Wahibre, and a daughter Ankhnesneferibre, who succeeded Neitiqerti I as God's Wife of Amun in 586.

Relatively little is known about events within Egypt prior to the last years of the reign of Haaibre Wahibre (Greek Apries, the Biblical Hophra), although a number of building projects can be attributed to the time.[55] Abroad, the king continued the policy of his father and his grandfather in intervening in Syria–Palestine against the Babylonians, as a result of which Egypt suffered a short-lived invasion by Nebuchadrezzar II in 582. However, between 574 and 571, Wahibre carried out successful campaigns along the Levantine coast, before embarking on a disastrous campaign to the west into Libya, which resulted in his army's defeat. This resulted in a revolt by the Egyptian elements of the army, who then proclaimed the official Ahmose (not Psamtik II's general), sent to quell the mutiny, as king.[56]

Wahibre led an army of Carian and Ionian mercenaries west from Sais to confront the rebels, but was defeated in the ensuing battle. Although Ahmose thus gained royal power in the north of Egypt around the beginning of February 570, Wahibre continued to be acknowledged as king further south (possibly maintaining a stronghold in his palace at Memphis). Then, in October/November 570, a final battle took place, after which Wahibre seems to have fled, ultimately finding his way to Babylon, where he was welcomed as a guest by his erstwhile foe, Nebuchadrezzar II.

Although Khnemibre Ahmose (II) was henceforth generally accepted as king, Wahibre attempted to regain power in the wake of a Babylonian invasion of Egypt in the spring of 567 and died in the process. However, Ahmose buried the former king in the royal cemetery at Sais (cf. p. 175), presumably to ritually legitimize his status as Wahibre's successor.[57]

Continuity was also maintained by Wahibre's sister Ankhnesneferibre's remaining God's Wife of Amun at Thebes (fig. 132), albeit Ahmose's own

Fig. 132. Last king of the Twenty-sixth Dynasty, Psamtik III, and last God's Wife of Amun, Ankhnesneferibre, both shown with Amun on the façade of the chapel of Ahmose II and Neitiqerti I at Karnak.

daughter, Neitiqerti (II), was adopted by her as her eventual successor. Notwithstanding the fact that Ahmose II came to power against a background of antipathy toward Greek soldiery, which formed the cornerstone of Wahibre's army, such troops continued to be employed, but Greek traders were henceforth concentrated at the northwestern Delta commercial center and fortress at Naukratis.[58] Ahmose also allied with various Greek states as bulwarks against Babylonian (and later Persian) threats to Egypt's independence, reinforcing his alliances by donations to key Greek sanctuaries, including Delphi.[59]

The king was an extensive builder, carrying out work throughout the Delta, including the capital city of Sais, as well as at Memphis and elsewhere in the Nile valley—and in the Western Desert oases, including the building at Aghurmi, in the Siwa Oasis, that became the famous Temple of the Oracle visited by Alexander the Great.[60] The number of temples built there suggests that a particular interest was being taken

Fig. 133. Persian emperor as pharaoh: Darius I depicted with Egyptian royal regalia and a cartouche in the inner gateway of the Hibis temple in Kharga Oasis.

by the Twenty-sixth Dynasty in the development of the Western Desert region, which was then enthusiastically continued by the Persians, Ptolemies, and Romans.

Ahmose II's last years were clouded by the steady advance of the Persians, who had long since disposed of Babylon, conquered the Greek states of Asia, and were now the sole great power in the Levant. By the time of the king's death in 526, Persian forces were bearing down upon Egypt, and would overrun the country not long after the accession of his son Psamtik III. Ahmose II's burial at Sais was allegedly desecrated by the Persian king Kambyses following the occupation.[61]

The brief reign of the son of Ahmose II, Ankhka(en)re Psamtik (III— fig. 132), during 526/525 BC thus saw the last phase of Egypt's struggle to avoid absorption into the Persian empire. His forces having been defeated in the northeast Delta, Psamtik withdrew to Memphis, where he surrendered after a siege. At first treated by the Persians as an honored guest, he fell into plotting against the Persian king and was executed.

Thus came to an end, for over a century, Egypt's status as an independent nation. Until 404, she formed an integral part of the Persian Empire, and while the earlier kings—in particular Darius I (fig. 133)—had themselves portrayed as proper pharaohs, this concept rapidly declined to such a degree that no hieroglyphic mentions of Xerxes II, Darius II, and Artaxerxes II appear to survive.[62] From 404 to 343, indigenous rule was restored under the Twenty-eighth through Thirtieth Dynasties, marked by significant building and successful resistance to the resurgent Persians, but troubled by incessant internal squabbling that inevitably weakened the state.[63]

In 343, however, king Nakhthorheb fled to Nubia in the face of, at last, a successful Persian invasion, leaving Egypt as just one part of the former Persian Empire to be conquered by Alexander the Great in 332. Falling to Ptolemy (I) Soter at the dissolution of the Alexandrine possessions, Egypt would form the core of a new Levantine empire until 30 BC, when she became part of the Roman imperial domains. It would not be until AD 1922 that she would once again become a freestanding state, and not until 1952 the untrammeled mistress of her own destinies.

APPENDICES

Appendix 1

The Absolute Chronology of the New Kingdom and Third Intermediate Period

The chronology of ancient Egypt prior to 690—the accession of Taharqa—remains uncertain. Prior to this, all relative and absolute dating is a matter for the subjective interpretation of contemporary Egyptian data, retrospective Egyptian data (family genealogies and suchlike), potential synchronisms with other parts of the Near East, records of astronomical phenomena, and the works of Classical writers, in particular Manetho. In some cases it is possible to construct 'islands' of solid chronology—e.g., the exact number of years (twenty-six) between Year 28 of Shoshenq III and Year 2 of Pamiu, as provided by the latter year's Apis epitaph (see p. 127)—but these are rare and not directly linked into absolute chronology (i.e., dates expressed in the Julian calendar). However, although there are various cross linkages between reigns, pontificates, periods of office, and lifespans, many are equivocal to a greater or lesser extent, and dead reckoning back from 690 can produce a range of options, not infrequently mutually exclusive.

Narrowing down the options is dependent on the view one takes of the overall chronological structure of the period—fundamentally the time that elapsed between the beginning of the Nineteenth Dynasty and Taharqa's accession. The generally accepted chronology of this period is ultimately based on two 'hooks' where an Egyptian ruler can be linked (or potentially be linked) into the broader chronological structure of the region. The earlier of the two is the reign of Rameses II, which lies within a network of synchronisms that link him into the Assyrian succession. The Assyrian king Ashur-uballit I corresponded with Akhenaten, while Ashur-uballit's father Eriba-Adad I is linked to Amenhotep III via the latter's Babylonian correspondents Kadashman-Enlil I and Burnaburiash II.[1] Rameses II's Hittite contemporaries, Muwatallish II and Hattushilish III, corresponded with Adad-nirari I of Assyria, while Hattushilish exchanged letters with the Assyrian Shalmaneser I.

Assyrian royal chronology has long been regarded as the keystone of the broader Near Eastern framework, since prior to the beginning of externally verified Assyrian chronology in the reign of Ashur-dan II (934–912), there exists the combination of a King List tradition (the Assyrian King List—AKL)[2] with a list of worthies for whom each year was named in the Assyrian dating system—the so-called *limmu* list[3]—that together purport to stretch back over a thousand years. As preserved, these derive from an overlapping set of individual documents that were compiled no earlier than the eighth century. On the basis of the AKL and the *limmu* list, Eriba-Adad I has been dated[4] to *c.* 1380–1353, Ashur-uballit I to *c.* 1353–1318, Adad-nirari I to *c.* 1295–1264, and Shalmaneser I to *c.* 1263–1234, leading to Rameses II's accession being assessed as falling between the end of the thirteenth century and the end of the first quarter of the twelfth.

This has been further refined via a record of a new moon in II *prt* of Rameses II's Year 52.[5] This can be converted into a series of potential Julian years based on the known lunar cycle, giving in turn a series of potential accession years for Rameses. Within the aforementioned 'target range,' the king's accession can thus have taken place only in 1304, 1290, or 1279. The last is generally accepted today as being the correct one, especially since Hattushilish III seems to have seized the Hittite throne around Rameses's Year 15, with Shalmaneser I becoming king soon after Hattushilish's coup. With the Assyrian's dates calculated, as noted above, from the AKL at *c.* 1263–1234, Rameses's own accession comes out at around *c.* 1280, neatly verifying the 1279 accession year derived from placing the Year 52 new moon in 1228.

However, all of this depends entirely on the correctness of the Assyrian regnal dates derived from the AKL and the *limmu* list. Although the kings listed in the period prior to Ashur-dan II possess significant contemporary documentation, between the death of Ashur-bel-kala and Ashur-dan's accession there is an almost complete lack of contemporary data. The AKL has lost a number of its reign lengths,[6] and the most that can be calculated is the total years elapsed. Even this is based on an estimate of the number of lines in a section of the *limmu* list that is very badly damaged,[7] having lost many of its entries and being thus largely incapable of independent data verification.

Given these issues, one cannot be certain either of the veracity of the total numbers of years recorded, or, even if the numbers are correct, whether they represent the aggregate of the reigns of a single sequence of kings, or two or more parallel lines that have been presented as a single line by the compiler of the AKL and the *limmu* list. If the latter, this would be very similar to the presentation of the Intermediate Periods in the Turin and Manethonic king lists in Egypt, where parallel lines were listed as though sequential (cf. p 124). In Assyria, the almost amuletic purpose of the AKL, purportedly demonstrating an unbroken line of succession from the earliest times to the current king, meant that such an approach was essentially *de rigeur*.[8]

That there was a single line of Assyrian kings from Ashur-dan II onward is absolutely certain, and highly likely prior to Tukulti-Ninurta I on the basis of external data. However, between these two reigns there are points where contemporary evidence could suggest a bifurcation of Assyrian kingship (or worse). In particular there survives a letter written by the "Great King" (of Babylon) Adadshumausur to the "[Smal]l Kings of Assyria," Ashur-nirari III and Ili-hadda.[9] As Ili-hadda does not appear as a king in the AKL, it has been assumed that such 'counter-kings' were omitted from the AKL. However, there are certainly cases where kings have been left out of the AKL—one definite example being the omission of Shalmaneser II from one version of the list (cf. below). It is thus quite possible that Ili-hadda's omission was simply an error, and does not imply that *no* such counter-kings were to be found within the AKL. Indeed, the knowledge that Ashur-nirari III was one of two Assyrian kings recognized by their Babylonian counterpart makes one suspicious of what might lie behind the complicated family relationships seen among those arranged in the AKL as successors of Tukulti-Ninurta I. Ashur-nadin-apil is listed there as Tukulti-Ninurta's son, but versions of the AKL disagree whether the king following Ashur-nadin-apil was the offspring of Ashur-nadin-apil himself, or of an otherwise unknown Ashur-nasir-apil. The next on the list, Enlil-kudurra-usur, was a son of Tukulti-Ninurta, and the next one, Ninurta-apil-Ekur, the son of Ili-hadda. It was Ninurta-apil-Ekur who was then the father of Ashur-dan I.[10] Against this background, arguments were once put forward for a fourfold division of Assyria after Tukulti-Ninurta's death.[11] While there is no direct evidence for this, the known duumvirate of Ashur-nirari III and Ili-hadda provides a clear possibility that the reigns of Ili-hadda's son, Ninurta-apil-Ekur, and perhaps the early years of Ninurta-apil-Ekur's son, Ashur-dan I, ran in parallel with those of Ashur-nirari III and Enlil-kudurra-usur. If so, a decade could be removed from the overall Assyrian chronology of the period, as the AKL is the sole extant source, the *limmu* list being hopelessly broken prior to the last years of Ashur-nasir-pal I.

A further potential case of division is to be seen some two centuries later, in the case of Ashur-rabi II. The AKL combines with the *limmu* list to give him a forty-one-year reign, separated from that of his father, Ashur-nasir-pal I, by the reigns of his brother Shalmaneser II (twelve years—missing from one version of the AKL) and Shalmaneser's son Ashur-nirari IV (six years: both reign lengths are securely recorded in KAV21). However, unlike Ashur-nasir-pal, Shalmaneser, and his own son Ashur-resha-ishi II, there is no attestation whatsoever of Ashur-rabi at the Assyrian capital of Ashur: his only contemporary monument is a broken cylinder referring to public works by a vassal apparently based near the river Khabur, some two hundred kilometers west of the capital city. Coupled with later kings' references to Ashur-rabi in connection with this area, one might suspect that he had been ruling in the west, while his brother Shalmaneser II and Shalmaneser's son Ashur-nirari IV ruled in Ashur. Thus, could the exclusion of Shalmaneser II from the Nassouhi version of the AKL (probably compiled under Ashur-rabi II's grandson) imply dissension as to which brother was legitimate heir on Ashur-nasir-pal I's death?

While this would of course imply a doubling up of the *limmu* list, the existence of rival lines could quite easily lead to parallel sets of *limmu*, as one king would surely reckon time in terms of his own officials, rather than those of a potentially rival ruler. Unfortunately, any attempt at detecting such a situation within the *limmu* list is thwarted by the fact that apart from its very beginning, Ashur-rabi's *limmu* list is in a very poor condition, with major lacunae extending through the reigns of Ashur-resha-ishi and Tiglath-Pileser II (neither of whose eponymous years survive) and beyond.

If these speculations were to prove to be correct, the dates of Rameses II's Assyrian contemporaries would be significantly lowered. Taking each of the aforementioned adjustments to the AKL chronology in turn, the following potential dates emerge:[12]

Option	Shalmaneser I accession date (~Year 15/16 of Rameses II)	Consequent Rameses II accession date	Fit with Rameses II lunar data-based accession date
Overlapping of successors of Tukulti-Ninurta I	1251/50	1266/5	1265
Overlapping of successors of Ashur-nasir-pal I	1241/40	1256/7	1254+2/3 yrs
Both of above	1233	1248/9	1254–5/6 yrs

Of course, if we are to assess these sections of the AKL as in error—or perhaps, better, misleading—it is quite possible that other parts of the tradition during the Ashur-bel-kala/Ashur-dan II 'dark ages' could also be flawed. Indeed, some scholars have suggested that the AKL chronology of this period should be entirely disregarded in the reconstruction of Egyptian history in view of the lack of contemporary corroborative data, especially as some of the listed reigns are of very considerable length.[13] However, while one is always nervous of apparently long reigns with few or no contemporary attestations, there are examples where an almost unknown king's only contemporary year-date is a high one—e.g., Iuput II's Year 21. Accordingly, one is nervous of second-guessing an ancient scribe unless there is some *prima facie* evidence to lead one to question his accuracy. On this basis, a wholesale disregard of the AKL data seems both methodologically unsound and undesirable, leaving, as it does, only dead reckoning as an historical means of determining both absolute and relative chronology.

As for scientific means of providing or verifying a macrochronological framework, although recent statistical approaches to the use of radiocarbon data have produced a structure that seems supportive of the broad consensus of placing Rameses II in the thirteenth century,[14] there remain concerns around the use of the calibration curve to convert 'BP' (radiocarbon) dates into 'BC' (historical) ones. Similarly, the results of a number of dendrochronological studies relevant to the period have been questioned, and currently it seems unwise to make use of them as primary dating material.[15] Thus, given the significant gap between the highest known regnal years of a number of Egyptian kings and the reign lengths extrapolated from the broad chronology provided by the AKL, abandoning the 'dark age' elements of the latter could lead to a lowering of dates that might run into centuries, given the 'floating' nature of many parts of the Egyptian relative chronology as noted above, and the potential for additional overlaps of reigns over and above those already known.

However, it has long been held that the chronology of the time is constrained by a further 'hook': the equation of the "Shishak king of Egypt" who "came up against Jerusalem" in the "fifth year of king Rehoboam" with Shoshenq I (cf. pp. 88–89). Rehoboam's Year 5 has been calculated to have corresponded to *c.* 925, on the basis of a synchronism between Shalmaneser III of Assyria and the last year of Ahab of Israel in 853— the earliest Biblical/Assyrian link known—and another synchronism, between Shalmaneser and the first year of Jehu of Israel, in 841. Biblical data links these Israelite reigns with those of their Judean contemporaries, allowing a back calculation to place Rehoboam's accession in 931.[16] Thus, depending on where one places Shoshenq I's Jerusalem campaign, his earliest accession date would be 946 and latest would be 926. The earlier date is probably the more likely (placing the campaign in the second decade of the reign: cf. pp. 92–93). Within these constraints, the record of a festival in Year 5 of Shoshenq I[17] has been interpreted as providing a lunar date whose only acceptable resolution between 950 and 930 is 939—thus refining Shoshenq I's accession to 944/3.[18] All this of course relies entirely on the accuracy of the Biblical data prior to the reign of Ahab and/or its transmission.[19]

Leaving aside these latter issues, the fact that Jerusalem seems not to have featured among the conquered towns listed on the Bubastite Portal has led, as already noted (p. 89), to proposals that "Shishak" and "Shoshenq" were different people, and that some other king should be sought as the prototype for the Biblical character. Both Rameses II and Rameses III have been put forward as candidates,[20] bringing their accession dates down respectively by three and a half and two and a half centuries. Such reductions are made possible only by the aforementioned option of disregarding the unverified portions of the AKL, together with some extremely radical overlapping of reigns and dynasties during the 250/350 years separating them from the accession of Taharqa. Others have denied the Shishak/Shoshenq equation—and produced a consequently unconstrained chronological revision of the latter part of the Third Intermediate Period—without providing an alternative candidate.[21]

However, as has again already been discussed, there is no reason to insist that the Bubastite Portal campaign was Shoshenq I's only foreign military venture. Also, the equation of the names "Shishak" and "Shoshenq" is straightforward (the missing 'n' being well attested in Egyptian sources as well), with the terminal 'q' not found in any other royal names—unlike the contortions needed to square the name with any other candidate.[22] Accordingly, the present author sees no reason to break the Shishak/Shoshenq link, placing the king's reign during the third quarter of the tenth century and defining the chronological upper limit for the chronology of the period down to the accession of Taharqa,[23] although acknowledging that there exists a tendency in Palestinian archaeology to lower the Late Bronze Age/Early Iron Age boundary, with a consequent preference for bringing Shoshenq I's campaign down into the ninth century.[24]

Retaining the Shishak/Shoshenq I equation, and thus a dating of Shoshenq's accession to 943, allows one to return to the question of the accession date of Rameses II. Dead reckoning back from 943 in the light of reanalyses of the history of the Nineteenth and Twentieth dynasties makes it apparent that the conventional Rameses II accession date of 1279 is untenable. First, it seems clear that Amenmeses's reign was entirely contained within that of Sethy II, removing four years from the conventional year count of the Nineteenth Dynasty.[25] Second, as discussed in Chapter 1, the conventional linear succession of Rameses IX-X-XI should almost certainly be replaced by a scheme that overlaps the reign of Rameses XI with those of Rameses IX and X, resulting in a further decade and a half being lost from the 'traditional' year-count. The interlocking sets of documentation available from Deir el-Medina allow no credible substantive compensatory upward adjustments to other Nineteenth/Twentieth Dynasty reign lengths and, as a result, it becomes arithmetically all but impossible to fill up the period between 1279 and 943 other than by gratuitously extending reigns during the Twenty-first Dynasty, where none of the reigns is of certainly known length (cf. Chapter 2). However, the paucity of material from the period points toward contracting them toward their minimum attested lengths, rather than extending them.[26] It therefore follows that the lower options for Rameses II's accession, based on potential reductions in the AKL-derived chronology set out above, should be considered further.[27]

The most conservative (1265) accommodates the Amenmeses and Rameses IX/X/XI compressions, while also retaining a Twenty-first Dynasty without any significant lengthening of the roughly 130 years for the period from Nesibanebdjedet I to Pasebkhanut II that can be derived from a mixture of contemporary dates and Manetho.[28] Placing Rameses II's accession in 1265 also gives an exact day-match for the Year 52 new-moon notation, rather than the one-day error needed for 1279. The consequences

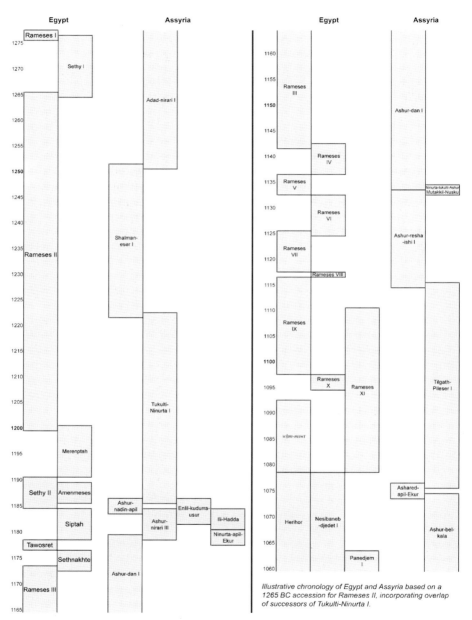

Fig. 134. Egyptian and Assyrian chronologies, based on a 1265 accession date for Rameses II.

for the chronologies of Rameside/early Third Intermediate Period Egypt and Assyria are shown in fig. 134. There would of course be corresponding reductions in date for the Eighteenth Dynasty (cf. Appendix 2).[29]

The yet lower options would permit a reduction of Twenty-first Dynasty reign lengths toward their contemporarily attested minima, but offer less satisfactory correlations with the new moon observation. Accordingly, the 1265 accession year for Rameses II and the 943 accession year for Shoshenq I have been adopted as the basis for the chronological structure proposed in this book and enshrined in the following two appendices. It is recognized, however, that both these 'hooks' continue to be potentially flawed. Thus, should new Assyrian and Palestinian data emerge to further undermine the validity of the AKL and the Biblical account of the period prior to Ahab, there is certainly scope for significant changes that might go some way to resolve some of the less than satisfactory loose ends that are a concomitant of the 1265/943 working hypothesis.[30]

Appendix 2

Outline Chronology of Ancient Egypt

LE = Lower Egypt only; UE = Upper Egypt

All dates are more or less uncertain prior to 690 BC (cf. Appendix 1).
Parentheses around a name and date indicate a co-ruler.

Early Dynastic Period
Dynasty 1	2900–2720 BC
Dynasty 2	2720–2580

Old Kingdom
Dynasty 3	2580–2515
Dynasty 4	2515–2405
Dynasty 5	2405–2275
Dynasty 6	2275–2120

First Intermediate Period
Dynasties 7/8	2120–2100
Dynasties 9/10 (LE)	2100–2000
Dynasty 11a (UE)	2080–2010

Middle Kingdom
Dynasty 11b	2010–1940
Dynasty 12	1940–1760
Dynasty 13	1760–1660

Second Intermediate Period
Dynasty 14 (LE)	1700–1650
Dynasty 15 (LE)	1650–1535
Dynasty 16 (UE)	1660–1590
Dynasty 17 (UE)	1585–1545

New Kingdom
Dynasty 18	
Ahmose I	1540–1516
Amenhotep I	1516–1496
Thutmose I	1496–1481
Thutmose II	1481–1468

Thutmose III	1468–1416
(Hatshepsut	1462–1447)
Amenhotep II	1415–1386
Thutmose IV	1386–1377
Amenhotep III	1377–1337
Akhenaten	1337–1321
(Smenkhkare	1325–1326)
(Neferneferuaten	1326–1319)
Tutankhamun	1321–1312
Ay	1311–1308
Horemheb	1308–1278

Dynasty 19

Rameses I	1278–1276
Sethy I	1276–1265
Rameses II	1265–1200
Merenptah	1200–1190
Sethy II	1190–1185
(Amenmeses	1189–1186)
Siptah	1186–1178
Tawosret	1178–1176

Dynasty 20

Sethnakhte	1176–1173
Rameses III	1173–1142
Rameses IV	1142–1136
Rameses V	1136–1132
Rameses VI	1132–1125
Rameses VII	1125–1118
Rameses VIII	1118–1116
Rameses IX	1116–1098
Rameses X	1098–1095
Rameses XI	1110–1095 (LE)+1095–1078

Third Intermediate Period

Dynasty 21

Herihor	1078–1065 (UE)
Nesibanebdjedet I	1078–1053 (LE)
Amenemnesut	1065–1049 (UE?)

Panedjem I	1063–1041 (UE)
Pasebkhanut I	1049–999
Amenemopet	1001–992
Osorkon the Elder	992–985
Siamun	985–967
Pasebkhanut II	967–941

Dynasty 22

Shoshenq I	943–922
Osorkon I	922–888
Takelot I	888–872
Osorkon II	872–831
Shoshenq III	831–791
Shoshenq IV	791–779
Pamiu	779–773
Shoshenq V	773–736

Dynasty 23

Osorkon IV	736–716+
Gemenefkhonsubak	
Padubast III	–666

Thebes

Horsieset I	–840?
Takelot II	834–810
Padubast I	824–800
Shoshenq VI	800–794
Osorkon III	791–762
Takelot III	768–753

South Delta(?)

Iuput I	810–799+
Padubast II	

Herakleopolis

Rudamun	753–
Peftjauawybast	–721

Hermopolis

Nimlot D	fl. 734
Thutemhat	

Leontopolis
Iuput II   fl. 734

Dynasty 24 (LE)
Tefnakhte   734–726
Bakenrenef   726–721

Dynasty 25
Kashta   –754
Piye   754–722
Shabaka   722–707
Shabataka   707–690
Taharqa   690–664
Tanutamun   664–656+

Saite Period
Dynasty 26
Nekau I   –664
Psamtik I   664–610
Nekau II   610–595
Psamtik II   595–589
Wahibre   589–570
Ahmose II   570–526
Psamtik III   526–525

Late Period
Dynasty 27 (Persians)   525–404
Dynasty 28   404–398
Dynasty 29   398–379
Dynasty 30   379–340
Dynasty 31 (Persians)   340–332

Hellenistic Period
Dynasty of Macedonia   332–310
Dynasty of Ptolemy   310–30

Roman Period   30 BC– AD 395

Appendix 3

Correlation of reigns, regnal years, and pontificates between Rameses IX and Psamtik I.

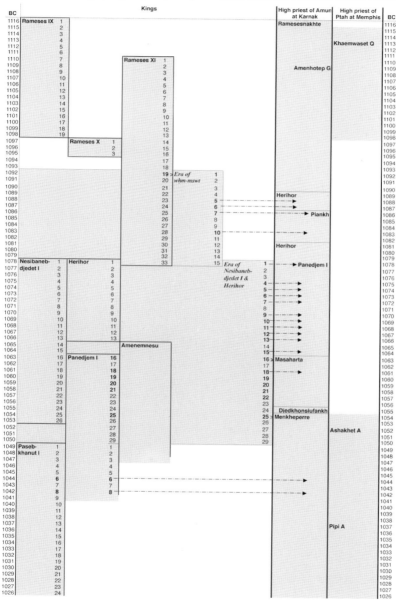

BC	Kings			High priest of Amun at Karnak	High priest of Ptah at Memphis	BC
1025	Paseb-	25		Menkheperre	Pipi A	1025
1024	khanut I	26				1024
1023		27				1023
1022		28				1022
1021		29			Horsieset J	1021
1020		30				1020
1019		31				1019
1018		32				1018
1017		33				1017
1016		34				1016
1015		35				1015
1014		36				1014
1013		37				1013
1012		38				1012
1011		39				1011
1010		40				1010
1009		41				1009
1008		42				1008
1007		43				1007
1006		44				1006
1005		45				1005
1004		46			Pipi B	1004
1003		47				1003
1002		48				1002
1001		49	Amenemopet 1			1001
1000		50	2			1000
999			3	Nesibanebdjedet II		999
998			4			998
997			5	Panedjem II		997
996			6			996
995			7			995
994			8			994
993			9			993
992	Osorkon	1	10			992
991	the Elder	2				991
990		3				990
989		4				989
988		3				988
987		4				987
986		5				986
985		6	Siamun 1			985
984			2			984
983			3			983
982			4			982
981			5			981
980			6		Ashakhet B	980
979			7			979
978			8			978
977			9			977
976			10			976
975			11			975
974			12			974
973			13	Pasebkhanut III/IV		973
972			14			972
971			15			971
970			16		Ankhefen	970
969			17		-sekhmet A	969
968			18			968
967	Paseb-	1	19			967
966	khanut II	2				966
965		3				965
964		4				964
963		5				963
962		6				962
961		7				961
960		8				960
959		9				959
958		10				958
957		11				957
956		12				956
955		13				955
954		14				954
953		15				953
952		16				952
951		17				951
950		18				950
949		19				949
948		20				948
947		21				947
946		22				946
945		23				945
944		24				944
943		25	Shoshenq I 1			943
942		26	2			942
941			3			941
940			4			940
939			5		Iuput A	939
938			6			938
937			7			937
936			8			936
935			9			935
934			10			934

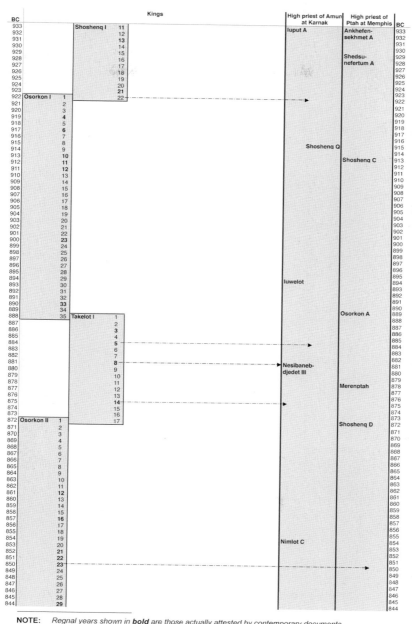

NOTE: Regnal years shown in **bold** are those actually attested by contemporary documents.

Arrows indicate synchronisms between individuals.

Unless marked by a solid line, transition-dates between pontificates are largely conjectural.

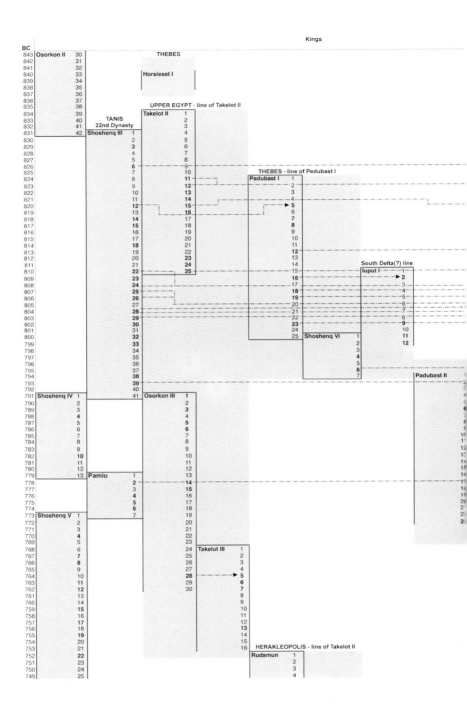

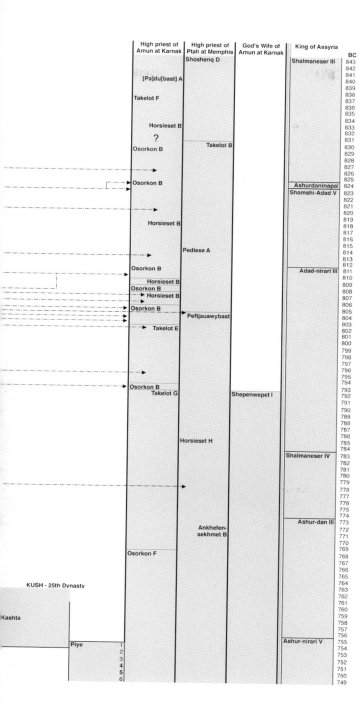

High priest of Amun at Karnak	High priest of Ptah at Memphis	God's Wife of Amun at Karnak	King of Assyria	BC
	Shoshenq D		Shalmaneser III	843
				842
[Pa]du[bast] A				841
				840
				839
Takelot F				838
				837
				836
				835
Horsieset B				834
				833
?				832
				831
Osorkon B	Takelot B			830
				829
				828
				827
				826
				825
Osorkon B			Ashurdaninapal	824
			Shamshi-Adad V	823
				822
				821
				820
Horsieset B				819
				818
				817
				816
				815
	Pediese A			814
				813
				812
Osorkon B			Adad-nirari III	811
				810
Horsieset B				809
Osorkon B				808
Horsieset B				807
				806
Osorkon B				805
	Peftjauawybast			804
				803
Takelot E				802
				801
				800
				799
				798
				797
				796
				795
				794
Osorkon B				793
Takelot G		Shepenwepet I		792
				791
				790
				789
				788
				787
				786
Horsieset H				785
				784
			Shalmaneser IV	783
				782
				781
				780
				779
				778
				777
				776
				775
				774
			Ashur-dan III	773
	Ankhefen-sekhmet B			772
				771
				770
Osorkon F				769
				768
				767
				766
				765
				764
				763
				762
				761
				760
				759
				758
				757
				756
			Ashur-nirari V	755
				754
				753
				752
				751
				750
				749

KUSH - 25th Dynasty

Kashta

Piye 1 2 3 4 5 6

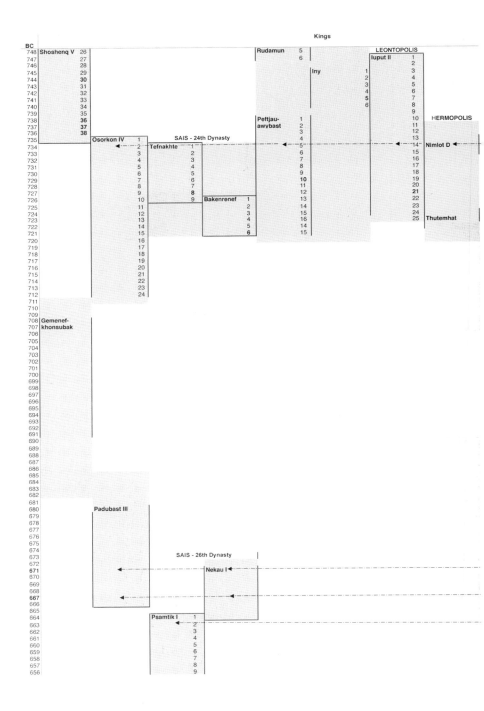

Kings

BC												
748	Shoshenq V	26					Rudamun	5		LEONTOPOLIS		
747		27						6		Iuput II	1	
746		28									2	
745		29					Iny		1		3	
744		30							2		4	
743		31							3		5	
742		32							4		6	
741		33							5		7	
740		34							6		8	
739		35									9	
738		36					Peftjau-	1			10	HERMOPOLIS
737		37					awybast	2			11	
736		38						3			12	
735			Osorkon IV	1	SAIS - 24th Dynasty			4			13	Nimlot D
734				2	Tefnakhte	1		5			14	
733				3		2		6			15	
732				4		3		7			16	
731				5		4		8			17	
730				6		5		9			18	
729				7		6		10			19	
728				8		7		11			20	
727				9		8		12			21	
726				10		9	Bakenrenef	1	13		22	
725				11				2	14		23	
724				12				3	15		24	
723				13				4	16		25	Thutemhat
722				14				5	14			
721				15				6	15			
720				16								
719				17								
718				18								
717				19								
716				20								
715				21								
714				22								
713				23								
712				24								
711												
710												
709												
708	Gemenef-											
707	khonsubak											
706												
705												
704												
703												
702												
701												
700												
699												
698												
697												
696												
695												
694												
693												
692												
691												
690												
689												
688												
687												
686												
685												
684												
683												
682												
681												
680			Padubast III									
679												
678												
677												
676												
675												
674												
673					SAIS - 26th Dynasty							
672												
671							Nekau I					
670												
669												
668												
667												
666												
665												
664					Psamtik I	1						
663						2						
662						3						
661						4						
660						5						
659						6						
658						7						
657						8						
656						9						

200 APPENDICES

King of Egypt	Regnal year	High priest of Amun at Karnak	High priest of Ptah at Memphis	God's Wife of Amun at Karnak	King of Assyria	BC
Piye	7	Osorkon F	Takelot H	Shepenwepet I	Ashur-nirari V	748
	8					747
	9					746
	10				Tilgath-pileser III	745
	11					744
	12					743
	13					742
	14					741
	15					740
	16					739
	17					738
	18					737
	19					736
	20					735
	21					734
	22					733
	23					732
	24					731
	25					730
	26					729
	27					728
	28				Shalmaneser V	727
	29					726
	30					725
	31					724
	32					723
Shabaka	33 / 1				Sargon II	722
	2					721
	3					720
	4					719
	5					718
	6					717
	7		Horemakhet			716
	8					715
	9					714
	10					713
	11			Amenirdis I		712
	12					711
	13					710
	14					709
	15					708
Shabataka	16 / 1					707
	2					706
	3				Sennacherib	705
	4					704
	5					703
	6					702
	7					701
	8					700
	9					699
	10					698
	11					697
	12					696
	13					695
	14					694
	15					693
	16			Shepenwepet II		692
	17					691
Taharqa	18 / 1					690
	2					689
	3					688
	4					687
	5					686
	6					685
	7					684
	8					683
	9					682
	10				Esarhaddon	681
	11					680
	12					679
	13					678
	14					677
	15					676
	16					675
	17					674
	18					673
	19					672
	20					**671**
	21					670
	22				Ashurbanipal	669
	23					668
	24					**667**
	25					666
	26					665
Tanutamun	27 / 1					664
	2					**663**
	3					662
	4					661
	5					660
	6		Horkhebi			659
	7					658
	8					657
	9					656

Appendix 4

Hieroglyphic Titularies of Kings and God's Wives

In its developed form, which came into consistent use in the latter part of the Old Kingdom, the titulary of the king comprised five names and associated titles. The first was the Horus name, sometimes written inside an enclosure known as a *serekh*, and referring to the king as the incarnation of Horus, the patron of the monarchy. The second was the Nebti-name, referring to him as the protégé of the emblematic goddesses of Upper and Lower Egypt. The third is probably to be read as Golden Falcon, but its significance is unclear. The two remaining names were enclosed in oval cartouches, usually referred to as the prenomen and nomen. The former comprised an epithet incorporating the name of the sun god Re, the latter was usually the king's birth name. They were preceded respectively by the titles Dual King (later also Lord of the Two Lands) and Son of Re (later also Lord of Appearances).

In the earliest times, the Horus name was the most frequently used, but for much of Egyptian history the prenomen was the name used where space permitted only one to be fitted in. However, from the Twenty-first Dynasty onward, the nomen starts being found—on occasion—as the sole designation of a king, a practice that becomes particularly common during the Twenty-fifth and Twenty-sixth Dynasties.

The common use of the prenomen as a single name clearly derived from the fact that, with a few exceptions, each prenomen down to the end of the New Kingdom was unique, although generally following 'themes,' with particular patterns popular during a given period. For example, names on the patterns "X-$\underline{h}pr(w)$-r^c," "X-$m3^ct$-r^c," "X-$\underline{h}^c(w)$-r^c," and "X-$k3$-r^c" account for a large proportion of known prenomina, while Thutmose IV's prenomen, Menkheperure, was clearly intended as an *hommage* to that of his grandfather, the great Thutmose III (Menkheperre).

However, after the early Nineteenth Dynasty, the enduring prestige of Rameses II meant that his 'core' prenomen, Usermaatre, was incorporated into a number of successors' prenomina. These names were, however, accompanied by immutable epithets (prior to the late Eighteenth Dynasty purely optional and often variable) which made these derivative names nevertheless unique. Thus we have Rameses II: Usermaatre-setepenre; Rameses III: Usermaatre-meryamun; Rameses IV: Usermaatre-setepenamun; Rameses V: Usermaatre-sekheperenre; Rameses VII: Usermaatre-setepenre-meryamun; and Rameses VIII: Usermaatre-akhenamun. Following the cue of Rameses VI (who borrowed the core prenomen of Amenhotep III), the last Ramesides cast their nets wider. Rameses IX added '-setepenre' to Pepy II's Neferkare, Rameses XI '-setepenptah' to Sethy I's Menmaatre, and Rameses X adopted the wholly new Khepermaatre as his prenomen.

Fresh or long-unused prenomina were employed by most of the earlier kings of the Third Intermediate Period, although those of Pasebkhanut I and Osorkon the Elder differed only in the epithet used (Akheperre-setepenamun vs. -setepenre). However, under the Twenty-second Dynasty, Takelot I re-employed his grandfather Shoshenq I's Hedjkheperre-setepenre (itself copying the previously unused prenomen taken by Nesibanebdjedet I) without change, after only three fallow decades. Both Osorkon II and Shoshenq III used Usermaatre, but while they were usually respectively '-setepenamun' and '-setepenre,' Shoshenq was occasionally '-setepenre,' making it necessary to have both prenomen and nomen present to be sure which king is involved. Shoshenq IV resurrected Hedjkheperre-setepenre once again, and in this case the only way to tell him from Shoshenq I was by the fact that the nomen of Shoshenq IV included the additional epithets '-sibast' and '-netjerheqaon.' These were taken directly from the nomen of Shoshenq III, and reflected a new feature introduced into nomina by Osorkon II: an epithet proclaiming the king the son of a goddess, usually Bastet, but sometimes Isis. The choice of goddess seems generally to reflect the northern or southern dominion of the king in question, but this is not always clear—cf. the debate as to whether '-sibast' versus '-sieset' is enough to distinguish between Usermaatre-setepenamun Padubast-*sibast*-meryamun and Usermaatre-setepenamun Padubast-*sieset*-meryamun (see p. 123).

These somewhat overblown sets of names were replaced progressively during the eighth century by much simpler ones based on Old and Middle Kingdom prototypes. Thus, although he used on occasion the long-form cartouches Akheperre-setepenre Shoshenq-sibast-meryamun-neterheqawaset, Shoshenq V was more usually simply Akheperre Shoshenq. In addition, the Horus, Nebti, and Golden Falcon names, which had become in the Eighteenth Dynasty extended and variable policy statements,[31] went back to being short mottoes, once again on ancient patterns. This practice would endure until the end of the Late Period.

This development of royal names during the Third Intermediate Period accordingly allows some assessment to be made of the likely placement of 'new' kings of doubtful affiliation. Thus, unique names of New Kingdom pattern should generally be placed prior to Osorkon II, 'complex' ones with banal prenomina should be placed between the mid-ninth and mid-eighth centuries, with 'simple' names of archaic pattern placed in the eighth century or later.

One other feature to be noted of royal names of the Third Intermediate Period is the adoption of double cartouches by at least some God's Wives of Amun. A prenomen, usually incorporating the name of the goddess Mut, was used by a number of the God's Wives, starting with Maatkare A (Mutemhat), with Neitiqerti I even on occasion affecting a Horus name. This development was combined with the addition of queenly titles, some of distinctly archaic nature, to the God's Wives titularies, which taken together reflected their ultimate position as second only to the pharaoh in status.

Names & titularies of kings and principal God's Wives of Amun of

Ahmose II

H.

Nb.

G.

P.

N.

Alara

N.

Amenemnesut

P.

N.

Amenemopet

P.

N.

Amenirdis I

P.

N.

Ankhnesneferibre

P.

N.

Bakenrenef

P.

N.

This list gives the principal variants and variant orthographies of the royal names of the period covered by this book. However, for reasons of space it has not proved possible to illustrate all variants, particularly where interchangeable signs are concerned. For more comprehensive coverage, see Gauthier 1914 and von Beckerath 1999

Ahmose II

H.   *smn-m^3^{c}t*

Nb. *s^3-nt spd-t^{3}wi*

G.   *stp-ntrw*

P.   *ḫnm-ib-r^c*

N.   *i^{c}ḥ-ms s^3-nt*

Alara

N.   *ilri*

Amenemnesut

P.   *nfr-k^3-r^c ḥq^3-w^{3}st*

N.   *imn-m-nsw mr-imn*

Amenemopet

P.   *wsr-m^3^{c}t-r^c stp-n-imn*

N.   *imn-m-ipt mr-imn*

Amenirdis I

P.   *ḫ^c-nfrw-mwt*

N.   *imn-ir-di.s*

Ankhnesneferibre

P.   *ḥk^3-nfrw-mwt*

N.   *^{c}nḫ-n.s-nfr-ib-r^c*

Bakenrenef

P.   *w^{3}ḥ-k^3-r^c*

N.   *b^3-kn-rn.f*

Gemenefkhonsubak

H.

P.

N.

Herihor

H.

Nb.

G.

P.

N.

Horsieset I

H.

P.

N.

Iuput I

N.

Iuput II

P.

N.

Karomama G

P.

N.

Kashta

P.

N.

Gemenefkhonsubak

H. *sꜥnḫ-tꜣwi*

P. *špss-kꜣ-rꜥ ir-n-rꜥ*

N. *gm-n.f-ḫnsw-bꜣk*

Herihor

H. *kꜣ-nḫt sꜣ-imn*

Nb. *sḥtp-nṯrw / swꜥb-bnbn-mḥ-sw-m-mnw*

G. *iri-ꜣḥw(t)-m-iptswt-n-it.f-imn / iri-mꜣꜥt-m-ḫt-tꜣwi*

P. *ḥm-nṯr-tpy-n-imn*

N. *ḥri-ḥr sꜣ-imn*

Horsieset I

H. *kꜣ-nḫt ḫꜥ-m-wꜣst*

P. *ḥḏ-ḫpr-rꜥ stp-n-imn*

N. *ḥr-sꜣ-ꜣst mr-imn*

Iuput I

N. *iwpwti mr-imn*

Iuput II

P. *wsr-mꜣꜥt-rꜥ stp-n-imn / rꜥ*

N. *iwpwt sꜣ-bꜣstt mr-imn*

Karomama G

P. *mwt-m-ḫꜣt sꜣt-imn*

N. *kꜣrmꜥmꜥ mr(t)-mwt*

Kashta

P. *(n-)mꜣꜥt-rꜥ*

N. *kꜣštꜣ*

Maatkare A

P.

N.

Neitiqerti I

P.

N.

Nekau I

P.

N.

Nekau II

H.

Nb.

G.

P.

N.

Nesibanebdjedet I

H.

Nb.

G.

P.

N.

Nimlot D

N.

Osorkon the Elder

P.

N. ?

Maatkare A

P.   *mwt-m-ḥȝt*

N.   *mȝꜥt-kȝ-rꜥ*

Neitiqerti I

P.   *nb(t)nfrw-mwt*

N.   *nt-iḳrt*

Nekau I

P.   *mn-ḫpr-rꜥ*

N.   *nkȝw*

Nekau II

H.   *mȝꜥ-ib*

Nb.   *mȝꜥ-ḫrw*

G.   *mr-nṯrw*

P.   *wḥm-ib-rꜥ*

N.   *nkȝw*

Nesibanebdjedet I

H.   *kȝ-nḫt mry-rꜥ swsr-imn-ḫpš.f-r-sqȝi-mȝꜥt*

Nb.   *sḫm-pḥti ḥwi-rqiw.f-bḥȝtw.f ḥtp-m-[...]*

G.   *[...]-ḫsf-dndn*

P.   *ḥḏ-ḫpr-rꜥ stp-n-rꜥ*

N.   *nsi-bȝ-(nb-)ḏdt mr-imn*

Nimlot D

N.   *nmlt*

Osorkon the Elder

P.   *ꜥȝ-ḫpr-rꜥ stp-n-rꜥ* / *ꜥȝ-ḫpr-rꜥ stp-n-imn*

N.   *wȝsȝirkn mr-imn*

Osorkon I

H.

Nb.

G.

P.

N.

Osorkon II

H.

Nb.

G.

P.

N.

Osorkon III

H.

Nb.

G.

P.

N.

Osorkon IV

P.

N.

Padinemty

N.

Padubast I

P.

N.

Osorkon I

H.   *k3-nḫt mry-rꜥ rdi.n-sw-itm-ḥr-nst.f-r-grg-t3wi*

Nb. *sꜥ3-ḫprw wr-bi3wt*

G.   *nḫt-ḫpš dr-pḏt-9*

P.   *sḫm-ḫpr-rꜥ stp-n-rꜥ*

N.   *w3s3irkn mr-imn*

Osorkon II

H.   *k3-nḫt mry-m3ꜥt sḫꜥ-sw-rꜥ-r-nsw-t3wi / k3-nḫt ḫꜥ-m-w3st*

Nb. *sm3-psšti-mi-s3-3st sḥtp-nṯrw / sm3-psšti-mi-s3-3st dmḏ.f-sḫmti-
                                                        -m-ḥtp*

G.   *wr-pḥti ḥwi-mnṯyw / sḫm-pḥti ḥwi-ḫftiw.f wsr 3w.f*

P.   *wsr-m3ꜥt-rꜥ stp-n-imn*

N.   *w3s3irkn s3-b3stt mr-imn*

Osorkon III

H.   *k3-nḫt ḫꜥ-m-w3st*

Nb. *st-ib-t3wi*

G.   *ms-nṯrw*

P.   *wsr-m3ꜥt-rꜥ stp-n-rꜥ*

N.   *w3srkn s3-3st mr-imn*

Osorkon IV

P.   *wsr-m3ꜥt-rꜥ*

N.   *w3srknw*

Padinemty

N.   *p3-di-nmty*

Padubast I

P.   *wsr-m3ꜥt-rꜥ stp-n-imn*

N.   *p3-di-b3stt mr-imn / p3-di-b3stt s3-3st mr-imn*

Padubast II

P.

N.

Padubast III

H.

G.

P.

N.

Pamiu

P.

N.

Panedjem I

H.

P.

N.

Pasebkhanut I

H.

Nb.

G.

P.

N.

Pasebkhanut II

P.

N.

Peftjauawybast

P.

N.

Padubast II

P.　*wsr-mꜣꜥt-rꜥ stp-n-imn*

N.　*pꜣ-di-bꜣstt mr-imn / pꜣ-di-bꜣstt sꜣ-bꜣstt mr-imn*

Padubast III

H.　*[...]-tꜣwi*

G.　*sḥtp-nṯrw*

P.　*sḥtp-ib-n-rꜥ*

N.　*pꜣ-di-bꜣstt*

Pamiu

P.　*wsr-mꜣꜥt-rꜥ stp-n-imn / rꜥ*

N.　*pꜣ-miy mr-imn*

Panedjem I

H.　*kꜣ-nḫt mr-imn / kꜣ-nḫt ḫꜥ-m-wꜣst*

P.　*ḫꜥ-ḫpr-rꜥ stp-n-imn*

N.　*pꜣy-nḏm mr-imn*

Pasebkhanut I

H.　*kꜣ-nḫt-m-ꜥwi-imn wsr-fꜣw sḫꜥi-m-wꜣst*

Nb.　*wr-mnw-m-iptswt*

G.　*smꜣ-ḫprw dr-pḏt-9 iṯi-m-sḫm.f-tꜣw-nbw*

P.　*ꜥꜣ-ḫpr-rꜥ stp-n-imn / ꜥꜣ-ḫpr-rꜥ mry-imn / ḥm-nṯr-tpy-n-imn*

N.　*pꜣ-sbꜣ-ḫꜥ-n-niwt mry-imn*

Pasebkhanut II

P.　*tit-ḫprw-rꜥ stp-n-rꜥ*

N.　*pꜣ-sbꜣ-ḫꜥ-n-niwt mry-imn / ḥr-pꜣ-sbꜣ-ḫꜥ-(n-)niwt mry-imn*

Peftjauawybast

P.　*nfr-kꜣ-rꜥ*

N.　*pf-ṯꜣw-ꜥwy-bꜣstt*

Piye

H.
Nb.
G.
P.
N.

Psamtik I

H.
Nb.
G.
P.
N.

Psamtik II

H.
Nb.
G.
P.
N.

Psamtik III

P.
N.

Rameses IX

H.
Nb.
G.
P.
N.

Piye

H. *kȝ-nḫt ḫʿ-m-npt / smȝ-tȝwi / sḥtp-tȝwy.f / kȝ-tȝwi.f / kȝ-nḫt ḫʿ-m-wȝst*

Nb. *wȝḥ-nsyt-mi-rʿ-m-pt / ms-ḥmwt / ḥkȝ-kmt*

G. *ḏsr-ḫʿw sḫm-pḥti / sʿšȝ-knw*

P. *mn-ḫpr-rʿ / wsr-mȝʿt-rʿ / snfr-rʿ*

N. *p{ʿnḫ}y-mr-imn / p{ʿnḫ]y-mr-imn-sȝ-bȝstt*

Psamtik I

H. *ʿȝ-ib*

Nb. *nb-ʿ*

G. *knw*

P. *wȝḥ-ib-rʿ*

N. *psmtk*

Psamtik II

H. *mnḫ-ib*

Nb. *wsr-ʿ*

G. *snfr-tȝwi*

P. *nfr-ib-rʿ*

N. *psmtk*

Psamtik III

P. *ʿnḫ-kȝ-rʿ*

N. *psmtk*

Rameses IX

H. *kȝ-nḫt ḫʿ-m-wȝst*

Nb. *wsr-ḫpš sʿnḫ-tȝwi*

G. *wsr-rnpwt-mi-rʿ-ḏt*

P. *nfr-kȝ-rʿ stp-n-rʿ*

N. *rʿ-mss ḫʿ-m-wȝst mrr-imn*

Rameses X

H.

P.

N.

Rameses XI

H.

Nb.

G.

P.

N.

Rudamun

P.   /

N.   /

Shabaka

H.

Nb.

G.

P.

N.   /

Shabataka

H.   /   /

Nb.   /   /

G.   /

P.

N.   /

Rameses X

H. *kȝ-nḫt sḫꜥꜥ-rꜥ*

P. *ḫpr-mȝꜥt-rꜥ stp-n-rꜥ*

N. *rꜥ-mss imn-(ḥr-)ḫpš.f mr-imn*

Rameses XI

H. *kȝ-nḫt mr-rꜥ*

Nb. *wsr-ḫpš ḥd-ḫfnw*

G. *wr-pḥti sꜥnḫ-tȝwi ity ḥrw-ḥir-mȝꜥt*

P. *mn-mȝꜥt-rꜥ stp-n-ptḥ*

N. *rꜥ-mss ḫꜥ-m-wȝst mrr-imn nṯr-ḥqȝ-iwnw*

Rudamun

P. *wsr-mȝꜥt-rꜥ / wsr-mȝꜥt-rꜥ stp-n-imn*

N. *rwḏ-imn / rwḏ-imn mr-imn*

Shabaka

H. *sbḳ-tȝwi*

Nb. *sbḳ-tȝwi*

G. *sbḳ-tȝwi*

P. *nfr-kȝ-rꜥ*

N. *šȝbȝkȝ mr-imn / šȝbȝkȝ*

Shabataka

H. *ḏd-ḫꜥ / ḏd-ḫꜥw / kȝ-nḫt ḫꜥ-m-wȝst*

Nb. *ḏd-ḫꜥ / ꜥȝ-šft-m-tȝw-nb(w) / sḫꜥ-mȝꜥt-mry-tȝwi*

G. *ꜥȝ-ḫpš ḥw-pḏt-9 / ḥrw-ḥr-nḫtw*

P. *ḏd-kȝw-rꜥ*

N. *šȝbȝtȝkȝ-mr-imn / šȝbȝtȝkȝ*

Shepenwepet I

P.

N.

Shepenwepet II

P.

N.

Shoshenq I

H.

Nb.

G.

P.   ?* /   /   /

N.

Shoshenq IIa

P.

N.

Shoshenq III

H.

P.   /

N.   /

Shoshenq IV

P.

N.

---

* Or the prenomen of a separare king Shoshenq IIb

Shepenwepet I

P. *ḥnm(t)-ib-imn*

N. *šp-(n-)wpt mr-mwt*

Shepenwepet II

P. *ḥnwt-nfrw-mwt*

N. *šp-n-wpt*

Shoshenq I

H. *kꜣ-nḫt mr-rꜥ sḫꜥ.f-m-nsw-r-smꜣ-tꜣwi*

Nb. *ḫꜥ-m-sḫmti-mi-ḥr-sꜣ-ꜣst sḥtp-nṯrw-n-mꜣꜥt*

G. *sḫm-pḥti ḥwi-pḏt-9 wr-nḫtw-m-tꜣw-nbw*

P. *twt-ḫpr-rꜥ [...]-n-[...]* / *ḥḏ-ḫpr-rꜥ stp-n-rꜥ* / *ḥḏ-ḫpr-rꜥ stp-n-imn* /

N. *ššnq mr-imn*   *ḥḏ-ḫpr-rꜥ stp-n-ptḥ*

Shoshenq IIa

P. *ḥqꜣ-ḫpr-rꜥ stp-n-rꜥ*

N. *ššnq mr-imn*

Shoshenq III

H. *kꜣ-nḫt mstiw-rꜥ*

P. *wsr-mꜣꜥt-rꜥ stp-n-rꜥ* / *wsr-mꜣꜥt-rꜥ stp-n-imn*

N. *ššnq sꜣ-bꜣstt mr-imn nṯr-ḥqꜣ-iwnw*

Shoshenq IV

P. *ḥḏ-ḫpr-rꜥ stp-n-rꜥ*

N. *ššnq sꜣ-bꜣstt mr-imn nṯr-ḥqꜣ-iwnw*

Shoshenq V

H.

Nb.

G.

P.

N.

Shoshenq VI

P.

N.

Siamun

H.

P.

N.

Taharqa

H.

Nb.

G.

P.

N.

Takelot I

P.

N.

Takelot II

H.

P.

N.

Shoshenq V

H.   *wsr-pḥtì / k₃-nḫt ḫꜥ-m-w₃st*

Nb.   *wsr-pḥtì*

G.   *wsr-pḥtì*

P.   *ꜥ₃-ḫpr-rꜥ / ꜥ₃-ḫpr-rꜥ stp-n-rꜥ*

N.   *ššnk / ššnk-s₃-b₃stt-mr-imn-nṯr-ḥk₃-w₃st*

Shoshenq VI

P.   *wsr-m₃ꜥt-rꜥ mr-imn*

N.   *šš(n)k-mr-imn*

Siamun

H.   *k₃-nḫt mr-m₃ꜥt s₃-mr-n-imn prì-m-ḫ₃w.f*

P.   *nṯr-ḫpr-rꜥ stp-n-imn / nṯr-ḫpr-rꜥ mr-imn*

N.   *s₃-imn mr-imn*

Taharqa

H.   *k₃-ḫꜥw*

Nb.   *k₃-ḫꜥw*

G.   *ḫw-t₃wì*

P.   *ḫw-nfrtm-rꜥ*

N.   *t₃hrk*

Takelot I

P.   *ḥḏ-ḫpr-rꜥ*

N.   *tìklt mr-imn*

Takelot II

H.   *k₃-nḫt ḫꜥ-m-w₃st*

P.   *ḥḏ-ḫpr-rꜥ stp-n-rꜥ / ḥḏ-ḫpr-rꜥ stp-n-rꜥ nṯr-ḥk₃-w₃st*

N.   *tklt s₃-₃st mr-imn*

Takelot III

H.

Nb.

G.

P.

N.

Tanutamun

H.

P.

N.

Tefnakhte

H.

Nb.

P.

N.

Thutemhat

P.

N.

Wahibre

H.

Nb.

G.

P.

N.

Takelot III

H. *w3ḏ-tꜥwi* / *nb-m3ꜥt-ḫrw* / *ꜥ3-b3w*

Nb. *w3ḏ-t3wi* / *ḥkn-m-m3ꜥt* / *iṯ-t3wi*

G. *w3ḏ-t3wi*

P. *wsr-m3ꜥt-rꜥ* / *wsr-m3ꜥt-rꜥ stp-n-imn*

N. *tklt* / *tklt s3-3st mr-imn*

Tanutamun

H. *w3ḥ-mrwt*

P. *b3-k3-rꜥ*

N. *t3nwt-imn*

Tefnakhte

H. *si3-ḫt*

Nb. *si3-ḫt*

P. *špss-rꜥ*

N. *t3.f nḫt*

Thutemhat

P. *nfr-ḫpr-rꜥ ḫꜥ-ḫꜥ(w)*

N. *ḏhwti-m-ḥ3t*

Wahibre

H. *w3ḥ-ib*

Nb. *nb-ḫpš*

G. *sw3ḏ-t3wi*

P. *ḥꜥꜥ-ib-rꜥ*

N. *w3ḥ-ib-rꜥ*

Appendix 5.1
Genealogy: Twentieth/Twenty-first Dynasties

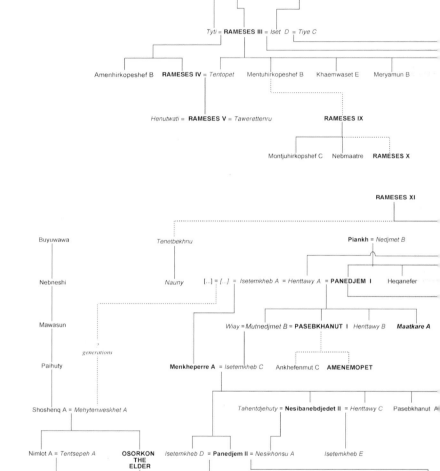

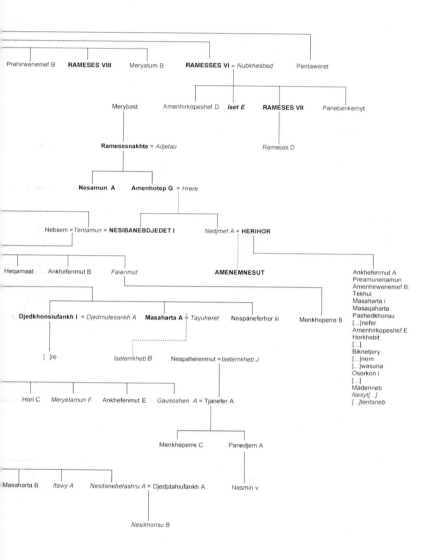

Prehirwenemef B **RAMESES VIII** Meryatum B **RAMESSES VI** = *Nubkhesbed* Pentaweret

Merybast Amenhirkopeshef D *Iset E* **RAMESES VII** Panebenkemyt

Ramesesnakhte = *Adjetau*

Rameses D

Nesamun A **Amenhotep G** = *Hrere*

Nebseni = *Tentamun* = **NESIBANEBDJEDET I** *Nedjmet A* = **HERIHOR**

Heqamaat Ankhefenmut B *Faienmut* **AMENEMNESUT**

Ankhefenmut A
Preamunenamun
Amenhirwenemef B:
Tekhui
Masaharta i
Masaqaharta
Pashedkhonsu
[...]nefer
Amenhirkopeshef E
Horkhebit
[...]
Biknetjery
[...]nem
[...]wasuna
Osorkon i
[...]
Madenneb
Nesyt[...]
[...]tentaneb

Djedkhonsiufankh I = *Djedmutesankh A* **Masaharta A** = *Tayuheret* Nespaneferhor iii Menkheperre B

[...]re *Isetemkheb B* Nespaherenmut = *Isetemkheb J*

Hori C *Meryetamun F* Ankhefenmut E *Gausoshen A* = Tjanefer A

Menkheperre C Panedjem A

Masaharta B *Itawy A* *Nesitanebetashru A* = Djedptahiufankh A Nesmin v

Nesikhonsu B

Appendix 5.2
Genealogy: Twenty-second Dynasty

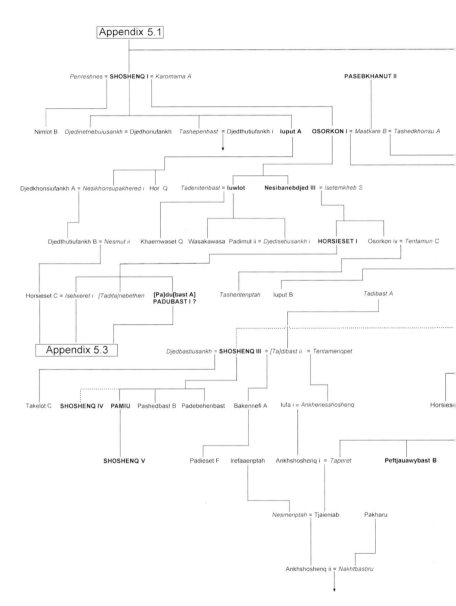

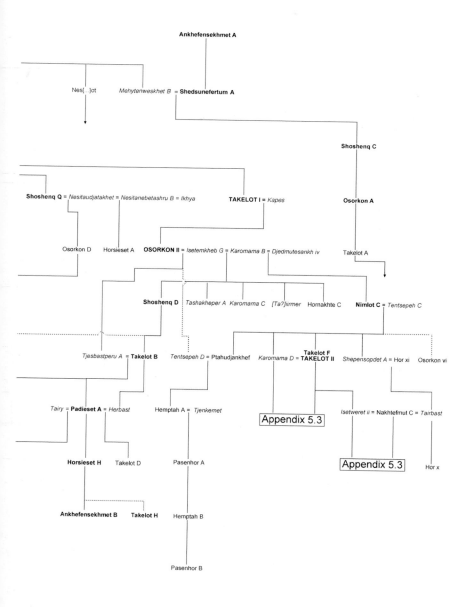

Appendix 5.3

Appendix 5.3

Appendix 5.3
Genealogy: Family of Takelot II

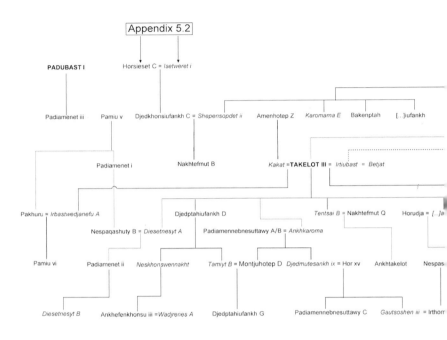

Appendix 5.4
Genealogy: Twenty-fifth Dynasty

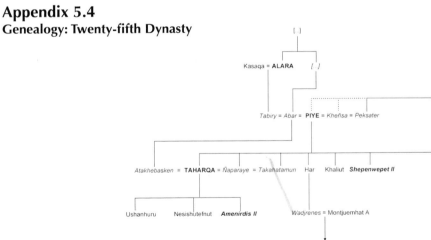

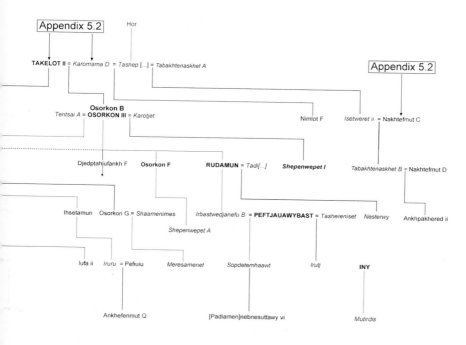

Appendix 5.2

Hor

TAKELOT II = Karomama D = Tashep [...] = Tabakhtenaskhet A

Appendix 5.2

Osorkon B
Tentsai A = **OSORKON III** = Karotjet

Nimlot F   Isetweret ii = Nakhtefmut C

Djedptahiufankh F   **Osorkon F**   **RUDAMUN** = Tadi[...]   **Shepenwepet I**   Tabakhtenaskhet B = Nakhtefmut D

Ihsetamun Osorkon G = Shaamenimes   Irbastwedjanefu B = **PEFTJAUAWYBAST** = Tashereniset   Nesterwy   Ankhpakhered ii

Shepenwepet A

Iufa ii   Iruru = Pefiuiu   Meresamenet   Sopdetemhaawt   Irutj   **INY**

Ankhefenmut Q   [Padiamen]nebnesuttawy vi   Mutirdis

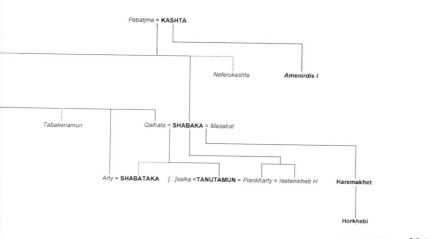

Pebatjma = **KASHTA**

Neferukashta   **Amenirdis I**

Tabakenamun   Qalhata = **SHABAKA** = Masabat

Arty = **SHABATAKA**   [...]salka = **TANUTAMUN** = Piankharty = Isetemkheb H   **Haremakhet**

Horkhebi

Appendix 5.5
Genealogy: Twenty-sixth Dynasty

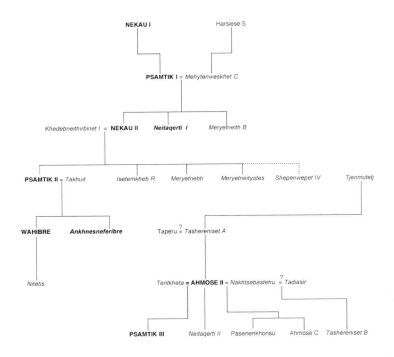

SOURCES OF IMAGES

All images by Aidan Dodson, except as follows:
5.   Caminos 1974: II, pl. 89.
6.   Nims 1948: pl. viii.
7.   Maspero 1889: pl. xb.
14. Drawing: adapted from Epigraphic Survey 1981: pl. 115–25, 135B, 137B; photograph: author.
15. Epigraphic Survey 1981: pl. 121B.
19. © Trustees of the British Museum.
20. Epigraphic Survey 1979: pl. 26.
21. Epigraphic Survey 1979: pl. 28.
28. Lepsius 1849–59: III, pl. 251[h, i, k].
31. Montet 1951: pl. lxxii.
35. After Romer [1979]: 19 and Ciccarello [1979].
36. Daressy 1909: pl. xlii.
37. Maspero and Brugsch 1881.
39. Maspero and Brugsch 1881: pl. 12.
42. Abdallah 1984: pl. xvii, courtesy Egyptian Museum.
43. Daressy 1909: pl. xxvi.
44. Moberly Bell 1888: 63.
50. © Trustees of the British Museum.
51. Lepsius 1849–59: III, pl. 258c.
52. Mariette 1857: pl. 31.
53. Adapted from Kruchten 1989: pl. 17–18.
55. Montet 1947: pl. ix[A].
58. Daressy 1909: pl. xlii-iii; Maspero and Brugsch 1881.

59. Photograph author/facsimile: Murray 1904: pl. xxi.
60. Rosellini 1834–36: pl. cxxvi[7].
64. Salima Ikram.
65. Ägyptologisches Institut der Universität Heidelberg.
67. Epigraphic Survey 1954: pl. 11C.
69. Adapted from Caminos 1952: pl. x–xiii.
72. Ägyptologisches Institut der Universität Heidelberg.
78. Budge 1909: pl. xxviii.
79. Adapted from Montet 1939: pl. xcii.
80. Montage by author after Bothmer 1960: pl. iii & vi[1].
81. © Trustees of the British Museum.
83. Naville 1892: frontispiece.
85. Salima Ikram.
89. Flinders Petrie, courtesy Egypt Exploration Society.
90. Mariette 1857: pl. 24.
92. Epigraphic Survey 1954: pl. 16–19.
95. Montet 1960: pl. xlix a.
96. Centre franco-égyptien d'Étude des Temples de Karnak.
102. Fazzini 1997: 137, fig. 4, courtesy Egyptian Museum.
103. Martin Davies.
104. Adapted from Caminos 1998: I, pl. 15, 18–19.
105. Ole Haupt, Ny Carlsberg Glyptotek.
108. Benson and Gourlay 1899: pl. xx[1], xxii[5]; Foucart 1924: pl. ix[B].
111. Adapted from Naville and Griffith 1890: pl. i.
114. Petrie 1925: 314, fig. 133.
119. Lepsius 1849–59: V, pl. 4c.
122. Dyan Hilton.
123. Martin Davies.
127. Adapted from Schweinfurth 1886: pl. ii.

NOTES

Notes to Preface

1   Dodson 2009a; 2010.
2   E.g., Spencer and Spencer 1986 and Aston 1989, which presented a fundamentally different model for the localization of the royal lines of the second half of the period; and various works by Karl Jansen-Winkeln.
3   James 1991; Rohl 1995; Morkot and James 2009; Thijs 2010. In the 1950s through 1970s, Immanuel Velikovsky (cf. Bauer 1984) had attempted a vastly more radical reordering of ancient history, making the Manethonic Twenty-sixth Dynasty Nechaô identical with Rameses II (rather than the usual Nekau II) and the Thirtieth Dynasty Nectanebês none other than Rameses III!
4   Often by lazily dubbing them the "sons of Velikovsky"—in spite of the fact that the "new radicals" had already unequivocally disowned his results.
5   E.g., Dodson 1996.
6   For an example, see note 7 below.
7   Dodson 1993b, taking as its starting point observations by the 'ultra radical' David Rohl (1986: 17–18 n. 2; 1989/90: 66–67).
8   Dodson 1987b; this was finally disproved by Payraudeau 2008; cf. Dodson 2009b: 103.
9   Dodson 2001 and Dodson and Hilton 2010: 195–240.
10   On the basis that much of it is without independent verification in the form of contemporary monuments and records.

Notes to Introduction

1   Ryholt 1997; Marée 2010: 127–31.
2   W.V. Davies 2003; 2005: 49–50.
3   D.B. Redford 2006; Weinstein 1998.
4   Spalinger 2006; O'Connor 1998.
5   Murnane 1990.

6 Including the dispatch of food aid from Egypt to Hatti under Merenptah (cf. Bryce 1998: 364–65).
7 Cf. Oren 2000.
8 Kitchen 1990a.
9 See Dodson 2010.
10 Cf. Frandsen 1991.
11 For one recent reconstruction of the events see S. Redford 2002. A 2011 television presentation of a CAT scan of Rameses III's mummy has stated that the king's throat appears to show a deep knife wound that reached his spine.
12 On the order of succession, cf. Kitchen 1972; 1982.
13 For whom, see Peden 1994a.
14 Cf. G.E. Smith, 1912: 90–92; on the other hand Černý confidently believed that Rameses V had been cut off prematurely by his successor (1965: 8–11).
15 Amer 1985.

Notes to Chapter One

1 Although cf. Kitchen 1972 and 1982 for the once fierce debates over the issue. It has now been established that queen Tyti was a wife of Rameses III (and mother of Rameses IV), rather than the spouse of a later king of the dynasty as had on occasion been proposed (see Collier, Dodson, and Hamernik 2010).
2 Kitchen 1968–90: VI, 463–65.
3 Kitchen 1984. The Montjuhirkopeshef (B) who was the son of Rameses III is likely to have been the prince of that name who was buried secondarily in tomb KV13; here he lay alongside an Amenhirkopeshef who was probably a son of Rameses VI. The tomb seems to have been appropriated under the latter, since a fragmentary text in the tomb names Queen Nubkhesbed, wife of Rameses VI (Altenmüller 1994: 5–6 who, however, associates the text with Montjuhirkopeshef's interment).
4 Kitchen 1968–90: VI, 465–67.
5 pTurin 2084 (Kitchen 1968–90: VI, 605): ro. 3.10; oCairo CG25236 (Kitchen 1968–90: VI, 839–40): see Gutgesell 1983: 246 n. 1.
6 pBM EA10221 [pAbbott] (Kitchen 1968–90: VI, 468–81, 764–67): §4.15–16; Nebmaatrenakhte may have been the northern vizier, in Thebes on a special commission (cf. Gnirs 1996: 202), and potentially identical with the southern vizier of the name under Rameses XI.
7 Kitchen 1968–90: VI, 525–27.
8 Cf. Reisner 1920: 50–52; Amer 1999: 28.
9 Kitchen 1968–90: VI, 527–28.
10 Khartoum 1847.
11 Kitchen 1968–90: VI, 451–55.
12 Kitchen 1968–90: VI, 543–53; Bács 1998; 2011.
13 Hori, Cairo JE29334–5; Setau, el-Kab tomb 4 (Kitchen 1968–90: VI, 554–58).
14 Wildung 1977: 1261.
15 See ch. 1, n. 6.
16 pBM EA10221: §1.1–4.10.

17 pBM EA10221: §4.11–5.11.
18 Porter and Moss 1960–64: 756.
19 pAmherst VI + pBrussels E6867 [pLeopold II-Amherst] (Kitchen 1968–90: VI, 481–89): §3.15.
20 Porter and Moss 1960–64: 268–71; Seele 1959.
21 Not yet identified.
22 pBM EA10054 (Kitchen 1968–90: VI, 489–97, 743–46): *vo.*1, *ro.*1–3.6; the date on the papyrus was initially misread as 'day 14' (Peet 1930: 60, cf. 57–58), but later correctly interpreted as 'day 19' (Capart, Gardiner, and van de Walle 1936: 184).
23 pBM EA10054: *ro.*2.1–6, *vo.*5–6.
24 pBM EA10221: §5.12–6.24.
25 pBM EA10221: §7.1–7.16: cf. Peet 1930: 32–36.
26 pAmherst VI + pBrussels E6867.
27 pBM EA10052 (Kitchen 1968–90: VI, 767–803): §8.17–24.
28 pBM EA10053 [pHarris A] (Kitchen 1968–90: VI, 755–63): *ro.*1–7.
29 pTurin C.2009+2029+2073+2076+2078+2082–3+2088+2096–7 [Turin Necropolis Journal] (Kitchen 1968–90: VI, 560–98): A *ro.*1–4; the loot is inventoried in pBM EA10068 (Kitchen 1968–90: VI, 747–55; J.J. Janssen 1992): *ro.*1–6.
30 Ibid B *ro.*7.
31 pBM EA10054: *ro.*3.7–17.
32 Based on pTurin C.2075+2056+2096 (Kitchen 1968–90: VI, 653–55, 681–84): see T. Schneider 2000: 81.
33 Porter and Moss 1960–64: 501–505; Abitz 1990; 1992.
34 Abitz 1990; 1992.
35 Mummy: Cairo unnumbered (Forbes 1998; 646–47; Graefe 2010: 59; Loring 2010: 70–71).
36 BM EA882; a number of *shabti*s (EA8570–1, 15304(?) and 34130) and a deity figure (EA61283) also derived from the king's funerary equipment (Reeves 1985).
37 Cf., conveniently, the list in T. Schneider 2000: 82–84.
38 The addition of a text to the bottom of the west face of the north tower and the usurpation of the stela of Rameses V in front of the south tower (Kitchen 1968–90: VI, 678).
39 Kitchen 1968–90: VI, 679.
40 Kitchen 1968–90: VI, 679.
41 Porter and Moss 1960–64: 545; Jenni 2000.
42 Kitchen 1968–90: VI, 680–81.
43 The suggestion that he actually had a nine-year reign (Parker 1957) is now generally rejected.
44 pTurin C.2075, 1900, 1932+1939 *ro.*, 1898 (Kitchen 1968–90: VI, 651–99); for discussion and additional bibliography, see T. Schneider 2000: 87–104; there are also fishermen's accounts running from the end of the reign of Rameses IX into Year 1 (pTurin C.2075+2056+2096—Kitchen 1968–90: VI, 653–55, 681–84).

45 pTurin C.2071+1960 (Kitchen 1968–90: VI, 633–44).

46 Manassa 2003.

47 Cf. Kitchen 1990a: 22.

48 Cf. the arrangements seen in various earlier tombs, where a corridor had been widened to turn it into a burial chamber: e.g., KV15 (Sethy II—see Dodson 2010: 33–34).

49 T. Schneider 2000: 104–108.

50 It is apparently used with this implication in the Horus name of Amenemhat I and one of the Nebti names of Sethy I.

51 pBM EA10052: §§1–4.

52 pBM EA10052: §§5–6 (see Collier, Dodson, and Hamernik 2010 for lost §§6.22–23); this papyrus contains further examinations in §§7–16, but it is not clear which tombs are involved.

53 pLiverpool M11162 [pMayer A] (Kitchen 1968–90: VI, 803–28): §4.3–4. On the identity of this queen, see p. 13.

54 pRochester 51.346.1 (Goelet 1996; Quack 2000); these thefts were attributed to the Doorkeeper Thuthotep, who also features among the accused in pBM EA10052 and pLiverpool M11162.

55 pBM EA10383 [pVan Burgh] (Kitchen 1968–90: VI, 833–36).

56 pBM EA10403 (Kitchen 1968–90: VI, 828–33).

57 pBM EA10053: *vo.*2–4 (Kitchen 1968–90: VI, 755–63).

58 pLiverpool M11186 [pMayer B] (Kitchen 1968–90: VI, 515–16).

59 Barwik 2011: 24–27.

60 pBM EA10221: §8.A.1; cf. §8.A.19 (day 24).

61 Porter and Moss 1972: 186[276].

62 Černý 1929; 1930; cf., however, Demidoff 2000, who attempts to resurrect an earlier idea (see Peet 1930: 130) that would make Year 19 of Rameses IX equivalent to Year 1 of the *wḥm-mswt*, with the years of the latter exactly equivalent to those of Rameses XI.

63 On pBM EA10221 (§8 A.1, 19).

64 Cf. Thijs 1998a; 1999a; much of the material on pp. 9–13 leans heavily on Thijs's discussions in these and other papers, cited below. I do, however, part company with Thijs on most other matters concerning the period—cf. Preface n. 3, ch. 1 nn. 135, 154, 169, ch. 4 n. 37. The resulting 'short chronology' has been opposed in Von Beckerath 2000 and 2001, Demidoff 2000, and Barwik 2011: 41–76. The latter volume appeared after the present work had been submitted to press, and it has thus not, with a few exceptions, generally been possible to cite or address its discussion of various issues concerning the Twentieth/Twenty-first Dynasty transition.

65 pBM EA10052: §14.10–18.

66 pLiverpool M11162: §5.9–12.

67 pBM EA10052: *vo.*10.1–10.

68 I.e., the last years of Rameses IX and the reign of Rameses X—see. p. 7.

69 pBM EA10052: §8.17–24.

70 Cf., however, Demidoff 2000.

71 Cf. Capart, Gardiner, and van de Walle 1936: 187 n. 7.

72 As proposed by Thijs (1998a; 1999a–b; 2000a–b; 2001a–b).

73 E.g., Daressy 1900: 143 (Shoshenq I, who is normally "setepenre," although there are two examples of "setepenamun" on statues from Karnak). In the Twenty-ninth Dynasty, the ephemeral Pasherenmut was Userre-setepenptah, perhaps tying in with regionalism suggested by the Thirtieth Dynasty Djehor and Nakhthorheb being uniquely "-setepenan-hur." Subsequently, however, Ptah is invoked in the standard prenomina of Ptolemy IV, V, VI, VIII, IX, X, XII, and XV, not to mention in various Roman imperial cartouches down to Nero.

74 On the other hand, Heliopolis-referencing royal epithets are far less common than Theban-referencing ones: during the Eighteenth and Nineteenth Dynasties only Amenhotep II regularly referenced the city in his nomen, while some post-Year 40 Lower-Egyptian records and monuments of Rameses II occasionally did so (von Beckerath 1999: 156–57). Later on, the city only reappears in the names of Shoshenq III and IV—both purely northern kings, following the Twenty-second/Twenty-third division of the kingship.

75 pAshmolean 1945.96 [the Adoption Papyrus] (Kitchen 1968–90: VI, 735–38).

76 Gardiner 1941a: 23.

77 pTurin C.1898+1937+2094/244 [pChabas-Lieblein] (Kitchen 1968–90: VI, 687–51, 850–51; von Beckerath 1994b).

78 pTurin C.2018 (Kitchen 1968–90: VI, 851–63).

79 pTurin C.1895+2006 [Turin Taxation Papyrus] (Gardiner 1948: 22–37; cf. Thijs 1999b: 186–88).

80 pBerlin P.10460 (Kitchen 1968–90: VI, 863–64).

81 pTurin C.1896 (Kitchen 1968–90: VI, 734–35); Cairo stela TR 11/11/24/2 (Kitchen 1968–90: VI, 701), whose date is normally read as Year 27 but may actually date to Year 17: see von Beckerath 1994a: 91.

82 Cf. Römer 1994: 6–7, on the oracle text of Herihor (see p. 22).

83 Cf. Thijs 1999a: 95–96; 1999b: 176–79.

84 In this connection, note that Hatshepsut did not start her own regnal reckoning when she took full kingly status during the reign of Thutmose III. Cf also pp. 18–19.

85 Cf. Thijs 1999b: 176–79.

86 pTurin C.2034 (Kitchen 1968–90: VI, 865): §1 (with *whm-mswt* explicitly mentioned); pBM EA10221: §A.1 (no mention of era or reign).

87 With the possible exception of Cairo TR 11/11/24/2 (ch. 1, n. 81), if the year-date is indeed to be read as "27."

88 pTurin C.1888 (Pleyte and Rossi 1869–76: pl. xli; Gardiner 1948: 64–88; see also Thijs 1999b: 179–84; 2001a: 93–94).

89 Almost certainly the son of the earlier vizier Montjuerhatef (see p. 3).

90 Cf. Thijs 1999b: 183; 2001b: 67–68.

91 Kitchen 1968–90: VI, 840–41.

92 See Thijs 1999b.

93 pBM EA10068.

94   pBM EA9997 (Kitchen 1968–90: VII, 389–94).

95   Dates after Thijs 2001a.

96   Known from the Medinet Habu procession of princes and his tomb in the Valley of the Queens (QV44—Porter and Moss 1960–64: 754–55; Hassanein and Nelson 1997).

97   E.g., Dodson 1987a: 225.

98   Although there is no contemporary evidence for Sethy having a wife of this name, there is only one (potential) attestation during his reign of Tuy, the mother of his son Rameses II. All of her undoubted memorials date after Sethy's death (see Brand 2000: 345). Another Queen Baketwernel, for whom KV10 (Amenmeses) was usurped, remains a lady of uncertain affiliations (cf. Dodson 2010: 48–51) but in any case cannot be the lady referred to in this document (taking "Menmaatre" as a miswriting of "Menmire"?Amenmeses) as it seems clear that the sepulcher in question was in the Valley of the Queens.

99   See Thijs 2003: 294–95.

100 Kitchen 1968–90: VI, 536–38.

101 Cf. Wente 1966.

102 Thijs 2003: 289–91.

103 Wente 1966: 82.

104 pBM EA10052: §11.8.

105 pBM EA10052: §11.18. It has been suggested that during this conflict Dra Abu'l-Naga tombs K93.11 and K93.12, which had been greatly expanded and adorned by Amenhotep, his father Ramesesnakhte, and the God's Wife Iset E (see ch.1, n. 116), were attacked and their decoration mutilated (Rummel 2011: 429–30).

106 For references to various views see Thijs 2003: 289 n. 9.

107 pBM EA10383: §2.5.

108 pTurin C.1896 (Kitchen 1968–90: VI, 734–35).

109 On the other hand, Niwiński (1992: 255–56) and Thijs (2003: 303–304) read more into this letter and make it some kind of test of Panehsy's loyalty to Rameses XI.

110 Gomaà 1977.

111 pLiverpool M11162: §13 B.2.

112 It has further been suggested that he was also the Panehsy mentioned as the husband of a certain Nesmut in pBM EA10052: §2.29 (Niwiński 1992: 244, seconded by Thijs 2003: 299 n. 67, largely on the basis of his name carrying the same determinative). However, from the context this is unlikely, as she is in a list of recipients of loot from a tomb robbery.

113 Bohleke 1985; cf. Caminos 1974: II, 109–10 on the impossibility of the viceroy in question being Panehsy.

114 Amenhotep's earliest appearance is in TT65, whose completion can be dated to Year 9 (see Bács 1995: 9–10, nn. 20, 22).

115 But cf. Thijs 2008; for an earlier discussion, see Bell 1980.

116 On Ramesesnakhte, see Polz 1998, who also discusses his appropriation of the earlier royal tomb-chapel K93.11 (to which his son Amenhotep G also

made additions—see also Rummel 2009; 2011; Bács 2011: 8–9). It should be noted that the tomb ascribed to Ramesesnakhte by Porter and Moss under the number TT293 (1960–64: 376), is actually the unnumbered monument of a scribe Huy, the number TT293 really belonging to K93.11 (Larkin and van Siclen 1975; Polz 1998: 272–73).

117 See ch. 1, n. 61. It may be noted, however, that Barwik 2011: 116–17 suggests that Piankh's figure may have been added later to the tableau, thus removing the evidence for his having been in office by Year 7. However, this would destroy the symmetry of the tableau, thus making this explanation perhaps unlikely.

118 E.g., Kitchen 1996: 248–52.

119 This appears only twice in Herihor titles in the Khonsu temple at Karnak—in the dedicatory inscription in the hypostyle hall and his oracle text at Karnak.

120 Cairo CG61019–20 (Porter and Moss 1960–64: 661; Ritner 2009a: 99–100[19]).

121 pPushkin 120 (Gardiner 1932: 60–76; Korostovtsev 1960; Ritner 2009a: 87–99[18]). The question of whether the document is a genuine report, a literary work based on fact, or even a work of fiction has been much debated. For a summary and bibliography of views, see Winand 2011, who notes that the language and paleography are more consistent with a date after the middle of the Twenty-first Dynasty than the late Twentieth, suggesting that "the chances for considering it as an administrative document . . . are virtually close to zero" (Winand 2011: 548).

122 For whom see pp. 5, 7.

123 On the other hand Ritner 2009a: 99 n. 12 and Egberts 1998: 102 prefer Rameses XI, Egberts believing the latter also now to be dead. This depends on a redating of the account to an era subsequent to the *wḥm-mswt*; on this and its problems, see pp. 18ff.

124 Although Niwiński (1979) argues that she is actually the wife of Rameses XI, holding some special commission alongside Nesibanebdjedet at Tanis.

125 Cairo (Mariette 1876: pl. 12–21).

126 Filiations frequently introduce the mother and father of a single individual in just such a way.

127 Dodson and Janssen 1989: 128–29.

128 Kitchen 1996: 537–38.

129 Jansen-Winkeln 1992.

130 E.g., Taylor 1998; Thijs 2003, albeit within a different overall framework.

131 E.g., Kitchen 1996: xiv–xvii; James and Morkot 2010: 235–42.

132 Particularly over the 'evolution' of high-priestly titles at this period.

133 Jansen-Winkeln 1992: 34–35; Egberts 1998: 97.

134 An affectation that Jansen-Winkeln (1992: 35–37) also attributes to Panedjem I and Menkheperre A.

135 Cf. Kitchen 1996: xvii–xviii; 2009: 192–94; Thijs 2005: 79; as an alternative, the latter proposes the novel solution that these Years 5 and 6 belong not to the *wḥm-mswt* but to the reign of Khakheperre Panedjem, which he

places directly after that of Rameses XI. Khakheperre is usually regarded as a prenomen affected by the high priest Panedjem I late in his career (see p. 50), but Thijs regards him as a distinct individual, perhaps a son of one of the last Rameside kings; cf. further pp. 29–30.

136 As proposed by Thijs 1998c; 2000a.

137 Published by Černý 1939, Wente 1967, and Wente 1990: 171–203.

138 The former had apparently been attached to the expedition to carry out various administrative functions.

139 pTurin C.1972 [LRL 4].

140 Given that it means "The Nubian"!

141 pTurin C.1895+2006: §1.4–5.

142 Assuming the correctness of the restoration of the title string as "Fan-Bearer on the Right of the King, Royal Scribe, General, Overseer of the Granaries of [Pharaoh, King's Son of] Kush, Commander of the Southern Lands, Army Leader [of Pharaoh]:" Gardiner 1941b: 23.

143 pTurin C.1895+2006: §1.4–5; see Thijs 2003: 295–302, including the observation that there is no evidence the Panehsy mentioned in pBM EA10053: vo. 2 as active in Thebes in Year 9 of what must be the *whm-mswt* was the viceroy, rather than some homonym.

144 Porter and Moss 1952: 79; Kitchen 1968–90: VI, 842; cf. Bohleke 1985: 23 n. 44.

145 Cf. Thijs 1998c; 2000a.

146 Cf. Thijs 2003: 300–302.

147 pBerlin 10487 [LRL21]; pBerlin 10489 [LRL35]; pBerlin 19488 [LRL34].

148 pBerlin 10487 [LRL21].

149 Cf. Thijs 2003: 300–302.

150 Leiden AP16, acquired with the Anastasi Collection in 1828 and of unknown provenance (Kitchen 1968–90: VI, 846–47; Boeser 1911–13: 13[50], pl. xxviii; Schneider and Raven 1981: 112–13[113]; Malek 2007ff: [803-055-420]).

151 Epigraphic Survey 1981: pl. 153, 156, 166, 172, 174, 178, 185, 188, 198A, 199, 201.

152 Strictly speaking, the king was the sole officiant in an Egyptian temple, and was thus shown as such, even though in reality the high priest would substitute.

153 Epigraphic Survey 1981: xviii, 14–17, pl. 132.

154 Cf. Thijs 2005: 85–87 for the suggestion that the thirty years comprises ten years as high priest and twenty as king.

155 Epigraphic Survey 1979; Ritner 2009a: 82–83[16].

156 Cf. Thijs 2005: 74–76 and Kitchen 2009: 194–95.

157 In pTurin C.1895+2006: see Thijs 1999b: 186–88, given that in Thebes the *whm-mswt* and the reign of Rameses XI were probably by then synonymous.

158 pBM EA9997 (see Thijs 1999b: 188–89).

159 Porter and Moss 1960–64: 501; Thomas 1966: 132–33; Ciccarello and Romer [1979]; Reeves 1990: 121–23.

160 Listed, conveniently, in Kitchen 1996: 415–19; note that the Year 15 text actually refers to R[ameses] II, not III as printed.

161 Jansen-Winkeln 2007–9: I, 7–10.
162 Cf. Thijs 2006: 81–83, albeit here supporting his proposal that this Panedjem was separate from the high priest: see pp. 29–30.
163 A not dissimilar reconstruction, with the Years 1–15 attributed to Herihor, has been suggested in James and Morkot 2010. However, they would overlap his reign with the *wḥm-mswt* from Herihor's Year 6, directly after the events related by Wenamun, thus placing Piankh's high priesthood within Herihor's actual reign rather than during a hiatus in his pontifical career.
164 The numerous mutilations of faces in the Khonsu temple are by Christian iconoclasts, while the probable usurpation of reliefs on the gate of the Khonsu temple pylon would have been a simple annexation of material into a new decorating project, with no malice intended.
165 Cairo TR 3/4/17/1 (Porter and Moss 1937: 51; Kitchen 1968–90: VI, 848).
166 Epigraphic Survey 1981: xix.
167 Epigraphic Survey 1981: xviii–xix, pl. 113–14, 117B, 118B, 120B, 121A, 122B, 124B, 125B.
168 E.g., by Epigraphic Survey 1981: xix; Kitchen, 2009: 196.
169 Thijs 2005, 2006, 2007. A significant point against creating this additional Panedjem is the fact that King Panedjem's wife Henttawy included among her titles that of Chief of the Harem of Amun, which is well attested as the designation of the wife of a high priest of Amun, and thus indicates that her husband had served as pontiff prior to becoming king. This fits the accepted scenario well, but under Thijs's scheme one would be forced to fit yet another pontificate into the late Twentieth Dynasty!
170 Thijs 2007: 54–55.
171 Cf. Thijs 2007: 52–53, nn. 20, 25.
172 pBerlin 10489 [LRL35].
173 In which Nedjmet is implicated by name in pBerlin 10487 [LRL21] and pBerlin 19488 [LRL34].
174 "I daily tell every god and every goddess by whom I pass to cause that you live, cause that you be in health and let (me) see (you) when I have returned and fill (my) eye with the sight of (you)."
175 Epigraphic Survey 1979: pl. 26, 28; she also has various other epithets.
176 pBM EA10541+Louvre E.6258+Munich ÄS825 [now lost] (Lenzo 2010).
177 pBM EA10490 (Budge 1899: pl. 1–10; Lenzo 2010).
178 Thijs 1998b, resurrecting an idea of Budge (1899: vi, 45).
179 Cf. Quirke 1993: 18–19.
180 As does Thijs 1998b; cf. Aston 2009b: 222.
181 Cf. Niwiński 1989a: 210, where comparable items are no earlier than the pontificate of Panedjem II.
182 Indeed, Niwiński (1989a: 210) has even suggested that this papyrus was produced for Nedjmet's reburial under Panedjem II, a view supported by Aston 2009b: 221–22.
183 Cairo CG61087 (G.E. Smith, 1912: 94–98).

184 G.E. Smith, 1912: 97. Unfortunately no transcription or even full translation is given and the date could refer to the reigns of Herihor and
Nesibanebdjedet I, of Amenemnesu, or of Pasebkhanut I.

185 In spite of Thijs's protestations (2006: 84–85): cf. pp. 42–43 for a bandage
used some two decades after its manufacture.

186 Cairo CG61024 (Porter and Moss 1960–64: 662; Niwiński 1988b: 116–17[72]).

187 Cairo TR 20/12/25/11, found holding *shabti*s of Panedjem I and Nesikhonsu
A (Aston 2009b: 221).

188 Cf. Niwiński 1979: 49; one of Nedjmet's *shabti*s seems also to have been
made around the same time (Aubert 1981: 17–18). Cf. further Aston 1991:
97; 2009: 221–22.

189 Both papyri had come through the antiquities market, EA10541+E.6258
surfacing in the 1870s and EA10490 in 1894, cf. Bickerstaffe 2010: 32–33.
Nedjmet may have been one of the first reburials in TT320, if the identification of various fragments found in the tomb's burial chamber as coming
from her coffins is correct (Graefe 2010: 53, cf. pl. Plan09).

190 But cf. Taylor 1998, for a suggestion that identifies Nedjmet, wife of Herihor,
with the similarly named lady associated with Piankh, allowing Nedjmet's
royal son to be Panedjem I.

191 Epigraphic Survey 1979: pl. 26; Ritner 2009a: 83–87[17].

192 Epigraphic Survey 1979: pl. 28.

193 Cf. Fisher 2001: I, 13–42.

194 Porter and Moss 1972: 502[104–107].

195 Which provides the basis for reconstructing her damaged name and titles in
the 'procession' relief.

196 pTurin [Unnumbered—LRL38] and C.2069 [LRL39] as author, with title;
pTurin C.1973 [LRL2]; pBM EA10100 [LRL30] as a protagonist—simply
by name but certainly the same lady.

197 The first two letters mentioned above have her dealing with a failure to
deliver rations to the Deir el-Medina workforce, while the third has her in the
company of Piankh at Elephantine, and in the fourth she is apparently acting
as his deputy in transferring some workmen to the Deir el-Medina workforce.

198 Kitchen 1996: 45, 536.

199 Porter and Moss 1972: 307–308.

200 Cf. Kitchen 1996: 41–42.

201 The two signs are very similar: 𓏏 versus 𓊮.

202 Taylor 1998: 1149–50.

203 Cf. Bell 1980 and Polz 1998: 282–83. On the other hand, Thijs 2008 argues
that Nesamun's tenure as (acting) high priest fell during his brother's 'suppression' and again for a short period afterward, with Nesamun retaining his
base title of Second Prophet throughout.

204 Unless some ephemeral pontiff held office between Amenhotep and
Herihor. Herere could also conceivably have been the relict of Nesamun
(Ramesesnakhte's wife was named Adjedt(aat): see Polz 1998: 272).

Notes to Chapter Two

1 From Africanus, Eusebius, and the Armenian version of Eusebius, respectively (Waddell 1940: 152–55).

2 Cf. Thijs 2005: 77–79, in spite of our rejection of his broader conclusions regarding these reigns.

3 Waddell 1940: 154–57.

4 Jansen-Winkeln 2007–2009: I, 111[8.1]; Ritner 2009a: 50–51.

5 Jansen-Winkeln 2007–2009: I, 156[9.56, 58]; Ritner 2009a: 50–51.

6 Payraudeau 2008.

7 Cf. Kitchen 1996: 421–23 and p. 68.

8 I.e., rejecting the second option set out on p. **Ch1** for the years associated with him in his kingly phase.

9 Unless Panedjem I started counting regnal years after Nesibanebdjedet's demise as an independent 'national' king; however, since he had already shared years with Nesibanebdjedet it seems more likely that he continued to do so with Nesibanebdjedet's successor (particularly as this successor was Panedjem's own son—cf. p. 25).

10 Porter and Moss 1937: 170; Jansen-Winkeln 2007–2009: I, 1–3[1.3]; Ritner 2009a: 101–104[20].

11 Varille 1943: 36, pl. 98; Christophe 1951: 77; Kitchen 1996: 256 n. 65, end.

12 Location unknown: formerly in the MacGregor Collection at Tamworth (Newberry 1902: 248[32b]).

13 Montet 1947.

14 MMA 47.60 and Aubert Collection, Paris (Jansen-Winkeln 2007–2009: I, 1[1.1]).

15 Epigraphic Survey 1979: pl. 21; cf. James and Morkot 2010: 246–47 on the scene's implications for the chronology of Herihor's career.

16 Kitchen 1996: 417–19; Ciccarello [1979]: second part; Jansen-Winkeln 2007–2009: I, 21–23[3.29–38]; Ritner 2009a: 114–17[24].

17 On suggestions that there might have been as many as three Butehamuns, all the sons of a Thutmose, see B.G. Davies, 1997 and Barwik 2011: 257–86.

18 See Kitchen 1996: 418–19; Jansen-Winkeln 2007–2009: I, 35–40[3.61–78].

19 A number of which were later displaced by the building of the forecourt and Pylon I (Ciccarello [1979]: Doc. 6–9; Jansen-Winkeln 2007–2009: I, 5[3.1–3]; Ritner 2009a: 112[22.IV]).

20 Epigraphic Survey 1998: 52–54, pl. 199–200; Jansen-Winkeln 2007–2009: I, 17[3.22]; Ritner 2009a: 109–11[22.I–II].

21 Although much more survived in the early 1890s when Georges Daressy copied the texts of the tableau.

22 Kitchen 1996: 55 takes this as referring to Amun-Re, as a contraction of his common epithet, "Lord of the Thrones of the Two Lands." On the other hand, it could be a mis-written "Lady of the Two Lands," and be a title of Henttawy.

23 Niwiński 1979: 52 proposed that the carving of the figures of Panedjem and Maatkare preceded the addition of the images of Henttawy and Mutnedjmet; however, this is refuted by Epigraphic Survey 1998: 53–54.

24 Although if Henttawy did indeed bear the Lady of the Two Lands title she might rather be Henttawy A, holding this queenly epithet prior to her husband's accession.

25 Cf. p. 18, for this extended meaning of the title.

26 Cairo CG61025A; see p. 50.

27 Cairo CG61088; see further p. 54.

28 Luxor, Museum of Mummification ex-Cairo CG61092 (G.E. Smith 1912: 106).

29 Which is known to have occurred under the pontificate of Menkheperre: see Aston 2009b: 224–25.

30 Cairo JE85894, from NRT-III (Montet 1951: 99, fig. 41, 100–102, pl. lxx[398]); cf. p. 43 for the possibility of her using the title Lady of the Two Lands prior to his accession.

31 Buried in tomb MMA60 at Deir el-Bahari alongside her probable sister-in-law Djedmutesankh A (p. 68) and niece Henttawy C (see Aston 2009b: 199–200); apparently the first person to be buried in the tomb (Winlock 1942: 113), Henttawy B's equipment is Cairo JE49100–2, 51948–9 and MMA 25.3.21.

32 A King's Daughter Nauny, daughter of a King's Daughter Tenetbekhnu, known only from her intrusive burial, in TT358 (Meryetamun B, wife of Amenhotep I) at Deir el-Bahari, has generally been regarded as a daughter of Panedjem I. However, she could equally have been a daughter of Herihor or Nesibanebdjedet I—or even someone other than a king, given the apparent inheritance of the King's Daughter title by the daughters of Panedjem through their maternal line. On the basis of its design, her funerary equipment (MMA 30.3.23–35, Cairo JE55044, 55080, 55146) seems to have been manufactured during the earlier part of the Twenty-first Dynasty (Aston 2009b: 202).

33 Cairo CG61026 (Porter and Moss 1960–64: 663).

34 A Twenty-third Dynasty priest, Ankhefenkhonsu, claimed to be descended from a "child of the mother" (*šrt mwt*) of Menkheperre in a now lost text from the roof of the Khonsu temple (Porter and Moss 1972: 242–43; Jansen-Winkeln 2007–2009: II, 326–28[30.12]; Ritner 2009a: 12–16); however, the number of generations cited in this line seems to be corrupt: see ch. 2, n. 199.

35 For past discussions, see Kitchen 1996: 50–52, 536–37.

36 Cairo (Montet 1951: 151, 152, fig. 56, pl. cxxi[543]); Henttawy is also named on a jar alongside Pasebkhanut and his wife Mutnedjmet, together with a further cartouche "*mwt-ntr n hnsw*" (Cairo JE85896—Montet 1951: 98, fig. 39, 101, pl. lxix[399]; Association Française d'Action Artistique 1987: 227, 229[72]).

37 Berlin ÄM1566, 1616 (Porter and Moss 1934: 124); they cannot refer to Panedjem II and his wife Isetemkheb D as they were found underneath bricks of Menkheperre (Lepsius 1897–1913: II, 46).

38 Cf. Kitchen 1996: 61–62.

39 Jansen-Winkeln 2007–2009: I, 18–21[24–5].

40 Cairo JE85886–7, from NRT-III (Montet 1951: 105, 108, fig. 44, pl. lxxii [413]).

41 Berlin ÄM23673 (Jansen-Winkeln 2007–2009: II, 278–80[28.24]; Ritner 2009a: 21–25[3]).

42 James and Morkot 2010 would have Panedjem I as the coregent (for some five years) and direct successor of Herihor as king. However, this does not address the problem of the reliefs on the interior of the Khonsu temple doorway.

43 Cf. Kitchen 1996: 419.

44 Cairo CG61005 (Porter and Moss 1960–64: 659).

45 Cairo CG42191 (Jansen-Winkeln 2007–2009: I, 6[3.5]; Ritner 2009a: 112–13[23.I]).

46 Jansen-Winkeln 2007–2009: I, 5–6[3.4]; Ritner 2009a: 113–14[23.II]).

47 Although generally regarded as having been made for Rameses, cf. Bernard Bothmer's confident dating of the piece to around the time of Panedjem (Kitchen 1996: 258 n. 80).

48 Romer [1979]: 18–19; Ciccarello [1979]; Jansen-Winkeln 2007–2009: I, 21[28]. Barwik 2011: 265 suggests tentatively, on the basis of the lack of any other attestation of Panedjem I with the 'high priestly' prenomen, that the text was actually prepared by Herihor, with Panedjem's nomen added secondarily; however, there seems no real evidence in the text itself for such a reconstruction.

49 Ciccarello and Romer [1979]: 2; Reeves 1990: 121–23.

50 Porter and Moss 1960–64: 662; Niwiński 1988b: 117; Manuelian and Loeben 1993: 127–28; Jansen-Winkeln 2007–2009: I, 23[3.39].

51 Cf. Niwiński 1979: 52.

52 Or possibly a complete inner coffin: Maspero speaks of a trough, "today no more than a shapeless mass of black wood [*n'en est plus aujourd'hui qu'une masse informe de bois noir*]" (1889: 570).

53 At least one coffin of Nedjmet A, prepared around the same time, also reused an earlier carcass (Niwiński 1988b: 117—he does not make it clear whether both or just one of the coffins had been "reused from an unknown man"), while there is no question that reuse of considerably earlier material was common during the Twenty-first Dynasty. Other examples include the outer coffin and sarcophagus used for Pasebkhanut I (see p. 67), and private coffins Copenhagen Nationalmuseet 3911 (Niwiński 1988b: 135–36[166], in which the foot of a Nineteenth Dynasty "daily life" coffin is visible below a much later mud-plaster surface), and NMS A.UC70A (Manley and Dodson 2010: 41–45[10], where a probably New Kingdom carcass has been similarly invested with a thick layer of mud plaster before complete reworking).

54 Mummy Cairo CG61065 (G.E. Smith, 1912: 25–28), which was found in Panedjem's coffin, was identified as that of Thutmose purely on grounds of its apparent physical likeness to the bodies of Thutmose II and III (Maspero 1889: 581–82). However, it has its arms by its side: the royal pose of arms crossed at the breast had already been adopted at the time of the mummification of Amenhotep I (Harris and Weeks 1973: 30–31), while it also appears to be the body of too young a man to be Thutmose I (Krogman

and Baer 1980: 206–207 make the body that of a "18:0–22:0"-year-old, although there are issues with such ages [cf. Dodson 2009c; 2010: 80–82]).

55 Goedicke 1971.

56 Dodson 1988a.

57 Porter and Moss 1972: 181–82, 186; Jansen-Winkeln 2007–2009: I, 27–28[3.48–49].

58 At Karnak and Brussels E.5188 (Porter and Moss 1972: 244; Jansen-Winkeln 2007–2009: I, 27, 28[3.47, 50]).

59 Cairo JE55181, 55155; MMA 30.3.9; Porter and Moss 1960–64: 630; Jansen-Winkeln 2007–2009: I, 28–29[3.52–53].

60 Theban Graffiti 1570–77 (Jansen-Winkeln 2007–2009: I, 39[3.75]).

61 Petrie UC16824 (Jansen-Winkeln 2007–2009: I, 29–30[3.55]).

62 Aston 2009b: 222–23.

63 Cairo JE26276 (Porter and Moss 1960–64: 664); Loring 2011.

64 Aston 2009b: 227.

65 Luxor Museum of Mummification ex-Cairo CG61027 (Porter and Moss 1960–64: 663). The body seems to have been partly plundered in its (unknown) original burial place before coming to rest in TT320; the typology of the *shabti*s found there with it may suggest that they had been provided as replacements at a reburial in the reign of Amenemopet or later (Aston 2009b: 222).

66 Luxor Museum of Mummification ex-Cairo CG61092 (G.E. Smith, 1912: 106).

67 Ikram and Dodson 1998: 124–27.

68 Cairo CG61088 (G.E. Smith, 1912: 99–101).

69 G.E. Smith, 1912: 100–101, seconding the view of Maspero 1889: 577.

70 Partly through a misunderstanding of the changing nature of the office of God's Wife, but also through a misreading of her title Daughter of the King's Great Wife as simply "King's Great Wife": see Kitchen 1996: 59 n. 276.

71 The first certain 'new style' God's Wife was Iset E, daughter of Rameses VI (Gitton and Leclant 1977: 804; Kitchen 1968–90: VI, 282, 347–48).

72 Cf. the references given by Kitchen 1996: 59 n. 277.

73 Harris and Weeks 1973: 53 (as a baboon); Ikram and Iskander 2002: 53 (correcting its identification as either a patas monkey or a savannah monkey type); on the burial of pets in tombs, cf. Ikram 2005: 1–4; Ikram and Iskander 2002: 25–28, 46.

74 Cf. Harris and Weeks 1973: 173–74.

75 Cf. Manchester 1781 (Kitchen 1968–90: VI, 282) and material from Dra Abu'l-Naga tomb K93.12 (Rummel 2011; cf. ch. 1, n. 116). Iset served as God's Wife until at least Year 9 of Rameses IX (Bács 1995: 9–10, nn. 20, 22), and may even have been Maatkare's immediate predecessor.

76 Jansen-Winkeln 2007–2009: I, 10[3.13], 11[3.15], 17[3.22], 81–84[6.24–27].

77 Jansen-Winkeln 2007–2009: I, 81[6.24]; a statue base dedicated by her steward, Horhotep, is Marseilles 432 (ibid. [6.25]; Porter and Moss 1960–64: 791).

78 Aston 2009b: 225–26.

79 pStrasbourg 21 (Jansen-Winkeln 2007–2009: I, 205–206; Ritner 2009a: 122–23); this has generally been linked to a further letter from Menkheperre to the same god (pMoscow 5660—Jansen-Winkeln 2007–2009: I, 205; Ritner 2009a: 123), thanking him for oracles and decisions on his behalf. Cf. Müller, M. 2009: 263–64.

80 Cf. the issues raised by Thijs 2005: 83.

81 Louvre C.256 (Porter and Moss 1972: 294; Jansen-Winkeln 2007–2009: I, 72–74[6.1]; Ritner 2009a: 124–29[28]]). Krauss 2008 takes this rather as the date of the erection of the stela; for objections cf. James (forthcoming).

82 von Beckerath 1968: 33–34.

83 James (forthcoming).

84 Given our rejection of a separate year-numbering for Panedjem I, to whose reign James assigns the two years.

85 Jansen-Winkeln 2007–2009: I, 21–22[3.31–33], 79[6.11–12].

86 E.g., Lull 2009: 241–45.

87 The latter's name was damaged, reading [. . .]re: see Kitchen 1996: 424–25. Djedkhonsiufankh's wife may have been the First Chief of the Harem of Amun, Djedmutesankh (A), the only holder of the title at this time without an obvious high-priestly husband. She was buried in tomb MMA60 at Deir el-Bahari alongside Henttawy B and C: see ch. 2, n. 31. Djedmutesankh's funerary equipment is now MMA 25.3.1–3, 17–18, 24, 27, 154A–D, 167–70, and Cairo JE49164–5, and seems to have been made no earlier than the pontificate of Panedjem II.

88 Although Niwiński (1984a: 83–86) has proposed that the filiation should be taken as (great-grand)son of Panedjem I, making him a son and successor of Panedjem II. Cf. Jansen-Winkeln 2006a: 225 n. 44; Kitchen 2009: 191.

89 As written in a few cases: e.g., Jansen-Winkeln 2007–2009: I, 44[7], 60[98].

90 Jansen-Winkeln 2007–2009: I, 43–44[4.44, 8, 10], 52–55 [4.36–40, 44, 45, 50, 53, 58, 62], 57–61 [4.72, 83, 84, 86–89, 96, 103(?), 104].

91 Cf. Kitchen 1996: 426–31.

92 Montet 1951: 9–18.

93 Cairo CG392–4, CG530, CG1243; and *in situ* at Tanis (Jansen-Winkeln 2007–2009: I, 45–47[4.13–20]).

94 Cf. Uphill 1984.

95 Cairo JE41644 (Jansen-Winkeln 2007–2009: I, 60[4.100]).

96 Porter and Moss 1974–81: 17–19.

97 Porter and Moss 1974–81: 845; Jansen-Winkeln 2007–2009: I, 70[4.134]).

98 Jansen-Winkeln 2007–2009: I, 63–67[4.113–29]; cf. Broekman 1998.

99 Jansen-Winkeln 2007–2009: I, 67–69[4.130–31].

100 Also recorded as such in another late Twenty-second Dynasty genealogy from the Serapeum at Saqqara (Louvre IM3429—Jansen-Winkeln 2007–2009: II, 394[44.27]).

101 Porter and Moss 1974–81: 781–805; Dodson 2005: 72–91.

102 For the numbering of the Apis, see Dodson 2005: 102 n. 7.

103 Porter and Moss 1974–81: 785.

104 Porter and Moss 1974–81: 785—or just possibly Apis 22.x+1/XXVIII under Takelot I (see Dodson 2005: 82).

105 Cf. Dodson 2005: 82.

106 On the basis of bulls whose life spans are known for certain, and the evidence of modern 'careful captivity' bulls (information courtesy Salima Ikram).

107 The three alleged Twenty-first Dynasty bulls were in a now collapsed room, and it is not impossible that this may have given access to additional rooms (cf. Dodson 2005: 82–83).

108 Jansen-Winkeln 2007–2009: I, 47[4.22], 53[4.40], 58–61[4.83, 90, 99, 107]; see also pp. 43, 45–46.

109 Jansen-Winkeln 2007–2009: I, 61–63[4.108].

110 Cf. Jansen-Winkeln 1997b; Lull 2009: 244–45.

111 Texts on linen from their mummy wrappings (Jansen-Winkeln 2007–2009: I, 22[3.32–33]).

112 Jansen-Winkeln 2007–2009: I, 21[3.31].

113 Jansen-Winkeln 2007–2009: I, 79[6.12]; cf. Reeves 1990: 94.

114 Jansen-Winkeln 2007–2009: I, 26[3.45]; one might suggest that these date to a building erected after Pasebkhanut I's accession.

115 Petrie UC16127 (Jansen-Winkeln 2007–2009: I, 25[3.42]).

116 Cairo JE71902 (Jansen-Winkeln 2007–2009: I, 25[3.41]; Ritner 2009a: 117–22[25]). From the photograph it appears possible that Henttawy's cartouche might be secondary, and that the immediately preceding titles have been altered as well. There is, however, no mention of this in the text of the publication of the piece (Abdallah 1984) and it may be that this is simply an artefact of the photograph. It has, to date, not been possible to examine the piece itself.

117 Jansen-Winkeln 2007–2009: I, 6–7[3.8, 6].

118 Cairo JE37509 (Jansen-Winkeln 2007–2009: I, 6[3.7]).

119 Jansen-Winkeln 2007–2009: I, 15[3.19].

120 Jansen-Winkeln 2007–2009: I, 16[3.21].

121 Jansen-Winkeln 2007–2009: I, 30[3.56].

122 Cf. Reeves 1990: 186–92; Graefe 2003a: 79–80.

123 Causing much more gross mutilation in the case of the first three named, which had extensive areas of gilding where the others had simply paint, their gilding being restricted to faces and hands. The outer lid of Henttawy is missing altogether.

124 Interestingly, while the faces and hands of the inner coffins and mummy boards of Maatkare and Masaharta were roughly removed, those of their outer coffins were left intact. The avoidance of religious texts on an otherwise totally despoiled (original) coffin is also seen on that of Thutmose III (CG61014—Porter and Moss 1960–64: 660).

125 Cf. Jansen-Winkeln 1995b; Graefe 2003a: 80–82.

126 Cf. the burial of Nauny in TT358 (see ch. 2, n. 32): although this deposit was certainly her original burial, and had never been entered by robbers, the coffin faces had all been wrenched out—presumably by the burial party itself

(Winlock 1942: 178–79). In MMA60 (see p. 68, ch. 2, n. 31), the mummies of both Henttawy B and Djedmutesankh A seem to have been rifled by those charged with burying Henttawy C, with the gilded faces of the three ladies' coffins then pilfered when the next burial, that of a certain Menkheperre (C), was added to the deposit. The venality of workers in the funerary business of the period is further illustrated by the pilfering from the mummy of Henttawy C herself during its original wrapping (Winlock 1942: 113–14). On the other hand, centuries earlier in the early Fourth Dynasty, the burial of the vizier Nefermaat may have been plundered and his mummy smashed by his own burial party, who then sealed the burial chamber, concealing the crime until AD 1910 (Harpur 2001: 44–46).

127   See Reeves 1990: 186, 191–92; for the Year 11 text, see Jansen-Winkeln 2007–2009: II, 30–31[12.42]; it is possible that an anonymous Year 13 on the wrappings of his wife(?: see pp. 85–86) Nesitanebetashru A could also be of Shoshenq's reign, pushing the date of the last primary interment even later (cf. Kitchen 1996: 423).

128   Cf. Reeves 1990: 185; Graefe 2010: 50–60.

129   The size of the entrance shaft of TT320 is such that mummies must have been removed from their coffins during the process of bringing them into the tomb. Given the number of bodies and coffins involved, it is not surprising that a number of mix-ups occurred.

130   Cairo, unnumbered: it was unwrapped in Bulaq on 27 June 1886 (Maspero 1889: 570; cf. Forbes 1998: 650–51), but was not among the royal mummies re-examined in 1909. The shroud and items found on the mummy are, however, in Cairo (JE46881; CG52089; an unnumbered Book of Amduat) and Paris (alleged collar): see Aston 2009b: 223.

131   Cairo CG61006 (Porter and Moss 1960–64: 660); see Maspero 1889: 545; cf. Graefe 2010: 54.

132   See ch. 2, n. 54. These coffins may have lain about halfway along the main corridor of the tomb, to judge from the discovery there of fragments of the foot of the inner lid (Graefe 2010: 54).

133   Cairo CG40006 (Saleh and Sourouzian 1987: [235]).

134   Cairo JE26253A–B and various collections. One of the boxes (JE26253A) seems to be typologically somewhat later than the other (Aston 2009b: 223–24, 366–69).

135   NMS A.1956.154 (Jansen-Winkeln 2007–2009: I, 92–94[6.43]; the handwriting on this label, and the others in the group (NMS A.1956.155–167) is certainly Twentieth/early Twenty-first Dynasty in date (Dodson and Janssen 1989: 134), although it is not impossible that the Year 27 refers to the reign of Rameses XI (cf. Jansen-Winkeln 2007–2009: I, 94 on the basis of the names of the personnel involved in the reburial). Cf., however, pp. 11–12 on the question of the year-count of Rameses XI vis-à-vis the *whm-mswt*.

136   Jansen-Winkeln 2007–2009: I, 74–75[6.3].

137   Cairo stela TR 3/12/24/2 (Jansen-Winkeln 2007–2009: I, 6.2]; Ritner 2009a: 136–37[32]).

138 Jansen-Winkeln 2007–2009: I, 78–79[6.8].
139 Jansen-Winkeln 2007–2009: I, 79[6.10].
140 Jansen-Winkeln 2007–2009: I, 80[6.18].
141 M. Müller 2009.
142 Jansen-Winkeln 2007–2009: I, 80–81[6.19–20, 22].
143 Jansen-Winkeln 2007–2009: I, 81[6.19–23].
144 Jansen-Winkeln 2007–2009: I, 75[4].
145 M. Müller 2009: 254.
146 Jansen-Winkeln 2007–2009: I, 167[11.5]; Aston 2009b: 141–42.
147 Jansen-Winkeln 2007–2009: I, 188[11.14]; Aston 2009b: 190–91.
148 Niwiński 1984b; 1988b: 25–27; Aston 2009b: 164–214.
149 Jansen-Winkeln 2007–2009: I, 188–89[11.15]; Aston 2009b: 191–92.
150 It is possible that a further daughter could have become God's Wife of Amun if the Higaza brick belonged to Isetemkheb C rather than D.
151 Jansen-Winkeln 2007–2009: I, 189[11.16]; Aston 2009b: 175–76.
152 Bierbrier 1975: 49–50; Jansen-Winkeln 2007–2009: I, 108[7.46], 187–88[11.13], 190[11.18], 244[11.109]; Aston 2009b: 192–95; on the Second, Third, and Fourth Prophets of the Twenty-first Dynasty, cf. Broekman 2000b, 2010: 127.
153 Rio de Janeiro 81 (Kitchen 1990b: 187–89, pl. 180–81, 203).
154 Jansen-Winkeln 2007–2009: I, 78–81[6.8, 18–22], which prints all these ovals as if they were cartouches, although only a few are actually potential cartouches.
155 Jansen-Winkeln 2007–2009: I, 80[6.18, top]; see Ritner 2009a: 135–36[31] regarding examples now found at Karnak-East.
156 Jansen-Winkeln 2007–2009: I, 72–78[6.1–7]. A figure of the god Nefertum has been cited by Lull (2009: 247) as potentially giving Menkheperre the prenomen Usermaatre-setepenamun (Durham N43—Malek 1999: 1048; Jansen-Winkeln 2007–2009: I, 80[15]). However, this seems more likely to name either Rameses IV or Amenemopet, who both used that prenomen, with either an amuletic use of the prenomen of Thutmose III or (in the latter case) a remembrance of the recently deceased pontiff. A similar combination of names is found on tablet Dresden, Japanese Palace, 44 (Jansen-Winkeln 2007–2009: I, 80[6.17]).
157 Cairo JE85779–80, 85781–82 (Montet 1951: 154–55[598–99, 600–601], pl. cxxii–iii).
158 As does Lull 2009: 246–49.
159 Cf. Lull 2009: 249, and Aston 2009b: 223 n. 1949 on the misattribution of Macclesfield *shabti*s 1846.77 and 1847.77 to Menkheperre (they actually belong to Panedjem I).
160 Montet 1951; Lull 2002: 27–33, 117–35; Aston 2009b: 41–54.
161 Cf. Lull 2002: 51–59.
162 Montet 1951: 69–89; Aston 2009b: 41–43.
163 Private burials had, however, abandoned this form of adornment by the reign of Thutmose III: see Dodson 2000a: 89–90.

164 Cairo JE85912 (Montet 1951: 130–32).

165 Cairo JE85911 (Montet 1951: 126–30).

166 Cairo JE87297 (Montet 1951: 111–26; Brock 1992); Montet proposed that the sarcophagus had actually come from a cenotaph at Per-Rameses; for the nonexistence of Montet's proposed royal cemetery there, see Černý 1973: 21–22).

167 This helps provide the latest possible date for the removal of the mummy of Merenptah from KV8 to the KV35 cache. The only dated material relating to this deposit consists of a Year 13 on blocks used to effect the final blocking of the room in which the nine mummies were placed, together with the Year 12(?) docket on the mummy of Amenhotep III—the latter clearly of the Nesibanebdjedet I/Herihor era. As Amenhotep was one of the first two bodies to be placed in the chamber (see Reeves 1990: 196–97, confirmed by Piacentini and Orsenigo 2004: 176–77), with Merenptah's mummy separated from that of Amenhotep only by the body of Sethy II, it may be that Merenptah was included in a group that arrived in Year 13, with other bodies added later. On the other hand, however, Reeves appears mistaken in his further deductions on the earlier movements of Merenptah's corpse (1990: 247), with the probable misdating of late Nineteenth Dynasty graffiti in KV14 to the *whm-mswt* (cf. Dodson 2010: 160 n. 10).

168 Cf. Brock 1992.

169 Cf. Aston 2009b: 44, 54.

170 Although some material attributed to the Twenty-second Dynasty pontiff Nesibanebdjedet III could possibly belong to him.

171 Jansen-Winkeln 2007–2009: I, 177–82[11.9]; Ritner 2009a: 138–43[33].

172 Tomb MMA60: see ch. 2, nn. 31, 87; her equipment is MFA 54.639–40, MMA 25.3.6, 19, 20, 28, 29, 35, 155, 162, and 171.

173 Jansen-Winkeln 2007–2009: I, 107–8[7.45]; Aston 2009b: 189.

174 Jansen-Winkeln 2007–2009: I, 108[7.47].

175 Kitchen 1996: 28–37.

176 Derry 1940/41. Remains are now Qasr el-Aini 2.

177 Jansen-Winkeln 2007–2009: I, 95[7.2], 101[7.32].

178 Cf. the suggestions surrounding Pasebkhanut I's use of the title, p. 57.

179 Qasr el-Aini 40 (Derry 1942).

180 Montet 1951: 173–75; Jansen-Winkeln 2007–2009: I, 95[7.3]; Aston 2009b: 54.

181 Cairo JE86058–62 (Montet 1951: 166).

182 Cairo JE86063 (Montet 1951: 166–67).

183 Montet 1951: 160–61; cf. Aston 2009b: 50.

184 Cairo TR 3/7/24/11 (Jansen-Winkeln 2007–2009: I, 99[7.23].

185 Berlin ÄM7973; Cairo JE4748, JE28161–2, TR 16/2/25/6; MFA Exc. 26-4-12, 29-7-3, 29-7-6, 29-7-1276; NMS A.1961.1069 (Jansen-Winkeln 2007–2009: I, 99[7.24–29]).

186 Jansen-Winkeln 2007–2009: I, 103–9[7.34–50].

187 See Niwiński 1988a.

188 Cairo CG61030 (Porter and Moss 1960–64: 664): one of this pair of cases was found occupied by the mummy of Rameses IX (Maspero 1889: 566–68, cf. Loring 2010: 70–71; see also p. 6).

189 For a complete list see Aston 2009b: 227–28.

190 Cairo CG58032 and JE46891 (Jansen-Winkeln 2007–2009: I, 122–41[9.122–3]).

191 Cf. Niwiński 1988a: 227 on tense issues within the text. There is also a pair of unusual *shabti* decrees (BM EA16672 and Louvre E.6858—Jansen-Winkeln 2007–2009: I, 119–21[9.27]) and a mention of Nesikhonsu in the property settlement of her aunt Henttawy C (see p. 68).

192 All explicitly mentioned in the aforementioned oracular decree.

193 Jansen-Winkeln 2007–2009: I, 194[11.23].

194 Cairo JE44670 (Jansen-Winkeln 2007–2009: I, 80–81[6.21]); this has also been taken to refer to Isetemkheb C, wife of Menkheperre.

195 So called today because of his identification after the ordinal numbering of later Osorkons had been settled: a few authors did attempt an up-numbering of the previously acknowledged Osorkons, but this seems now to have been abandoned in view of the confusion thus generated among the uninitiated.

196 Jansen-Winkeln 2007–2009: II, 326–28[30.12]; Ritner 2009a: 11–16[1].

197 Cf. p. 113.

198 Louvre IM2846 (Jansen-Winkeln 2007–2009: II, 271[28.12]).

199 *šrt mwt*: see Ritner 2009a: 12–13; however, Ritner's reconstruction of this badly broken part of the text gives eight generations between Menkheperre and Nimlot A, which is by any measure excessive. The text is thus here either corrupt or Ritner's reconstruction is incorrect; in the case of the latter it is possible that *two* lines of descent are involved, giving a much more reasonable figure of four generations.

200 For which see Kruchten 1989.

201 Jansen-Winkeln 2007–2009: I, 111[8.1].

202 RMO F1971/9.1; AO10a (Jansen-Winkeln 2007–2009: II, 369[1–2]; Ritner 2009a: 411–12[107]). Both items—naming Akheperre-setepenamun Osorkon-meryamun—were allocated to Osorkon IV before the identification of Osorkon the Elder as having an Akheperre prenomen (albeit otherwise with the epithet -setepen*re*). Certainly the formats of the names are more appropriate to the early than to the late Third Intermediate Period; cf. Payraudeau 2000; 2008: 305. For Osorkon IV's likely actual prenomen, see p. 150.

203 It is possible that Osorkon was buried in tomb NRT-VI, which in view of its similarity to Amenemopet's NRT-IV should probably be dated to the Twenty-first Dynasty, but lacks any other evidence as to its owner.

204 Cairo CG741 (Jansen-Winkeln 2007–2009: II, 33–34[12.45]; cf. Kitchen 1996: 113–14.

205 Jansen-Winklen 2007–2009: I, 114[9.13], 151–56[9.44–54].

206 Cairo JE70218 (Jansen-Winkeln 2007–2009: I, 150–1[9.43]).

207 Jansen-Winkeln 2007–2009: I, 112–13[9.1–6, 8].

208 Jansen-Winkeln 2007–2009: I, 113[9.11].

209 Now in London (Embankment) and New York (Central Park—Jansen-Winkeln 2007–2009: I, 114[9.12]).

210 Jansen-Winkeln 2007–2009: I, 156[9.56].

211 Jansen-Winkeln 2007–2009: I, 169–77[11.8].

212 Payraudeau 2008: 305.

213 Cf. Niwiński 1984b; Graefe 2003a, Graefe 2010: 46–48.

214 Jansen-Winkeln 2007–2009: I, 118[9.20]; Ritner 2009a: 144[34.II].

215 Jansen-Winkeln 2007–2009: I, 117[9.18]; cf. ch. 2, n. 188.

216 On the other hand, a text on the old shroud of Rameses's mummy (Jansen-Winkeln 2007–2009: I, 114[9.14]) records the mummy's restoration in a temple in a Year 7: this is generally assumed to be of the reign of Siamun, but might reflect an earlier restoration under Amenemopet or an earlier king. Cf. Graefe 2010: 59; Loring 2010: 70–71.

217 Aston 2009b: 229–30.

218 Jansen-Winkeln 2007–2009: I, 141–42[9.33]; Ritner 2009a: 160–61[37]; Graefe and Belova 2010: 82–83, pl. 05–09.

219 The long-held view that the tomb of Inhapy and TT320 were one and the same has now been generally rejected (cf. Dewachter 1975; Reeves 1990: 187; Niwiński 1984b; Graefe 2003a, 2005, 2010: 46–48; Aston 2009b: 220). While various suggestions have been made for the location of the tomb of Inhapy, none has proved definitive.

220 As recorded on dockets on the kings' coffins (Jansen-Winkeln 2007–2009: I, 114–17[9.15]; Ritner 2009a: 158–59[36]).

221 Jansen-Winkeln 2007–2009: I, 157[9.59]; Aston 2009b: 186–87; this mummy also included linen of the reign of Amenemopet, thus indicating the problems of dating a burial by a single piece of linen.

222 Pasebkhanut's filiation from Panedjem is included on a bandage epigraph from mummy A.17 in the Bab el-Gasus (Jansen-Winkeln 2007–2009: I, 162–63[10.12]).

223 See Dodson 2009b for a more extensive treatment of the following discussions; I have now withdrawn the proposals set out in Dodson 1987b; cf. Payraudeau 2008: 302–304.

224 Cf. Dodson 2009b: 107.

225 Daressy 1896: 77[17].

226 The date is printed as {⌒ⁱ₁₁; it is possible that a stroke dropped out from a typesetting error, meaning that the date should have been "Year 5."

227 Daressy 1907: 23[17], printing the date as {⌒ (?).

228 From Bab el-Gasus mummy A.65 (Jansen-Winkeln 2007–2009: I, 230[11.83]).

229 Much as Panedjem I passed his priestly office to his son Masaharta when he became king.

230 Payraudeau 2008.

231 Jansen-Winkeln 2007–2009: I, 162[10.10–11].

232 Jansen-Winkeln 2007–2009: I, 158[10.4]; Naville 1911: 2 reports finding "Two inscribed potsherds . . . giving the names of one of the Psusennes

(XXIst Dynasty) and of Osorkon I. (XXIInd Dynasty)" nearby—it is unclear which Pasebkhanut is involved.

233 Cairo JE66285 (Jansen-Winkeln 2007–2009: I, 159–62[10.7]; Ritner 2009a: 166–72[41]); although no date survives, the stela most probably dates to the reign of Pasebkhanut II, although Siamun cannot be ruled out.

234 Jansen-Winkeln 2007–2009: I, 162[10.9].

235 Cf. Payraudeau 2008: 299–302.

236 Ashmolean 1894.107a [the Larger Dakhla Stela], from Mut in the Dakhla oasis (Jansen-Winkeln 2007–2009: II, 23–26[12.28]).

237 Krauss 2006b: 412.

238 Cf. Payraudeau 2008: 300.

239 Jansen-Winkeln 2007–2009: I, 182–83[11.10]; Ritner 2009a: 163–66[40].

240 A block from near Tell el-Daba, referred to in Leclant 1980: 354 as naming Pasebkhanut II, actually refers to either the first king of the name or Panedjem I (personal communication, Manfred Bietak, 24 February 2008).

241 Association Française d'Action Artistique 1987: 136–37[19]; Aston 2009b: 51. A purported *shabti* of Pasebkhanut II, Fitzwilliam E.445.1982, published in Dodson 1987b, has been shown to be a forgery (Yoyotte 1988a). A scarab of Siamun was also found in the chamber (Jansen-Winkeln 2007–2009: I, 113[19.10]; Aston 2009b: 51).

242 Montet 1951: 50–52 states that "[l]es ossements du personnage de gauche m'ont paru être ceux d'une femme," but given the state of the skeletons, and lack of any published anatomical report, this is unlikely to be a definitive assessment. Some of the thirteen canopic jars in the room not belonging to Shoshenq IIa are also likely to be associated with these burials (cf. Dodson 1994: 85–86; Aston 2009b: 53–54).

243 At this time simple nomina were for the first time being used to denote a king, rather than the usually more distinctive prenomen.

244 Cairo CG42192 (Jansen-Winkeln 2007–2009: II, 58[13.33]; see also ch. 3, n. 9).

245 Dodson 1993a; Jansen-Winkeln 2007–2009: II, 37[12.51].

246 Jansen-Winkeln 2007–2009: I, 218–20[11.64]; Manniche 2011: 70–86.

247 Now known only from early-nineteenth-century copies.

248 TTs68, 70, 117(?), 307, 337, and 348 (Porter and Moss 1960–64: 133–34, 139, 233, 385, 405–406, 415; Kampp 1996: 292–94, 297–98, 397–405, 572, 586). There is a possibility, however, that TT307's unfinished decoration could be 'original' (cf. Manniche 2011: 73).

249 Seyfried 1991; Jansen-Winkeln 2007–2009: I, 220[11.65]; Aston 2009b: 411. The tomb had originally been constructed by one Meryptah in the time of Amenhotep III.

250 See Manniche 2011: 73–74.

251 Cf. Manniche 2011: 73, who suggests that it refers to a visit to the north at the time of Shoshenq I's accession. Iuput A, son of Shoshenq I, cannot be wholly ruled out, however, as the date at which he succeeded Pasebkhanut III/IV is unknown: cf. p. 83.

252 Menkheperre or a successor, on the basis of *shabti*s provisionally attributed to the tomb owner (Aston 2009b: 411 n. 3182).

Notes to Chapter 3

1 Kruchten 1989: 49–50, pl. 3, 18.

2 E.g., Kitchen 1996: 288.

3 On the other hand, cf. Broekman's suggestion (2000a) that he might rather have been in dispute with a putative son of Pasebkhanut II, "Maatkheperre Shoshenq": cf. ch. 3, n. 9.

4 There is no real evidence for the date of Iuput's appointment as High Priest, other than it must have been before Year 10 of Shoshenq I, in which he appears on a bandage from the mummy of Djedptahiufankh A (CG61097) in TT320 (Jansen-Winkeln 2007–2009: II, 30–31[12.42]). He then remained in office until at least Year 21 (Silsila stela 100—Jansen-Winkeln 2007–2009: II, 20–22[12.27]).

5 Bandage epigraph from mummy CG61097 (Jansen-Winkeln 2007–2009: II, 31[12.42]); Ashmolean 1894.107a (ch. 2, n. 236), certainly to be attributed to Shoshenq I's reign, is simply dated to 'Year 5 . . . of Pharaoh Shoshenq, l.p.h., beloved of Amun', with no prenomen, but generally accepted to be Shoshenq I. Karnak Nile Level text 3, formerly attributed to Year 5 of Shoshenq I, now appears to be that of a later king of uncertain nomen—see p. 118.

6 Louvre E.31886 (Jansen-Winkeln 2007–2009: II, 75[15.2]).

7 Jansen-Winkeln 2007–2009: II, 75[15.1]; Lange 2010.

8 Following Kitchen's suggestion that Shoshenq was hailing himself as "another Smendes" (1996: 287). The alternative interpretation of the Tutkheperre cartouche is to make him an ephemeral king of the first half of the Twenty-second Dynasty ("Shoshenq IIb": cf. Aston 2009a: 21–22).

9 The prenomen cartouche actually reads "Maatkheperre." While this is probably best read as a mistake for "Hedjkheperre" (von Beckerath 1994c: 86–87 suggested "Heqakheperre"), Broekman (2000a) has proposed that he might be an ephemeral son of Pasebkhanut II, and Jansen-Winkeln (1995c: 147–48) of Shoshenq Q, grandson of Pasebkhanut II (as "Shoshenq IIc").

10 NMS A.1967.2 (Jansen-Winkeln 2007–2009: II, 26–27[12.31]).

11 Cairo JE37966; Vienna ÄS5791; BM EA14594-5 (Jansen-Winkeln 2007–2009: II, 84–85[17.1–3]).

12 Cairo CG42221 (Jansen-Winkeln 2007–2009: II, 243–45[25.51]).

13 BM EA26811 (Jansen-Winkeln 2007–2009: II, 27[12.34]).

14 Jansen-Winkeln 2007–2009: II, 29[12.37], sometimes regarded as a cenotaph. A coffin fragment from the Ramesseum at Thebes-West naming Iuput (Petrie UC14225—Jansen-Winkeln 2007–2009: II, 30[41]) is of a type not found until long after Iuput's death, and probably belonged to a descendant (Taylor 2003: 97). Cf. also the burial at Abydos of Pasebkhanut A, a son of the earlier Theban high priest Menkheperre (pp. 64–65).

15 On the basis of their placement in the genealogy on statue Cairo CG42218 (Jansen-Winkeln 2007–2009: III, 509–10[52.288]). Cf. Broekman 2010: 137–38, reaffirming the dating of CG42218 prior to the Twenty-fifth Dynasty.

16 Broekman 2010: 129.

17 Dodson 1994: 83–84, 131[44], 178–79; on Shoshenq's burial, cf. p. 95.

18 For the typological evolution of the Yellow coffin, see Niwiński 1988b.

19 Cf. Dodson 2000a.

20 Harvard 2230=901.9.1 (Hollis 1987).

21 No mixed deposit of both types has as yet been recorded.

22 Taylor 2003: 103–11; 2009.

23 Jansen-Winkeln 2007–2009: II, 1–2[12.1–7], 4[12.13–14], 410[45.1]; NMS A.1967.2 (see above, ch. 3, n. 10) came from Zagazig, adjacent to Bubastis. A block naming a King Hedjkheperre-setep[en . . .] from Tell Tebilla (Cairo TR 25/11/18/6—ibid. 411[45.6]) could also attest to Shoshenq's work—although Nesibanebdjedet I and Takelot I cannot be ruled out as owners.

24 Jansen-Winkeln 2007–2009: II, 2–3[8–10], 32–36[12.43–48].

25 Jansen-Winkeln 2007–2009: II, 3[12.12].

26 Jansen-Winkeln 2007–2009: II, 4–7[12.15].

27 Porter and Moss 1934: 124; Jansen-Winkeln 2007–2009: II, 7–10[12.16]; Ritner 2009a: 220–27[53].

28 Jansen-Winkeln 2007–2009: II, 16–19[12.21]; Ritner 2009a: 193–200[48A–C].

29 Whose figure had originally been added in high relief in plaster, now missing (Epigraphic Survey 1954: viii).

30 Jansen-Winkeln 2007–2009: II, 11–16[12.20]; Ritner 2009a: 200–13[48D–E].

31 Cf. Aḥituv 1984; Kitchen 1996: 432–47, 587; K.A. Wilson 2005.

32 I Kings 14:25–26; a longer version is given at II Chronicles 12:2–9. Shishak is also mentioned slightly earlier, during the reign of Solomon: "Solomon sought therefore to kill Jeroboam. And Jeroboam arose, and fled into Egypt, unto Shishak king of Egypt, and was in Egypt until the death of Solomon" (I Kings 11:40). Jeroboam went on to found the kingdom of Israel as a rival to Judah.

33 Champollion 1868: 81.

34 The omission of the 'n' is also found in Egyptian sources.

35 Champollion had misread a name ring as giving that city.

36 Being instead identified with Rameses II (Rohl 1995: 120–28, 162–63) or Rameses III (James 1991: 229–31, 257)—with far-reaching chronological implications within the so-called 'new chronology' (cf. p. ix). Kitchen has opined that the omission was due to the fact that Jerusalem had been "cowed; but unconquered" (1996: 298).

37 See further Dodson forthcoming.

38 Porter and Moss 1937: 213; Jansen-Winkeln 2007–2009: II, 20–22[12.27]; Ritner 2009a: 187–93[47].

39 Epigraphic Survey 1954: vii–ix.

40 Cf. Epigraphic Survey 1954: ix. The pylon is generally regarded as a Thirtieth Dynasty/Ptolemaic confection (cf. Arnold 1999: 96–97, 115), although some

have suggested attribution to Taharqa (cf. p. 163), or even that it was actually the structure projected by Shoshenq I (Shubert 1981: 146–47).

41 Cf. Kitchen 1996: 72–76.

42 Cf. D.B. Redford 1973: 10.

43 A similar conclusion is reached by Ben-Dor Evian 2011a in her analysis of the Bubastite Portal tableau.

44 Cairo TR 3/12/24/1=JE59635 (Jansen-Winkeln 2007–2009: II 10–11[12.19]; Ritner 2009a: 215–18[50]).

45 Heidelberg 1343, 1345 & 1970 and *in situ* (Feucht 1981).

46 Fitzwilliam E.8.1896; although found in the Twenty-second Dynasty necropolis around the Ramesseum at Thebes, it seems to have been made in the north (Jansen-Winkeln 2007–2009: II 101[17.27]; Ritner 2009a: 227–28[54]; Taylor 2009: 398, 415, pl. xiv).

47 Ben-Dor Evian 2011b.

48 Jerusalem I.3554 (Porter and Moss 1952: 381; Jansen-Winkeln 2007–2009: II, 26[12.29]; Ritner 2009a: 218–19[51]).

49 Chapman 2009, who argues that the piece (found on a spoil heap) must originally have come from Stratum VA, indicating the erection of the stela in Stratum VB.

50 Cf. Broekman 2011a: 70–71.

51 Berlin VA3361, formerly in the Loytved Collection (Aimé-Giron 1926: 1–5; Porter and Moss 1952: 388; Jansen-Winkeln 2007–2009: II, 26[12.30]; Ritner 2009a: 219–20[52]; Lemaire 2006). My thanks go to Peter Van der Veen for knowledge of the current location of this piece and additional bibliography.

52 The canopic jar fragments and a heart scarab from NRT-V that were once ascribed to him actually belonged to Shoshenq IV: see pp. 127–28; cf. Sagrillo 2011: 246. On the unlikely proposal that the king was buried with a new prenomen, Heqakheperre, see p. 101.

53 Brunton 1939: 546–47.

54 But cf. Sagrillo 2009: 341–42, 349–50.

55 As once suggested by the present writer (Dodson 1988b: 229–31), seconded by Aston 2009b: 61.

56 Sagrillo 2009: 357–58.

57 Jansen-Winkeln 2007–2009: II, 55[13.25].

58 On whom see Dodson 2009a: 60–64.

59 Jansen-Winkeln 2007–2009: II, 62[13.42]; Ritner 2009a: 60[9/Text 34].

60 Cairo CG42193–4 (Jansen-Winkeln 2007–2009: II, 57[30–31]). The second piece names both his parents, as do a graffito and a statue base at Luxor temple (Jansen-Winkeln 2007–2009: II, 56 [28–29]; Ritner 2009a: 264[65]).

61 BM EA8 (Jansen-Winkeln 2007–2009: II, 57–58[13.32]; Ritner 2009a: 264–67[66]).

62 Cartouches were only ever used for kings until the end of the Twelfth Dynasty, when we find Amenemhat III's daughter Neferuptah granted it—potentially as female heir to the throne as a precursor to the reign of the female king Sobekneferu (cf. Ryholt 1997: 210; Dodson 2000b). Cartouches then become

increasingly usual for kings' wives during the Second Intermediate Period and then normal from the New Kingdom onward. A few royal sons and daughters also employ cartouches around this time, but only a few Eighteenth Dynasty princes are so honored—in particular Amenmose, son of Thutmose I, and "Prince B" [Amenhotep B?] (see Dodson 1990). No Rameside royal sons are known to have used a cartouche, nor any others in the Third Intermediate Period save Shoshenq Q, emphasizing his exceptional status.

63   Or even the 'Maatkheperre' Shoshenq (IIc) of Cairo statue CG42192: see ch. 3, n. 9.

64   While one could resort to special pleading to argue that the brevity and/or non-independence of the putative reign of the former Shoshenq Q meant that to his descendants he was "high priest par excellence," rather than an ephemeral king (as does Kitchen 1996: 119–20, 545) this seems unlikely.

65   Cairo CG42193 (see ch. 3, n. 60).

66   Durham N313 (Malek 1999: 1029[802-006-100]; Jansen-Winkeln 2007–2009: II, 56[13.27]; Ritner 2009a: 267–69[67]); it is possible to read the text on this piece as indicating that Shoshenq was still alive when it was carved.

67   pSt Petersburg, National Library of Russia SPL 1–2 (Denon 1802: pl. cxxxvii–viii; Coenen 1995; Dodson 2009a: 54–60; Solkin 2011–12: 44–49).

68   Known from fragments of his cartonnage mummy case in a private collection, giving his full male-line descent from Osorkon I (Dodson 2009a: 51–54).

69   Broekman 2010: 128.

70   Cairo CG884, Berlin ÄM22461, Louvre E.25479, etc., (Jansen-Winkeln 2007–2009: II, 89–93[17.10–14) and mentions by descendants: cf. Broekman 2010: 130–31.

71   Cairo CG884; cf. Broekman 2010: 130.

72   Cf. Broekman 2010: 132–33, who prefers the first of these options.

73   Broekman 2010: 130–31.

74   Petrie UC14496 (Jansen-Winkeln 2007–2009: II, 59[13.34]; Ritner 2009a: 261–62[63]); Broekman 2010: 139.

75   Known from the monuments of various descendants (cf. Kitchen 1996: 217–20; Broekman 2010: 139–40).

76   Jansen-Winkeln 2007–2009: II, 61–68[13.39–46].

77   Jansen-Winkeln 2007–2009: II, 52–54[13.17–19]; Ritner 2009a: 229–32[56], 258[61].

78   Goyon and Traunecker 1982.

79   Jansen-Winkeln 2007–2009: II, 52[13.15].

80   Jansen-Winkeln 2007–2009: II, 52[13.14].

81   Jansen-Winkeln 2007–2009: II, 49–52[13.11–13]; Ritner 2009a: 235–37[58].

82   The genealogical succession is set out in stela Louvre IM3429 from the Serapeum (see ch. 2, n. 100).

83   MMA 10.176.42 (Jansen-Winkeln 2007–2009: II, 60–61[13.38]).

84   Jansen-Winkeln 2007–2009: II, 38–49[13.4–9]; Ritner 2009a: 237–58 [59–60].

85   Louvre AO.9502 (Jansen-Winkeln 2007–2009: II, 54–55[13.21]; Ritner 2009a: 233–34[57]).

86 II Chronicles 14:9–15.
87 Cf. Kitchen 1996: 309 n. 371. For the reliability of such datings, cf. p. 186.
88 Of the God's Father Nakhtefmut E from the Ramesseum (Fitzwilliam E.64.1896, E.70-293.1896—Jansen-Winkeln 2007–2009: II, 69–70[13.49]; Aston 2009b: 239; Ritner 2009a: 262–64[64]). A Year 3 on another bandage has generally been attributed to a coregent—but is more likely to be an old piece from Osorkon's own reign, or that of Takelot I. Another mummy including Osorkon's name incorporated bandages with dates of Years 11, 12, and 23 (of the *waab* priest of Amun, Khonsumakheru, Hamburg C3835-9—Jansen-Winkeln 2007–2009: II, 70[50]), the latter also arguing against a reign as short as fifteen years. For other burials datable to Osorkon I's reign, see Jansen-Winkeln 2007–2009: II, 69[13.48], 70–72[13.51–55].
89 Cf. Broekman 2010.
90 Cf. Kitchen 1996: 110–11, although his third point becomes invalid under our view that Shoshenq Q and king Shoshenq IIa were separate people.
91 Jansen-Winkeln 1987; Kitchen 1996: xxii–xxiii. The cartouches of the later Takelot II differed only by addition of the epithet '-siese' (Son of Isis) to the nomen.
92 Jansen-Winkeln 2007–2009: II, 76–77[16.5–7], 81[16.12–14].
93 Moscow I.1.a.5000(4154) (Jansen-Winkeln 2007–2009: II, 81[16.10]).
94 From Umm el-Qaab (Jansen-Winkeln 2007–2009: II, 81[16.11]).
95 BM EA1224 (Jansen-Winkeln 2007–2009: II, 81–81[16.9]; Ritner 2009a: 278–80[70]). Another son, Wasakawasa, is attested by a pectoral (Petrie UC13124—Jansen-Winkeln 2007–2009: II, 230[25.23]; Ritner 2009a: 280–81[71]); and a daughter, Djedisetesankh i, by a statue of her son (Cairo CG42215—Jansen-Winkeln 2007–2009: II, 240–41[25.46]).
96 Cairo JE31882 [the 'stela de l'apenage'] (Jansen-Winkeln 2007–2009: II, 77–80[16.8]; Ritner 2009a: 271–78[69]).
97 Cairo CG42215 (n. 95, just above).
98 Louvre SN82 (Jansen-Winkeln 2007–2009: II, 82[16.18]).
99 Cf. Malinine, Posener, and Vercoutter 1968: 18–19; if so, a stela fragment in Alexandria (Jansen-Winkeln 2007–2009: II, 82[19]) dated to a nameless Year 14 may belong to this putative burial.
100 Cairo JE86161 (Jansen-Winkeln 2007–2009: II, 82[16.17]).
101 Copenhagen Nationalmuseet 332; Berlin ÄM8437+Aberdeen 1337=1551; Cairo JE31653 (Jansen-Winkeln 2007–2009: II, 82–83[16.20–22]).
102 Although Lull has suggested (2002: 39–40) that Takelot might have first been buried in NRT-VI, which was dismantled after his removal to NRT-I. There seems, however, no real evidence for such a scenario.
103 Jansen-Winkeln 2007–2009: II, 76[16.2].
104 Jansen-Winkeln 2007–2009: II, 76[3]; Ritner 2009a: 282[75].
105 Stolen in 1943 and never recovered (Dodson 1994: 90, 134–35[46/1–4]).
106 Aston 2009b: 54–55.
107 Of a man apparently around fifty years of age, who had died from an infected head wound (Derry 1939). Now Qasr el-Aini 3.

108 Cf. Broekman 2009b.

109 Cairo JE72154–97, 86956, TR 27/4/44/3 (Aston 2009b: 51–54).

110 Gardiner 1961: 448; Jacquet-Gordon 1975: 359; Edwards 1982: 549; Broekman 2006–2007.

111 Cf. Sagrillo 2009: 356.

112 Cf. Aston 2009a: 21; Shoshenq IIb (Tutkheperre) has also been placed here, but see p. 84 for the view that he may rather be an earlier titulary of Shoshenq I.

113 Jansen-Winkeln 2007–2009: II, 110[18.6]; Ritner 2009a: 282–82[73].

114 Montet 1947: 46–47; 1951: 27–30.

115 Fragments of offering scenes, probably from this court, were found in the Sacred Lake (Jansen-Winkeln 2007–2009: II, 108[18.1–2]).

116 Jansen-Winkeln 2007–2009: II, 110[18.4].

117 Cf. Graefe 1975.

118 Vienna ÄS3561–4 (Jansen-Winkeln 2007–2009: II, 222[25.1]).

119 See n. 123.

120 Jansen-Winkeln 2007–2009: II, 124–26[18.46–52]; Aston 2009b: 55–58.

121 Perez Die 2009.

122 Cf. Sagrillo 2009.

123 Cairo JE45327 (Jansen-Winkeln 2007–2009: II, 131–33[18.69]; Ritner 2009a: 344–47[80]).

124 Although called "Crown Prince" in Kitchen 1996, none of his titles unequivocally gives him this status (cf. Jansen-Winkeln 2007–2009: II, 123–24[18.41–45], 184–86[22.15–18]).

125 Budapest 51.2050 (Jansen-Winkeln 2007–2009: II, 123[18.41], 129–30[18.63]).

126 Cairo JE86786 (Jansen-Winkeln 2007–2009: II, 185[22.18]).

127 Cairo JE88131 (Aston 2009b: 78–80; Jansen-Winkeln 2007–2009: II, 184–85[22.15]).

128 Although a fragment of stela with Osorkon's name was found there (Cairo JE28582—Porter and Moss 1974–81: 839).

129 Jansen-Winkeln 2007–2009: II, 112–6, 477[18.13–20a]); Ritner 2009a: 291–344[78–79]; Lange 2009.

130 BM EA1146 (Jansen-Winkeln 2007–2009: II, 116–7[18.21]).

131 Aston 2009a: 11–12; 2009b: 64–65; Jansen-Winkeln 2007–2009: II, 126–28[18.53, 56–85].

132 Jansen-Winkeln 2007–2009: II, 121[18.35]; Ritner 2009a: 288[75].

133 Jansen-Winkeln 2007–2009: II, 121[34].

134 Jansen-Winkeln 2007–2009: II, 120–21[18.33].

135 Jansen-Winkeln 2007–2009: II, 118–9[18.29]; Ritner 2009a: 288–90[76].

136 Jansen-Winkeln 2007–2009: II, 119–20[18.30–32].

137 Cf. Aston 1989: 151–52.

138 Jansen-Winkeln 2007–2009: II, 133[18.70–72].

139 Jansen-Winkeln 2007–2009: II, 118[18.24–28]; Ritner 2009a: 36–37.

140 Jansen-Winkeln 2007–2009: II, 133–51[18.73–83]; Ritner 2009a: 51–52.

141 Jansen-Winkeln 2007–2009: II, 154–59[19.1–8].

142 The inscription on statue Durham N313 had been misread to give him the high-priestly title (see Jansen-Winkeln 1995c: 129–32).

143 On Cairo statue CG42225 (Jansen-Winkeln 2007–2009: II, 135–39[18.75]).

144 Jansen-Winkeln 1995c: 135–36.

145 Jansen-Winkeln 2007–2009: II, 225[25.8, end].

146 Jansen-Winkeln 2006b: 241 n. 64.

147 Jansen-Winkeln 2007–2009: II, 156, 25[25.10]; Aston 2009b: 111.

148 Known from statues of her descendants (Cairo CG42210 and CG42211—Jansen-Winkeln 2007–2009: II, 234[25.36], 323[30.7]).

149 Known from a fragment of coffin from Abydos (UPMAA E.16186—Jansen-Winkeln 2007–2009: II, 226[25.12]).

150 Cairo JE37516, from Koptos (Jansen-Winkeln 2007–2009: II, 155–56[19.6]).

151 On stela Berlin ÄM14995 (Jansen-Winkeln 2007–2009: II, 154[19.1]).

152 Jansen-Winkeln 2007–2009: II, 226–28[25.13–17]; she was buried in the area of the Ramesseum (Aston 2009b: 237–38).

153 Jansen-Winkeln 2007–2009: II, 113[18.13].

154 Cairo CG42208 (Jansen-Winkeln 2007–2009: II, 141–44[18.78]).

155 Cf. Broekman 2010: 140–41, 146–47 on whether the Osorkon named on Cairo statue JE91720 is to be taken as Osorkon II or as Osorkon III.

156 The damage to [Pa?]du[bast?]'s name seems to have been due purely to wear and tear.

157 Hölscher 1954: 10.

158 Porter and Moss 1960–64: 772.

159 Cairo JE59900A–D; JE59716–9 and Chicago OIM 15639–53; Cairo JE59896, 60137 (Jansen-Winkeln 2007–2009: II, 154–55[19.5]; Aston 2009b: 260).

160 Jansen-Winkeln 2007–2009: II, 119–20[18.32].

161 Louvre IM3090 (Jansen-Winkeln 2007–2009: II, 129–30[18.63]).

162 Jansen-Winkeln 2007–2009: II, 118[18.28].

163 Lull 2002: 74–117; Aston 2009b: 54–58.

164 Jansen-Winkeln 2007–2009: II, 110[18.5]; Ritner 2009a: 347–48[81].

165 Cf. Aston 2009b: 55–58.

166 Aston 2009b: 58; the canopic jars were stolen in 1943 and have never been recovered.

167 Montet 1947: 58–59, fig. 7. On size alone they cannot be Osorkon II and others, as is proposed by Aston 2009b: 58 n. 246.

168 von Känel 1987: 57.

169 Aston 2009b: 58.

170 Cf. Aston 2009b: 58–59.

Notes to Chapter 4

1 For a summary, see Ritner 2009b; cf. also Lange 2008.

2 Cf. Ritner's point (2009b: 336–37) regarding the way in which Padieset A passed on his Egyptian pontifical title to his son, while retaining his Libyan one and wearing a Libyan feather on his principal monuments: cf. pp. 116–17.

3   And even more so about projecting the onset of the Libya-influenced fissiparous traits back as far as the end of the Rameside Period, as set out in Jansen-Winkeln 1994. Although there is no doubt that Libyan elements were already present in the ruling families at that time, the appearance of Libyan titles in those circles seems to date only to the latter part of the Twenty-first Dynasty.

4   Cf. the issue of Shoshenq IIa (see pp. 99, 101).

5   Unlike the Twenty-first Dynasty (see pp. 39–40), Manetho is of no real help for the Twenty-second: his most extensive list (cf. p. 123, with ch. 4, nn. 54–55) simply runs Sesonchosis—Osorthon—"three other kings"—Takelothis—"three other kings."

6   Jansen-Winkeln 1987.

7   Aston 1989, refreshed in Aston 2009a.

8   E.g., Jansen-Winkeln 2006b: 242–43.

9   Especially Kitchen 1996: xxiii–xxv; 2009: 167–76; cf. Aston 2009a: 2.

10   Petrie UC14661; Cairo JE36728 (Jansen-Winkeln 2007–2009: II, 196[22.22]; III, 371–72[52.43].

11   Cairo JE45610 (Jansen-Winkeln 2007–2009: II, 196–97[22.23]; Ritner 2009a: 385–86[87]).

12   Louvre E.20905 (Jansen-Winkeln 2007–2009: II, 197–98[22.25]).

13   Berlin ÄM7344 (Jansen-Winkeln 2007–2009: II, 201[22.30]).

14   Cairo CG9430 (Jansen-Winkeln 2007–2009: II, 415[45.33]).

15   Jansen-Winkeln 2007–2009: II, 175[22.1–2]; Ritner 2009a: 390–92[90].

16   Montet 1960.

17   Jansen-Winkeln 2007–2009: II, 179–82[22.6–10]; blocks from a building at Memphis (Cairo JE46915) often attributed to Shoshenq III more probably belong to Shoshenq V (see p. 135).

18   Jansen-Winkeln 2007–2009: II, 196–203[22.23–34]; Ritner 2009a: 383–85[86–88].

19   Jansen-Winkeln 2007–2009: II, 185–86[22.19]; Ritner 2009a: 388–90[89].

20   A quarter-century appears to be the maximum possible life span of a bull, while the gap between burials is approximately four decades. As already noted (pp. 59–60), there also seem to be a number of 'missing' bulls directly preceding that of Osorkon II. From Apis XXIX onward, however, an essentially unbroken series of bulls stretches into the Late Period.

21   See ch. 4, n. 2.

22   Porter and Moss 1974–81: 847; Aston 2009b: 80. His brother Horsieset i was buried in an adjacent tomb (Aston 2009b: 80–81). Interestingly, Padieset and and Horsieset were interred respectively in the sarcophagus and stone outer coffin of the Eighteenth Dynasty Steward of Memphis Amenhotep-Huy (Memphis open air museum and Cairo JE59128).

23   Jansen-Winkeln 2007–2009: II, 203[22.36].

24   Cairo CG42225: see ch. 3, n. 143.

25   Jansen-Winkeln 2007–2009: II, 332[32.1]; although definitely belonging to a king Hedjkheperre, the nomen is badly damaged and only [. . .]-sieset

meryamun is certain. The traces have been read as giving an otherwise unknown Shoshenq (VIa—Broekman 1988: 176–77; 2005), but may actually refer to Takelot II (Payraudeau 2009: 296; cf. Broekman 2009a: 97–99).

26 Jansen-Winkeln 2007–2009: II, 160[20.2].

27 Elephantine Museum (Jansen-Winkeln 2007–2009: II, 172[20.15]).

28 Jansen-Winkeln 2007–2009: II, 161–68[20.7], 186–96[22.21]; Ritner 2009a: 348–77[82]; Broekman 2008.

29 Stela Turin C.1468+Vatican 329 (Jansen-Winkeln 2007–2009: II, 229[25.21]).

30 Stone fragment Stockholm MM32010 (Jansen-Winkeln 2007–2009: II, 229[25.20]).

31 Named in Karnak Priestly Annals 7 = Cairo JE36493 and stela Cairo TR 11/9/21/17 (Jansen-Winkeln 2007–2009: II, 203[22.38], 225–26[25.11]).

32 Stela Cairo JE36195 (Jansen-Winkeln 2007–2009: II, 161[20.6]; Ritner 2009a: 379–80[84]).

33 Named on the coffins of their daughter and grandson (Berlin 20132–6—Jansen-Winkeln 2007–2009: II, 390–91[44.19–20]; Aston 2009b: 250). Isetweret's mother was named Tabakhtenaskhet (A), perhaps the same woman buried in the high-priestly cemetery at Memphis (Aston 2009b: 81).

34 Statue Cairo CG42211 (ch. 3 n. 148); cf. Broekman 2010: 141.

35 Louvre E.3336=C258 (Jansen-Winkeln 2007–2009: II, 168–69[20.10]; Ritner 2009a: 377–79[83]). Year 11 also saw an entry in the Karnak Priestly Annals (Jansen-Winkeln 2007–2009: II, 168 [20.9]; Ritner 2009a: 59).

36 Jansen-Winkeln 2007–2009: II, 182–83[22.11]; Ritner 2009a: 37.

37 Cf. Krauss 2006a: 377. The wording is unclear. What does appear certain, however, is that no 'normal' eclipse is being reported in the text, as has sometimes been proposed (cf. Kitchen 1996: 181–82). On the other hand, Thijs (2010: 181–82) has put forward the proposal that what is being referred to is the penumbral eclipse of 756. This, however, requires a radical change to the overall chronology of the period that creates what appear to be wholly untenable knock-on effects earlier in the Third Intermediate Period and New Kingdom.

38 Jansen-Winkeln 2007–2009: II, 208[23.2]; Ritner 2009a: 37.

39 Jansen-Winkeln 2007–2009: II, 212–13[23.15]; Ritner 2009a: 48–9.

40 Jansen-Winkeln 2007–2009: II, 208[23.1]; Ritner 2009a: 413[108].

41 Jansen-Winkeln 2007–2009: II, 213[23.16]; Ritner 2009a: 49.

42 Cairo JE36159: see ch. 4, n. 32.

43 Jansen-Winkeln 2007–2009: II, 250–51[25.57]; Ritner 2009a: 380–82[85].

44 Jansen-Winkeln 2007–2009: II, 174, 208[23.3]; Ritner 2009a: 38.

45 Jansen-Winkeln 2007–2009: II, 173 [21.3–4].

46 Jansen-Winkeln 2007–2009: II, 17[21.1]; Ritner 2009a: 51–52. This could also, however, be Year 11 of Takelot II.

47 Jansen-Winkeln 2007–2009: II, 209–12[23.10–13]; an unprovenanced statuette also bears the name (ibid. 209[23.8]).

48 Cf. Aston 2009b: 14–15.

49 Cf. von Beckerath 1995; Muhs 1998.

50 Kahn 2006.

51 Cairo JE45530; Ny Carlsberg ÆIN917 (Jansen-Winkeln 2007–2009: II, 209–12[23.10, 13]).

52 For a simple 'Padubast' in Dakhla Oasis, see Jansen-Winkeln 2007–2009: II, 209[23.7].

53 Cf. the objections to making Padubast I and II the same person pointed out in Kahn 2006 and Aston 2009a.

54 Eusebius and the Armenian version of Eusebius.

55 Africanus (Waddell 1940: 158–61); cf. ch. 4, n. 5.

56 Waddell 1940: 161–63.

57 E.g., Kitchen 1996: 450–52.

58 Cf. Aston 1989.

59 E.g., probably statue Cairo CG42212, bought at Luxor but bearing the name of king Thutemhat of Hermopolis (Jansen-Winkeln 2007–2009: II, 367–68[37.3]).

60 Moscow I.1.a.5647 (Jansen-Winkeln 2007–2009: II, 203–3[22.34]).

61 BMA 67.118 (Jansen-Winkeln 2007–2009: II, 198–99[22.26]; Ritner 2009a: 386–88[88]).

62 Cairo TR 11/1/25/13 (Jansen-Winkeln 2007–2009: II, 200[22.28]).

63 Jansen-Winkeln 2007–2009: II, 208[23.3–5]; Ritner 2009a: 38.

64 Jansen-Winkeln 2007–2009: II, 208[23.6]; Ritner 2009a: 38.

65 Once regarded as potentially simply Shoshenq III employing a variant prenomen epithet (cf. Aston 1989: 151).

66 Jansen-Winkeln 2007–2009: II, 219–20[24.1–6]; Ritner 2009a: 39, 57.

67 Jansen-Winkeln 2007–2009: II, 220[24.7]; cf. Aston 1989: 151–52.

68 Cairo JE36439 (Jansen-Winkeln 2007–2009: II, 203–204[22.38]; Ritner 2009a: 52–54.

69 From Tihna el-Gebel (Jansen-Winkeln 2007–2009: II, 296[29.9]; Ritner 2009a: 421–23[111]).

70 Louvre IM3697, 3736, 4205, 3441 (Jansen-Winkeln 2007–2009: II, 261–63, 265 [27.5–6, 9–10]; Ritner 2009a: 394–400[94–97]).

71 Cf. Kitchen 1996: 102–103.

72 Dodson 1993b; the nomen was long thought to be simply a long version of that of Shoshenq I.

73 Jansen-Winkeln 2007–2009: II, 175–79, 256 [22.3–4, 26.2–3]; Lull 2002: 135–55; Aston 2009b: 59–60; Sagrillo 2009: 355.

74 Jansen-Winkeln 2007–2009: II, 256–58[26.1–8]; Ritner 2009a: 392–93[91–92].

75 Hermitage 5630 (Jansen-Winkeln 2007–2009: II, 257[26.6]; Ritner 2009a: 393[92]).

76 Jansen-Winkeln 2007–2009: II, 273–74[28.16], assigned to Shoshenq V on the basis of the epithet '-netjerheqwaset' (cf. p. 135)—there is no prenomen on the stela; however, as noted above, there seems to be at least one example of this epithet being used by Shoshenq IV.

77 Jansen-Winkeln 2007–2009: II, 293[29.1–3]; Ritner 2009a: 39.

78   Jansen-Winkeln 2007–2009: II, 295[29.8], 315[30.3].
79   Jansen-Winkeln 2007–2009: II, 297[29.11].
80   Jansen-Winkeln 2007–2009: II, 331[31.4].
81   Jansen-Winkeln 2007–2009: II, 295[29.8].
82   MFA 94.321 (D'Auria, Lacovara, and Roehrig 1988: 171–72[123]).
83   Jansen-Winkeln 2007–2009: II, 393[44.23]; they were the parents of a Prophet of Amun, Osorkon (see pp. 132–33).
84   Jansen-Winkeln 2007–2009: II, 294, 297[29.5, 11–13].
85   Jansen-Winkeln 2007–2009: II, 314–18[30.3], 366[36.1], 385[44.1]; III, 259[51.2], 263[51.16], 269[51.17], 334[51.128], 335[51.129], 568[51.6a].
86   Cf. Jansen-Winkeln 2007–2009: I, 81[6.25].
87   Cf. Jansen-Winkeln 2007–2009: II, 226–28[25.13–16].
88   She is first attested around half a century previously, and if appointed in her youth could easily have lived this long (cf. the long lives of many later God's Wives, freed by their status from the perils of childbearing: cf. pp. 171, 177).
89   Berlin statue ÄM17272 (Jansen-Winkeln 2007–2009: II, 301–302[29.16]; cf. Broekman 2010: 135).
90   Jansen-Winkeln 2007–2009: II, 301–11[29.15–30].
91   Broekman 2010: 141.
92   Jansen-Winkeln 2007–2009: II, 298–301[29.14]; Ritner 2009a: 415–21[111]; Bickel 2009.
93   Jansen-Winkeln 2007–2009: II, 313[30.1]; Ritner 2009a: 39–40.
94   Jansen-Winkeln 2007–2009: II, 313–19[30.3]; Ayad 2009a.
95   Although Porter 2011 suggests that he is to be found with a short-form nomen with a unique terminal '-nw' on blocks from Tanis. For the greater likelihood that these actually belong to Osorkon IV see p. 150.
96   For full titularies—as far as preserved—see Appendix 4.
97   Cf. von Beckerath 1999.
98   Payraudeau 2009: 299–301; the latter name has usually been taken as belonging to Rudamun, but from its context in the Osiris-Heqadjet chapel it, and the associated Nebty-name ḥkn-m³ʿt, can only belong to Takelot III (see also Jurman 2006: 78–85).
99   Jansen-Winkeln 2007–2009: II, 313[30.2].
100 Jansen-Winkeln 2007–2009: II, 294.
101 Although no obvious remains can be identified from among the various tombs excavated in the area (Hölscher 1954: 16–33).
102 Jansen-Winkeln 2007–2009: II, 329[30.14]; Kaper 2009: 150–53; the protagonist, the Chief of the Shamin, Nesthuty, was still in office in Year 23 of Piye (Payraudeau 2009: 291–96; cf. p. 152).
103 This date/name combination lies adjacent to a similar pair linking a Year 12 with the God's Wife Amenirdis I (Jansen-Winkeln 2007–2009: II, 355[44.1]), and was long regarded as a single double-dated inscription, providing a synchronism between an Egyptian king (the Shepenwepet date) and a Nubian king (the Amenirdis date—e.g., Kitchen 1996: 543–44, proposing

Piye/Iuput II; Piye/Takelot III and Piye/Rudamun have also been put forward). However, the two pairs have now been shown to be almost certainly independent (see Jurman 2006: 86–91).

104 Jansen-Winkeln 2007–2009: II, 393[44.24]; III, 359[52.21].
105 Jansen-Winkeln 2007–2009: II, 319[30.4].
106 Cf. Aston and Taylor 1990.
107 Bruyère 1957: 16–18.
108 Jansen-Winkeln 2007–2009: III, 357–8[52.19], 362–63[52.26].
109 Jansen-Winkeln 2007–2009: III, 357–8[52.19].
110 Jansen-Winkeln 2007–2009: III, 355–57[52.17].
111 BM EA74892 (ex-Croydon Public Library—Aston and Taylor 1990: 135–36).
112 Jansen-Winkeln 2007–2009: III, 208[48.150], 355[52.16].
113 BM EA22913 (Jansen-Winkeln 2007–2009: II, 398–99[44.38]).
114 Broekman 2010: 136–37.
115 Payraudeau 2009: 297–99.
116 Jansen-Winkeln 2007–2009: II, 320–26[30.7–8].
117 Jansen-Winkeln 2007–2009: II, 319–20[30.5], 328[30.13].
118 Leiden C.I.280, 283, and 284 (Jansen-Winkeln 2007–2009: II, 320[30.6]). Given their curious form and the poor spelling of their texts, one must retain a degree of scepticism regarding their origins. It is not impossible that they belonged to Takelot II, although the short form of the name supports the later king.
119 Turin C.1632 (Jansen-Winkeln 2007–2009: III, 408[52.132]).
120 Cairo JE37163 (De Meulenaere 1978).
121 Coffins Cairo CG41035 and formerly Berlin NN (Jansen-Winkeln 2007–2009: III, 357[52.18], 393[44.23]); ch. 4, n. 83.
122 Aston and Taylor 1990: 134.
123 Cf. Yoyotte 1988a.
124 Reused in the Bab el-Nasr gateway at Cairo (Jansen-Winkeln 2007–2009: II, 259–61[27.3]).
125 Jansen-Winkeln 2007–2009: II, 259[27.1]; Ritner 2009a: 394[93].
126 Cairo TR 2/2/21/13 (Jansen-Winkeln 2007–2009: II, 267[27.13]); Ritner 2009a: 402–403[100]).
127 Louvre IM3697, 3736.
128 A *shabti* of Peftjauawybast is in Cairo (Jansen-Winkeln 2007–2009: II, 156[22.20]). While one would assume that he had died in the interim, Morkot and James suggest (2009) that Peftjauawybast might rather have translated to Herakleopolis and become the king of that name (p. 149); this, however, requires a radical change in the chronology of the period that does not seem credible (cf. Appendix 1), leaving aside the fact that the only real argument is of the similarity of names. For a detailed critique, see Broekman 2011a.
129 Louvre IM4205, 3441, 3083, NN (Jansen-Winkeln 2007–2009: II, 265–67[27.9–12]; Ritner 2009a: 398–400[96–97]).
130 Louvre E.20368, E.11139 (Jansen-Winkeln 2007–2009: II, 263–65[27.7–8]; Ritner 2009a: 401–402[99]).

131 Jansen-Winkeln 2007–2009: II, 259[27.2]; Ritner 2009a: 403–404[101].
132 Amenemopet: NRT-III & IV; Osorkon II-NRT-I; Shoshenq III-NRT-V.
133 Aston 2009b: 60.
134 As explicitly stated in Serapeum stela Louvre IM3049 (Jansen-Winkeln 2007–2009: II, 280–81[28.26]).
135 Jansen-Winkeln 2007–2009: II, 268–69[28.1].
136 Although *wsr-pḥty*, used for all three minor names, had not actually been used before, except as one element of one of Rameses III's variant Nebty names.
137 Jurman 2009: 129–32.
138 Jansen-Winkeln 2007–2009: II, 179[22.5]—dated to Shoshenq III; Jurman 2009: 128.
139 Jurman 2009: 127–29.
140 De Meulenaere 1985.
141 Cf. Jurman 2009: 128–29.
142 Jansen-Winkeln 2007–2009: II, 271–72[28.12], 283–91[28.32–46]. This Apis burial plays a crucial role in the radical chronological revision in Thijs 2010, for which cf. ch. 4, n. 37.
143 Jansen-Winkeln 2007–2009: II, 272–78[28.13–23], 291–92[28.47].
144 Jansen-Winkeln 2007–2009: II, 280–83[28.26–31].
145 Jansen-Winkeln 2007–2009: II, 269–70[28.3–8].
146 Jansen-Winkeln 2007–2009: II, 269[28.2].
147 Cf. Aston 2009a: 58–59.
148 BMA 67.119 (Jansen-Winkeln 2007–2009: II, 274[28.18]).
149 Cairo JE30972 (Jansen-Winkeln 2007–2009: II, 276–77[28.21]).
150 IFAO 14456 (Jansen-Winkeln 2007–2009: II, 275–76[28.20]).
151 Louvre IM3078 (Jansen-Winkeln 2007–2009: II, 286–87[28.37]).
152 Jansen-Winkeln 2007–2009: II, 270[28.9–10]; Ritner 2009a: 435–36[123–24].
153 Florence 1777 (Jansen-Winkeln 2007–2009: II, 270–71[28.11]).
154 Location uncertain (Jansen-Winkeln 2007–2009: II, 273[28.15]; Ritner 2009a: 437–38[126]).
155 Formerly King Faruq Collection (Jansen-Winkeln 2007–2009: II, 272–73[28.14]; Ritner 2009a: 436–37[125]).
156 Cf. Kitchen 1996: 355.
157 Jansen-Winkeln 2007–2009: II, 330–31[31.3].
158 See ch. 4, n. 102 for what has in the past been regarded as a potential Year 19.
159 Jansen-Winkeln 2007–2009: II, 385[44.3].
160 Jansen-Winkeln 2007–2009: II, 382–83[42.1–5]; Ritner 2009a: 66[10/11]. The stela (Louvre C.100) may, however, belong to the Kushite king Piye (cf. Eide et al. 1994–2000: I, 47).

Notes to Chapter 5
1 pLouvre E.25365+pAberdeen 171i (M. Müller 2009: 254).
2 Cf. Morkot 2000: 129–66; 2003.
3 Horton 1991: 264–65.
4 Caminos 1998: I, pl. 15, 18–19; Darnell 2006; Eide et al. 1994–2000: I, 35–41.

5   Or possibly Karimala—see Darnell 2006: 12–14.

6   Darnell 2006: 17–44, 55–71.

7   Darnell 2006: 45–48; cf. Morkot 2000: 153.

8   In situ, BM EA1777, and Ny Carlsberg ÆIN1709 (Porter and Moss 1952: 181[3–4], with latter number misquoted as 1708).

9   Cf. Morkot 2000: 149.

10 The reading of the nomen is unclear: cf. Morkot 2000: 147.

11 Khartoum 5225, 5227 (Porter and Moss 1952: 216[18], 222); Dunham 1970: 34, pl. xxxvii.

12 Priese 1977, from an unpublished Lepsius expedition copy.

13 Morkot 2000: 145–46.

14 With Morkot 2000: 147–50.

15 Napatan prenomina follow the 'simple' pattern that reappeared in Egypt under Takelot III and Shoshenq V.

16 For early theories on the post-New Kingdom history of Nubia and the origins of the Kushite state, cf. Morkot 2003.

17 Dunham 1950; there is also a pair of pyramids of uncertain, but probably fourth-century, date.

18 Plus the later Ku1 and 2.

19 Dunham 1950: 1–3.

20 Kendall 1982: 22–23, a view later recanted; Hakem 1988: 253–55; Török 1995. Cf. Lull 2002: 197–210.

21 Cf. Morkot 2000: 140–44.

22 Cf. Morkot 2000: 143.

23 Khartoum 2678 [Kawa IV]: §§16–17; Khartoum 2679 [Kawa VI]: §§23–24 (Jansen-Winkeln 2007–2009: III, 132–35[48.74], 138–41[48.76]; Eide et al. 1994–2000: I, 140–51, 173–74); Kawa IX: §54 (Eide et al. 1994–2000: II, 400–428[71]).

24 Often read in the past as 'Piankhy,' depending on how one reads the ʿnḫ-sign in his cartouche (cf. Vittmann 1974).

25 Stela Khartoum 1901, from her tomb, el-Kurru Ku53 (Jansen-Winkeln 2007–2009: II, 358–59; Eide et al. 1994–2000: I, 119–20[11]). This names her mother as Kasaqa.

26 Kendall (1999: 64) and Morkot (2000: 149, 157) have raised the possibility that Alara might be equated with the aforementioned Iry, but this seems unlikely on chronological grounds; also, as Morkot points out, Alara is never given a prenomen in these sources.

27 The reading of the prenomen is not altogether clear—cf. Eide et al. 1994–2000: I, 43.

28 Although a stray fragment (MFA exc. 19-3-537) possibly naming Kashta was found in pyramid Ku1, potentially suggesting his interment at el-Kurru (Dunham 1950: 23–24, pl. xxxiic); cf. Lull 2002: 180–82.

29 Jansen-Winkeln 2007–2009: II, 336[34.2–3].

30 Cairo JE41013 (Jansen-Winkeln 2007–2009: II, 336[34.1]; Eide et al. 1994–2000: I, 45–47[4]).

31   Morkot argues for the *a priori* likelihood of a God's Wife being installed by her father (1999: 194–96).

32   Museo Barracco, Rome (Jansen-Winkeln 2007–2009: II, 366[36.1]).

33   Cairo JE31886 (Jansen-Winkeln 2007–2009: II, 354–57[35.17]).

34   Jansen-Winkeln 2007–2009: II, 355; Broekman 2009a: 100–101, a view opposed by Olivier Perdu (Broekman 2009a: 101 n. 50).

35   Filiation on statue Cairo CG42498 (Jansen-Winkeln 2007–2009: III, 259[51.2]).

36   Cairo JE32022–3, from Pekasater's tomb at Abydos (Jansen-Winkeln 2007–2009: II, 360[35.29]).

37   Cf. Leahy 1994: 182–87; Morkot 2000: 159–61.

38   Respectively buried in tombs D48 and D9 at Abydos (Jansen-Winkeln 2007–2009: III, 352–53[52.12–13]).

39   According to Paabtameri's stela, her son was only twenty when she died.

40   Cf. Dodson 1990: 88–89.

41   Given that Shepenwepet II held an office for some six and a half decades, she may indeed have been born to a younger wife of Piye who could still have been of childbearing age following that king's death.

42   Or even Taharqa (father of Amenirdis II), if the stelae could be of a date sufficiently late (cf. Leahy 1994: 187).

43   Buried in Ku52 (Dunham 1950: 81–85).

44   Block from chapel of Osiris-Nebankh at Karnak (Jansen-Winkeln 2007–2009: III, 11–12[46.24]).

45   Louvre statuette E.3915 (Jansen-Winkeln 2007–2009: II, 357–58[35.19]).

46   el-Kurru Ku4 (Jansen-Winkeln 2007–2009: III, 191[48.423]): the orthographies of the names are significantly different, but that could be explained by the vagaries of transliterating Nubian names into Egyptian hieroglyphs.

47   Khartoum 1851 (Jansen-Winkeln 2007–2009: II, 350–51[35.2]; Eide et al. 1994–2000: I, 55–62[8]; Ritner 2009a: 461–64[143]).

48   Cf. Eide et al. 1994–2000: I, 48–52; unfortunately the prenomen is missing from Khartoum 1851: whether it might have been Thutmose III's Menkheperre depends in part on whether stela Louvre C.100 is attributed to him rather than Iny (cf. ch. 4, n. 160).

49   Berlin ÄM1068+Cairo JE47085 (Jansen-Winkeln 2007–2009: II, 351–52[35.3]; Eide et al. 1994–2000: I, 118–19[10]; Ritner 2009a: 464–65[144]).

50   Cairo JE48862+47086–9 (Jansen-Winkeln 2007–2009: II, 337–50[35.1]; Eide et al. 1994–2000: I, 62–118[9]; Ritner 2009a: 465–92[145]). Morkot suggests (2000: 171–72) that the Year 21 stela may actually be a retelling of the Year 4 campaign, but it seems unlikely that the date of the stela would have been so far removed from the events related.

51   Dunham 1950: 110–17.

52   Porter and Moss 1952: 123.

53   On the question of the ritual ban on fish in certain localities at certain times, cf. Brewer 2001: 535.

54 MFA 06.2408 (gold) and 1977.16 (bronze—Jansen-Winkeln 2007–2009: II, 333[33.1–2]; Ritner 2009a: 423–24[112]).

55 Cairo JE45948 and TR 11/9/21/14 (Jansen-Winkeln 2007–2009: II, 333–34[33.4–5]; Ritner 2009a: 424–26[113]).

56 Possibly to be read as "Ilot."

57 Mentioned on statue Moscow I.1.a.5736=4491 and fragments of her own coffin and that of her son (Jansen-Winkeln 2007–2009: II, 334–35[33.6]).

58 Cf. Aston 2009a: 18.

59 Jansen-Winkeln 2007–2009: II, 366[36.1–2]; cf. p. 144.

60 Cf. P.A. Spencer and A.J. Spencer 1986: 199; Aston 2009a: 20.

61 Jansen-Winkeln 2007–2009: II, 367–68[37.1–3]; cf. ch. 4, n. 59. It is interesting that Thutemhat's prenomen echoes that of Akhenaten ('Neferkheperure'), whose city of Tell el-Amarna lay almost opposite Hermopolis, and blocks from which formed the cores of many of the Rameside walls and pylons of Thoth's city.

62 BMA 59.17 (Jansen-Winkeln 2007–2009: II, 370[39.1–3]).

63 Geneva 23473 (Jansen-Winkeln 2007–2009: II, 370–71[39.4]).

64 Cf. P.A. Spencer and A.J. Spencer 1986: 199–201. Cf. p. 104 on the possible tomb of Osorkon II's wife at the site.

65 See images at http://affinitiz.net/space/tanis/content/deux-nouveaux-blocs-du-lac-de-mout-a-parrainer---photos-en-exclusivite_7934DDB2-C16D-4C6D-AA41-20759B240B8D. Osorkon IV has in the past been allocated the titulary Akheperre-setepenamun Osorkon-meryamun (Jansen-Winkeln 2007–2009: II, 369[38.1–2]), but the monuments in question may more likely belong to Osorkon the Elder (cf. pp. 73–74). Cf. ch. 4, n. 95 for a view that makes the blocks a thus-far unique northern attestation of Osorkon III.

66 Louvre E.7167 (Jansen-Winkeln 2007–2009: II, 369[38.3]).

67 See Kitchen 1996: 366 n. 710.

68 As proposed by Leahy 1990: 188–89.

69 II Kings 17:4.

70 Kitchen 1996: xxxiv–ix, 372–75, 582–83.

71 Sargon's Annals and Display Inscriptions at Khorsabad (Pritchard 1969: 284–85).

72 Botta and Flandin 1849–50: II, pl. 87.

73 Cf. Kahn 2001: 12.

74 Sargon's Annals; prism Assur 16587 (Pritchard 1969: 285–86).

75 Jansen-Winkeln 2007–2009: III, 252–55[50.11–14, 16]; also of this group may be a king Neferkare (Jansen-Winkeln 2007–2009: III, 256[50.17–19a]).

76 Jansen-Winkeln 2007–2009: III, 255[50.15].

77 Jansen-Winkeln 2007–2009: II, 353[35.7], 357[35.19].

78 BM EA6640 (Jansen-Winkeln 2007–2009: II, 363[35.33]). This prenomen also appears on slab Khartoum 5220 (Jansen-Winkeln 2007–2009: II, 354[35.12]).

79 Cf. Parkinson 1999: 97[21].

80 Ashmolean 1894.107b (Jansen-Winkeln 2007–2009: II, 36365[35.34]; Ritner 2009a: 492–94[146]).

81 Known from a stela of the reign of Aspelta in the approach to temple Barkal B500, which established a mortuary cult for him (Porter and Moss 1952: 216; Eide et al. 1994–2000: I, 268–78[40]).

82 Known from an inscription of his daughter Wadjrenes in the tomb of her husband, Montjuemhat A (TT34—Jansen-Winkeln 2007–2009: III, 483[52.238]).

83 Jansen-Winkeln 2007–2009: III, 301–22.

84 Named on statue Cairo JE49157 of the high priest Horemakhet, who probably served during the reigns of Shabaka through Tanutamun (Jansen-Winkeln 2007–2009: III, 348[52.5]). Cf. Morkot 2000: 205.

85 Dunham 1950: 64–66; Lull 2002: 182–83.

86 MFA NN (exc. 19-13-261, 19-3-720—Dodson 1994: 98, 139[53].

87 Jansen-Winkeln 2007–2009: II, 354[35.16–17].

88 Dunham 1950: 30–37, 78–80, 86–90.

89 Jansen-Winkeln 2007–2009: II, 372–73[40.1–2].

90 Priese 1970: 19–20; von Beckerath 1997: 93; Perdu 2002; cf. ch. 5, n. 231.

91 See the discussion in Kahn 2009.

92 Diodorus Siculus i, 45, 65, 69.

93 Cf. Moret 1903; Hölbl 1981; J.M.A. Janssen 1954; Gill and Vickers 1996; Ridgway 1999.

94 Manetho, all versions; cf. Waddell 1940: 164–65.

95 Jansen-Winkeln 2007–2009: II, 375[41.1], 376–81[41.11–24].

96 Hamm 5770 (Jansen-Winkeln 2007–2009: II, 381[41.25]).

97 Jansen-Winkeln 2007–2009: II, 375[41.2].

98 Cf. Gill and Vickers 1996; Ridgway 1999.

99 For an alleged alternate Wahibre, cf. Kitchen 1996: 152.

100 Jansen-Winkeln 2007–2009: III, 2[46.4].

101 Cf. Vercoutter 1960: 65–69.

102 Macadam 1949–55: I, 119–32; Dunham and Macadam 1949.

103 Cf. Morkot's comprehensive review (1999).

104 Coffin fragments Cairo JE34431=TR 9/2/15/11, from Abydos tomb D3 (Jansen-Winkeln 2007–2009: III, 351[52.10]).

105 Rassam Cylinder A of Ashur-banipal (Pritchard 1969: 295[ii]).

106 Variant in Rassam Cylinder B (ibid). However, some (e.g., Kitchen 1996: 150–51) have proposed to emend the king's name to 'Shabataka.' Such emendations, however, should be avoided unless absolutely necessary.

107 Stela Cairo JE48863 (ch. 6 n. 1).

108 Statue Cairo CG42204 and coffin lid Cairo JE55194 (Jansen-Winkeln 2007–2009: III, 347[52.4], 350[52.8]).

109 Jansen-Winkeln 2007–2009: III, 4[46.11].

110 Louvre E.10571 (Jansen-Winkeln 2007–2009: III, 29[46.72]).

111 From near Bubastis (Jansen-Winkeln 2007–2009: III, 28[46.71]).

112 Moscow I.1.a.5646=4118 (Jansen-Winkeln 2007–2009: III, 28[46.69]).

113 From Tell Farain (MMA 55.144.6—Jansen-Winkeln 2007–2009: III, 28[46.70]).

114 Jansen-Winkeln 2007–2009: III, 1[46.1–3], inc. Berlin ÄM31235.
115 Louvre N.2541; Cairo CG38020; Berlin ÄM7742 (Jansen-Winkeln 2007–2009: III, 2–3[46.5, 8–3]).
116 BM EA498 (Jansen-Winkeln 2007–2009: III, 2[46.6]).
117 Cf. Manuelian 1993.
118 Jansen-Winkeln 2007–2009: III, 4–12[46.11–25].
119 Jansen-Winkeln 2007–2009: III, 12–17[46.26–27].
120 Jansen-Winkeln 2007–2009: III, 17–19[46.28].
121 Jansen-Winkeln 2007–2009: III, 21[46.35].
122 Jansen-Winkeln 2007–2009: III, 21–22[46.37].
123 Jansen-Winkeln 2007–2009: III, 38[46.83].
124 Porter and Moss 1960–64: 772; Aston 2009b: 263.
125 Jansen-Winkeln 2007–2009: III, 347–51[52.4–8].
126 Given that some fifty years separate the earliest credible date of appointment of Horemakhet from the laying down of his pontificate by Takelot G on becoming king, it is likely (but of course not certain) that at least one high priest other than Osorkon officiated during that period.
127 Khorsabad Display Inscription 90-112; Prism A (Pritchard 1969: 286–87).
128 Although it has also been argued that Bakenrenef might have been the king in question, this is chronologically impossible on the overall reconstruction adopted here.
129 Khorsabad Display Inscription 90-112; it is noted that Egypt "now belongs to" Nubia, which was to the Assyrians "an unapproachable region" that had never previously had dealings with them.
130 Assyrian texts refer to Nubia as both 'Meluhha' and 'Kush'; the reason behind this distinction is unclear.
131 Inscription at Tang-i Var in Iran, lines 19–21 (Frame 1999); it is paralleled—without the Nubian being named—in the Great Display Inscription and the Room XIV Small Display Inscription in Sargon II's palace at Khorsabad (Pritchard 1969: 285–86).
132 E.g., Kitchen 2009: 162–64.
133 Cf. Kitchen's special pleading based on his prior assumptions on the chronology of the period.
134 E.g., Morkot 2000: 224. A coregency between Shabaka and Shabataka had previously been posited for other reasons, but not widely accepted (cf. Kitchen 1996: 170–71; Morkot 2000: 319 n. 6).
135 See the full discussion in Kahn 2001. The month is provided by the dating of the Khorsabad versions of the account of Iamani's extradition to Sargon's Year 15 (April 707 to March 706).
136 Cf. Zibelius-Chen 2006: 291.
137 Statue of Iti, BM EA24429 (Jansen-Winkeln 2007–2009: III, 30[46.76]).
138 Manetho gives 'Sabacôn' only twelve years, which is of no help given the absolutely secure Year 15.
139 Dunham 1950: 55–59; Lull 2002: 183.
140 Exc. 19-2-676, 677 (Dodson 1994: 99, 139[54/1–2]).

141 Dunham 1950: 99–100.
142 Dunham 1950: 111–12; on the matter of Nubians and horses, cf. pp. 147–48.
143 Jansen-Winkeln 2007–2009: III, 40[47.5]; Eide et al. 1994–2000: I, 125–29[17]; Ritner 2009a: 41.
144 The excerptors of Manetho gives variously twelve and fourteen years for Sebichôs.
145 Cairo JE49157 (ch. 5 n. 84).
146 Dunham 1950: 42–43.
147 Khartoum 2678: l.7–10; Ny Carlsberg ÆIN1712 [Kawa V], l.13–14 (Jansen-Winkeln 2007–2009: III, 135–38[48.75]; Eide et al. 1994–2000: I, 135–45[21], 145–58[22]; Ritner 2009a: 535–45[161–62]); further copies of the latter text are Cairo JE37488, 38269, and 48400 (Jansen-Winkeln 2007–2009: III, 54–55[48.1], 121–23[48.60], 61–63[48.13]; Eide et al. 1994–2000: I, 156).
148 Apparently provided by more than one Egyptian king—presumably including the current Tanite.
149 Chicago Prism of Sennacherib and Taylor Prism ii 37–iii 49 (Pritchard 1969: 287–88).
150 II Kings 18–19; Isaiah 36–37; II Chronicles 32.
151 II Kings 19:9; Isaiah 37:9.
152 Basic arguments summarized in Kitchen 1996: 158–161, 552–54 but coming down firmly in favor of the second option.
153 MMA 65.45 (Jansen-Winkeln 2007–2009: III, 53[47.21]).
154 Cairo CG655 and *in situ*(?) (Jansen-Winkeln 2007–2009: III, 39–40[47.2–3]; Jeffreys 2010: 175, fig. 37).
155 Jansen-Winkeln 2007–2009: III, 39[47.1].
156 Louvre IM3440, 3019, and 3146 (Jansen-Winkeln 2007–2009: II, 192–93[48.127–29]—there attributed to Taharqa).
157 Macadam 1949–55: I, 19, 20;
158 Cf. Kitchen 1996: 170–71.
159 Jansen-Winkeln 2007–2009: III, 40–46[47.6].
160 Cf. Ayad 2009a: 41, 48–49.
161 Parts now Berlin ÄM1480 (Jansen-Winkeln 2007–2009: III, 46–50[47.7]).
162 Jansen-Winkeln 2007–2009: III, 50[47.8].
163 Porter and Moss 1960–64: 441–42; Eigner 1984: 40–41, 95; Pischikova 2009.
164 On the last Fourth Prophets of this line, see Broekman 2010: 141–42, although it is certainly not impossible that Nakhtefmut B did indeed live long enough to be the father of Djedkhonsiufankh D, last of the family.
165 Porter and Moss 1960–64: 223; Eigner 1984: 41–42, 135, 140, 176; Pischikova 2008; 2009.
166 Cf. Aston 2003.
167 Strudwick 1995.
168 Sheikholeslami 2003.
169 Jansen-Winkeln 2007–2009: III, 51[47.10–13].
170 Dunham 1950: 67–71.
171 Exc. 19-2-239; MFA 21.2813–4 (Dodson 1994: 99–100, 139–40[55/1–3]).

172 Dunham 1950: 118. It was also noted that "[m]uch difficulty was experienced in the reconstruction because of the implausible outline of the nasal root. A considerable part of this region was lacking, and had to be interpolated. The way in which the surrounding parts developed as reconstruction progressed made it very difficult to restore the missing part in a convincing way. Attention was not called to the existence of portraits of King Shebitku till after the reconstruction was completed. Comparison with one of these showed that the peculiarity in this region was a genuine one, and constituted a good mark of personal identification."

173 For whom, in general, see Dallibor 2005.

174 Cf. Morkot 1999: 200, and pp. 154–55.

175 Ny Carlsberg ÆIN1712.

176 Cairo JE36327 (Porter and Moss 1972: 27); cf. p. 152.

177 Khartoum 2678–9 [Kawa IV, VI] (Jansen-Winkeln 2007–2009: III, 74–35[48.74], 138–41[48.76]; Eide et al. 1994–2000: I, 135–45[21], 164–76[24]; Ritner 2009a: 535–39[161], 545–52[163]).

178 Cf. Morkot 1999; 2000: 156.

179 Porter and Moss 1952: 209[5].

180 Cairo CG42203 (Jansen-Winkeln 2007–2009: III, 192[48.126]); the name of the prince's mother has been erased, but her title of King's Great Wife remains.

181 Nuri Nu36 (Dunham 1955: 19–24).

182 el-Kurru Ku3 (Dunham 1950: 27–29).

183 Other children have been identified on the basis of assumptions concerning the antecedents of the later king Atlanersa: cf. Morkot 2000: 290–91.

184 Leclant 1961.

185 Russman 1997.

186 Suggestions that he may have had even wider responsibilities, on the basis of a stela at Semna-West (MFA 29.1130 [Porter and Moss 1952: 145]: see Dallibor 2005: 230[1]; Török 1997: 140, 250; 2009: 344–45) have been shown to be incorrect, since the stela in question actually belonged to a Middle Kingdom homonym (Pope 2011).

187 Pischikova 1998; Jansen-Winkeln 2007–2009: III, 395–96[52.102], 491[52.255], 493[52.256], 507[52.283].

188 Jansen-Winkeln 2007–2009: III, 366–97[52.103], 494–92[52.255–56].

189 Ny Carlsberg ÆIN1712: l.11–13.

190 Cairo JE37488, 38269, and 48400 and Ny Carlsberg ÆIN1712.

191 Jansen-Winkeln 2007–2009: III, 59–61[48.12]; Eide et al. 1994–2000: I, 158–63[23].

192 Jansen-Winkeln 2007–2009: III, 55–56[48.3].

193 Jansen-Winkeln 2007–2009: III, 54–55[48.1–2].

194 Jansen-Winkeln 2007–2009: III, 58–59[48.8–10].

195 Cf. Spencer 1989: 70.

196 Florence 7655 (Russman 1974: 54[31]).

197 Ibrahim Aly unpublished: 72–73, 315.

198 Jansen-Winkeln 2007–2009: III, 83[48.31].
199 Cf. Leclant 1965: 14; Lauffray 1970.
200 Jansen-Winkeln 2007–2009: III, 102–10[48.37].
201 Jansen-Winkeln 2007–2009: III, 92–101[48.35].
202 Jansen-Winkeln 2007–2009: III, 309–13[51.74].
203 Jansen-Winkeln 2007–2009: III, 87–92[48.34].
204 Jansen-Winkeln 2007–2009: III, 63–81[48.16–22].
205 Jansen-Winkeln 2007–2009: III, 112[48.43–45].
206 Jansen-Winkeln 2007–2009: III, 113–15[48.47–49].
207 Jansen-Winkeln 2007–2009: III, 115–18[48.50].
208 Jansen-Winkeln 2007–2009: III, 264–76[48.18].
209 Jansen-Winkeln 2007–2009: III, 464–69[52.210–12].
210 Jansen-Winkeln 2007–2009: III, 324–29[51.110–18].
211 Jansen-Winkeln 2007–2009: III, 123–24[48.62–63].
212 Jansen-Winkeln 2007–2009: III, 125–26[48.65].
213 Jansen-Winkeln 2007–2009: III, 127–28[48.69–70].
214 To judge from some blocks of Taharqa reused in a Meroitic pyramid there (Jansen-Winkeln 2007–2009: III, 128–29[48.71]).
215 Jacquet-Gordon, Bonnet, and Jacquet 1969.
216 Macadam 1949–55; Jansen-Winkeln 2007–2009: III, 129–61[48.73–88].
217 A number of them have been discussed above, pp. 143, 158, 162, with ch. 5, nn. 23, 147, 177.
218 Jansen-Winkeln 2007–2009: III, 162–79[48.91].
219 Jansen-Winkeln 2007–2009: III, 173–80[48.96].
220 Jansen-Winkeln 2007–2009: III, 181–82[48.97].
221 Jansen-Winkeln 2007–2009: III, 183[48.99].
222 Jansen-Winkeln 2007–2009: III, 182–83[48.98].
223 Dunham 1955: 7–16.
224 The form of the substructure of the pyramid is unique in the Kushite burial record, but is reminiscent of the Osireion, the cenotaph built by Sethy I at Abydos (Porter and Moss 1939: 29–31). Intriguingly, Abydos is the one cemetery in Egypt known to have contained burials of members of the Twenty-fifth Dynasty royal family (Leahy 1994)—all other known interments of this kind are at el-Kurru or Nuri in Sudan.
225 Cf. Pritchard 1969: 288–90.
226 Babylonian Chronicle iv.16 (Pritchard 1969: 302).
227 Annalistic Text BM K3082+S2027+K3086 (Pritchard 1969: 292–93).
228 Two in the National Museum, Aleppo, one Berlin-Vorderasiatisches VA2708; the vanquished figure has also been identified as Taharqa himself.
229 Cylinder E (Pritchard 1969: 296[2]). On the toponyms in the Assyrian sources, see Verreth 1999.
230 Cf. Yoyotte 1961.
231 Where he seems to have succeeded an earlier local king Nekauba (Jansen-Winkeln 2007–2009: III, 250[50.1]), presumably the Nechepsôs of Manetho, who places as his predecessors a Stephinatês (="Tefnakhte II"—cf. p. 153) and

Ammeris the Nubian—perhaps a governor installed following Bakenrenef's alleged end by immolation, prior to the reinstatement of a local princely/kingly line.

232 The identity of this individual has been much debated; cf. Kahn 2006.

233 Rassam Cylinder of Ashur-banipal; BM K228 + K2675 (Pritchard 1969: 294–95, 296–97).

234 Cf. Kitchen 1996: 392 n. 874.

235 Louvre IM2640; other stelae from the burial give only the bare year (Porter and Moss 1974–81: 791).

236 Cf. Depuydt 2006.

237 At some point acquiring the prenomen Menkheperre.

238 Louvre IM3733 (Porter and Moss 1974–81: 791–92).

239 Cf. Kitchen 1996: 161–62.

240 Probably directly, although cf. Kitchen 1996: 173 regarding suggestions of a brief coregency.

241 Cf. Leahy 1984a.

Notes to Chapter 6

1 Nubian Museum ex-JE48863 (Jansen-Winkeln 2007–2009: III, 236–40[49.8]; Eide 1994–2000: I, 193–209[29]; Ritner 2009a: 566–73[169]).

2 Interestingly, the Assyrians are never mentioned—only the Egyptian "rebels" (cf. the Assyrians also being missing from Herodotus's account of the career of Psamtik I—cf. Lloyd 1975–88: III, 132–33).

3 Herodotus II: 152, although he attributes his killing to "Sabacos the Ethiopian" (i.e., Shabaka, perhaps through some confusion with his killing of Bakenrenef—another Saite dynast); cf. ch. 6, n. 7.

4 Rassam Cylinder (Pritchard 1969: 295).

5 Jansen-Winkeln 2007–2009: III, 229–34[49.1–3].

6 Jansen-Winkeln 2007–2009: III, 256[50.17–19a]; cf. Kitchen 1996: 396–97, n. 904.

7 On Herodotus's account of the career of Psamtik I (II: 147–57), cf. Lloyd 1975–88: III, 116–49. Herodotus makes no mention of the involvement of the Assyrians in Psamtik's career, although he records his exile following the killing of Nekau I (cf. ch. 6, n. 3). The "twelve kings" mentioned by Herodotus, of whom Psamtik was one, are clearly a remembrance of the fragmented politics of the early seventh century, although the details are certainly derived from a later folkloric narrative, as is the 'accidental' manner in which Psamtik engaged the Carians.

8 Based on Polyaenus §7.3 and Pseudo-Aristeas 14 (Sauneron and Yoyotte 1952a: 199–200; 1952b: 131–35; Burstein 1984).

9 Cairo JE36327 (ch. 5 n. 176); a series of blocks from the temple of Mut at Karnak also in their current state refer to these events (Cairo JE31886—Porter and Moss 1972: 257–58[9]; Kitchen 1996: 236–39). It is presently a matter for debate whether they were carved under Psamtik I, or represent a usurpation of scenes that originally depicted the arrival of the earlier God's

Wife Amenirdis I under Piye (Broekman 2009a: 100–101; Jansen-Winkeln 2007–2009: II, 354–57[35.17]); cf. p. 144.

10 Porter and Moss 1952: 339.

11 Graefe 1994: 96–97.

12 Porter and Moss 1972: 478–80.

13 Habachi 1977. The unlikelihood of this reconstruction is pointed out by Morkot 1999: 197, noting that the Amenirdis in question is only a *s3t-nsw*,and not necessarily linked with Taharqa. The scenario is, however, accepted by Teeter 1999: 411—but see Dodson 2002: 181–82 n. 21.

14 Christophe 1953: 147–48.

15 Morkot 1999: 194–200.

16 Dodson 2002, but cf. Graefe 2003b.

17 Cf. Eide et al. 1994–2000: I, 210–11.

18 Dunham 1950: 60–63. The pyramids of a further king and a queen (names unknown—Ku1 and 2) were erected there during the fourth century.

19 Gasm El Seed 1985.

20 For an overview, see Zibelius-Chen 2006.

21 Heidorn 1991.

22 Cairo JE48864 (Eide et al. 1994–2000: II, 438–64[78]).

23 Berlin ÄM2268 (Eide et al. 1994–2000: II, 471–501[84]). The attacker, "Kambasawden," has on occasion been identified with the Egyptian king Khabbash (replacing earlier speculations that he might be the Persian king Kambyses), but this remains a matter for debate.

24 Including expeditions to the south by Ptolemy I (c. 319/8) and II (c. 274), but nevertheless subject to Nubian raids—e.g., one on Elephantine under Ptolemy II (Eide et al. 1994–2000: II, 536–41[97–99]).

25 Porter and Moss 1952: 46–47; 1939: 211; Winter 1981; Eide et al. 1994–2000: II, 588–90.

26 Porter and Moss 1952: 4; Farid 1978; Eide et al. 1994–2000: II, 591, 592–96[132].

27 Eide et al. 1994–2000: II, 596–60[134–35].

28 Eide et al. 1994–2000: II, 614–31[137–38], 631–38[140–41].

29 Dunham 1955: 1–3.

30 Dunham 1952; 1957.

31 Eide et al. 1994–2000: II, 687–738[162–85].

32 Adams 1977: 382–591.

33 Cf. Smoláriková 2008: 28–30, 84–99.

34 Oren 1984: 28; Valbelle and Defernez 1995: 96–97; Smoláriková 2008: 48–54.

35 Porter and Moss 1934: 7; Smoláriková 2008: 77–82; http://www.deltasurvey.ees.ac.uk/dafana212.html

36 Spencer 1996–2009; Smoláriková 2008: 65–70.

37 Herodotus II: 30–31.

38 Ritner 2009a: 585–87[174].

39 Herodotus II: 157 (Lloyd 1975–88: III, 146–49).

40   Herodotus I: 103–106.

41   Lloyd 1975–88: III, 147.

42   Cf. Lloyd 1975–88: I, 24–32.

43   P. Wilson 2006.

44   The probable source of the earliest of a series of slabs found at Rashid (Porter and Moss 1934: 1–2).

45   Montet 1966: pl. xciv–vii[314–22].

46   Porter and Moss 1972: 13–14, 19–20.

47   Ritner 1990.

48   Cf. P. Wilson 2006: 19–150, 259–66.

49   Herodotus II: 159; II Kings 23:29, 33; II Chronicles 35:20–24.

50   Jeremiah 46:2; II Kings 24:7; Smoláriková 2008: 31–34; cf. Lloyd 1975–88: I, 20–21, on the use of Greeks in this campaign.

51   Herodotus II: 158; Lloyd 1977; cf. the pair of forged scarabs relating this activity (Petrie 1908).

52   Yoyotte and Sauneron 1952; Smoláriková 2008: 34–38.

53   Cf. Rowe 1938; Lloyd 1975–88: I, 21–23.

54   II Kings 23:29–30; II Chronicles 35:20–24; Smoláriková 2008: 38–39.

55   Arnold 1999: 80–83.

56   Leahy 1988; Smoláriková 2008: 39–41.

57   The burial may, nevertheless, have been an austere one, lacking some of its intended equipment: one of the canopic jars ended up being used to bury a falcon at Saqqara some centuries later and another found its way into an Etruscan tomb in Italy (Dodson 1994: 104–105).

58   Cf. Lloyd 1975–88: I, 26–28; Smoláriková 2008: 70–77.

59   On Ahmose II's foreign policy, cf. Smoláriková 2008: 44.

60   Arnold 1999: 83–91.

61   Herodotus III: 16. Material has, nevertheless, survived from the burial, e.g., *shabti* Kestner 2191.

62   Cf. Ray 1987.

63   Amenirdis (Amyrtaios), Hagar, Naefarud II, and Djehir (Teos) were all the subject of coups d'état—although Hagar was able to regain power (cf. Traunecker 1979; Ray 1986; Klotz 2010: 247–51).

Notes to Appendices

1   Cf. Giles 1997: 76–101.

2   Grayson 1980–83: 101–16.

3   Ungnad 1938.

4   According to the so-called 'low' chronology: cf. Grayson 1987.

5   pLeiden I 350, *vs.* III, 6 (Kitchen 1968–90: II, 809).

6   Grayson 1980–83: 101–15; cf. Brinkman 1973.

7   KAV21/22.

8   Cf. Henige 1996; Yamada 1994.

9   Poebel 1943: 56.

10   On issues with the King Lists genealogical data, cf. Landsberger 1954: 31–73.

11 Poebel 1943: 56–57.
12 The following represent the consequential accession dates of bringing the next four lunar cycles into consideration; I owe this data to the kindness of Rolf Krauss.

Year 52 option	Day of new moon*	Consequent accession year
1228	II *prt* 28	1279 BC
1214	II *prt* 27	1265 BC
1203	II *prt* 28	1254 BC
1189	II *prt* 27	1240 BC
1178	II *prt* 27	1229 BC

* The actual report is dated II *prt* 27, but the vagaries of observation allow some leeway.

13 James 1991: 293–308; Rohl 1995: 393–98; Newgrosh 1999.
14 Bronk Ramsey et al. 2010.
15 For example, a piece of wood from the Uluburun shipwreck off Asia Minor was initially dated to 1316 (Kuniholm et al. 1996). The ship's cargo included a gold scarab of Nefertiti—probably as scrap—with the date implying that the queen's career ended prior to the last years of the fourteenth century (Weinstein 1989). However, there has since been a complete collapse of confidence in the dating of the wood (Manning et al. 2001: 2535 n. 38; cf. Wiener 2003: 244–45; Bietak 2004: 221–22) and it now seems clear that the Uluburun evidence can no longer be called in support of any dates proposed for the general period of the Eighteenth/Nineteenth Dynasty transition.
16 Thiele 1965: 53–76. However, other calculations have been made, potentially placing Year 5 of Rehoboam within the extremes of 970 to 915 (see references in Ben-Dor Evian 2011: 18 n. 49).
17 Ashmolean 1894.107a.
18 Krauss 2006b: 411–12.
19 Cf. Thiele 1965: 197–201 on variations between dates given in the Greek versions of the Books of Kings.
20 Respectively by Rohl 1995 and James 1991.
21 Thijs 2010: 185–86, 189.
22 Suggestions have nevertheless been made to derive 'Shishak' from a pet form of the name Rameses or from a Hebrew pun (e.g., Van der Veen 1999).
23 For a recent review of the key chronological data of this span of time, see Broekman 2011 (in its origin a critique of Morkot and James 2009).
24 Cf. Chapman 2009.
25 Dodson 2010: 31–37.
26 The only other option would be to reject the aforementioned adjustments to the Nineteenth and Twentieth Dynasties, for which there is clear prima facie evidence, purely on the grounds that they will not fit the established macro-chronological picture—clearly a poor starting point methodologically.
27 On the potential desirability of a reduction from the point of view of Babylonian history, cf. Klinger 2006: 323–24.

28 Cf. pp. 39–40; the only place where the Manethonic data cannot be squared with contemporary records is Psin(n)achês's nine years: he would seem to be identical with Siamun, for whom a Year 17 survives. One would therefore probably emend the reign length here to *19.

29 A priori the lunar-based 1479 accession date for Thutmose III should shift down to 1468—cf. Krauss 2006b: 420–22. The further implications for Eighteenth Dynasty chronology are beyond the scope of the present work.

30 For example, interpreting Osorkon B's mention of a lunar phenomenon as a 'non-phenomenon' (p. 121) leaves the author uncomfortable—but he finds the macrochronological consequences of an intriguing recent alternate explanation (Thijs 2010) wholly untenable on the basis of current data.

31 With the Horus name invariably prefixed by the phrase *k3-nḫt*—"The Strong Bull."

BIBLIOGRAPHY

Abbreviations used for periodicals in bibliography

Ä&L *Ägypten und Levante: Zeitschrift für ägyptische Archäologie und deren Nachbargebiete.* Vienna: Verlag der Österreichischen Akademie der Wissenschaften.

AJA *American Journal of Archaeology.* New York, &c.: Archaeological Institute of America.

AncEg *Ancient Egypt.* Manchester: Ancient Egypt Magazine.

AnnBSA *Annual of the British School at Athens.* London: MacMillan & Co.

AO *Acta Orientalia.* Copenhagen: Munksgaard.

ASAE *Annales du Service des Antiquités de l'Égypte.* Cairo: Institut français d'Archéologie orientale/Supreme Council of Antiquities Press.

BACE *Bulletin of the Australian Centre for Egyptology.* North Ryde: Australian Centre for Egyptology, Macquarie University.

BASOR *Bulletin of the American Schools of Oriental Research.* Ann Arbor: American Schools of Oriental Research.

BES *Bulletin of the Egyptological Seminar.* New York: Egyptological Seminar of New York.

BIÉ *Bulletin de l'Institut d'Égypte.* Cairo.

BIFAO *Bulletin de l'Institut français d'Archéologie orientale du Caire.* Cairo: Institut français d'Archéologie orientale.

BiOr *Bibliotheca Orientalis.* Leiden: Nederlands Instituut voor het Nabije Oosten.

BMSAES   *British Museum Studies in Ancient Egypt and Sudan.* http://www. britishmuseum.org/research/online_journals/bmsaes.aspx

BSFE   *Bulletin de la Societé française d'Égyptologie.* Paris: Societé française d'Égyptologie.

BSFFT   *Bulletin de la Société française des fouilles de Tanis.* Paris: Société française des fouilles de Tanis.

CAJ   *Cambridge Archaeological Journal.* Cambridge: Cambridge University Press.

CdE   *Chronique d'Égypte.* Brussels: Fondation égyptologique Reine Élisabeth.

CRAIBL   *Comptes rendus de l'Académie des Inscriptions et Belles-Lettres.* Paris: l'Académie des Inscriptions et Belles-Lettres.

CRIPEL   *Cahiers de Recherches de l'Institut de Papyrologie et d'Égyptologie de Lille.* Lille: Université de Lille III.

DE   *Discussions in Egyptology.* Oxford: DE Publications.

EgArch   *Egyptian Archaeology: Bulletin of the Egypt Exploration Society.* London: Egypt Exploration Society.

GM   *Göttinger Miszellen.* Göttingen: Universität Göttingen. Ägyptologisches Seminar.

JACF   *Journal of the Ancient Chronology Forum.* Basingstoke: Institute for the Study of Interdisciplinary Sciences.

JAOS   *Journal of the American Oriental Society.* New Haven, Conn. and Ann Arbor, Mich.: American Oriental Society.

JARCE   *Journal of the American Research Center in Egypt.* New York: Eisenbraun.

JEA   *Journal of Egyptian Archaeology.* London: Egypt Exploration Fund/Society.

JEgH   *Journal of Egyptian History.* Leiden: Brill.

JMFA   *Journal of the Museum of Fine Arts, Boston.* Boston: Museum of Fine Arts.

JNES   *Journal of Near Eastern Studies.* Chicago: Chicago University Press.

JSSEA   *Journal of the Society for the Study of Egyptian Antiquities.* Toronto: Society for the Study of Egyptian Antiquities.

Kmt   *Kmt: A Modern Journal of Ancient Egypt.* San Francisco: Kmt Communications.

LÄ   *Lexikon der Ägyptologie.* Wiesbaden: Otto Harrassowitz.

MDAIK   *Mitteilungen des Deutschen Archäologischen Instituts, Kairo.* Mainz: Philipp von Zabern.

MMJ	*Metropolitan Museum Journal*. New York: Metropolitan Museum of Art.
NARCE	*Newsletter of the American Research Center in Egypt*. Varous locations: American Research Center in Egypt.
OMRO	*Oudheidkundige Mededelingen uit het Rijksmuseum van Oudheden te Leiden*. Leiden: Rijksmuseum van Oudheden.
PEQ	*Palestine Exploration Quarterly*. London: Palestine Exploration Fund.
PSBA	*Proceedings of the Society of Biblical Archaeology*. London: Society of Biblical Archaeology.
RdE	*Revue d'Égyptologie*. Leuven: Peeters.
RevArch	*Revue archéologique*. Paris: Ernest Leroux.
RT	*Recueil de travaux relatifs à la Philologie et à l'Archéologie égyptiennes et assyriennes*. Paris: A. Franck.
SAK	*Studien zur altägyptischen Kultur*. Hamburg: H. Buske Verlag.
TSBA	*Transactions of the Society for Biblical Archaeology*. London: Longmans, Green, Reader and Dyer.
VA	*Varia Aegyptiaca*. San Antonio, TX: Van Siclen Books.
ZA	*Zeitschrift für Assyriologie und vorderasiatische Archäologie*. Berlin: W. de Gruyter.
ZÄS	*Zeitschrift für Ägyptische Sprache und Altertumskunde*. Leipzig: J. C. Hinrichs'sche Buchhandlung; Berlin: Akademie Verlag.
ZDMG	*Zeitschrift der Deutschen Morgenländischen Gesellschaft*. Wiesbaden: Kommissionsverlag F. Steiner.
ZDPV	*Zeitschrift des Deutschen Palästina-Vereins*. Wiesbaden: Harrassowitz Verlag.

List of works cited

Abdallah, A.O.A. 1984. "An Unusual Private Stela of the Twenty-First Dynasty from Coptos." *JEA* 70:65–72.

Abitz, F. 1990. "Der Bauablauf und die Dekorationen des Grabes Ramesses' IX." *SAK* 17:1–40.

———. 1992. "The Structure of the Decoration in the Tomb of Ramesses IX." In Reeves 1992: 165–85.

Adams, W.Y. 1977. *Nubia: Corridor to Africa*. London: Allen Lane.

Aḥituv, S. 1984. *Canaanite Toponyms in Ancient Egyptian Documents*. Jerusalem: Magnes Press.

Aimé-Giron, N. 1926. "Note sur les inscriptions de Aḥiram." *BIFAO* 26: 1–13.

Altenmüller, H. 1994. "Prinz Mentu-her-chopeschef aus der 20. Dynastie." *MDAIK* 50:1–12.

Amer, A.A. 1985. "Reflections on the Reign of Ramesses VI." *JEA* 71:66–70.

———. 1999. "Wentawat, Viceroy of Nubia, and His Family." *SAK* 27:27–31.

Arnold, D. 1999. *Temples of the Last Pharaohs*. New York: Oxford University Press.

Association Française d'Action Artistique. 1987. *Tanis: L'or des pharaons*. Paris: Ministère des Affaires Étrangères/Association Française d'Action Artistique.

Aston, D.A. 1989. "Takeloth II—A King of the 'Theban Twenty-third Dynasty'?" *JEA* 75:139–53.

———. 1991. "Two Osiris Figures of the Third Intermediate Period." *JEA* 77:95–107.

———. 2000. "Canopic Chests from the Twenty-first Dynasty to the Ptolemaic Period." *Ä&L* 10:159–78.

———. 2003. "The Theban West Bank from the Twenty-fifth Dynasty to the Ptolemaic Period." In Strudwick and Taylor 2003: 138–66.

———. 2009a. "Takeloth II, a King of the Herakleopolitan/Theban Twenty-third Dynasty Revisited: The Chronology of Dynasties 22 and 23." In Broekman, Demarée, and Kaper 2009: 1–28.

———. 2009b. *Burial Assemblages of Dynasty 21–25: Chronology—Typology—Developments*. Vienna: Verlag der Österreichischen Akademie der Wissenschaften.

Aston, D.A. and J.H. Taylor. 1990. "The Family of Takeloth III and the 'Theban' Twenty-third Dynasty." In Leahy 1990: 131–54.

Aubert, J.-F. 1981. "Nouvelles observations sur les chaouabtis de Deir el-Bahari et autres de la 21e dynastie." *CdE* 56, no. 111: 15–30.

Aubert, J.-F. and L. Aubert. 1974. *Statuettes égyptiennes, chaouabtis, ouchebtis*. Paris: Librairie d'Amérique et d'Orient Adrien Maisonneuve.

Ayad, M.F. 2009a. "The Transition from Libyan to Nubian Rule: The Role of the God's Wife of Amun." In Broekman, Demarée, and Kaper 2009: 29–49.

———. 2009b. *God's Wife, God's Servant: The God's Wife of Amun*. London: Routledge.

Bács, T.A. 1995. "A Note on the Divine Adoratrix Isis, Daughter of Ramesses VI." *GM* 148:7–11.

———. 1998. "First Preliminary Report on the Work of the Hungarian Mission in Thebes in Theban Tomb No. 65 (Nebamun/Imiseba)." *MDAIK* 54:49–64.

————. 2011. "The Last New Kingdom Tomb at Thebes: The End of a Great Tradition?" *BMSAES* 16:1–46. http://www.britishmuseum.org/research/online_journals/bmsaes/issue_16/bacs.aspx

Barnes, W.H. 1991. *Studies in the Divided Monarchy of Israel*. Atlanta: Scholars Press.

Barwik, M. 2011. *The Twilight of Ramesside Egypt: Studies on the History of Egypt at the End of the Ramesside Period*. Warsaw: Agade.

Bauer, H.H. 1984. *Beyond Velikovsky: The History of a Public Controversy*. Champaign: University of Illinois Press.

Bell, L. 1980. "Only One High Priest Ramessenakht and the Second Prophet Nesamun His Younger Son." *Serapis* 6:7–27.

Ben-Dor Evian, S. 2011a. "Shishak's Karnak Relief—More Than Just Name-rings." In *Egypt, Canaan and Israel: History, Imperialism, Ideology and Literature, Culture and History of the Ancient Near East*, edited by S. Bar, D. Kahn, and J. J. Shirley, 11–22. Leiden: Brill.

————. 2011b. "Egypt and the Levant in the Iron Age I-IIA: The Ceramic Evidence." *Tel Aviv* 38:94–119.

Benson, M. and J. Gourlay. 1899. *The Temple of Mut in Asher*. London: Murray.

Bickel, S. 2009. "The Inundation Inscription in Luxor Temple." In Broekman, Demarée, and Kaper 2009: 51–55.

Bickerstaffe, D. 2010. "The History of the Discovery of the Cache." In Graefe and Belova, 2010: 13–36.

Bierbrier, M.L. 1975. *The Late New Kingdom in Egypt (c. 1300–664 BC)*. Warminster: Aris and Phillips.

Bietak, M. 2004. Review of S.W. Manning: *A Test of Time* (Oxford: Oxbow Books). In *Bibliotheca Orientalis* 61, no. 1–2: 200–22.

Boeser, P.A.A. 1911–13. *Beschreibung der Ägyptischen Sammlung des Niederländischen Reichsmuseums der Altertümer in Leiden*. Vol. 6: *Die Denkmäler des Neuen Reiches*, 3: *Stelen*. The Hague: Nijhoff.

Bohleke, B. 1985. "An Ex Voto of the Previously Unrecognized Viceroy Setmose." *GM* 85:13–24.

Bothmer, B.V. 1960. "The Philadelphia–Cairo Statue of Osorkon II (Membra Dispersa III)." *JEA* 46:3–11.

Botta, P.É. and E. Flandin. 1849–50. *Monument de Ninive*. 5 vols. Paris: Imprimerie nationale.

Botti, G. and T.E. Peet. 1928. *Il Giornale della Necropoli di Tebe*. Turin: Bocca.

Botti, G. and P. Romanelli. 1951. *Le sculture del Museo Gregoriano Egizio*. Vatican City: Tip. poliglotta vaticana.

Brand, P.J. 2000. *The Monuments of Seti I: Epigraphic, Historical and Art Historical Analysis*. Leiden: Brill.

Brewer, D.J. 2001. "Fish." In *The Oxford Encyclopedia of Ancient Egypt*, edited by D.B. Redford, vol. 1: 532–35. New York: Oxford University Press.

Brinkman, J.A. 1973. "Comments on the Nassouhi Kinglist and the Assyrian Kinglist Tradition." *Orientalia* 42:306–19.

Brock, E.C. 1992. "The Tomb of Merenptaḥ and its Sarcophagi." In Reeves 1992: 122–40.

Broekman, G.P.F. 1988. "The Nile Level Records of the Twenty-second and Twenty-third Dynasties in Karnak: A Reconsideration of the Chronological Order." *JEA* 88:161–78.

———. 1998. "Facts and Questions about Wen-djeba-en-djed." *GM* 167:25–27.

———. 2000a. "Shoshenq Maäkheperre and Shoshenq Heqakheperre: Contemplations on the Question of Which of Them (If One of the Two) Was Identical with the High Priest of Amun, Shoshenq Son of King Osorkon I." *GM* 176:39–46.

———. 2000b. "On the Chronology and Genealogy of the Second, Third, and Fourth Prophets in Thebes during the Twenty-first Dynasty in Egypt." *GM* 174:25–36.

———. 2002. "The Founders of the Twenty-first Dynasty and Their Family Relationships." *GM* 191:11–18.

———. 2005. "The Chronological Position of King Shoshenq Mentioned in Nile Level Record No. 3 on the Quay Wall of the Great Temple of Amun at Karnak." *SAK* 33:75–89.

———. 2006–7. "On the Identity of King Shoshenq Buried in the Vestibule of the Tomb of Psusennes I in Tanis (NRT III)." *GM* 211:11–20; 212:9–28.

———. 2008. "The Chronicle of Prince Osorkon and its Historical Context." *JEgH* 1:209–34.

———. 2009a. "Takeloth III and the End of the 23rd Dynasty." In Broekman, Demarée, and Kaper 2009: 91–101.

———. 2009b. "Falcon-Headed Coffins and Cartonnages." *JEA* 95:67–81.

———. 2010. "The Leading Theban Priests of Amun and their Families under Libyan Rule." *JEA* 96:125–48.

———. 2011a. "The Egyptian Chronology from the Start of the Twenty-second until the End of the Twenty-fifth Dynasty: Facts, Suppositions and Arguments." *JEgH* 4:41–81.

————. 2011b. "Theban Priestly and Governmental Offices and Titles in the Libyan Period." *ZÄS* 138:93–115.

Broekman, G.P.F., R.J. Demarée, and O.E. Kaper. 2008. "The Numbering of the Kings Called Shoshenq." *GM* 216:9.

Broekman, G.P.F., R.J. Demarée, and O.E. Kaper, eds. 2009. *The Libyan Period in Egypt: Historical and Cultural Studies into the 21st—24th Dynasties. Proceedings of a Conference at Leiden University, 25–27 October 2007*. Leiden: Nederlands Instituut voor het Nabije Oosten; Louvain: Peeters.

Bronk Ramsey, C., M.W. Dee, J.M. Rowland, T.F.G. Higham, S.A. Harris, F. Brock, A. Quiles, E.M. Wild, E.S. Marcus, and A.J. Shortland. 2010. "Radiocarbon-based Chronology for Dynastic Egypt." *Science* 328:1554–57.

Brunton, G. 1939. "Some Notes on the Burial of Shashanq Heqa-kheper-Re'." *ASAE* 39:541–47.

Bruyère, B. 1957. "Une nouvelle famille de prêtres de Montou trouvée par Baraize à Deir el Bahri." *ASAE* 54:11–33.

Bryce, T.R. 1998. *The Kingdom of the Hittites*. Oxford: Clarendon Press.

Budge, E.A.W. 1899. *The Book of the Dead: Facsimiles of the Papyri of Hunefer, Ȧnhai, Ḳerāsher and Netchmet with Supplementary Text from the Payrus of Nu*. London: British Museum.

————. 1909. *A Guide to the Egyptian Galleries (Sculpture)*. London: Trustees of the British Museum.

Burstein, S.M. 1984. "Psamtek I and the End of Nubian Domination in Egypt." *JSSEA* 14: 31–34.

Caminos, R. 1952. "Gebel es-Silsilah No. 100." *JEA* 38:46–61.

————. 1974. *The New Kingdom Temples of Buhen*. 2 vols. London: Egypt Exploration Society.

————. 1998. *Semna-Kumma*. 2 vols. London: Egypt Exploration Society.

Capart, J., A.H. Gardiner, and B. van de Walle. 1936. "New Light on the Ramesside Tomb-Robberies." *JEA* 22:169–93.

Černý, J. 1929. "A Note on the 'Repeating of Births'." *JEA* 15:194–98.

————. 1930. "Zu den Ausführungen von Sethe über die *whm msw.t* Datierungen in den thebanischen Grabberaubungsakten der 20. Dynastie." *ZÄS* 65:129–30.

————. 1939. *Late Ramesside Letters*. Brussels: Fondation égyptologique Reine Élisabeth.

————. 1952. *Paper and Books in Ancient Egypt*. London: H.K. Lewis & Co., Ltd.

———. 1965. *Egypt: From the Death of Ramesses III to the End of the Twenty-first Dynasty*. Cambridge, U.K.: Cambridge University Press.

———. 1973. *A Community of Workmen at Thebes in the Ramesside Period*. Cairo: Institut français d'Archéologie orientale.

Champollion, J.-F. 1868. *Lettres écrites d'Égypte et de Nubie en 1828 et 1829*. New ed. Paris: Didier et Cie.

Chapman, R.P. 2009. "Putting Sheshonq I in His Place." *PEQ* 141, no. 1: 3–17.

Christophe, L.A. 1951. *Karnak-Nord (1945–1949)*. Cairo: Institut français d'Archéologie orientale.

———. 1953. "La double datation du Ouadi Gassous." *BIÉ* 35:141–52.

Ciccarello, M. [1979]. *The Graffito of Pinutem I in the Tomb of Ramesses XI*. Privately printed.

Ciccarello, M. and J. Romer. [1979]. *A Preliminary Report of the Recent Work in the Tombs of Ramesses X and XI in the Valley of the Kings*. Privately printed.

Coenen, M. 1995. "The So-called Denon Papyri." *JEA* 81:237–41.

Collier, M., A. Dodson, and G. Hamernik. 2010. "P. BM EA 10052. Anthony Harris and Queen Tyti." *JEA* 96:242–47.

Cryer, F.H. 1995. "Chronology: Issues and Problems." In *Civilizations of the Ancient Near East*, edited by J.M. Sasson, J. Baines, G. Beckman, and K.S. Rubinson, vol. 2, 651–64. New York: Scribner.

Dallibor, K. 2005. *Taharqo, Pharao aus Kusch: ein Beitrag zur Geschichte und Kultur der 25. Dynastie*. Berlin: Achet.

Daressy, G. 1896. "Contribution à l'étude de la XXIe Dynastie égyptienne." *RevArch* 28:72–90.

———. 1900. "Remarques et notes." *RT* 22:137–43.

———. 1907. "Les cercueils des prêtres d'Ammon (deuxième trouvaille de Deir el-Bahari)." *ASAE* 8:3–38.

———. 1909. *Cercueils des cachettes royales*. Cairo: Institut français d'Archéologie orientale.

Darnell, J.C. 2006. *The Inscription of Katimala at Semna: Textual Evidence for the Origins of the Napatan State*. New Haven, Conn.: Yale Egyptological Seminar.

D'Auria, S., P. Lacovara, and C.H. Roehrig. 1988. *Mummies and Magic: The Funerary Arts of Ancient Egypt*. Boston: Museum of Fine Arts.

Davies, B.G. 1997. "Two Many Butehamuns? Additional Observations on Their Identity." *SAK* 24:49–68.

Davies, N. de G. and M.F.L. Macadam. 1957. *A Corpus of Inscribed Egyptian Funerary Cones*. Oxford: Griffith Institute.

Davies, W.V. 2003. "Sobeknakht of Elkab and the Coming of Kush." *EgArch* 23:3–6.

———. 2005. "Egypt and Nubia: Conflict with the Kingdom of Kush." In *Hatshepsut: From Queen to Pharaoh*, edited by C.H. Roehrig, R. Dreyfus, and C.A. Keller, 49–56. New York: Metropolitan Museum of Art.

Davies, W.V., ed. 1991. *Egypt and Africa: Nubia from Prehistory to Islam.* London: British Museum Press.

De Meulenaere, J. 1977. "Harwa." *LÄ* 2:1021–22.

———. 1978. "La statuette JE 37163 du Musée du Caire." *SAK* 6:63–68.

———. 1985. "Les grands-prêtres de Ptah à l'époque saïto-perse." In *Mélanges offerts à Jean Vercoutter*, edited by F. Geus and F. Thill, 263–66. Paris: Éditions Recherche sur les Civilisations.

Demidoff, G. 2000. "Pour une révision de la chronologie de la fin de l'époque Ramesside." *GM* 177:91–101.

Denon, V. 1802. *Voyage dans las Basse et la Haute Égypte pendant les campagnes de Général Bonaparte.* Paris: P. Didot l'aîné.

Depuydt, L. 2006. "Saite and Persian Egypt, 664 BC–332 BC (Dyns. 26–31, Psammetichus I to Alexander's Conquest of Egypt)." In Hornung, Krauss, and Warburton 2006: 265–83.

Derry, D.E. 1939. "Note on the Remains of Shashanq." *ASAE* 39:549–51.

———. 1940–41. "An Examination of the Bones of King Psusennes I." *ASAE* 40:969–70.

———. 1942. "Report on the Skeleton of King Amenemopet." *ASAE* 41:149.

Dewachter, M. 1975. "Contribution à l'histoire de la cachette royale de Deir el-Bahari." *BSFE* 74:19–32.

Dodson, A. 1987a. "The Takhats and Some Other Royal Ladies of the Ramesside Period." *JEA* 73:224–29.

———. 1987b. "Psusennes II." *RdE* 38:49–54.

———. 1988a. "Egypt's First Antiquarians?" *Antiquity* 62, no. 236: 513–17.

———. 1988b. "Some Notes Concerning the Royal Necropolis at Tanis." *CdE* 63, no. 126: 221–33.

———. 1990. "Crown Prince Djhutmose and the Royal Sons of the Eighteenth Dynasty." *JEA* 76:87–96.

———. 1993a. "Psusennes II and Shoshenq I." *JEA* 79:267–68.

———. 1993b. "A New King Shoshenq Confirmed?" *GM* 137:53–58.

———. 1994. *The Canopic Equipment of the Kings of Egypt.* London and New York: Kegan Paul International.

———. 1996. "Coffin Development: A Problem for the New Chronology." In *A Test of Time: The London Debate*, edited by M. Rowland, 23–26. Basingstoke: Institute for the Study of Interdisciplinary Sciences.

———. 2000a. "The Late Eighteenth Necropolis at Deir el-Medina and the Earliest 'Yellow' Coffin of the New Kingdom." In *Deir el-Medina in the Third Millennium AD*, edited by R. Demarée and A. Egberts, 89–100. Leiden: Nederlands Instituut voor het Nabije Oosten.

———. 2000b. "The Intact Pyramid Burial at Hawara of 12th Dynasty Princess Neferuptah." *Kmt* 11, no. 4: 40–47.

———. 2001. "Third Intermediate Period." In *The Oxford Encyclopedia of Ancient Egypt*, edited by D.B. Redford, vol. 3, 388–94. New York: Oxford University Press.

———. 2002. "The Problem of Amenirdis II and the Heirs to the Office of God's Wife of Amun during the Twenty-sixth Dynasty." *JEA* 88:179–86.

———. 2005. "Bull Cults." In *Divine Creatures: Animal Mummies in Ancient Egypt*, edited by S. Ikram, 72–105. Cairo: American University in Cairo Press.

———. 2009a. "The Priest of Amun Iuput and His Distinguished Ancestors." *JEA* 95:51–66.

———. 2009b. "The Transition between the 21st and 22nd Dynasties Revisited." In Broekman, Demareé, and Kaper 2009: 103–12.

———. 2009c. "How Old is That Mummy in the Coffin?" *AncEg* 10, no. 2: 66–67.

———. 2010. *Poisoned Legacy: The Fall of the Nineteenth Egyptian Dynasty*. Cairo: American University in Cairo Press.

———. forthcoming. "The Palestinian Campaign(s) of Shoshenq I." In *Studies in Memory of Cathleen A. Keller*, edited by C. Redmount and D. Kiser-Go.

Dodson, A. and D. Hilton. 2010. *The Complete Royal Families of Ancient Egypt*. London and New York: Thames & Hudson; Cairo: American University in Cairo Press.

Dodson, A. and S. Ikram. 2008. *The Tomb in Ancient Egypt*. London and New York: Thames & Hudson; Cairo: American University in Cairo Press.

Dodson, A. and J.J. Janssen. 1989. "A Theban Tomb and Its Tenants." *JEA* 75:125–38.

Dunham, D. 1950. *The Royal Cemeteries of Kush*. Vol. 1: *El Kurru*. Cambridge, Mass.: Harvard University Press.

————. 1952. *The Royal Cemeteries of Kush*. Vol. 3: *Decorated Chapels at the Meroitic Pyramids at Meroë and Barkal*. Boston: Museum of Fine Arts.

————. 1955. *The Royal Cemeteries of Kush*. Vol. 2: *Nuri*. Boston: Museum of Fine Arts.

————. 1957. *The Royal Cemeteries of Kush*. Vol. 4: *Royal Tombs at Meroë and Barkal*. Boston: Museum of Fine Arts.

————. 1970. *The Barkal Temples*. Boston: Museum of Fine Arts.

Dunham, D. and M.F.L. Macadam. 1949. "Names and Relationships of the Royal Family of Napata." *JEA* 35:139–49.

Edwards, I.E.S. 1982. "Egypt: From the Twenty-second to the Twenty-fourth Dynasty." In *Cambridge Ancient History*. Vol. 3, no. 1: *The Prehistory of the Balkans, the Middle East and the Aegean World, Tenth to Eighth Centuries BC*, edited by J. Boardman, I.E.S. Edwards, N.G.L. Hammond, and E. Sollberger, 534–77. Cambridge, U.K.: Cambridge University Press.

Egberts, A. 1991. "The Chronology of *The Report of Wenamun*." *JEA* 77:57–67.

————. 1998. "Hard Times: The Chronology of 'The Report of Wenamun' Revised." *ZÄS* 125:93–108.

Eide, T., T. Hägg, R. Holton Pierce, and L. Török, eds. 1994–2000. *Fontes Historiae Nubiorum: Textual Sources for the History of the Middle Nile Region between the Eighth Century BC and the Sixth Century AD*. 4 vols. Bergen: Klassisk Institutt, Universitetet i Bergen.

Eigner, D. 1984. *Die monumentalen Grabbauten der Spätzeit in der Thebanischen Nekropole*. Vienna: Akademie der Wissenschaften.

Epigraphic Survey. 1954. *Reliefs and Inscriptions at Karnak*. Vol. 3: *The Bubastite Portal*. Chicago: University of Chicago Press.

————. 1979. *The Temple of Khonsu*. Vol. 1: *Scenes of King Herihor in the Court*. Chicago: Oriental Institute.

————. 1981. *The Temple of Khonsu*. Vol. 2: *Scenes and Inscriptions in the Court and the First Hypostyle Hall*. Chicago: Oriental Institute.

————. 1998. *Reliefs and Inscriptions at Luxor Temple*. Vol. 2: *The Facade, Portals, Upper Register Scenes, Columns, Marginalia, and Statuary in the Colonnade Hall*. Chicago: Oriental Institute.

Farid, A. 1978. "The Stela of Adikhalamani Found at Philae." *MDAIK* 34:53–56.

Fazzini, R. 1997. "Several Objects, and Some Aspects of the Art of the Third Intermediate Period." In *Chief of Seers: Egyptian Studies in Memory of Cyril Aldred*, edited by E. Goring, N. Reeves, and J. Ruffle, 113–37. London: Kegan Paul International.

Feucht, E. 1981. "Ein Relief Scheschonqs I. beim Erschlagen der Feinde aus El-Hibe." *SAK* 9:105–17.

Finkelstein, I. 2002. "The Campaign of Shoshenq I to Palestine: A Guide to the 10th Century BCE Polity." *ZDPV* 118, no. 2: 109–35.

Finkelstein, I., Z. Herzog, L. Singer-Avitz, and D. Ussishkin. 2007. "Has King David's Palace in Jerusalem Been Found?" *Tel Aviv* 37, no. 2: 142–64.

Finkelstein, I. and N.A. Silberman. 2006. *David and Solomon: In Search of the Bible's Sacred Kings and the Roots of the Western Tradition*. London: Free Press.

Fisher, M.M. 2001. *The Sons of Ramesses II*. 2 vols. Wiesbaden: Harrassowitz.

Forbes, D.C. 1998. *Tombs, Treasures, Mummies: Seven Great Discoveries of Egyptian Archaeology*. Sevastopol and Santa Fe: KMT Communications.

Foucart, G. 1924. "Études thébaines: La belle fête de la vallée." *BIFAO* 24:1–209.

Frame, G. 1999. "The Inscription of Sargon II at Tang-i Var." *Orientalia* 68:31–57.

Frandsen, P.J. 1991. "Editing Reality: The Turin Strike Papyrus." In *Studies in Egyptology Presented to Miriam Lichtheim*, edited by S. Israelit-Groll, 166–99. Jerusalem: The Agnes Press.

Gardiner, A. H. 1932. *Late-Egyptian Stories*. Brussels: Fondation égyptologique Reine Élisabeth.

———. 1941a. "Adoption Extraordinary." *JEA* 26:23–59.

———. 1941b. "Ramesside Texts Relating to the Taxation and Transport of Corn." *JEA* 27:19–73.

———. 1948. *Ramesside Administrative Documents*. Oxford: Griffith Institute.

———. 1961. *Egypt of the Pharaohs: An Introduction*. Oxford: Oxford University Press.

Gasm El Seed, A.A. 1985. "La tombe de Tanoutamon à El Kurru (Ku. 16)." *RdÉ* 36:67–72.

Gauthier, H. 1914. *Le Livre des rois d'Égypte*. Vol. 3. Cairo: Institut français d'Archéologie orientale.

Giles, F.J. 1997. *The Amarna Age: Western Asia*. Warminster: Aris & Phillips.

Gill, D. and M. Vickers. 1996. "Bocchoris the Wise and Absolute Chronology." *Römische Mitteilungen* 103:1–9.

Gitton, M. and J. Leclant. 1977. "Gottesgemahlin." *LÄ* 2:792–812.

Gnirs, A, 1996. *Militär und Gesellschaft: Ein Beitrag zur Sozialgeschichte des Neuen Reiches*. Heidelberg: Heidelberger Orientverlag.

Goedicke, H. 1971. *Re-used Blocks from the Pyramid of Amenemhat I at Lisht*. New York: Metropolitan Museum of Art.

————. 1975. *The Report of Wenamun*. Baltimore and London: Johns Hopkins University Press.

Goelet, O. 1996. "A New 'Robbery' Papyrus: Rochester MAG 51.346.1." *JEA* 82:107–27.

Gomaà, F. 1977. "Hardai." *LÄ* 2:962.

Goyon, J.-C. and C. Traunecker. 1982. "La chapelle de Thot et d'Amon au sud-ouest du Lac Sacré." In *Cahiers de Karnak*, vol. 7, 1978–81, 355–66. Paris: Éditions Recherche sur les Civilisations.

Graefe, E. 1975. "Der libysche Stammesname *p(j)d(j)/pjt* im spätzeitlichen Onomastikon." *Enchoria* 5:13–17.

————. 1994. "Der autobiographische Text des Ibi, Obervermögensverwalter der Gottesgemahlin Nitokris, auf Kairo JE 36158." *MDAIK* 50:85–99.

————. 2003a. "The Royal Cache and the Tomb Robberies." In Strudwick and Taylor 2003: 74–82.

————. 2003b. "Nochmals zum Gebrauch des Titels *dw3t-ntr* in der Spätzeit." *JEA* 89:246–47.

————. 2005. "'Der Hügel (*q3y*) der Inhapi, der der Heilige Ort ist, in dem Amenhotep ruht.'" *MDAIK* 61:207–10.

————. 2010. "Description, Clearance and Finds." In Graefe and Belova, 2010: 37–60.

Graefe, E. and G. Belova. 2010. "Catalogue of Finds." In Graefe and Belova, eds., 2010: 77–187.

Graefe, E. and G. Belova, eds. 2010. *The Royal Cache TT320: A Re-examination*. Cairo: Supreme Council of Antiquities Press.

Grandet, P. 1993. *Ramsès III: Histoire d'un règne*. Paris: Pygmalion/Gérard Watelet.

Grayson, A.K. 1980–83. "Königslisten und Chroniken. B. Akkadisch." *Reallexikon der Assyriologie*, vol. 6: 86–135. Berlin and New York: Walter de Gruyter.

————. 1987. *Assyrian Rulers of the Third and Second Millennia BC*. Toronto: University of Toronto Press.

Gutgesell, M. 1983. *Die Datierung der Ostraka und Papyri aus Deir el-Medineh und ihre ökonomische Interpretation*. Hildesheim: Gerstenberg Verlag.

Habachi, L. 1977. "Mentuhotep, the Vizier and Son-in-law of Taharqa." In *Ägypten und Kusch. Schriften zur Geschichte und Kultur des Alten Orients*, edited by E. Endesfelder, K.-H. Priese, W.F. Reineke, and S. Wenig, 165–70. Berlin: Akademie-Verlag.

Hakem, A M.A. 1988. *Meroitic Architecture: A Background of an African Civilisation*. Khartoum: Khartoum University Press.

Harpur, Y. 2001. *The Tombs of Nefermaat and Rahotep at Maidum: Discovery, Destruction and Reconstruction*. Oxford: Oxford Expedition to Egypt.

Harris, J.E. and K.R. Weeks. 1973. *X-raying the Pharaohs*. London: MacDonald.

Harris, J.E. and E.F. Wente (eds). 1980. *An X-ray Atlas of the Pharaohs*. Chicago: University Press.

Hassanein, F. and M. Nelson. 1997. *La tombe du prince Khaemouaset [VdR n° 44]*. Cairo: Conseil Supérieur des Antiquités.

Heidorn, L.A. 1991. "The Saite and Persian Period Forts at Dorginarti." In W.V. Davies, 1991: 205–19.

Henige, D. 1996. "Comparative Chronology and the Ancient Near East." *BASOR* 262:57–68.

Hölbl, G. 1981. "Die Aegyptiaca des griechischen, italischen und westphönikischen Raumes aus der Zeit des Pharao Bocchoris (718/17–712 v. Chr.)." *Grazer Beiträge* 10:1–20.

Hollis, S.T. 1987. "The Cartonnage Case of Pa-di-Mut, Harvard Semitic Museum 2230." In *'Working with No Data': Semitic and Egyptian Studies Presented to Thomas O. Lambdin*, 165–79. Winona Lake: Eisenbrauns.

Hölscher, U. 1954. *The Excavation of Medinet Habu*. Vol. 5: *The Post-Ramessid Remains*. Chicago: Chicago University Press.

Hornung, E. 2006. "The New Kingdom." In Hornung, Krauss, and Warburton, 2006: 197–217.

Hornung, E., R. Krauss, and D.A. Warburton, eds. 2006. *Ancient Egyptian Chronology*. Leiden: Brill.

Horton, M. 1991. "Africa in Egypt: New Evidence from Qasr Ibrim." In W.V. Davies 1991: 264–77.

Ibrahim Aly, M. "Les petits souterrains du Sérapéum de Memphis, étude d'archéologie, religion et histoire: Textes inédits." PhD thesis, Université de Lyon.

Ikram, S. 2005. "Divine Creatures: Animal Mummies." In *Divine Creatures: Animal Mummies in Ancient Egypt*, edited by S. Ikram, 1–15. Cairo: American University in Cairo Press.

Ikram, S. and A. Dodson. 1998. *The Mummy in Ancient Egypt: Equipping the Dead for Eternity*. London and New York: Thames and Hudson; Cairo: American University in Cairo Press.

Ikram, S. and N. Iskander. 2002. *Non-human Mummies*. Cairo: Supreme Council of Antiquities Press.

Jacquet-Gordon, C. 1975. Review of Kitchen, K.A. *The Third Intermediate Period in Egypt (1100–650 BC.)* (Warminster: Aris & Phillips, 1973). *BiOr* 32:358–60.

Jacquet-Gordon, C., C. Bonnet, and J. Jacquet 1969. "Pnubs and the Temple of Tabo on Argo Island." *JEA* 55:103–11.

James, P. 1991. *Centuries of Darkness: A Challenge to the Conventional Chronology of Old World Archaeology.* London: Jonathan Cape.

———. (forthcoming). "The Date of the Oracle on the Maunier ('Banishment') Stela."

James, P. and R. Morkot. 2010. "Herihor's Kingship and the High Priest of Amun Piankh." *JEgH* 3:231–60.

Jansen-Winkeln, K. 1985. *Ägyptische Biographien der 22. und 23. Dynastie.* Wiesbaden: Otto Harrassowitz.

———. 1987. "Thronname und Begräbnis Takeloths I." *VA* 3:253–58.

———. 1988. "Weiteres zum Grab Osorkons II." *GM* 102:31–39.

———. 1989. "Zwei Bemerkungen zu Gebel es-Silsila Nr. 100." *JEA* 75:237–39.

———. 1990. "Zu den biographischen Texten der 3. Zwischenzeit." *GM* 117/118:165–90.

———. 1992. "Das Ende des Neuen Reiches." *ZÄS* 119:22–37.

———. 1994. "Der Beginn der libyschen Herrschaft in Ägypten." *Biblische Notizen* 71:78–97.

———. 1995a. "Neue biographische Texte der 22./23. Dynastie." *SAK* 22:169–94.

———. 1995b. "Die Plünderung der Königsgräber des Neuen Reiches." *ZÄS* 122:62–78.

———. 1995c. "Historische Probleme der 3. Zwischenzeit." *JEA* 81:129–49.

———. 1997a. "Die thebanischen Gründer der 21. Dynastie." *GM* 157:49–74.

———. 1997b. "Der Majordomus des Amun Anchefenmut." *DE* 38:29–36.

———. 2001a. *Biographische und religiöse Inschriften der Spätzeit aus dem Ägyptischen Museum Kairo.* Wiesbaden: Harrassowitz.

———. 2001b. "Der thebanische 'Gottesstaat'." *Orientalia* 70:153–82.

———. 2006a. "Dynasty 21." In Hornung, Krauss, and Warburton 2006: 218–33.

———. 2006b. "Third Intermediate Period." In Hornung, Krauss, and Warburton 2006: 234–65.

———. 2007–2009. *Inschriften der Spätzeit.* 3 vols. Wiesbaden: Harrassowitz.

Janssen, J.J. 1992. "A New Kingdom Settlement. The Verso of Pap. BM. 10068." *Altorientalische Forschungen* 19:8–23.

Janssen, J.M.A. 1954. "Over farao Bocchoris." In *Varia Historica aange-boden aan Professor Doctor A. W. Byvanck ter gelegenheid van zijn zeventigste verjaardag door de Historische Kring te Leiden*, 17–29. Assen: Van Gorcum.

Jeffreys, D. 2010. *The Survey of Memphis*. Vol. 7: *The Hekekyan Papers and Other Sources for the Survey of Memphis*. London: Egypt Explora-tion Society.

Jenni, H., ed. 2000. *Das Grab Ramses' X. (KV 18)*. Basel: Schwabe & Co.

Jurman, C. 2006. "Die Namen des Rudjamun in der Kapelle des Osi-ris-Hekadjet. Bemerkungen zu Titulaturen der 3. Zwischenzeit und dem Wadi Gasus-Graffito." *GM* 210:69–91.

———. 2009. "From the Libyan Dynasties to the Kushites in Memphis: Historical Problems and Cultural Issues." In Broekman, Demarée, and Kaper 2009: 113–38.

Kahn, D. 2001. "The Inscription of Sargon II at Tang-i Var and the Chro-nology of Dynasty 25." *Orientalia* 70:1–18.

———. 2006. "A Problem of Pedubasts?" *Antiguo Oriente* 4:21–40.

———. 2009. "The Transition from Libyan to Nubian Rule in Egypt: Revisiting the Reign of Tefnakht." In Broekman, Demarée, and Kaper 2009: 139–48.

Kampp, F. 1996. *Die thebanische Nekropole: zum Wandel des Grabgedankens von der XVIII. bis zur XX. Dynastie*. 2 vols. Mainz: Phillipp von Zabern.

Kaper, O. 2009. "Epigraphic Evidence from the Dahleh Oasis in the Lib-yan Period." In Broekman, Demarée, and Kaper 2009: 149–59.

Kendall, T. 1982. *Kush: Lost Kingdom of the Nile*. Brockton, Mass.: Brockton Art Museum/Fuller Memorial.

———. 1999. "The Origin of the Napatan State: El Kurru and the Evi-dence for the Royal Ancestors." In *Meroitica 15: Studien zum antiken Sudan: Akten der 7. Internationalen Tagung für meroitischen Forschun-gen vom 14. bis September 1992 in Gosen/bei Berlin*, edited by S. Wenig, 3–117. Wiesbaden: Harrassowitz.

Kitchen, K.A. 1968–90. *Ramesside Inscriptions: Historical and Biographical*. 8 vols. Oxford: Blackwell.

———. 1972. "Ramesses VII and the Twentieth Dynasty." *JEA* 58:182–94

———. 1982. "The Twentieth Dynasty Revisited." *JEA* 68:116–25.

———. 1984. "Family Relationships of Ramesses IX and the Late Twenti-eth Dynasty." *SAK* 11:127–134.

———. 1990a. "The Arrival of the Libyans in Late New Kingdom Egypt." In Leahy 1990: 15–27.

———. 1990b. *Catálogo da Coleção de Egito Antigo existente no Museu Nacional, Rio de Janiero/Catalogue of the Egyptian Collection in the National Museum, Rio de Janiero*. Warminster: Aris & Phillips.

———. 1993ff(a). *Ramesside Inscriptions: Translated and Annotated. Translations*. Oxford: Blackwell.

———. 1993ff(b). *Ramesside Inscriptions: Translated and Annotated. Notes and Comments*. Oxford: Blackwell.

———. 1996. *The Third Intermediate Period in Egypt (1100–650 BC)*. 3rd ed. Warminster: Aris and Phillips.

———. 2009. "The Third Intermediate Period in Egypt: An Overview of Fact and Fiction." In Broekman, Demareé, and Kaper 2009: 161–202.

Klinger. J. 2006. "Chronological Links between the Cuneiform World of the Ancient Near East and Ancient Egypt." In Hornung, Krauss, and Warburton 2006: 304–24.

Klotz, D. 2010. "Two Overlooked Oracles." *JEA* 96:247–54.

Korostovtsev, M.A. 1960. *Нутешествие Ун-Амуна в Библ*. Moscow: Academy of Sciences.

Krauss, R. 2006a. "Dates Relating to a Seasonal Phenomena." In Hornung, Krauss, and Warburton 2006: 369–79.

———. 2006b. "Lunar Dates." In Hornung, Krauss, and Warburton 2006: 395–431.

———. 2008. "Ein Modell für die chronologische Einordnung der Maunier-Stele (Stele der Verbannten)." *GM* 219:41–48.

Krogman, W.M. and M.J. Baer. 1980. "Age at Death of Pharaohs of the New Kingdom, Determined from X-Ray Films." In Harris and Wente 1980: 188–212.

Kruchten, J.-M. 1989. *Les annales des prêtres de Karnak (XXI–XXIIImes dynasties) et autres textes contemporains relatifs à l'initiation des prêtres d'Amon*. Leuven: Departement Oriëntalistiek.

Kuniholm, P.I., B. Kromer, S.W. Manning, M. Newton, C.E. Latini, and M.J. Bruce. 1996. "Anatolian Tree Rings and the Absolute Chronology of the Eastern Mediterranean, 2220–718 BC." *Nature* 381:780–83.

Lacau, P. 1906–25. *Statues et Statuettes des rois et des particuliers*. 3 vols. Cairo: Institut français d'Archéologie orientale.

Landsberger, B. 1954. "Assyrische Königslisten und 'Dunkles' Zeitalter." *Journal of Cuneiform Studies* 8:31–73.

Lange, E. 2008. "Legitimation und Herrschaft in der Libyerzeit: Eine neue Inschrift Osorkons I. aus Bubastis (Tell Basta)." *ZÄS* 135:131–41.

———. 2009. "The Sed-Festival Reliefs of Osorkon II at Bubastis: New Investigations." In Broekman, Demarée, and Kaper 2009: 203–18.

———. 2010. "King Shoshenqs at Bubastis." *EgArch* 37:19–20.

Larkin, D.B. and C.C. van Siclen III. 1975. "Theban Tomb 293 and the Tomb of the Scribe Huy." *JNES* 34:129–34.

Lauffray, J. 1970. "Note sur les portes du 1er pylône de Karnak." *Kêmi* 20 [= *Karnak* 3]:101–10.

Leahy, A. 1984a. "Tanutamon, son of Shabako?" *GM* 83:43–45.

———. 1984b. "Saite Royal Sculptue: A Review." *GM* 80:69–70.

———. 1988. "The Earliest Dated Monument of Amasis and the End of the Reign of Apries." *JEA* 74:183–99.

———. 1990. "Abydos in the Libyan Period." In Leahy 1990: 155–200.

———. 1994. "Kushite Monuments at Abydos." In *The Unbroken Reed: Studies in the Culture and Heritage of Ancient Egypt in Honour of A.F. Shore*, edited by C. Eyre, A. Leahy, and L. M. Leahy, 171–92. London: Egypt Exploration Society.

Leahy, A., ed. 1990. *Libya and Egypt, c. 1300–750 BC*. London: Centre of Near and Middle Eastern Studies, School of Oriental and African Studies, University of London; and the Society for Libyan Studies.

Leclant, J. 1961. *Montouemhat, quatrième Prophète d'Amuon, Prince de la Ville*. Cairo: Institut français d'Archéologie orientale.

———. 1965. *Recherches sur les Monuments thébains de la XXVe Dynastie dite éthiopienne*. Cairo: Institut français d'Archéologie orientale.

———. 1975. "Achamonrau." *LÄ* 1:52–53.

———. 1980. "Fouilles et Travaux en Égypte et au Soudan, 1978–1979." *Orientalia* 49:346–420.

Legrain, G. 1914. *Statues et Statuettes des rois et particuliers*. Vol. 3. Cairo: Institut français d'Archéologie orientale.

Lemaire, A. 2006. "La datation des Rois de Byblos Abibaal et Élibaal et les relations entre l'Égypte et le Levant au Xe siècle av. notre ère." *CRAIBL* 150:1697–1716.

Lenzo, G. 2010. "The Two Funerary Papyri of Queen Nedjmet (P. BM EA 10490 and P. BM EA 10541 + Louvre E. 6258)." *BMSAES* 15:63–83. http://www.britishmuseum.org/research/online_journals/bmsaes/issue_15/lenzo.aspx

Lepsius, C.R. 1849–59. *Denkmaeler aus Aegypten und Aethiopien*. 6 vols. Berlin/Leipzig: Nicolaische Buchandlung.

———. 1897–1913. *Denkmaeler aus Aegypten und Aethiopien, Textband*. 5 vols. Leipzig: J.C. Hinrichs.

Lloyd, A.B. 1975–88. *Herodotus. Book II.* 3 vols. Leiden: Brill.

———. 1977. "Necho and the Red Sea: Some Considerations." *JEA* 63:142–55.

Loring, E. 2010. "The Dynasty of Piankh and the Royal Cache." In Graefe and Belova, 2010: 61–76.

———. 2011. "The Leather Funerary Baldachin of Isetemkheb." *AncEg* 11, no. 6: 52–58.

Lull, J. 2002. *Las tumbas reales egipcias del Tercer Período Intermedio (dinastías XXI–XXV).* Oxford: Archaeopress.

———. 2006. *Los sumos sacerdotes de Amón tebanos de la wḥm nswt y dinastia XXI (ca. 1083–1045 a.C.).* Oxford: Archaeopress.

———. 2009. "Beginning and End of the High Priest of Amun Menkheperre." In Broekman, Demareé, and Kaper 2009: 241–49.

Macadam, M.F.L. 1949–55. *The Temples of Kawa.* 2 vols. London: Oxford University Press.

Malek, J. 1999. *Topographical Bibliography of Ancient Egyptian Hieroglyphic Texts, Reliefs and Paintings.* Vol. 8: 1–2, *Objects of Provenance Unknown, Statues.* Oxford: Griffith Institute.

———. 2007ff. *Topographical Bibliography of Ancient Egyptian Hieroglyphic Texts, Reliefs and Paintings.* Vol. 8: 3–4, *Objects of Provenance Unknown, Stelae.* Oxford: Griffith Institute.

Malinine, M., G. Posener, and J. Vercoutter. 1968. *Catalogue des steles du Sérapéum de Memphis.* Vol. 1. Paris: Imprimerie Nationale.

Manassa, C. 2003. *The Great Karnak Inscription of Merenptah: Grand Strategy in the 13th Century BC.* New Haven: Yale Egyptological Seminar.

Manley, B. and A. Dodson. 2010. *Ancient Egypt in National Museums Scotland: Life Everlasting—Ancient Egyptian Coffins.* Edinburgh: National Museums Scotland.

Manniche, L. 2011. *Lost Ramessid and Post-Ramessid Provate Tombs in the Theban Necropolis.* Copenhagen: Museum Tusculanum Press.

Manning, S.W., B. Kromer, P.I. Kuniholm, and M.W. Newton. 2001. "Anatolian Tree Rings and a New Chronology for the East Mediterranean Bronze–Iron Ages." *Science* 294, no. 5551: 2532–35.

Manuelian, P. Der. 1993. *Living in the Past: Studies in Archaism of the Egyptian Twenty-sixth Dynasty.* London: Kegan Paul International.

Manuelian, P. Der and C.E. Loeben. 1993. "New Light on the Recarved Sarcophagus of Hatshepsut and Thutmose I in the Museum of Fine Arts, Boston." *JEA* 79:121–55.

Marée, M. 2010. *The Second Intermediate Period (Thirteenth–Seventeenth Dynasties): Current Research, Future Prospects.* Leuven: Uitgeverij Peeters and Departement Oosterse Studies.

Mariette, A. 1857. *Le Sérapeum de Memphis decouvert et décrit par Aug. Mariette. Ouvrage dédié à S. A. I. Mgr. le Prince Napoléon et publié sous les auspices de S.E.M. Achille Fould, ministre d'état.* Paris: Gide.

———. 1876. *Les papyrus égyptiens du Musée de Boulaq.* Vol. 3. Paris: Franck.

Maspero, G. 1889. *Les momies royales de Déir el-Baharî.* Paris: Ernest Leroux.

Maspero, G. and E. Brugsch. 1881. *La Trouvaille de Deir el-Bahari.* Cairo: F. Mourès & Cie.

Moberly Bell, C.F. 1888. *From Pharaoh to Fellah.* London: Wells Gardner, Darton.

Montet. P. 1939. "Découverte d'une nécropole royale à Tanis." *ASAE* 39:529–39.

———. 1947. *La nécropole royale de Tanis I: Les constructions et le tombeau de Osorkon II à Tanis.* Paris: n.p.

———. 1951. *La nécropole royale de Tanis II: Les constructions et le tombeau de Psousennes à Tanis.* Paris: n.p.

———. 1960. *La nécropole royale de Tanis III: Les constructions et le tombeau de Chéchanq III à Tanis.* Paris: n.p.

———. 1966. *Le lac sacré de Tanis.* Paris: Imprimerie Nationale.

Moret, A. 1903. *De Bocchori rege.* Paris: Leroux.

Morkot, R. 1999. "Kingship and Kinship in the Empire of Kush." In *Studien zum antiken Sudan: Akten der 7. Internationalen Tagung für meroitische Forschungen vom 14. bis 19. September 1992 in Gosen/bei Berlin,* edited by S. Wenig, 179–229. Wiesbaden: Harrassowitz.

———. 2000. *The Black Pharaohs: Egypt's Nubian Rulers.* London: Rubicon.

———. 2003. "On the Priestly Origin of the Napatan Kings: The Adaptation, Demise and Resurrection of Ideas in Writing Nubian History." In *Ancient Egypt in Africa,* edited by D. O'Connor and A. Reid, 151–68. London: UCL Press.

———. 2006. "A Kushite Royal Woman, Perhaps a God's Wife of Amun." In *Egyptian Art in the Nicholson Museum, Sydney,* edited by K.N. Sowada and B.G. Okinga, 147–58. Sydney: Mediterranean Archaeology.

Morkot, R. and P. James. 2009. "Peftjauawybast, King of Nen-nesut: Genealogy, Art History, and the Chronology of Late Libyan Egypt." *Antiguo Oriente* 7:13–55.

Muhs, B. 1998. "Partisan Royal Epithets in the Late Third Intermediate Period and the Dynastic Affiliations of Pedubast I and Iuput II." *JEA* 84:220–23.

Müller, M. 2009. "The 'El-Hibeh' Archive: Introduction and Preliminary Information." In Broekman, Demareé, and Kaper 2009: 251–64.

Müller, V. 2006. "Wie gut fixiert ist die Chronologie des Neuen Reiches wirklich?" *Ä&L* 16:203–30.

Murnane, W. J. 1990. *The Road to Kadesh: A Historical Interpretation of the Battle Reliefs of King Sety I at Karnak*. 2nd ed. Chicago: Oriental Institute.

Murray, M.A. 1904. *The Osireion*. London: Egyptian Research Account.

Naville, E. 1892. *The Festival Hall of Osorkon II in the Great Temple of Bubastis (1887–1889)*. London: Egypt Exploration Fund.

———. 1911. "Excavations at Abydos: Work at the Royal Tombs." *Egypt Exploration Fund Annual Report* 1910/11: 1–2.

Naville, E. and F.Ll. Griffith. 1890. *The Mound of the Jew and the City of Onias: Belbeis, Samanood, Abusir, Tukh el Karmus, 1887 & The Antiquities of Tell el Yahûdîyeh*. London: Egypt Exploration Fund.

Newberry, P.E. 1902. "Extracts from My Notebooks." *PSBA* 24:244–52.

Newgrosh, B. 1999. "The Chronology of Ancient Assyria Re-assessed." *JACF* 8:78–106.

Nims, C.F. 1948. "An Oracle Dated in 'The Repeating of Births'." *JNES* 7:157–62.

Niwiński, A. 1979. "Problems in the Chronology and Genealogy of the XXIst Dynasty: New Proposals for Their Interpretation." *JARCE* 16:49–68.

———. 1984a. "Three More Remarks in the Discussion of the History of the Twenty-first Dynasty." *BES* 6:81–88.

———. 1984b. "The Bab el-Gusus Tomb and the Royal Cache in Deir el-Bahri." *JEA* 70:73–81.

———. 1988a. "The Wives of Pinudjem II: A Topic for Discussion." *JEA* 74:226–30.

———. 1988b. *21st Dynasty Coffins from Thebes. Chronological and Typological Studies*. Mainz: Philipp von Zabern.

———. 1989a. *Studies on the Illustrated Theban Funerary Papyri of the 11th and 10th Centuries BC*. Freiburg: Universitätsverlag; Göttingen: Vandenhoeck & Ruprecht.

———. 1989b. "Some Remarks on Rank and Titles of Women in the Twenty-first Dynasty Theban 'State of Amun'." *DE* 14:79–89.

————. 1992. "Bürgerkrieg, militärischer Staatsstreich und Ausnahmezustand in Ägypten unter Rameses XI." In *Gegengabe (Festschrift Emma Brunner-Traut)*, edited by I. Gamer-Wallert and W. Helck, 235–62. Tübingen: Attempto.

O'Connor, D. 1998. "Amenhotep III and Nubia." In *Amenhotep III: Perspectives on His Reign*, edited by D. O'Connor and E.H. Cline, 261–70. Ann Arbor: University of Michigan Press.

Ōhshiro, M. 1999. "The Identity of Osorkon III: The Revival of an Old Theory (Prince Osorkon = Osorkon III)." 古代オリエント博物館紀要 [*Bulletin of the Ancient Orient Museum*] 20:33–49.

Oren, E.D. 1984. "Migdol: A New Fortress on the Edge of the Eastern Nile Delta." *BASOR* 256:7–44.

Oren, E.D., ed. 2000. *The Sea Peoples and Their World: A Reassessment*. Philadelphia: The University Museum, University of Pennsylvania.

Parker, R.A. 1957. "The Length of the Reign of Ramses X." *RdE* 11:163–64.

Parkinson, R. 1999. *Cracking Codes: The Rosetta Stone and Decipherment*. London: British Museum Press.

Payraudeau, F. 2000. "Remarques sur l'identité du premier et du dernier Osorkon." *GM* 178:175–80.

————. 2008. "Des nouvelles annales sacerdotales des règnes de Siamon, Psousennès II et Osorkon Ier." *BIFAO* 108:293–308.

————. 2009. "Takeloth III: Considerations on Old and New Documents." In Broekman, Demareé, and Kaper 2009: 291–302.

Peden, A.J. 1994a. *The Reign of Ramesses IV*. Warminster: Aris & Phillips.

————. 1994b. *Egyptian Historical Inscriptions of the Twentieth Dynasty*. Jonsered: Paul Åströms Förlag.

Peet, T.E. 1930. *The Great Tomb-Robberies of the Twentieth Egyptian Dynasty: Being a Critical Study, with Translations and Commentaries, of the Papyri in Which These Are Recorded*. Oxford: Clarendon Press.

Perdu, O. 2002. "De Stéphinates à Necho ou les débuts de la XXVIe Dynastie." *CRAIBL* 2002:1215–44.

Perez Die, M.C. 2009. "The Third Intermediate Period Necropolis at Herakleopolis Magna." In Broekman, Demarée, and Kaper 2009: 301–26.

Petrie, W.M.F. 1908. "The First Circuit of Africa and the Supposed Record of It." *Geographical Journal* 32:480–85.

————. 1925. *A History of Egypt*. Vol. 3. 3rd ed. London: Methuen.

Piacentini, P. and C. Orsenigo. 2004. *La Valle dei Re Riscoperta: i giornali scavo di Victor Loret (1898–1899) e altri inediti*. Milan: Università degli Studi di Milano/Skira.

Pischikova, E. 1998. "Reliefs from the Tomb of the Vizier Nespakashuty: Reconstruction, Iconography, and Style." *MMJ* 33:57–101.

———. 2008. "Tomb of Karakhamun (TT 223) in the South Asasif and a 'Lost' Capital." *JARCE* 44:185–92.

———. 2009. "The Early Kushite Tombs of South Asasif." *BMSAES* 12:11–30. http://www.britishmuseum.org/research/online_journals/bmsaes/issue_12/pischikova.aspx

Pleyte, W. and F. Rossi. 1869–76. *Papyrus de Turin.* Leiden: Brill.

Poebel, A. 1943. "The Assyrian King List from Khorsabad—Concluded." *JNES* 2:56–90.

Polz, D. 1998. "The Ramsesnakht Dynasty and the Fall of the New Kingdom: A New Monument in Thebes." *SAK* 25:257–93.

Pope, J. 2011. "Montuemhat's Semna Stela: The Double Life of an Artifact." Paper delivered at 62nd Annual Meeting of the American Research Center in Egypt, Chicago, 3 April 2011.

Porter, B. and R.L.B. Moss. 1934. *Topographical Bibliography of Ancient Egyptian Hieroglyphic Texts, Reliefs and Paintings.* Vol. 4: *Lower and Middle Egypt.* Oxford: Clarendon Press.

———. 1937. *Topographical Bibliography of Ancient Egyptian Hieroglyphic Texts, Reliefs and Paintings.* Vol. 5: *Upper Egypt: Sites.* Oxford: Clarendon Press.

———. 1939. *Topographical Bibliography of Ancient Egyptian Hieroglyphic Texts, Reliefs and Paintings.* Vol. 6: *Upper Egypt: Chief Temples (excl. Thebes).* Oxford: Clarendon Press.

———. 1952. *Topographical Bibliography of Ancient Egyptian Hieroglyphic Texts, Reliefs and Paintings.* Vol. 7: *Nubia, Deserts, and Outside Egypt.* Oxford: Clarendon Press/Griffith Institute.

———. 1960–64. *Topographical Bibliography of Ancient Egyptian Hieroglyphic Texts, Reliefs and Paintings.* Vol. 1: *The Theban Necropolis.* 2nd ed. Oxford: Clarendon Press/Griffith Institute.

———. 1972. *Topographical Bibliography of Ancient Egyptian Hieroglyphic Texts, Reliefs and Paintings.* Vol. 2: *Theban Temples.* 2nd ed. Oxford: Griffith Institute.

———. 1974–81. *Topographical Bibliography of Ancient Egyptian Hieroglyphic Texts, Reliefs and Paintings.* Vol. 3: *Memphis.* 2nd ed. by J. Málek. Oxford: Griffith Institute.

Porter, R.M. 2011. "Osorkon III of Tanis: The Contemporary of Piye?" *GM* 230:111–12.

Postgate, N. 1991. "The Chronology of Assyria: An Insurmountable Obstacle." *CAJ* 1, no. 2: 22–53.

Priese, K.-H. 1970. "Der Beginn der Kuschitischen Herrschaft." *ZÄS* 98, no. 1: 16–32.

———. 1977. "Eine verschollene Bauinscrift des frühmerotischen Königs Aktisanes vom Gebel Barkal." In *Ägypten und Kusch*, edited by E. Endesfelder, K.-H. Priese, W.-F. Reineke, and S. Wenig, 343–67. Berlin: Akademie-Verlag.

Pritchard, J.B., ed. 1969. *Ancient Near Eastern Texts Relating to the Old Testament*. 3rd ed. Princeton, N.J.: Princeton University Press.

Quack, J.F. 2000. "Eine Revision im Tempel von Karnak (Neuanalyse von Papyrus Rochester MAG 51.346.1)." *SAK* 28:219–32.

Quirke, S.G.J. 1993. *Owners of Funerary Papyri in the British Museum, London*. London: British Museum Publications.

Ray, J.D. 1986. "Psammuthis and Hakoris." *JEA* 72:149–58.

———. 1987. "Egypt: Dependence and Independence (425–343 BC)" In *Achaemenid History*, I: *Sources, Structures and Synthesis. Proceedings of the Groningen 1983 Achaemenid History Workshop*, edited by H. Sancisi-Weerdenburg, 79–95. Leiden: Brill.

Redford, D.B. 1973. "Studies in Relations between Palestine and Egypt during the First Millenium BC. Vol. 2: The Twenty-second Dynasty." *JAOS* 93:3–17.

———. 2006. "The Northern Wars of Thutmose III." In *Thutmose III: A New Biography*, edited by E. H. Cline and D. O'Connor, 325–43. Ann Arbor: University of Michigan Press.

Redford, S. 2002. *The Harem Conspiracy: The Murder of Ramesses III*. DeKalb, Ill.: Northern Illinois University Press.

Reeves, C.N. 1985. "Tut'ankhamūn and His Papyri." *GM* 88:39–45.

———. 1990. *Valley of the Kings: The Decline of a Royal Necropolis*. London: Kegan Paul International.

Reeves, C.N., ed. 1992. *After Tut'ankhamūn*. London and New York: Kegan Paul International.

Reisner, G.A. 1920. "The Viceroys of Ethiopia." *JEA* 6:28–55.

Ridgway, D. 1999. "The Rehabilitation of Bocchoris: Notes and Queries from Italy." *JEA* 85:143–52.

Ritner, R.K. 1990. "The End of the Libyan 'Anarchy' in Egypt: P. Rylands IX, cols. 11–12." *Enchoria* 17:101–108.

———. 2009a. *The Libyan Anarchy: Inscriptions from Egypt's Third Intermediate Period*. Atlanta: Society of Biblical Literature.

———. 2009b. "Fragmentation and Re-integration in the Third Intermediate Period." In Broekman, Demarée, and Kaper 2009: 327–40.

Rohl, D.M. 1986. "Forum: David Rohl Replies." *Chronology & Catastrophism Workshop* 1986/1: 17–23.

———. 1989/90. "The Early Third Intermediate Period: Some Chronological Considerations." *JACF* 3:45–70.

———. 1995. *A Test of Time*. Vol. 1: *The Bible: From Myth to History*. London: Century.

Römer, M. 1994. *Gottes- und Priesterherrschaft in Ägypten am Ende des Neuen Reiches: Ein religionsgeschichtliches Phänomen und seine Grundlagen.* Wiesbaden: Harrassowitz.

Romer, J. [1979]. *The Brooklyn Museum Theban Expedition: The Theban Royal Tomb Project—A Report of the First Two Seasons*. San Francisco: privately published.

Rosellini, I. 1834–36. *I monumenti dell'Egitto e della Nubia*. Vol. 2: *Monumenti civili*. Pisa: Capurro.

Rowe, A. 1938. "New Light on Objects Belonging to the Generals Potasimto and Amasis in the Egyptian Museum." *ASAE* 38:157–95.

Rummel, U. 2009. "Grab oder Tempel? Die funeräre Anlage des Hohenpriesters des Amun Amenophis in Dra' Abu el-Naga (Theben–West). In *Texte—Theben—Tonfragmente: Festschrift für Günter Burkard*, edited by D. Kessler, 348–60. Wiesbaden: Harrassowitz.

———. 2011. "Two Re-Used Blocks of the God's Wife Isis at Deir el-Bakhit/Dra' Abu el-Naga (Western Thebes)." In *Ramesside Studies in Honour of K.A. Kitchen*, edited by M. Collier and S. Snape, 423–31. Bolton: Rutherford Press.

Russman, E.R. 1974. *The Representation of the King in the XXVth Dynasty.* Bruxelles: Fondation égyptologique Reine Élisabeth; Brooklyn: The Brooklyn Museum.

———. 1997. "Mentuemhat's Kushite Wife (Further Remarks on the Decoration of the Tomb of Mentuemhat, 2)." *JARCE* 34:21–39.

Ryholt, K.S.B. 1997. *The Political Situation in Egypt During the Second Intermediate Period, c. 1800–1550 BC*. Copenhagen: Museum Tusculanum Press.

Sagrillo, T.L. 2009. "The Geographic Origins of the 'Bubastite' Dynasty." In Broekman, Demarée, and Kaper 2009: 341–59.

———. 2011. "The Heart Scarab of King Shoshenq III (Brooklyn Museum 61.10)." *JEA* 97:240–46.

Saleh, M. and H. Sourouzian. 1987. *The Egyptian Museum Cairo: Official Catalogue*. Mainz: Philipp von Zabern.

Sauneron, S. and J. Yoyotte. 1952a. "La campagne nubienne de Psammétique II et sa signification historique." *BIFAO* 50:157–207.

————. 1952b. "Sur la politique palestinienne des rois saïtes." *Vetus Testamentum* 2:131–36.

Schneider, H.D. and M.J. Raven. 1981. *De Egyptische Oudheid*. The Hague: Staatsuitgeverij.

Schneider, T. 2000. "Ramses X.: Person und Geschichte." In Jenni 2000: 81–108.

Schweinfurth, G. 1886. *Alte Baureste und hieroglyphische Inschriften im Uadi Gasus*. Berlin: Königliche Preussische Akademie der Wissenschaften.

Seele, K.C. 1959. *The Tomb of Tjanefer at Thebes*. Chicago: University of Chicago Press.

Seyfried, K.-J. 1991. *Das Grab des Pa-en-khemenu (TT 68) und die Anlage TT 227*. Mainz: Philipp von Zabern.

Sheikholeslami, C.M. 2003. "The Burial of Priests of Montu at Deir el-Bahari in the Theban Necropolis." In Strudwick and Taylor 2003: 131–37.

Shubert, S.B. 1981. "Studies on the Egyptian Pylon." *JSSEA* 11:135–64.

Smith, G.E. 1912. *The Royal Mummies*. London: Constable.

Smith, H.S. 1976. *The Fortress of Buhen*. Vol. 2: *The Inscriptions*. London: Egypt Exploration Society.

Smoláriková, K. 2008. *Saite Forts in Egypt: Political-Military History of the Saite Dynasty*. Prague: Czech Institute of Egyptology.

Solkin, V.V. 2011–12. "Four Ancient Egyptian Papyri in the Collection of the Russian National Library, St. Petersburg." *Kmt* 22, no. 4: 43–52.

Spalinger, A.J. 2006. "Covetous Eyes South: The Background to Egypt's Dominion over Nubia by the Reign of Thutmose III." In *Thutmose III: A New Biography*, edited by E.H. Cline and D. O'Connor, 344–69. Ann Arbor: University of Michigan Press.

Spencer, A.J. 1989. *Excavations at El-Ashmunein*. Vol. 2: *The Temple Area*. London: British Museum Publications.

————. 1996. *Excavations at Tell El-Balamun, 1991–1994*. London: British Museum Press.

————. 1999. *Excavations at Tell El-Balamun, 1995–1998*. London: British Museum Press.

————. 2003. *Excavations at Tell El-Balamun, 1999–2001*. London: British Museum Press.

————. 2009. *Excavations at Tell El-Balamun 2003–2008*. http://www.britishmuseum.org/pdf/Book%201.pdf

Spencer, P.A. and A.J. Spencer. 1986. "Notes on Late Libyan Egypt." *JEA* 72:198–201.

Strudwick, N. 1995. "The Fourth Priest of Amun, Wedjahor." *GM* 148: 91–94.

Strudwick N. and J.H. Taylor, eds. 2003. *The Theban Necropolis: Past, Present and Future*. London: British Museum Press.

Taylor, J.H. 1998. "Nodjmet, Payankh and Herihor: The End of the New Kingdom Reconsidered." In *Proceedings of the Seventh International Congress of Egyptologists*, edited by C.J. Eyre, 1143–55. Louvain: Peeters.

———. 2003. "Theban Coffins from the Twenty-second to the Twenty-sixth Dynasty." In Strudwick and Taylor 2003: 95–121.

———. 2009. "Coffins as Evidence for a 'North-South Divide' in the 22nd–25th Dynasties." In Broekman, Demarée, and Kaper 2009: 375–415.

Teeter, E. 1999. "Celibacy and Adoption among God's Wives of Amun and Singers in the Temple of Amun: A Re-examination of the Evidence." In *Gold of Praise: Studies on Ancient Egypt in Honor of Edward F. Wente*, edited by E. Teeter and J.A. Larsen, 405–14. Chicago: Oriental Institute.

Thiele, E.R. 1965. *The Mysterious Numbers of the Hebrew Kings*. 2nd ed. London: Paternoster Press.

Thijs, A. 1998a. "Reconsidering the End of the Twentieth Dynasty, Part I: The Fisherman Pnekhtemope and the Date of BM 10054." *GM* 167:95–108.

———. 1998b. "Two Books for One Lady: The Mother of Herihor Rediscovered." *GM* 163:101–10.

———. 1998c. "Piankh's Second Nubian Campaign." *GM* 165:99–103.

———. 1999a. "Reconsidering the End of the Twentieth Dynasty, Part II." *GM* 170:83–100.

———. 1999b. "Reconsidering the End of the Twentieth Dynasty, Part III: Some Hitherto Unrecognised Documents from the *wḥm mswt*." *GM* 173:175–92.

———. 2000a. "'Please Tell Amon to Bring Me Back from Yar.' Dhutmose's Visits to Nubia." *GM* 177:63–70.

———. 2000b. "Reconsidering the End of the Twentieth Dynasty, Part IV: The Harshire Family as a Test for the Shorter Chronology." *GM* 175:99–104.

———. 2000c. "Reconsidering the End of the Twentieth Dynasty, Part V: P. Ambras as an Advocate of a Shorter Chronology." *GM* 179:69–84.

———. 2001a. "Reconsidering the End of the Twentieth Dynasty, Part VI: Some Minor Adjustments and Observations Concerning the Chronology of the Last Ramessides and the *wḥm-mswt*." *GM* 181:95–103.

———. 2001b. "Reconsidering the End of the Twentieth Dynasty, Part VII: The History of the Viziers and the Politics of Menmare." *GM* 184:65–73.

———. 2003. "The Troubled Careers of Amenhotep and Panehsy: The High Priest of Amun and the Viceroy of Kush under the Last Ramessides." *SAK* 31:289–306.

———. 2004a. "Pap. Turin 2018, the Journeys of the Scribe Dhutmose and the Career of the Chief Workman Bekenmut." *GM* 199:79–88.

———. 2004b. "'My Father Was Buried during Your Reign': The Burial of the High Priest Ramessesnakht under Ramses XI." *DE* 60:87–95.

———. 2005. "In Search of King Herihor and the Penultimate Ruler of the 20th Dynasty." *ZÄS* 132:73–91.

———. 2006. "King or High Priest? The Problematic Career of Pinuzem." *GM* 211:81–88.

———. 2007. "The Scenes of the High Priest Pinuzem in the Temple of Khonsu." *ZÄS* 134:66–81.

———. 2008. "The Second Prophet Nesamun and His Claim to the High-Priesthood." *SAK* 38:343–53.

———. 2010. "The Lunar Eclipse of Takeloth II and the Chronology of the Libyan Period." *ZÄS* 137:171–90.

Thomas, E. 1966. *Royal Necropoleis of Thebes*. Princeton: privately printed.

Török, L. 1995. "The Emergence of the Kingdom of Kush and Her Myth of the State in the First Millennium BC." In *Actes de la VIIIe conférence internationale des études nubiennes*. Vol. 1: *Communications principales*. [= *CRIPEL* 17]: 203–28.

———. 1997. *The Kingdom of Kush: Handbook of the Napatan-Meroitic Civilization*. Leiden: Brill.

———. 2009. *Between Two Worlds: The Frontier Region between Ancient Nubia and Egypt, 3700 BC–AD 500*. Leiden: Brill.

Traunecker, C. 1979. "Essai sur l'histoire de la XXIXe dynastie." *BIFAO* 79:395–436.

Ungnad, A. 1938. "Eponymen." In *Reallexikon der Assyriologie*, vol. 2: 412–57. Berlin and Leipzig: Walter de Gruyter.

Uphill, E.P. 1984. *The Temples of Per Ramesses*. Warminster: Aris & Phillips.

Valbelle, D. and C. Defernez. 1995. "Les sites de la frontière Égypto-palestinienne à l'époque perse." *Transeuphratène* 9:93–100.

Van der Veen, P. 1999. "The Name Shishak." *JACF* 8:22–25.

Van Dijk, J. 2008. "New Evidence on the Length of the Reign of Horemheb." *JARCE* 44:193–200.

Varille, A. 1943. *Karnak*. Cairo: Institut français d'Archéologie orientale.

Vercoutter, J. 1960. "The Napatan Kings and Apis Worship (Serapeum Burials of the Napatan Period)." *Kush* 8:62–76.

Verreth, H. 1999. "The Eastern Egyptian Border Region in Assyrian Sources." *JAOS* 119:234–47.

Vittmann, G. 1974. "Zur Lesung des Königsnamen ⌐𓏏𓋹𓎺⌐ ." *Orientalia* 43:12–16.

———. 1987. *Priester und Beamte im Theben der Spätzeit: Genealogische und prosopographische Untersuchungen zum Thebanische Priester- und Beamtentum der 25. und 26. Dynastie.* Vienna: Afro-Pub.

von Beckerath, J. 1951. *Tanis und Theben. Historische Grundlagen der Ramessidenzeit in Ägypten.* Glückstadt: J.J. Augustin.

———. 1966. "The Nile Level Records at Karnak and Their Importance for the History of the Libyan Period (Dynasties XXII and XXIII)." *JARCE* 5:43–55.

———. 1968. "Die Stele der Verbannten im Museum des Louvre." *RdE* 20:7–36.

———. 1984. "Drei Thronbesteigungsdaten der XX. Dynastie." *GM* 79:7–9.

———. 1994a. *Chronologie des ägyptischen Neuen Reiches.* Hildesheim: Gerstenberg.

———. 1994b. "Papyrus Turin 1898+, Verso." *SAK* 21:29–33.

———. 1994c. "Zur Rückeninschrift der Statuette Kairo CG 42192." *Orientalia* 63:84–87.

———. 1995. "Beiträge zur Geschichte der Libyerzeit, 3. Die Könige namens Pedubaste." *GM* 147:9–13.

———. 1997. "Zur Datierung des Grabräuberpapyrus Brit. Mus. 10054." *GM* 159:5–9.

———. 1999. *Handbuch der ägyptischen Königsnamen.* 2nd ed. Mainz: Philipp von Zabern.

———. 2000. "Bemerkungen zur Chronologie der Grabräuberpapyri." *ZÄS* 127:111–16.

———. 2001. "Überlegungen zum Zeitabstand zwischen Ramses II. und dem Ende der XXI. Dynastie." *GM* 181:15–18.

von Känel, F. 1987. "Notes épigraphiques." *Cahiers de Tanis* 1:45–60.

Waddell, W.G. 1940. *Manetho.* Cambridge, Mass.: Harvard University Press; London: William Heinmann.

Weinstein, J. 1989. "The Bronze Age Shipwreck at Ulu Burun: 1986 Campaign. Vol. 3. The Gold Scarab of Nefertiti from Ulu Burun: Its Implications for Egyptian History and Egyptian-Aegean Relations." *AJA* 93:17–20.

————. 1998. "Egypt and the Levant in the Reign of Amenhotep III." In *Amenhotep III: Perspectives on His Reign*, edited by D. O'Connor and E.H. Cline, 223–36. Ann Arbor: University of Michigan Press.

Wente, E.F. 1966. "The Suppression of the High Priest Amenhotep." *JNES* 25:73–87.

————. 1967. *Late Ramesside Letters*. Chicago: Oriental Institute.

————. 1990. *Letters from Ancient Egypt*. Atlanta: Scholars Press.

Wiener, M. 1998. "The Absolute Chronology of Late Helladic IIIA2." In *Sardinian and Aegean Chronology: Towards the Resolution of Relative and Absolute Dating in the Mediterranean*, edited by M.S. Balmuth and R.H. Tykot, 309–19. Oxford: Oxbow Books.

————. 2003. "The Absolute Chronology of Late Helladic III A2 Revisited." *AnnBSA* 98:239–50.

Wildung, D. 1977. "Hoherpriester von Memphis." *LÄ* 2:1256–63.

Wilson, K.A. 2005. *The Campaign of Pharaoh Shoshenq I into Palestine*. Tübingen: Mohr Siebeck.

Wilson, P. 2006. *The Survey of Saïs (Sa el-Hagar) 1997–2002*. London: Egypt Exploration Society.

Winand, J. 2011. "The *Report of Wenamun*: A Journey in Ancient Egyptian Literature." In *Ramesside Studies in Honour of K.A. Kitchen*, edited by M. Collier and S. Snape, 541–59. Bolton: Rutherford Press.

Winlock, H E. 1942. *Excavations at Deir el Baḥri 1911–1931*. New York: Macmillan.

Winter, E. 1981. "Ergamenes II., seine Datierung und seine Bautätigkeit in Nubien." *MDAIK* 37:509–13.

Yamada, S. 1994. "The Editorial History of the Assyrian King List." *ZA* 84:11–37.

Yoyotte, J. 1961. "Les principautés du Delta au temps de l'anarchie libyenne." In *Mélanges Maspero* 1, no. 4: 121–81. Cairo: Institut français d'Archéologie orientale.

————. 1988a. "A propos de Psousennes II." *BSFFT* 1:41–53.

————. 1988b. "Des lions et des chats: Contribution à la prosopographie de l'époque libyenne." *RdÉ* 39:155–78.

Yoyotte, J. and S. Sauneron. 1952. "La campagne nubienne de Psammétique II et sa signification historique." *BIFAO* 50:157–207.

Zibelius-Chen, Z. 2006. "The Chronology of Nubian Kingdoms from Dyn. 25 to the End of the Kingdom of Meroe." In Hornung, Krauss, and Warburton 2006: 284–303.

INDEX

Names of Egyptian kings are CAPITALIZED; prenomina are only given for kings where this element is non-unique or for other reasons of clarity.

Argo Island 164
el-Arish 151
Arqamani, king of Kush 173
ARTAXERXES II 180
Arty, wife of Shabataka 143, 152, 158
Asa, king of Judah 99
Asasif xxvii, 160, 163–64
Ashakhet A, high priest of Ptah 49, 59
Ashdod 156, 158, 175
Ashmolean Museum, Oxford *see*
    Oxford, Ashmolean Museum
Ashmunein *see* Hermopolis
Ashur-banipal, king of Assyria 167,
    169, 273 n. 105, 278 n. 233
Ashur-bel-kala, king of Assyria 182,
    185
Ashur-dan I, king of Assyria 184
Ashur-dan II, king of Assyria xi, 182,
    183, 185
Ashur-nadin-apil, king of Assyria 183
Ashur-nasir-apil, king of Assyria 183
Ashur-nasir-pal I, king of Assyria 184,
    185
Ashur-nirari III, king of Assyria 183–84
Ashur-nirari IV, king of Assyria 184
Ashur-rabi II, king of Assyria 184
Ashur-resha-ishi II, king of Assyria 184
Ashur-uballit I, king of Assyria 182
Aspelta, king of Kush 172, 273 n. 81
Assyria xi, 151, 155–59, 162, 165–67,
    169–70, 176, 182–84, 186,
    188–89, 274 nn. 129, 130, 277
    n. 229, 278 n. 1, 278 n. 7
Assyrian King List (AKL) xi, 124, 182
Aswan 118, 137, 174
    Elephantine 104, 118, 144, 155,
        244 n. 197, 279 n. 24
    Elephantine Museum, stela of
        Takelot II 118

Nubian Museum, objects:
    ex-CG560 162
    ex-JE48863 273 n. 107
Atakhebasken, wife of Taharqa 162
Atfih 98, 148
Athens, National Archaeological
    Museum, stela of
    Tefnakhte 153
Athribis (Tell Atrib) 86, 148, 163, 167
Atlanersa, king of Kush 172, 276 n.
    183

Bab el-Gasus *see* Deir el-Bahari, Bab
    el-Gasus
Babylon 176–79, 182–83, 281 n. 27
Bahariya Oasis 136, 155
Bahnasa *see* Oxyrhynkhos
Bahr Yusuf 148
Bakennefi A, son of Shoshenq III 115
Bakennefi C, ruler of Athribis 167
Bakenptah, son of Takelot II 119, 126
BAKENRENEF (BOKKHORIS)
    153–54, 193, 274 n. 128, 278
    n. 231
Bakenwernel, Treasurer of the Lord
    of the Two Lands in Kush 4
Baketwernel A, wife of Sethy I 9, 13
Baketwernel B (KV10) 240 n. 98
Ballana 148
Banebdjedet 41
Banishment Stela *see* Louvre C.256
Bendariya 115
Beni Mazar 15
Berlin, Ägyptisches Museum und
    Papyrussamlung, objects:
    ÄM1068 271 n. 49
    ÄM1480 161, 275 n. 161
    ÄM1566 46, 246 n. 37
    ÄM1572 46

JE46891 254 n. 190
JE46915 137, 264 n. 17
JE47085 271 n. 49
JE47086–9 271 n. 50
JE48400 275 n. 147
JE48862 147, 271 n. 50
JE48863 273 n. 107, 278 n. 1
JE48864 279 n. 22
JE49100–2 246 n. 31
JE49157 273 n. 84, 275 n. 145
JE49164–5 249 n. 87
JE51948–9 246 n. 31
JE55044 246 n. 32
JE55080 246 n. 32
JE55146 246 n. 32
JE55155 248 n. 59
JE55181 248 n. 59
JE55194 273 n. 108
JE59128 264 n. 22
JE59635 259 n. 44
JE59716–9 263 n. 159
JE59896 263 n. 159
JE59900 263 n. 159
JE60137 109, 263 n. 159
JE66285 256 n. 233
JE70218 254 n. 206
JE71902 61, 250 n. 116
JE72154–97 262 n. 109
JE85779–82 252 n. 157
JE85886–7 48, 246 n. 40
JE85894 246 n. 30
JE85911 253 n. 165
JE85912 253 n. 164
JE86058–62 253 n. 181
JE86063 70, 253 n. 182
JE86161 261 n. 100
JE86956 262 n. 109
JE87297 253 n. 166
JE88131 105, 262 n. 127

JE91720 263 n. 155
TR 2/2/21/13 268 n. 126
TR 3/4/17/1 243 n. 165
TR 3/7/24/11 253 n. 184
TR 3/12/24/1 *see* JE59635
TR 3/12/24/2 251 n. 137
TR 9/2/15/11 *see* JE34431
TR 11/1/25/13 266 n. 62
TR 11/9/21/14 272 n. 55
TR 11/9/21/17 265 n. 31
TR 11/11/24/2 239 n. 81, 239 n. 87
TR 16/2/25/6 253 n. 185
TR 20/12/25/11 244 n. 187
TR 25/11/18/6 258 n. 23
TR 27/4/44/3 262 n. 109
Cairo, Institut français d'Archéologie
    orientale, object 14456 269
    n. 150
Cairo, King Faruq Collection 269
    n. 155
Cairo, Qasr el-Aini Medical School,
    human remains:
    2 253 n. 176
    3 261 n. 107
    40 253 n. 179
Cambridge, Fitzwilliam Museum,
    objects:
    E.8.1896 259 n. 46
    E.64.1896 261 n. 88
    E.70-293.1896 261 n. 88
    E.445.1982 256 n. 241
Cambridge, MA, Harvard Semitic
    Museum, object 2230=901.9.1
    258 n. 20
canopic equipment 33, 41, 43, 69, 70,
    85, 95, 101, 102, 108, 111, 128,
    133, 134, 152, 158, 161, 256
    n. 242, 259 n. 52, 263 n. 166,
    280 n. 57

Re'u, army commander 151
reuse of funerary equipment 52, 67, 69, 101, 102, 247 n. 53, 253 n. 166, 264 n. 22
Rijksmuseum van Oudheden, Leiden, Netherlands *see* Leiden, Rijksmuseum van Oudheden
Rio de Janeiro, Museu Nacional, object 81 252 n. 153
Rochester University Memorial Art Gallery, Rochester NY, object 51.346.1 238 n. 54
Rockefeller Archaeological Museum, Jerusalem *see* Jerusalem, Rockefeller Archaeological Museum
Rome, Museo Barracco 271 n. 32
Rosetta *see* Rashid
RUDAMUN 128, 134, 137–38, 146, 149, 192, 267 n. 98, 267–68 n. 103
Rudamun B, Great Chief of the Libu 136

Sa el-Hagar *see* Sais
Sabacôn *see* SHABAKA
Sabacos 278 n. 3
Saft el-Henna 80, 84
Sais 136, 148, 153, 162, 166, 167, 169, 175, 177, 178
    royal necropolis 175–76, 177, 179
Samaria 104
Sammlung des Ägyptologischen Instituts, Universität Heidelberg *see* Heidelberg, Sammlung des Ägyptologischen Instituts
Sanam 164
San el-Hagar *see* Tanis

Saqqara 136, 280 n. 57
    Serapeum 59, 72, 87, 100, 115, 117, 134, 154, 159, 249 n. 100, 260 n. 82, 269 n. 134
Sargon II, king of Assyria 151, 156–58, 272 nn. 71, 74, 274 nn. 131, 135
Sedeinga 164
Sematawytefnakhte, Shipmaster of Herakleopolis 144, 145
Semna-West 139, 140, 164, 276 n. 186
SENEFERU 131
Sennacherib, king of Assyria 158, 165, 275 n. 149
SENWOSRET I 50
SENWOSRET III 52, 104
Setau (El-Kab tomb 4) 236 n. 13
Sethhirkopeshef, son of Rameses III 3; *see also* RAMESES VIII
Sethmose, King's Son of Kush 14, 16
SETHNAKHTE 2, 39, 191
SETHY I 13, 16, 17, 41, 42, 43, 62, 76–77, 78, 79, 92, 94, 187, 191, 203, 238 n. 50, 240 n. 98
SETHY II 187, 191, 238 n. 48, 253 n. 167
SHABAKA 143, 145, 152, 154–58, 159, 160, 161, 172, 193, 273 n. 84, 274 n. 134, 274 n. 138, 278 n. 3
Shabaka Stone *see* London, British Museum, EA498
SHABATAKA 143, 152, 158–61, 163, 193, 273 n. 106, 274 n. 134
Shalmaneser I, king of Assyria 182, 185
Shalmaneser II, king of Assyria 184
Shalmaneser III, king of Assyria 186
Shalmaneser V, king of Assyria 151
Shashaq, Chief of the Ma *see* SHOSHENQ I